T0319737

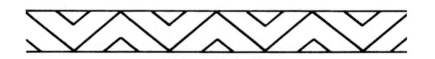

Land, Governance, Conflict
& the Nuba
of Sudan

EASTERN AFRICA SERIES

* forthcoming

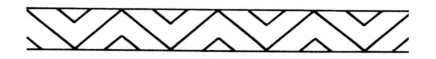

Land, Governance, Conflict
& the Nuba
of Sudan

GUMA KUNDA KOMEY

Assistant Professor of Human Geography
Juba University, Sudan

JC JAMES CURREY

James Currey
www.jamescurrey.com
is an imprint of Boydell & Brewer Ltd
PO Box 9, Woodbridge, Suffolk IP12 3DF, UK
and of Boydell & Brewer Inc.
668 Mt Hope Avenue, Rochester, NY 14620, USA
www.boydellandbrewer.com

© Guma Kunda Komey Kalo 2010
First published 2010

1 2 3 4 5 14 13 12 11 10

All Rights Reserved. Except as permitted under current legislation
no part of this work may be photocopied, stored in a retrieval system,
published, performed in public, adapted, broadcast,
transmitted, recorded or reproduced in any form or by any means,
without the prior permission of the copyright owner.

The right of Guma Kunda Komey to be identified as
the author of this work has been asserted in accordance with
sections 77 and 78 of the Copyright, Designs and Patents Act 1998

The publisher has no responsibility for the continued existence or accuracy of URLs for
external or third-party internet websites referred to in this book, and does not guarantee
that any content on such websites is, or will remain, accurate or appropriate.

British Library Cataloguing in Publication Data

Komey, Guma Kunda.
Land, governance, conflict & the Nuba of Sudan. -- (Eastern
Africa series)
1. Public lands--Sudan--Nuba Mountains--History--20th
century. 2. Sudan--History--Civil War, 1983-2005.
I. Title II. Series
333.1'09628-dc22

ISBN 978-1-84701-026-1 (James Currey Hardcover)

Papers used by Boydell and Brewer are natural, recyclable products
made from wood grown in sustainable forests

Typeset in 10/11 pt Baskerville
by Tina Ranft, Woodbridge, Suffolk, UK
Printed and bound in Great Britain
by CPI Antony Rowe, Chippenham, Wiltshire

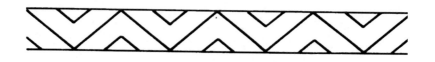

In Memory of
Yusuf Kuwa Mekki (1945–2001)
Philip Abbas Ghabush (1922–2008)

&

John Garang De Mabior (1945–2005)

Contents

Contents

Contents

7
Contested Communal Lands, Identity Politics & Conflicts

ix

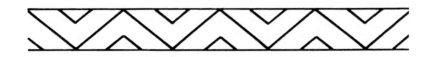

List of Tables & Maps

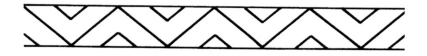

Preface

The Making & Object of the Book

Since gaining independence in 1956, Sudan has undergone a troubled socio-political process that culminated in the longest civil war in the contemporary Africa. Today, Sudan is a living case of a state in political disarray with an uncertain future. This gloomy political situation is an inevitable manifestation of its failing nation-building process. Instead of promoting national integration and unity through cherishing its normal societal ingredients of socio-cultural, ethnic and religious diversities, the postcolonial Sudanese state resorted to force national unity through uniformity. This false start ossified the processes of nation-building, arrested national integration and, therefore, impeded the realization of the Sudanese state formation as a cohesive political entity. Thus, Sudan remains a highly contested political unit that continues a brutal fight against its own people for its mere survival. The first civil war in southern Sudan (1955–1972), the second civil war (1983–2005) which started initially in southern Sudan and extended gradually to northern Sudan via Nuba Mountains and Blue Nile, and the current political, social and humanitarian crisis in Darfur are full proof.

Taking the marginalized indigenous people and their war-torn region in southern Kordofan as a case study, this book attempts to examine state–society relations and their political and social repercussions on the involved communities. The author's field work reveals what went on in the Nuba Mountains before, during, and after the period of the civil war in the Sudan. The strength of the book is on the empirical side, with its historical overviews, combined with ethnographic detail all relating to the political, social and economic strivings of the indigenous Nuba people. Thus, this is not another political overview of the postcolonial Sudan but an original case study of the disadvantaged Nuba people and their historical and contemporary processes of socioeconomic and political marginalization and exclusion by the state, and their various responses to such negatives. In a number of ways, a model for this study is found in Wendy James' *War and Survival in Sudan's Frontierlands:*

Voices from the Blue Nile (2007). Both works focus on one of the two contested, marginalized, and frontier regions of the Nuba Mountains and southern Blue Nile which share the dilemma of being situated along Sudan's north–south socio-political and geographic divides.

The main argument advanced here is that although the root causes of the conflicts and civil wars in Sudan are multifaceted, access to land is the core issue within the wider context of state overall political system and governance. This centrality stems from the fact that access to land is crucial to human survival in agrarian societies. Besides its economic utilities, land is a symbol of social and political identification for the majority of rural peoples. Despite this, the interests and rights of such communities, whether sedentary like the Nuba or nomadic like the Baqqara, are barely harmonized with the state's land policies. At the same time, their very habitats are overly exploited by state in the course of development process in the name of 'public interest'. This results in state driven conflicts that force the victims themselves to fight a proxy war against each other for reasons externally generated and reinforced by the state.

The analysis in this book reveals that neither land resource nor any other single factor should be accepted at face value as a single root cause of a conflict. Rather, the contribution of this study is precisely to demonstrate that the role of any contributing factor to a conflict, at its different levels of scale, is correctly understood when situated in wider socio-economic and politico-administrative analytical context. The ethnographic material in this book reveals that the way in which the conflicts have evolved in the Nuba Mountain requires a focus on the state governance, in this case 'bad governance'. Focusing on Nuba–Baqqara relations in their shared but contested territory of the Nuba Mountains, the book traces the people's use and control of resources at many different levels of their social organizations, thus permitting a consideration of processes of inter-communal cooperation and/or competition in the wider context of state-society relations, power and authority.

This study was conducted over many years, divided between field work in Sudan, archival scrutiny in Durham, London and desk work including the final analysis in Halle, Germany. Guided by a set of central questions outlined in the Introduction, a period of sixteen months of ethnographic fieldwork was carried out, in three stages between 2005–2008. The process was intentionally interrupted, and therefore, supplemented by an extensive literature review at the Institute of Social Anthropology, University of Halle, Germany, coupled with research at the Sudan Archive, Durham University Library in the United Kingdom. Thus the ethnographic material presented here is combination of (i) systematic participatory observations of certain events and agents in diverse but interrelated social fields, such as local markets which are viewed here as economic, socio-cultural, and political intermediaries; (ii) informal and semi-structured but guided interviews with local people as well as community leaders; and (iii) records of the daily life, social organization, with the discourses and practices related to claims of land rights and their disputations between sedentary Nuba and nomadic Baqqara Arabs.

During the field work, the focus was on monitoring and tracing cases of land-based conflicts, discourses, competition, and/or cooperation, not only within the limited sphere of shared land and water resources, but also within the broader shared social space as a set of intersecting ecological, social, economic, and political fields. Toward that end, the first stage of the field work (March to June 2005) was devoted to conducting a preliminary survey in which a set of criteria was developed and tested in order to ensure the suitability and practicality of some potential field sites as viable ethnographic case studies. The criteria include, among others, the history of ethnic settlement successions among the competing ethnic groups; the current pattern of inter-ethnic settlement and mixtures; the traceability of frequent boundary shifts; documented or verbal claims to collective land rights in terms of firstcomer or even autochthonous status, and the existence of some form of socio-economic or ecological interactive intermediaries that impose a consistent mode of encounter between the various competing actors. Such intermediaries include shared market places, state institutions, socio-cultural events, water points, farming activities and grazing.

Based on these criteria, the al-Azraq, Umm Derafi, Reikha and Keiga Tummero local areas were finally selected as sites for an in-depth field-centred ethnographic work (see Map 6.1 in Chapter 6). The first task, in 2005, was to collect theoretically relevant cases of contested access to land and water rights. In the second stage (October 2005 to June 2006), detailed ethnographic investigations were carried out at the selected sites with a focus on observing certain events and their interconnections at various levels of scale. This was followed by a more detailed ethnographic analysis with the intention of identifying some information and data gaps. Between December 2006 and March 2007, final fieldwork was carried out to fill in the gaps identified through analysis of the main fieldwork of 2006. The drafting of this study began in June 2008 at the Institute of Social Anthropology in Halle, Germany and continued up to 2010, although the research sub-project ended in September 2008.

During field work, certain issues were pursued in more detail, while always paying special attention to the variations found in the field site localities, and to the state policies and reactions to the local dynamics. These were, first, the issue of claiming communal land rights, related conflicts, and their implications for the relations between the nomadic Baqqara and the sedentary Nuba groups in a situation without state legal recognition of customary land rights. The most challenging question is the clarification of what exactly communal land rights mean in the context of present day negotiations in the locations selected. Identity discourses and collective memories in relation to ethnicity, strongly linked with territoriality, play an important role here and are often articulated in terms of autochthony and or other forms of identities and belongings.

Second, the case studies are analyzed through longstanding or emerging strategic groups with common economic and/or political interests who sometimes crosscut the stereotypical nomadic-sedentary and ethnic dichotomies and are linked into networks which reach outside the localities. Special attention is given to traders of various ethnicities who cross existing borders and partly did so during the war. Of equal importance is the role of the elite from the urban centres along the Nile and protagonists from diasporas abroad who influence local developments. Special attention is also given to the emergence of new forms of politically avowed religiosities (Christian and Islamic) and their role in emerging power networks which influence local phenomena. The dynamics of separation and integration of state as national social space, and religion as a social field in Southern Kordofan and the Sudan as a whole are important features of the overall analysis.

Third, in the context of the post-conflict situation that followed the Comprehensive Peace Agreement of January 2005, a new political-administrative system is in the making with significant impact on social groups' relations and local developments. Thus, the case studies are analyzed in view of the recorded history of disputed developments coupled with recent emerging patterns of conflicts over access to and control of land and water resources. Fourth, each locality is analyzed as just one field among others, to allow for the discovery of social fields at a larger or smaller scale. Particularly important here is the role of international organizations since they also played an important role in the reconfiguration of the social order in the region during the civil war and continue to do so in the post-conflict situation, which is characterized by political fluidity and social fragility despite the Comprehensive Peace Agreement.

The overall analytical perspective of this work is informed by a set of interrelated social anthropological and geographic approaches and concepts found is the following works: Barth (1969/1998, 1978), Pounds (1972), Grönhaug (1978), Cloke et al., (1991), Schlee (2001, 2002a, 2002b, 2008), Gertel (2007) and Rottenburg (2009). The analysis is constructed around the theory of social world/space/fields advanced by Strauss (1978), Grønhaug (1978), and Bourdieu (1985) and Clarke (1991), among others, as well as around the concept of region proposed by Murphy (1991) and William and Smith (1993).

The premise of this social world/field perspective is that society as a social reality is a complex, fluid, and multi-dimensional organization with various active agents, relationships, field forces, positions, resources, scale and power structures in a continuous process of segmenting and regrouping. Using this theoretical approach, the present study follows the trajectories of continuing communal land claims and their broader connections beyond the locations selected to distant actors (the Nuba in diaspora, global actors, and the international NGOs) all of whom are involved in local events in a number of ways. The basic proposition of this analytical perspective is that individuals, groups, and organizations situate themselves in relation to what they perceive as a highly contested, burning issue which then becomes an ongoing concern for all of them. Once this situation is established, a social field or arena emerges around it where new groups and organizations emerge and build networks to deal with the issue. In the case of this study, the ongoing concern is the controversial and frequently conflictive relation between territoriality (land), ethnicity (identity) and the state (governance).

Guma Kunda Komey
Khartoum/Halle

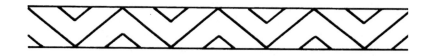

Acknowledgements

The completion of this book is a result of the support and collaborative involvement of various institutions, individual colleagues and informants. It is an ethnographical study within a sub-project entitled 'Contested autochthony: land and water rights in the relation of the sedentary Nuba and the nomadic Baqqara of the South Kordofan/Nuba Mountains, Sudan'. The sub-project was headed by Professor Richard Rottenburg of the Institute of Social Anthropology at the University of Halle-Wittenberg in Germany. It was part of a larger multi-disciplinary research project 'SFB586: Difference and Integration' conducted by the Collaborative Research Centre at the Universities of Halle-Wittenberg and Leipzig in Germany. The project was generously funded by the German Research Foundation for the period 2004–2008. This financial support is much appreciated as the work would not have materialized without it.

Equally, I am indebted to a wide range of support received from the academic, administrative and support staff of the above-mentioned academic and research institutions, especially Professor Stefan Leder, former Director of the Collaborative Research Centre Project, his successor and the current Director, Professor Jörg Gertel, and their entire staff. Special thanks and appreciation is due to Conny Gropp at the Institute of Social Anthropology, the University of Halle-Wittenberg for she was among that small circle who made my stay in Germany comfortable, and my research work a successful undertaking. In my own country, I would like to acknowledge the support of the administration of the University of Juba, where I am based, for allowing me to pursue my post-doctoral research during the period of 2005–2008.

Although the book bears my name and the views expressed here are solely my responsibility, a number of colleagues both in Sudan and Germany have provided me with invaluable intellectual insights that enriched the final product. First and foremost, my profound gratitude is owed to Professor Richard Rottenburg, our research team leader and the initiator and principal investigator of the sub-project. His inspirational guidance, scholarly contributions, marvellous support and unending encouragement motivated me in a number of ways to work with stronger commitment and focus during the entire course of this work and beyond.

While writing the manuscript, I received constructive comments from many colleagues at various symposiums, conferences and colloquiums held at the Institute of Social Anthropology, the Max Plank Institute for Social Anthropology, the Universities of Halle-Wittenberg, Leipzig and Bremen in Germany; and the Universities of Bergen in Norway, and of Texas in the USA as well as the Universities of Khartoum and Juba in Sudan. I would like to make special reference to the inspirational critiques, received over many years, from my colleagues: Enrico Ille, Andrea Behrends, Bert Turner, Markus Hoehne, Dereje Feyissa, Olaf and Julia Zanker, during our regular colloquia at the Institute of Social Anthropology. In addition, I would like to express my sincere gratitude to Professor Leif Manger of the Social Anthropology department at Bergen University in Norway for his constant support, valuable advice and academic comments that refined and enriched the content and focus of this work at different stages of its evolution. I am also grateful to Günther Schlee and John Eidson of the Max-Planck Institute of Social Anthropology for valuable comments on parts of the manuscript.

Moreover, while doing my field work, I benefited significantly from guidance, advice, support and intellectual input from a group of distinguished Sudanese scholars at the University of Khartoum who willingly accepted being committed members of an advisory entity (the Sudan Reference Group) for the sub-project during the period of the research. I am particularly grateful to Drs Musa Abdul Jalil and Idriss Salim at the department of Social Anthropology, Professor al-Amin Abu Manga of the Institute of African-Asian Studies, Professor Adam al-Zain of the Institute of Federal Governance Studies, Professor Ali Suliman of Faculty of Law, and Dr. Atta M. H. al-Battahani of Political Science at Khartoum University.

I am also thankful for the detailed constructive comments contributed by two anonymous reviewers to the final manuscript. Special appreciation is due to the copy editor, Frances Kennett, for her shrewd and insightful input while refining the final version of the manuscript and to my proofreader and indexer, Margaret Cornell. The ethnographic material was enriched by the wealth of archival documents from the Sudan Archive at Durham University Library in the UK. Thus, special thanks and appreciation are due to Jane Hogan of the Sudan Archive at Durham University for her generous support and assistance in my research there. I would also like to acknowledge the cooperation and enthusiasm of many informants in their different capacities during my field work in Kadugli, Keiga Tummero, Keiga Luban, Umm Derafi, Reikha, al-Azraq, Kauda, Heiban and Umm Berembeita in the Nuba Mountains, as well as in 'Aloba in Northern Kordofan and in Khartoum.

Finally, my deepest gratitude is due to my family: my lovely wife Hanan Timothous and our lively five 'Js': Julia, Judy, Jessica, Jesse and Jonas for their patience, sacrifices and support. Their endless love is not only the motive of my being but was and still is a source of my intellectual inspirations, strength and encouragement that continue to keep me from failing or falling while encountering various kinds of challenges and stresses at different stages of work.

Abbreviations & Acronyms

ABC	Abyei Boundary Commission
ABS	Agricultural Bank of Sudan
ACTS	African Centre for Technology Studies
CBOs	Community-Based Organizations
CFA	Ceasefire Agreement
CFV	Ceasefire Violation
CPA	Comprehensive Peace Agreement
DOP	Declaration of Principles
EU	European Union
GNPOC	Greater Nile Petroleum Operating Corporation
GONU	Government of National Unity
GOS	Government of Sudan
GOSS	Government of Southern Sudan
GUNM	General Union of the Nuba Mountains
ICG	International Crisis Group
IDPs	Internally Displaced Persons
IGAD	Inter-Governmental Authority on Development
JEM	Justice and Equality Movement
JMC	Joint Military Commission
JMM	Joint Monitoring Mission
NCP	National Congress Party
NIF	National Islamic Front
NGOs	Non-Governmental Organizations
NMAPs	Nuba Mountains Alliance Parties
NMPACT	Nuba Mountains Programme for Advancing Conflict Transformation
NRRDO	Nuba Relief, Rehabilitation and Development Organization
OECD	Organization for Economic Co-operation and Development
OLS	Operation Lifeline Sudan
PCA	Permanent Court of Arbitration
PDFs	Peoples' Defence Forces
SAD	Sudan Archive, Durham

Abbreviations & Acronyms

SANU	Sudan African National Union
SFCSs	Small Farmers' Collective Schemes
SLM	Sudan Liberation Movement
SNP	Sudanese National Party
SPLM/A	Sudan People's Liberation Movement/Army
UK	United Kingdom
UN	United Nations
UNMIS	United Nations Mission in Sudan
UNOCHA	United Nations Office for Coordination of Humanitarian Affairs
USA	United States of America
USDA	United States Department of Agriculture
USAID	United States Agency for International Development

Introduction

National Context, Key Questions
& Arguments

The basis of the contemporary Sudanese state can be traced back to its ancient, precolonial and colonial history and related legacies. The ancient and precolonial eras were characterized by independent feudal systems of governance, each occupying its own territory. From its establishment in 1899, the colonial administration subjected the peoples of Sudan to new spatial and socio-political arrangements which persisted under successive postcolonial regimes. The legacy of this history, particularly that of the colonial period, continues to shape the social, economic and political spaces of contemporary Sudan. The country's current problems of retarded statehood, the failure of its nation-building, its underdevelopment and the sharp disparities in development,together with recurring internal conflicts and protracted civil wars, are the most conspicuous issues that continue to challenge Sudan.

The historical dimension of these persistent problems is well documented (Abd al-Rahim 1970; Lees and Brooks 1977; Beshir 1979a, 1979b, 1984; Beshir et al., 1984, Mohamed Salih and Harir 1994; Johnson 2006). Whatever the scale of these challenges, they have mostly involved economic, social and political struggles for all disadvantaged communities and regions of Sudan, including the subject of this book: the Nuba people and their homeland.

Falsehood of the independent Sudan

History informs us that modern Sudan as a clearly defined political entity and as an object of national loyalty did not exist before Darfur was brought under colonial administration in 1916. During the Condominium rule (1898–1956), the British administration pursued a policy of concentrated development in northern and central Sudan, fostering this area as the

1

emerging political, cultural, and economic core, and subsequently as a centre of Sudanese nationalism (Roden 1974; Beshir 1979b, 1984; Abd al-Rahim 1970; Niblock 1987; Mohamed Salih and Harir 1994). Thus, the modern Sudanese nationalist movement was to a large degree a northern phenomenon, oriented more to the Arab cultural and political worlds in northern Sudan than to the African areas in southern Sudan, together with other marginalized communities in the Nuba Mountains, Darfur, southern Blue Nile and eastern Sudan. This configuration established a basis for multiple processes of political and cultural marginalization and socio-economic underdevelopment in the under-privileged areas.

As it started its march towards independence, the Sudan was already in political disarray, with the northern region acting as the seat for the country's politico-administrative and socio-economic functions. At the same time, the remaining regions, as listed above, were left on the periphery. This colonial legacy came to have a far-reaching impact on postcolonial Sudan, and continues to do so, with persistent socio-political instability and protracted civil wars along ethno-regional divides throughout the country.

It is useful to map out some of the key historical, political, socio-cultural, economic and geographic factors that have shaped and continue to shape the formation of the Sudanese state since its independence. The birth of an independence movement in Sudan was shaky, a false start that subsequently retarded the overall process of nation-building. This is attributed primarily to poor governance structure and a lack of political will on the part of successive ruling elites, who have failed to establish strong foundations for a pluralistic state that not only recognizes but cherishes and celebrates the Sudan's social, cultural, religious, economic and environmental diversity.

A direct result of this false start was that the people of southern Sudan resisted the newly independent entity, fearing that it would simply signify a change of masters, from the British to the northern ruling elites. That fear gained momentum when it became apparent that the northern elites lacked the political will and commitment to fulfil their promise of establishing a federal system in the country, to which they had committed themselves before independence. The consequences were the first southern rebellion during 1955–72 and the emergence of serious mistrust between the south and the north that persists to the present day (Abd al-Rahim 1970; Beshir 1979a; Beshir et al., 1984; Alier 1990; Johnson 2006). In 1956, on the eve of independence, Sudan was already in a state of civil war coupled with a host of internal problems,

> [...] chief amongst which is the erosion of nationalism, in the sense of loyalty to the homeland as a whole, and the resurgence or development of a variety of particularistic tendencies, loyalty to which has in some cases equalled or even surpassed loyalty to the nationalism under whose banner independence was won. (Abd al-Rahim 1970: 233)

Introduction

The upsurge of a violent political movement in the southern Sudan, at this early stage of the state's formation, suggests that the vision of an independent Sudan as an integrated entity was a myth and not a reality. The country was unprepared for a viable national political project that would lead it through successfully to a postcolonial future. Seeking political independence without safeguarding even a minimum national consensus on fundamental questions such as national identity and political orientation led to a national identity crisis and consequently a failure of the nation-building project in Sudan.

At the heart of this national crisis was the question of fair representation and participation of sub-national communities of the peripheral regions in the formation of national identity, and in wealth and power sharing. Despite the fact that Sudan is a multi-ethnic, multi-linguistic, and multi-religious state, several Sudanese politicians and/or writers such as Abbas (1973), Deng (1973, 1995), Beshir (1984), Beshir et al., 1984; Alier (1990), Mohamed Salih and Harir (1994), Khalid (2003), and Kameir (2006), among others, insist that the Sudanese state formation was narrowly and wrongly constructed out of Islamism and Arabism rather than on an all-encompassing Sudanese cultural base, because the northern ruling elites were unwilling to promote such a pluralistic society. Instead, they pursued a policy of presenting Sudan as an Islamic and Arab country, with only token representation or even misrepresentation of the majority indigenous identities. Many critics have argued that the northern ruling elites sought to impose Arabization and Islamization nationwide in an attempt to achieve national unity through uniformity. In the opinion of Makris (2001: 55) 'Sudanization, or becoming a citizen, essentially means Arabization and concomitantly, Islamization.'

In consequence, the marginality of communities of the peripheral regions is multi-dimensional, affecting socio-cultural, religious, economic and political aspects (Abbas 1973; Roden 1974; Ibrahim A. A. 1985; Umbada 1988; Komey 2005a; Johnson 2006). This has led to the emergence of strong tendencies in the peripheral regions to the formation of political movements and other markers of loyalty derived from ethnic identities. These are usually tied strongly to specific regions as sources of identification and livelihoods (Deng 1973, 1995; Beshir 1984; Lesch 1998; Ajawin and de Waal 2002; James 2007; Komey 2008b).

Thus, instead of promoting national integration and unity by cherishing the socio-cultural, ethnic and religious diversity of the Sudanese, systematic attempts to force national unity through uniformity have restricted the processes of nation-building, arrested national integration and, therefore, impeded the realization of the Sudanese state as a cohesive political entity. The contest over national identity remains intense and bitter (Deng 1973; Beshir et al., 1984; Lesch 1998; Khalid 2003), resulting in 'increasing unrest in underprivileged areas which, for a time, threatened the integrity of the state' (Roden 1974: 499).

Conceptually, nation-building is a process of spatial integration of a national territory with respect to key social, economic and political variables that must be functionally and territorially integrated in order to constitute a base for a viable state (Pounds 1972). The integration of social space is achieved nationwide when the ultimate loyalties of all communities are transferred from the local to the national level. The integration of economic space is achieved when the whole economy returns to factors of production that are approximately equal nationwide. Lastly, the integration of political space is achieved when a common political framework is territorially and functionally extended nationwide, and the relative accessibility to power, wealth, political influence, and participation is approximately equal across the territory. In short, the nation-building process is a political endeavour aiming at integrating the population of a defined territory into a cohesive political unit (Friedmann 1967; Pounds 1972; Murphy 1991; William and Smith 1993; Komey 2005a). Failure to accomplish this is likely to foster loyalties other than that of the state, which then tend to act as centrifugal forces that may weaken or even lead to the disintegration of the state. In summary, when applying this theoretical model to the current situation in the Sudan , it is hard to avoid the evidence that it is a failing state, with no political record of good governance, which is the precondition for building a cohesive and viable political unit for the long run.

National disparity in development and its political implications

A critical factor overlooked by the northern elites at the initial stage of reshaping newly independent Sudan was the colonial legacy of sharp and multifaceted regional disparity in national development. The disparity was not only maintained, but has been exacerbated under successive national governments to the present day (Lees and Brooks 1977; A. A. Ibrahim 1985; Fadalla 1986; Niblock 1987; Umbada 1988; Abdel Ati 2005; Komey 2005a). Some examples follow.

First, the concentration of economic development in the core region was clearly maintaine in the first national development plan (The Ten Year Plan 1961–70) with 70% of agricultural investment concentrated in the core region. By the end of the plan, 81.8% of the total agro-industrial establishments, 82.2% of total industrial production, 80.6% of its value added, 84.5% of workers, and 71.5% of total investments in manufacturing were concentrated in the core region, within the confines of the Kosti–Sennar–Atbara Triangle, with Khartoum as its core (Komey 2005a). This pattern remains virtually unchanged to the present day.

Second, social development, particularly in education and health services, continued to be highly concentrated in the core region. For instance, in 1996, intake ratios in the primary school sector amounted to

116%, 80.32%, 75.4% for the core areas of the Northern, Khartoum and Gezira (Central) regions respectively, far above the national average of 66.45%. Figures for the periphery remain far below the national average, with Darfur trailing behind with 53.5%. There are no available data for the South, although it is reasonable to suggest that it is likely to be below that of Darfur (Komey 2005a). Similarly, health services show striking regional disparities in major variables. For instances, in 1998 while the national averages for the general doctors, the specialist physicians, and hospital beds per 100,000 persons were 2.2, 12, and 79 respectively, regional distribution demonstrated sharp disparity. Data ranged from 30 general doctors per 100,000 persons in Khartoum to a mere 1.1 in the South; from 8.6 specialists per 100,000 persons in Khartoum to a mere 0.3 in Darfur; and from 206 hospital beds per 100,000 in the Northern region to 24.7 in Darfur (Komey 2005a: 188).

Third, the northern elites continue to dominate the politico-administrative apparatus as sources of power, wealth and socio-economic status. A study conducted in 1988 revealed that 84% of the surveyed senior civil servants in the Sudan were from the core regions of Khartoum (50%), Gezira (20%), and the greater Northern region (14%) (Komey 2005a: 68).

A direct consequence of these multifaceted, sharp and persistent regional disparities in national socio-economic development has been the widespread discontent of the peripheral regions. The absence of a political will to address these grievances has stimulated the emergence of the regional political movements that appeal to ethno-regional loyalties, with a tendency to articulate collective identity through strengthening ties to local territory in political discourse.

The ramifications of misrepresentation of sub-national identities and regional disparities in national development have stirred up successive regional political movements such as the Sudan African National Union (SANU) of southern Sudan, which arose as early as 1947. In the west and in the east, a less-publicized dissidence involving indigenous communities such as the Fur, Nuba, Funj, Igassana, and Beja started to increase from the 1950s, including the Union of North and South of Funj in 1953, the General Union of the Nuba Mountains (GUNM) in 1965, the Beja Congress in Eastern Sudan in 1958, and the Fur Development Front in Darfur in 1965 (Abbas 1973: 33; Roden 1974: 513; Beshir 1984: 22; Komey 2008b: 993–94).

A major feature of the emergence of these ethno-political movements is that they continue to pursue their issues with the central governments on the basis of their ethno-territorial affiliation, with each region progressively becoming a spatial expression of belonging and attachment, a source of economic livelihood, and an icon for socio-cultural identification. This has fostered a shift of loyalties from the national to the regional level, with each region being concretized as a political category with a specific character, image, and status in the minds of its inhabitants (Komey 2008b). This is the inevitable result of successive postcolonial regimes aggressively suppressing such regional movements with a systematic policy of undermining their political demands instead of redressing them.

As a result of this response, there has been a gradual shift of regional movements from peaceful and political to violent and armed struggle. This is manifested in the southern-based Anya Nya One in 1955, and the Sudan Peoples' Liberation Army/Movement (SPLM/A), set up in 1983, with subsequent extension to the Nuba Mountains and the southern Blue Nile in the 1980s; the Beja in the East in the 1990s; the Justice and Equality Movement (JEM) and the Sudan Liberation Movement (SLM) in Darfur in the 2000s. As the Nuba Mountains case demonstrates, the aggregate consequences have been recurring conflicts, leading to a protracted civil war with destructive effects, not only during the formal wars but also after the conclusion and implementation of the Comprehensive Peace Agreement (CPA) signed on 9 January 2005.

In summary, four common features characterize the various ethno-political movements in Sudan. First, they arose in the regions whose populations are largely of African origins in response to persistent exclusion and marginalization by the central state. Second, in pursuing their political endeavours, these regions form a loose political solidarity in some national issues of common interest, particularly in their demand for a federal system (Abbas 1973; Roden 1974). Third, these movements pursue their demands to the central government on the basis of their ethno-territorial affiliations, with each region progressively becoming a spatial expression of belonging and attachment, a source of economic livelihood, and an icon for socio-cultural identification. Finally, in response to their persistent political marginality and socio-economic deprivation, these regional movements gradually shifted from peaceful and political to armed movements coupled with a change of loyalties from national to regional levels, with each region (land) being concretized as a political category with a specific character, image, and status in the minds of its inhabitants.

Land factor in conflicts and wars

This study departs, to some degree, from the conventional perspective that tends to overstress a single cause such as ethnicity, religion or power struggle as a prime factor that triggers and sustains a conflict. This approach places land, in its broader context, at the centre of the analysis while simultaneously paying attention to other key causes of Sudan's conflicts at their various levels of scale. It suggests that, despite the multiplicity of the root causes of Sudan's recurrent political instability, coupled with its protracted civil wars, land-based grievances remain one of the motivating factors which trigger political instability and civil war particularly in the Nuba Mountains and Darfur. The significance of this approach lies in the fact that land is a cross-cutting theme that allows for a multi-layered analysis of different, yet intermingled, social spaces and fields at different levels of scale of Sudan's social organization.

This multi-layered analysis brings together various key elements including governance, ethnicity, material and symbolic resources, and their social, economic and political dimensions. Thus, a focus on the land factor in this analysis of Sudan's protracted conflicts and civil wars captures the dynamic role of local, national and international actors in triggering and subsequently sustaining conflicts at their various level of scale. The importance of situating land at the centre of this analysis stems from the fact that land, in its broader context, is a source of power, material and symbolic wealth, an icon for identification, and a base for livelihood and survival for the bulk of the rural communities in Sudan, in particular, and the Third World in general (Babiker 2001; Kjosavik 2006; Lentz 2002, 2007; Pantuliano 2007; Chapal et al., 2007; Komey 2008b, 2009a, 2010b; Falola and Njoko 2010).

The study demonstrates empirically that a single or a combination of factors such as ethnicity, religion, cultural differences or even land may be initiating or stimulating factors in a conflict. In the process, however, other factors may be raised, then gradually ascend to occupy a central position, while the initial triggering factor/s recede. This implies that the triggers are not necessarily the factors that sustain war. In this way, the causes of a conflict in a given socio-political setting become more complex, with an internal self-generating capacity, so that the conflict itself is promoted to a larger scale and effect in both temporal and spatial dimensions.

Thus, complexity is a key feature of the root causes of many communal conflicts in the world, whatever their scale. At the centre of these multifaceted causes, particularly in Africa, is the question of land rights in terms (among others) of ownership or access to use. Recent literature on this topic is substantial: for example, Suliman (1999, 2002); Toulmin and Quan (2000); Mohamed Salih et al. (2001); de Wit (2001); ACTS (2005); Manger (2002, 2008b); Komey (2008a, 2008b, 2009a, 2009b, 2010a, 2010b; Mamdani 2009). In demonstrating the centrality of land in conflicts as a symbolic and a material factor, Shipton (1994: 347–8) insists that 'Nothing excites deeper passions or gives rise to more bloodshed than do disagreements about territory, boundaries, or access to land resources.' This is so because '[what] people seek in land is not just material satisfaction but also power, wealth, and meaning ... people relate to land not just as individuals, but also as members of groups, networks, and categories.'

Lentz suggests, along the same lines that land rights are not about things but about relationships between and among persons with regard to things (2007: 37). Rights concerning land are 'nested', pertaining to different economic and ritual activities. They are also intimately tied to membership of specific communities, ranging from the nuclear or extended family, clan, or ethnic group to the nation-state. As a result, control over land has been and is still used as a means of defining identity and belonging. Membership in these groups, however, is not a given. Rather, it is contested, negotiable, and changeable over time.

For national governments, land in its broad context is a national economic resource-base for public and private development in areas such as large-scale farming and oil exploration and exploitation. The key issue is that the interests and the rights of the rural majorities and their sedentary and nomadic subsistence forms of life are rarely integrated into the land policies pursued by many national governments (Ahmed 1980; Håland 1980, 1991; Toulmin and Quan 2000; Mohamed Salih et al. 2001; International Crisis Group 2002; Muñoz 2007; Komey 2009b). In rural societies of Africa, livelihood, wealth, power, and identity are often determined by the ability of different competing stakeholders to exercise some sort of access to, use of, and ownership rights over a piece of land in question. Thus, issues of land tenure, policies, distribution patterns, and rights of ownership or access for use, are becoming critically important in political and public arenas in Africa. Numerous studies (Shipton 1994; Toulmin and Quan 2000; Dafinger and Pelican 2002; OECD 2005, Abdul Jalil 2005, 2008; Kupa and Lentz 2006; Pelican 2007; Komey 2008b, 2009a, 2009b, 2010a, 2010b), confirm that in many African countries, tension may occur or recur over land tenure and access rights when the rights grounded in formal state law contradict traditional or customary claims, or when overlapping and competitive rights exist for the use of the same land, as is the case for traditional farmers and nomadic pastoralists.

Recent works, for example, Shipton (1994); Mohamed Salih (1995, 1999); de Wit (2001); Pantuliano (2007) and Komey (2008a, 2009b, 2010b) indicate that land-related conflicts are significantly increased when land rights (statutory or customary), or government appropriation and resettlement schemes are seen to benefit certain social or ethnic groups or when they discriminate against specific stakeholders, especially communities with an indigenous claim to the land in question. Moreover, writers such as Azarya (1996); Mohamed Salih et al. (2001); Egemi (2004, 2006); Adam and Turner (2005) and Komey (2008b, 2009a) have revealed that, in many instances, the state finds itself implicated in local politics when it asserts control over certain critical land resources, which leads in turn to the emergence of a sense of marginality and exclusion among the communities affected. The link between governance, in this case bad governance, and land-related conflict is obvious.

In a situation of bad governance, some of the excluded or disadvantaged rural groups tend to employ different survival strategies, including articulating various forms of belongings and identities (Schlee 2001, 2002a, 2002b; Kjosavik 2006, Kupa and Lentz 2007; Pelican 2007; Komey 2009b). They may claim autochthonous identity (Geschiere and Nyamnjoh 2000; Mbembe 2000; Geschiere 2005; Geschiere and Jackson 2006; Komey 2008a, 2009a). In fact, several African states' exclusionary and discriminatory land policies and development interventions seem to have acted as primary factors evoking all kinds of emotional appeals to land/property rights, including some mythical autochthonous/indigenous notions inscribed in the oral history of these disadvantaged communities.

Thus, the states' exclusionary land policies and politics of limiting or denying the communities their land rights play a crucial role in causing local conflicts. With the passage of time, these state-induced local conflicts tend to escalate into large-scale wars. To paraphrase Suliman (2002: 182), land as a central factor can invert, with the progress of a conflict, to become an intrinsic cause and, in the process, increase its complexity, thereby reducing the possibility of managing, resolving, and ultimately transforming it. The conflict in the Nuba Mountains in central Sudan, a regional focus in this study, is living proof of this transformation (see below).

In the process of prolonged conflict, endangered communities may obsessively activate other forms of belonging, such as ethnic or autochthonous identities, to promote their political struggle through a strong tie to their territoriality. However, such forms of belonging and associated claims have their own logic of the inevitable territorial exclusion of other groups sharing the same contested land (Geschiere and Nyamnjoh 2000; Geschiere 2005; Geschiere and Jackson 2006; Komey 2008a, 2009b). More often than not, the result is the emergence of claims and counter-claims which are extremely difficult to substantiate empirically or negate specifically in a situation characterized by social and territorial boundary fluidity. This, in turn, inevitably instigates another chain of conflicts between the claimants of autochthonous rights and the other excluded groups (Komey 2008a, 2009a, 2009b).

State governance and land-based conflicts

The intrinsic relationship between land resource, governance and conflict in Africa is well substantiated (Mohamed Salih et al., 2001; Wily 2003, 2004). Several studies such as those of Suliman (1998, 1999, 2001, 2002); Mohamed Salih et al. (2001); Adams and Turner (2005) have pointed out that in many cases, local groups marginalized by state development policies may find themselves inevitably fighting against each other in the process of their competition over land and its meagre resources. A typical example of such state-induced land-based conflict is that between sedentary and nomadic groups in the subsistence economies of Africa.

Land-motivated conflict between symbiotic sedentary and nomadic ways of life and the way it tends to shift from a low-scale to a more complex pattern is the focal theme of this study. In this respect, a growing body of literature on Africa and elsewhere reveals that relations between sedentary and nomadic groups that share the same land resources have always oscillated between cooperation, competition, conflict, inclusion and exclusion. Reference can be made, for example, to the works of Ahmed (1976); Azarya (1996); Hussein (1998); Mohamed Salih et al., (2001); Dafinger and Pelican (2002); Tonah (2002); Benda-Beckmann (2004);

Abdul Jalil (2005, 2008) and Komey (2008a, 2008b, 2009a, 2009b, 2010b).
Nomadic groups and sedentary communities struggle to retain their
distinctive identities and compete for limited resources, while
complementarily relying on each other for the provision of essential
services and products.

The sedentary–nomadic land-based conflict, however, is not a new
type, but an old one, and has been present throughout the history of rural
societies. This is due to the fact that competition, on the one hand, together
with complementarity and cooperation, on the other, are normal historic
forms of interaction between farmers and nomads. Occasionally, these
forms of interaction escalate into violent but locally managed conflicts
(Håland 1980, 1991; Hussein 1998; Ahmed 2001; Mohamed 2002; Abdul
Jalil 2005, 2008). What is new, particularly in the semi-arid zone of Africa,
is the mounting trend of land-based conflicts to shift from local to large-
scale civil wars, beyond the capacity of local communal institutions to
manage them, and with swift change in the relations between sedentary
and nomadic groups, as well as between these local competing stakeholders
and the state (Azarya 1996; Hussein 1998; Mohamed Salih et al. 2001;
Dafinger and Pelican 2002; Schlee 2002a, 2002b, 2008; Mamdani 2009).

The crux of the matter is that when such conflicts are left unmanaged
or mismanaged by the different stakeholders, including the state, they tend
to escalate to the very worst conflict imaginable. According to Prunier
(2005), the current gross human rights violations in Darfur that have
amounted to genocide in intent were triggered by sedentary–nomadic
dynamics in their bitter competition for meagre resources.

The semi-arid zone of Africa can be roughly described as a strip north
of the equator but below the Sahara desert, stretching from the coast across
sub-Saharan Africa and characterized by an annual rainfall of 250–800
mm. This region favours contact between traditional farmers and pastoral
nomads as a prime area both to find new grazing pastures and to expand
crop cultivation. It is a zone that is often characterized by multiple and,
therefore, contested customary land rights. It has permanent natural
resources, namely grass and water on which pastoral production depends
during the dry season or droughts, while also providing conditions for
traditional farming for sedentary communities. As Shipton (1994: 359)
comments,

> Typically, in these contested areas, farmers delimiting spaces for cropping
> have neglected to leave access routes for herders to pass through; and
> herders, assuming such routes to be natural rights, have, willingly or not,
> allowed their animals to trample or eat those crops. What farmers see as
> turf disputes, the herders see as trail disputes.

Most importantly, the semi-arid zone of Africa possesses some strategic
natural resources, particularly oil, and large-scale arable land coupled with
interventions from the states of the region in the name of 'public interest'.
As a result, the zone continues to experience consistent expansion of

private and public agricultural development projects coupled with growing oil and minerals exploration and other exploitations on behalf of national and international actors over the last three decades. A wide range of literature describes these development patterns including Shipton (1994); Suliman (2001); Mbembe (2000); Hibou (2002); ACTS (2005); Johnson (2006); Ylonen (2007); Muñoz (2007); Patey (2007). Obviously, this development has been at the expense of sedentary and nomadic communities, to a large degree, with far-reaching and multifaceted repercussions on their social organizations, economic livelihoods, ecological systems – in other words, on their entire ways of living.

In Sudan, the semi-arid zone, stretching from its western border in southern Darfur to the southern Kordofan/Nuba Mountains across to the central part of the eastern border, is no exception in this respect. The Nuba Mountains region has been part of a platform for the longest civil war in contemporary Africa, with the land question being one of the key contributing factors, particularly between the sedentary and nomadic communities. Various publications confirm this reading, as in Ahmed (1980, 2001); Babiker (1998, 2001); Suliman (1999, 2002); Manger (2001, 2002); Abdul Jalil (2005, 2008); and Mamadani (2009).

As in many developing societies, the land tenure system in the Sudan is characterized by sharp dualism: (i) the communal traditional land tenure pattern regulated by customary laws and institutions, with no legal recognition when it comes to ownership rights, and (ii) the modern state land tenure pattern based on civil laws and institutions. Since its gradual introduction, the latter has continued to concentrate functionally on central and northern Sudan and on limited urban areas in the remaining parts of the Sudan (Bolton 1954; MacMichael 1954; Warburg 1970; Simpson 1976; el Mahdi 1979; Spaulding 1982; Gordon 1986; Goldflam 1988; Komey 2010b). Thus, the bulk of Sudanese rural communities remain beyond modern land policies (Adams 1982; Abdul-Jalil 1985, 2005; Håland 1991; Babiker 1998; Abdel Salam et al. 2002; Manger 2003a).

In this rural setting, land is communally owned, with individual use rights in accordance with the customs and traditions of the tribal community. Therefore, tribal land is the main constituent of land tenure with a strong link to the practice of native administration (Bolton 1954; Simpson 1965; Mohamed 1998; Miller 2005). Within the tribal homeland, the collective security of the community is constituted by individual use and inheritance rights without alienating the land from the collective ownership of the community (Nadel 1947; Spaulding 1982; Goldflam 1988; Simpson 1991). Hence, tribal land, or tribal *dar* in Arabic, demonstrates the link between tribal identity and territory and provides the base upon which the colonial administration relied in order to exercise indirect rule over the Sudan.

After independence in 1956, land tenure policy and legislation did not deviate much from the colonial legacy. With the sharp rise in demand for arable land for public and private projects, however, the land tenure system became a bone of contention between the state and rural communities. Of great significance was the introduction of the 1970 Unregistered Land Act: it stipulates that all land of any kind, whether waste, forest, occupied, or unoccupied, which was not registered before the commencement of this Act would, on its commencement, become the property of the government (Gordon 1986; Simpson 1991; Egemi 2004, 2006).

According to Simpson (1991: 102), the Act made it 'easier for the Government to expropriate land for large agricultural schemes regardless of claims to ownership'. The result was a multifaceted crisis in subsistence economies with serious socio-economic, ecological, and political repercussions in these regions (Duffield 1990; Harragin 2003). The policy fostered the formation of regional political movements and recurrent ethno-regional conflicts, particularly in Darfur (Harir and Tvedt 1994; Prunier 2005; Abdul-Jalil 2008); the Southern Blue Nile, and the Nuba Mountains (African Rights 1995; Mohamed Salih 1995, 1999; Suliman 1999; Rahhal 2001a; Johnson 2006). The same pattern is found in other regions in the Sudan (de Wit 2001; Adel Salam et al. 2002; Miller 2005; Pantuliano 2007).

Core questions and line of argument

It has already been pointed out that this study departs, to some degree, from the conventional perspective that tends to overstress a single cause as a prime factor that triggers and sustains a conflict. It thus places land, in its broader context, at the centre of the analysis while simultaneously paying attention to other key causes of Sudan's conflicts at their various levels of scale. Thus, many land-based conflicts in the Nuba Mountains region require a broader analytical perspective that allows us to understand the way people deal with access to, the use, and management of natural resources at local level and the social structures in which they are embedded. This more complex perspective reveals that not all resource conflicts are based on a situation of resource scarcity, or land grabbing as such; rather, they are political in nature and have to do with the system of governance at different levels of the state. However, once conflicts erupt they tend also to be interpreted in tribal and ethnic terms which can be linked to other types of conflicts, and leads to their escalation. Thus, an increase in levels of conflicts, which we have seen in the Nuba Mountains, cannot automatically be interpreted as another example of the many gloomy accounts of the 'degradation' of African environments or the view that all conflicts are environmental in nature, and requiring resource management solutions (see Suliman 1998, 1999, 2002). The way in which conflicts have evolved in the Nuba Mountains also requires a focus on the state and its bad governance in terms of the reproduction of autocratic leadership, mismanagement of national resources and the collapse of the state structure into warring factions fighting their own people.

Thus, the continuous alienation of Nuba lands and their appropriation by the state and outside investors is analysed in this study, within the wider context and perspective developed in this chapter. Land has been singled out by many observers as the root cause and key motivating factor for the Nuba to join the Sudan People's Liberation Movement/Army in the mid 1980s (SPLM/A) (Mohamed Salih 1995, 1999; Rahhal 2001; Manger 2001a,b, 2003, 2004, 2007, 2008a,b; NMPACT 2002; Suliman 2002; Harragin 2003; Pantuliano 2007; Komey 2008a, 2008b, 2009b, 2010b).

The extension of the civil war from the south to the Nuba Mountains region from the mid-1980s was the greatest event in the region's recent history, reshaping its entire public space. It brought about new dynamics with significant repercussions on the historical, political, economic, and territorial relationships between the state and society and equally between the various communal groups in the region. Most destructive was the collapse of the co-existence between the sedentary Nuba and the nomadic Baqqara. The failure of the symbiotic relationship that had always existed between them led to a near complete breakdown of their market, economic complementarities, and social interactions and ties.

Moreover, as the war intensified, the Nuba Mountains territory was progressively divided into two ethno-political and geo-administrative territories. These areas had been controlled and administered by successive governments of the Sudan, with the Baqqara having the upper hand in public affairs, and other areas controlled and administered by the Nuba-led SLPM/A. Thus, Baqqara nomads had no access to their traditional seasonal grazing lands and water. Whereas the land question, in terms of customary communal rights, was not a major factor in the outbreak of the civil war in southern Sudan (1983–2005), substantial literature and field-centred ethnographic material confirm its prime role in extending the civil war into the Nuba Mountains. While there were other significant causes in the larger conflict, from combined historical and contemporary factors, for the Nuba area, this ethnic rupture was the key factor.

After peace was achieved, the commonly held conviction was that the underlying root causes of Sudan's civil war, including the land question, had been diagnosed, negotiated, and finally transformed into the Comprehensive Peace Agreement (CPA) signed on 9 January 2005. Thus, during the period after the formal end of the war, two closely related questions relevant to this study have arisen. First, to what extent has the CPA been successful in addressing the land question as one of the root causes of the civil wars particularly in the Nuba Mountains region? Second, how will the conflict between the nomadic Baqqara and the sedentary Nuba people of Southern Kordofan/Nuba Mountains and the contradictions between traditional land rights and modern state land rights policy be resolved in practice? The issue involves aspects of governance, state legality, social legitimacy, territoriality, land rights, and ethnic identities and conflicts together with all their political, economic, cultural, and ecological dimensions.

In view of these core questions, the main objective of this study is to examine the mechanisms of simultaneous differentiation and adjustment between the nomadic Arabs of the Baqqara and the sedentary Nuba of the region within the broad context of Sudanese state formation. Within this frame, the study explores local discourses and practices of social and political belongings and attachments in the region since the early 1980s, during the civil war, and thereafter. The questions of access, control, and/or use rights for land and water are the main focus of this study of autochthonous identity politics. Emphasis is placed precisely on the autochthonous claim to land rights by the sedentary Nuba and the persistent questioning of those rights not only by the nomadic Baqqara in the region but also by the state. The core issue is the legal status and the practice of claiming communal land rights in a context of legal pluralism and ever-fluid boundaries among coexisting groups. Instead of concentrating on patterns and causes of confrontation, the study traces some patterns of inter-communal cooperation, co-existence, and adjustment which endured or even emerged locally before, during, and after the war.

This implies that the focus is not only on relations in a normal situation, but also on the large-scale war context and the subsequent post-conflict period. The investigation centres on land ownership as a source of material and symbolic power, wealth, local identities and livelihoods. Simultaneously, special attention is paid to governance, land laws, policies and practices in relation to communal customary rights, claims and counter-claims over the same lands, and subsequent ramifications. The contentious issue here is that most of these claims are articulated in terms of autochthonous rights. Autochthony is the claim to collective rights on the basis of belonging to an indigenous group with strong ties to an ancestral homeland (Rosivach 1987; Geschiere and Nyamnjoh 2002; Geschiere 2005; Geschiere and Jackson 2006; Ceuppens 2006; Komey 2008a, 2009a).

Autochthony is a notion associated with an ever-increasing articulation of collective rights in categories difficult to reconcile with the principles of modern statehood. To be specific, the land rights claims are presented within categories of ethnicity, culture, and religion, among others. The difficulty of reconciling these categories with the principles of the modern state stems from the fact that all these categories have doubtful references, are far from being clear, and are not simply bestowed to be used but instead emerge when invoked. Another point of contention is that the Nuba Mountains, a case in focus, is a region with several centuries of migration, forced displacements, and all kinds of settlement, social mixtures and miscegenation. Thus, the claim of autochthony, as a tie between territory and collective identity, is always not only contested, but also difficult to prove empirically. There are no clear-cut social and territorial boundaries, coupled with constant situational or strategic shifts in identities, alliances or enemy makings (Manger 1994, 2001, 2001/2002, 2003, 2008b; Mohamed Salih 1998a, 1998b; Schlee 2001, 2002a, 2002b, 2008; Elsayed 2005).

Seen from the outside, the Nuba and the Baqqara should be in the same position vis-à-vis the state policy of consistent grabbing of the best available farm and pasture lands in their region. Large-scale commercial mechanized farming and oil exploration and exploitation, are coupled with persistent policies of economic, social, and political marginalization. The success of such policies should be, as it indeed has been, of equal damage to the socio-economic basis of both the traditional nomadic and sedentary communities in the region. Therefore, national policies and politics in the region and their role in shaping state-society relations as well as inter-communal group relations will receive special attention throughout this analysis.

Thinking in rigid and dichotomous categories of Baqqara versus Nuba, nomadic versus sedentary, Arab versus African, perpetrator versus victim is avoided in this work. Instead, it explores the region during the war as social space full of 'connections, continuity, discontinuity, commonalities and dissimilarities among the various elements in the conflict zone' (Jennings 2007: 7). Thus, it analyzes these categories as social fields interrelated to and causative of each other in the Nuba Mountains region; a social world generated by the disputed results of both historical and contemporary developments.

In view of the above, the following core questions are of great significance in directing the content of this overall discussion:

1. Why and how have the traditional relations between the sedentary Nuba and the nomadic Baqqara groups witnessed such a drastic shift from amicable co-existence, complementarities, and self-management of local conflicts towards large-scale civil war, coupled with growing exclusionary tendencies along ethnic lines?

2. Why have these two major groups, previously co-existing in the Nuba Mountains region, been unwilling to pursue jointly what is apparently their clear common interest and to confront the central government's systematic policy of grabbing farming and grazing lands alike for public and private mechanized farming and oil investment? Why don't they pursue this, given the fact that the state has consistently placed both of them, as social forces, on the periphery of social space by means of a broader centre-periphery dynamic process of unequal economic, social, and political relationships?

3. How has the autochthony notion come to be articulated in identity politics by the Nuba people? Why do the emerging autochthony movement and other forms of belonging, with their exclusionary consequences, seem to have grown in dominance over the current politics in the region? Which outside ideas are adopted or challenged in local discourses on identity politics and autochthony?

4. How and why are collective identities linked with territories? How are

traditionally fluid boundaries negotiated under the pressure to fix them? By whom, in what way, and for what reasons, are they introduced into local negotiations and confrontations? And on the basis of which interpretations and interests are they transformed and applied locally?

5. The subject matter also raises the normative question of how an entangled confrontation can develop in a situation that started with peaceful negotiations and an intent to restore sustainable socio-economic development and political settlement in the Nuba Mountains region in particular and the whole of the Sudan in general.

On the basis of the central questions and main line of argument set out above, three premises can be stated:

1. The question of land, in terms of customary communal rights in a situation of sharp legal pluralism in the land tenure system coupled with exclusionary state policies and politics that consistently undermine the interests and rights of rural communities, is one among many root causes of the large-scale conflicts experienced in the Nuba Mountains in particular and in similar regions of the Sudan in general.

2. In spite of their intrinsically symbiotic life forms, shared socio-economic marginalization and underdevelopment, and poor political representation, the two disadvantaged local communities, the sedentary Nuba and the nomadic Baqqara, were brought to fight each other for reasons externally generated at the centre by the state through its bad governance.

3. Although the civil war stirred up and perpetuated the upsurge of the ethno-political movement among the Nuba in claiming land rights in the region, the premise here is that the emergence of ethno-political and autochthonous movements among the politically suppressed Nuba can be viewed as a survival mechanism or 'strategic use of essentialism' (Spivak 1988; Werbner 1997) against, and an inevitable ramification of, exclusionary state institutions and their disguised/misguided development policies before, during, and after the civil war.

Organization of the book

In addition to this introduction and the conclusion, the core of the book is divided into three parts comprising seven chapters. The first two chapters provide the background. Chapter 1 introduces and synthesizes the Nuba Mountains region as a social world composed of sets of separate, yet closely linked, spatial and social sub-worlds/fields/spaces in historical and contemporary perspectives. Chapter 2 presents a critical synopsis of historical and contemporary forces that shaped, and are still shaping, land tenure policies, rights of ownership and or access to use and their socio-political and economic trajectories.

In the second part, Chapters 3 and 4 set out an historical analysis. Chapter 3 examines the civil war as a great and unprecedented event, its root causes, dynamics, and its subsequent ramifications on the various ethnic communities in the Nuba Mountains region, particularly the sedentary Nuba and the nomadic Baqqara and their social, economic, political, and territorial relations. It gives a detailed analysis of the tragic developments of the state-induced large-scale war which rampaged in the region from 1985–2002 and subsequently transformed the relatively peaceful and symbiotic Nuba-Baqqara relationship into an antagonistic one. Chapter 4 traces various economically driven cooperations, interests, and ties between the Nuba and the Baqqara during the war. These interactions were made possible by some individuals situating themselves along the divides and doing trade and market exchange across borders, despite the intensity of war. Attention is paid to some survival strategies and coping mechanisms deployed by the parties involved while interacting in a situation characterized by excessive insecurity and mounting risk.

Part Three consists of three ethnographic chapters, drawn from the author's field work. Chapter 5 is devoted to a discursive analysis of the Sudan peace as initiative, process, and outcome that resulted in the Comprehensive Peace Agreement (CPA) in 2005. The focus is on the attempt of the peace agreement to address the question of the Nuba political and armed struggle in general and the issue of communal land rights in the Nuba Mountains in particular. Chapter 6 attempts to trace analytically Nuba autochthonous identity politics driven by the 'doctrine of liberation' embedded in the SPLM concept of 'New Sudan' and its salient political, social, and territorial features in the post-war situation. At the same time, attention is given to the Baqqara counter-responses to the Nuba's emerging ethno-political and social movement. This movement, which is still in the making, is represented as a unified agency capable of 'essentializing' the Nuba in order to take collective, strategic action in the context of their self-identification and self-representation as groups indigenous to the region.

Chapter 7 follows Nuba–Baqqara socio-economic and political discourses and trajectories in the post-conflict situation. More precisely it focuses on the discourse of an upsurge of Nuba claims to communal land ownership and the Baqqara counter-claims and disputations, and subsequent land-driven conflicts between these two groups after the peace agreement. In doing so, two competing lines of argumentation are examined in this chapter. First, the Nuba's firstcomer or even autochthonous claim of communal land rights is deeply rooted in their historical and traditional legitimacy. Second, the Baqqara Arabs raise the counter-claim of having rights not only in terms of their traditional secondary rights of access to and use of land and water, but also in terms of equal and first rights of ownership of the same land. In the process of these claims and counter-claims, at various levels of scale in the social organizations of the two groups, a range of land-motivated conflicts occur of varying scale despite the Comprehensive Peace Agreement of 2005.

In conclusion, some major findings are summarized in order to provide empirically grounded and theoretically informed insights. These findings point to further important research agendas and have implications for policy-making in the reconstruction of post-conflict Sudan, with special emphasis on the interconnected questions of state governance, communal identity politics, land and conflicts.

Part I

Background

1

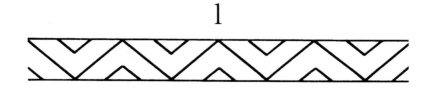

The Nuba Mountains Region as Social World

A Synthesis

Introduction

The Nuba Mountains region of South Kordofan in central Sudan represents at least three major features of contemporary Sudan as outlined in this introduction. It demonstrates the African and Arab character of Sudanese society; it signifies the unequal and exploitative forms of centre-periphery relations within an overall socio-spatial system. Further, it manifests the consequences of political marginality, disguised or distorted forms of development, coupled with excessive land grabbing and alienation by the state (Baumann 1982, 1984, 1987; Ibrahim 1988; Battahani 1986; Mohamed Salih 1999; Saavedra 1998; Suliman 1999, 2002; Mohamed and Fisher 2002; Manger 2003b, 2008b; Komey 2005a, 2005b; Jedrej 2006; Patey 2007).

This chapter provides a bird's eye view, or generalized picture, of the Nuba Mountains region as a whole entity, composed of physical and cultural landscapes. Nevertheless, the focus is on its major socio-economic organizations within their temporal and spatial settings. It outlines topographic features, ethnic composition, settlement and land use patterns, and the socio-political landscape of the past and present. At the centre of this multi-dimensional analysis is the land factor, in its wider context, as a connecting feature between these various spatial and social fields.

The region is first introduced in its spatial aspect which contains sets of ecological agents, interconnected and causative to each other as a whole natural resource base. Second, the present social setting is sketched while paying attention to the multifaceted historical and contemporary socio-political forces that continue to shape the region in the process of state formation. Third, through land use patterning, the spatial aspect, with its natural endowments as resource base, is functionally linked with social organizations to form a whole social world in a spatial-social continuum. Using the concepts of 'social space' (Bourdieu 1985) or 'social world/arena' (Strauss 1978; Clarke 1991) as analytical perspectives, the Nuba Mountains region is delineated as a social space consisting of intersecting social fields (ecological, economic, social, and political) of active forces both in the past and present, with their respective roles and attributes. Within this wider presentation of the Nuba Mountains region, the dynamic relationship between its various socio-political entities can be understood and investigated further in subsequent chapters.

Land as source and basis of livelihoods

As an ecological field, the Nuba Mountains region lies in the geographical centre of the Sudan. In older literature, it was referred to as Dar Nuba (Lloyd 1908: 140, Sagar 1922: 138). It is situated between longitudes 29° and 31°30'E and latitudes 10° and 12°30'N and covers an area of approximately 88,000 km2 (roughly 30,000 square miles) within the savanna summer rain belt. It is bordered by North Kordofan in the north, White Nile State in the east, Upper Nile State in the southeast, Warrap, Jonglei and Unity States in the south, and South Darfur State in the west (Map 1.1).

Its mountainous topographical features give it unique physical characteristics in relation to its surroundings. It forms an irregular, broken pattern of long mountain ranges, squat massifs and rugged rocks, separated by broad valleys and stretches of plains.[1] Several mountain masses and isolated hills separated by plains of various sizes are the distinct topographic features in the region. The mountainous masses and hills represent 18.5% of the total area, which is part of a basement complex formation (Babiker et al., 1985: 38; Komey 2005a: 199–200). The plains areas are covered with muddy, cracking and/or non-cracking soils with some alluvial deposits at the edges, close to the Bahr al-Arab River in the south and the White Nile in the east. The fertile clay and alluvial soils account for about 45% of the total land area in the region. A second land type of sandy soils covers the western and northern parts of the region and composes approximately 32% of the total land area of the region. These soils include stabilized quz, mobile quz, windblown sand sheets, and alluvial sands in valleys vulnerable to degradation.

Generally, arable land in the region constitutes 15% of the total arable land in the Sudan. It is divided into the fertile clay soils of the plains known locally as hadaba (black cotton soils), the sandy/clay pediment soils found at the foot of the mountain, known as gardud, broad wadi as well as small

---

[1] For some details of the physical and land use features in the region, see Lloyd (1910a: 254–59); March (1944: 1–3, 1954: 832–40); Nadel (1947: 1); Tothill (1954: 832); Lebon (1959: 63–5); Babiker et al. (1985: 35–6).

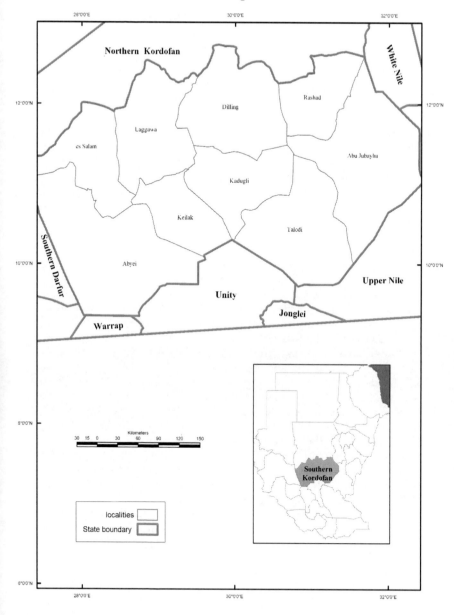

Map 1.1 Southern Kordofan State location
Source: Survey department, Sudan 2009

wadi soil systems known as bat-ha or faw, and the rocky mountain soils known as karkar. Over 20% of the total area of the region is grazing land, whereas 14–22% of the area is either cultivated or lies fallow (Harragin 2003: 4; March 1944: 1–3). The vegetation cover varies according to the level of soil fertility and rainfall; it is generally richer to the south, while along the water courses the stratified alluvial soils support moderately various types of dense, tall trees, including horticultural species (Hassan 1963; Babiker et al., 1985).

Rainfall is the main source of surface water, and its availability depends on the amount of precipitation, temperature, evaporation, and drainage system. The relatively high rainfall and the mountainous nature of the terrain give rise to many seasonal streams (in Arabic, khiran [pl.], khur [sg.] dissecting the plains. They provide very fertile silt soils for irrigated farming including horticulture. Along some of these water courses, a few water reservoirs and dams have been constructed to capture some water resources for human, animal, and horticultural use during the dry season (Bolton 1954; March 1954).

In addition, there are a number of natural depressions filled with rainfall or run-off, locally known as fula, rihud, and turda. There are also man-made water stores in the traditional local reservoirs known as hafirs, and different types of wells that represent the main source of water during the dry season, particularly in the northern parts of the region (Colvin 1939; Hassan 1963; Babiker et al., 1985). These distinctive ecological features determine the pattern of human settlement, land use, and overall socio-economic activities and organizations.

Land-use patterns in the region are predominantly two, co-existing subsistence systems: rain-fed cultivation, practised chiefly by the sedentary Nuba, and pastoralism, which is the main way of life for the nomadic Baqqara. These complementary traditional modes of life are supplemented by the cultivation of gardens, irrigated by seasonal water courses or shallow aquifers. Since the 1960s, there has been a successive introduction of modern mechanized rain-fed farming systems in the region (Saeed 1980; Battahani 1980, 1983; Salih 1982; Ibrahim 1988). Mechanized rain-fed farming and trade businesses are in the hands of small but extremely influential groups of the Jillaba, from northern and central Sudan, and the Fellata who are migrants from West Africa (Kursany 1983; Battahani 1986; Manger 1984, 1988).

As a promising agricultural region strategically located between equatorial southern Sudan and the northern desert areas, this region is one of the major economic bases for the country's agrarian economy. Moreover, rich oil fields recently discovered and exploited in the southwestern portion in the 1980s have added more economic, political, and strategic significance to the region at national as well as global levels (Suliman 2001; Mohamed and Fisher 2002; Johnson 2006; Patey 2007).

The sedentary Nuba

The region is predominantly inhabited by a cluster of Nuba peoples who identify themselves as indigenous to the area. Classic literature attests to the status of the Nuba as the firstcomers, which is undisputed.[2] The people are composed of more than fifty different ethnic groups (Nadel 1947: 1) and constitute ten distinct linguistic groups (MacDiarmid and MacDiarmid 1931:160–1). They are of African origin and followers of Islam, Christianity, and traditional religions.

In 1927, the Nuba population was estimated at 270,000, representing 72% of the total population in the region at that time, including the former Nuba Mountains Province (1914–28), part of Jebel al-Dair, and the Nuba hills of al-Haraza, Um Duraq, Abu Hadid, and Kaja (Gillan 1931: 8) in the present North Kordofan. In the 1955 population census, the Nuba population was estimated at 572,935, representing 6% of the total population of the Sudan (Republic of the Sudan 1958).

Since independence, however, population censuses in the region have become a highly contested topic, due to ethno-politics that tend to manipulate statistics for various interests. In view of this, in the 1983 census, the population of the region was described as 'more than a million, nearly five percent of the total population of Sudan, before war engulfed the region in the early 1990s' (Meyer 2005: 25). In 1993, the Sudanese government estimated the total Nuba in the region to be 1.1 million in number, while a UN census in 1998 put the figure at 1,025,772. Later, in 2006, the government of Sudan estimated the total population of the region to be 1.7 million (Republic of Sudan 2006: 6), with Nuba peoples representing about 70% of that total. Johnson (2006: 131) cites a range between 1.3 and 1.6 million for the Nuba population, excluding internally displaced peoples and refugees. In 2008, the Minority Rights Group International estimated the total number of Nuba to be around 3.7 million (Ylonen 2009: 14). According to a fifth population census conducted in 2009, the total population of the region stands at 1,406,404. The process and results of this last census have been controversial, and it has been officially cancelled with an agreement to be redone later.

Despite their statistical majority, the Nuba 'constitute a political minority due to their social and economic marginalization' (Mohamed Salih 1999: 1). The history of the Nuba reviewed below shows that their political struggle has been characterized by a series of violent phases. These rest consistently on two main pillars: identity and territory, both of which contribute to a constant striving for sovereignty and for the right to manage their own development (Manger 2007: 72).

---

[2] See Pallme (1844); Seligmann (1910, 1932/65); Lloyd (1908, 1910a, 1910b); MacMichael (1912/67, 1922/67, 1954); Sagar (1922); Hillelson (1930); Nadel (1947); Stevenson (1965); Spaulding (1987).

NUBA HISTORY, ORIGINS, AND ATTACHMENT
TO THE REGION

A wide range of literature agrees that the Nuba peoples were the first to settle in greater Kordofan, thousands of years before other groups came in. At the very least, the geographical area where the Nuba tribes live in southern Kordofan has been known as Dar Nuba, or the Nuba homeland, for more than six centuries (Lloyd 1908: 55; Seligmann 1910; MacMichael 1912/67: 3, also see Hawkesworth 1932, Henderson 1931, 1935). Moreover, some writers, such as MacMichael (1922/67: 197), Trimingham (1949/83: 6) and recently Saavedra (1998: 225) are certain that the Nuba are not only the firstcomers but autochthones to the region in particular and, indeed, to the Sudan as a whole.

MacMichael (1912/67: 3) confirmed that '[the] area at present known as Kordofan may very roughly be divided into three parallel latitudinal belts, viz – the southern mountains inhabited by sedentary autochthonous Nuba and in part by nomad Bakkara.' Nevertheless, little is known about the ancient history of the Nuba, as their own traditions and recollections yield sparse information (Lloyd 1908: 55, Nadel 1947:5; Salih 1982: 19). This might be ascribed to successive historical events which, as outlined below, significantly disturbed the memory of their history of movement and subsequent settlement patterns. For Nadel (1947: 5), 'it often seems as if historical traditions had been cut short by the overpowering experience of the Mahdist regime (1881–98), which must have severed all links with a more distant – and possibly less disturbed – past.'

Spaulding reinforced this view: '...no scholar has yet deliberately undertaken to write a history of the Nuba, but many have found themselves constrained to make tangential statements of assumptions about the Nuba history in the course of constructing studies with some other primary focus' (1987: 369). Despite this, some sort of collective mythology still exists, vaguely linking the origin and past of the different Nuba groups in a common historical trajectory (Sagar 1922, Nadel 1947, Kramer 1987).

Different yet interrelated views and theses have been developed about the Nuba origins, history, and migratory patterns. One is represented by Hillelson (1930: 137–40), who assumes a racial connection between the Nuba and the Nilotic Nubians on the basis of partial linguistic affinities between the two groups. This is manifested in the diffusion of the Nubian language in three main dialects, the Nilotic Nubian of the Northern Sudan, the Hill Nubian of the Nuba Mountains, and the Nubians of south-west Darfur, the Bergid and Midob (Hillelson 1930; MacMichael 1922/67). Apparently, the linguistic connection between the Nuba of the northern-western part of South Kordofan (Dilling, Ghulfan, and Kadaro, among others) and the Nubians of the northern Nile Valley is well-established from historical records (Hillelson 1930: 137–40; MacDiarmid and MacDiarmid 1931: 161; Seligmanns 1932/65: 373; Stevenson 1965).

What is still in dispute is the racial connection between these two groups, because language is an acquired skill. Nevertheless, the link between these two groups exists by virtue of more than linguistic affinities alone. Arkell (1961: 178) reported that

> [... in] the third century A.D. we hear of a people called Nubades or Nobatae, who have hitherto usually been taken to be the same people as the Nuba or Nubians. But whether they are the same people or have a different origin is uncertain, and in the present state of our ignorance an open mind should be kept on the matter.

The second view attributes the linguistic affinities of the two groups to the influence of the Nilotic Nubians, who infiltrated Southern Kordofan and imposed their own language on the local Nuba around their settlements in the most northerly of the Nuba Mountains (Seligmann 1913: 620, 1917: 402, MacMichael 1922/67: 14–15). It is evident that the Nuba had occupied the whole of Kordofan before they were 'beaten back by other races that ruled the Nile banks in successive generations, or by tribes from the interior, and finally by the nomads Arabs, the Nuba have now retired to the mountains of Southern Kordofan' (MacMichael 1912/67: 3; also see Trimingham 1949: 244).

As the Arabs conquered Northern Sudan, the Nuba were killed, enslaved, or driven by force into Kordofan, where they remained until the invasion of the Fung and their kindred tribes. Some of their number eventually succumbed to the Kababish or to the Dervishes (Sagar 1922: 139; Lloyd 1908: 55). This view is substantiated by two factors: the existence of the Nuba remnants in northern Kordofan today in 'Jebels Al-Haraza, Um Duraq, Abu Hadid, and Kaqa' (Trimingham 1949: 245), and the oral narratives of the Nuba themselves. Trimingham goes on to comment that 'the inhabitants of Harraza are of Nuba origin but are now quite Arabicized, having lost the qualities which endear the pagan Nuba to those living among them and become debased' (Trimingham 1949: 245). This same narrative was reported by MacMichael (1922/67: 34) and Seligmanns (1932/65: 367–412).

One common point among these diverse views is the prevalence of some major historical incursions of outsiders who continuously and aggressively de-territorialized the Nuba, and eventually pushed them out of their flat and fertile lands into the hilly areas of southern Kordofan. Their traditional lands were progressively occupied by others, including the present Baqqara.

NUBA PRESENT SETTLEMENT, LAND TENURE, AND USE PATTERNS

Following the Nuba's enforced retreat to the hilly areas in southern Kordofan, they enjoyed a period of comparative tranquility and peace which allowed them to cultivate huge tracts of the land with 'their crops stretching for miles into the plains around their Jebels' (Lloyd 1908: 55,

Sagar 1922: 139). This pattern continued until the penetration of the Baqqara into the Dar Nuba from the west in the 1780s (Lloyd 1908; Hederson 1935, 1939; Cunnison 1966). Upon their arrival,

> [the] Baqqara at once began to raid the Nubas, enslaving all on whom they could lay hands, and taking all their grain and cattle they could find. The Nubas in defense retired into Jebels and terraced them for cultivation in remote parts where horsemen could not approach them. (Lloyd 1908: 55)

This suggests that, due to the 'institutionalized insecurity' imposed by external forces (Spaulding 1987: 373), the majority of Nuba hill communities were forced to confine themselves to their respective hilltops while cultivating in long, narrow, terraced strips. At best, the Nuba extended downwards to the adjacent plains and fertile lands (Sudan Archive 1934b: SAD 631/10/4) with a measure of uncertainty and caution. Today, the majority of the Nuba tribes live in straggling settlements, scattered over the valleys and hillsides. The heart of the matter is that the Nuba present settlement patterns, land tenure practices, and social organizations are a result of historical forces that imposed on them multifaceted forms of pressure and violence. Therefore, the spatial distribution of Nuba settlement and land use patterns, as they exist today, should not be interpreted as the norm, but rather as an anomaly brought about by successive violent external forces and their related practices, including slave trading. In Manger's words: this is 'not as a result of any natural situation but rather because of unequal strength during periods of slavery' (2007: 72).

Paradoxically, the civil war (1983–2005) proved that the persistence of the Nuba in preserving their historical settlement pattern is not only a past legacy but a present necessity. Their fortifications in their inaccessible hills during the civil war kept down their casualties during the government's intentional campaign of genocide and ethnocide, particularly during the early 1990s (see Chapter 3). As a result of this war, the collective mind of the Nuba has come to equate the obsessive marginalization and discrimination forced on them by the state and the coercive control exercised by national governments with what prevailed during the precolonial and colonial eras.

In adapting to their imposed hilly settlements, the Nuba developed a number of agricultural land uses and tenure patterns in the areas of the massif and other extensive mountain ranges, by enclosing large tracts of arable lands or by encroaching on the open plain areas in the foothills (Roden 1969, 1972, 1975; Rottenburg 1983; Harragin 2003). At least five distinctive types of traditional farming practised by the sedentary Nuba communities may be identified in the region.

First, there are 'house farms', known locally as jubraka and usually located close to the house compound. The land here is fertilized annually with animal and human waste and ashes. Second, there are 'near or hillside farms' on the inhabited slopes or in the higher terraced valleys. Third, there are 'far farms' in the plains which began to flourish following the downhill movement caused by the colonial administration. As their name indicates, the far farms are situated at a great distance from the settlement in the plains areas, known as bat-ha or gardud. This type is usually situated on clay soil where a system of crop rotation is adopted within a pattern of shifting cultivation. There is a fourth category, the 'cattle camp farms' which mainly benefit from animal waste and are usually the direct responsibility of very young family members who tend the livestock during the cultivation period. Fifth, there are irrigated plots and gardens situated close to wells or stream courses (Nadel 1947:16–17; Stevenson 1965: 47).

Land is communally owned within customary traditions and norms regulating individual, family, or community access. Despite the fact that there is no formal land authority or institution among Nuba communities, three types of land ownership are recognized (Nadel 1947; Roden 1975; Harragin 2003). First, there is individually owned land, over which a certain individual holds complete and absolute property rights. Individual land holdings are marked by clearly visible boundaries, i.e., rows of stones, tree stumps, hedges, or strips of grass between neighbouring cultivated fields. Every tract of land in the region that is, or has once been, under cultivation, is individually owned.

Second, community-owned land is usually vacant and uninhabited land. Local groups hold certain pre-emptive claims over this type of 'corporate land', regarding it as a communal asset belonging to their members. Corporate property rights are those vested in varying degrees in a village, hill community, or at the tribal level. These are shared by all group members, by virtue of membership in a wider community within whose territory the land is situated.

Third is the vacant, ownerless, 'no man's land' which does not belong to any individual or community. Usually, this is the uninhabited and unclaimed stretches between the territories occupied by the tribes or hill communities. Such areas continue to serve as corridor zones for pastoral movement, without interference, for the protection of crops.

In the majority of tribes, land inheritance is based on patrilineal traditions. Inheritance in the matrilineal system is followed by distinct groups, mostly in the western and southern hills (Nadel 1947; Roden 1975). Despite the fact that the land tenure patterns described are still practised, they have recently undergone significant transformation. This has been brought about by numerous external and internal factors, particularly the increasing trends of Nuba down-hill movement, mechanized farming expansion, and the gradual settlement pattern of the Baqqara (Roden 1975; Saeed 1980; Kursany 1983; Ibrahim 1988, 1998; Manger 2003a). These factors have provoked a hardening of Nuba tribal boundaries, and even, in some areas, the appearance of fixed boundaries for the first time, as the arable territory of one tribe gradually impinges upon that of another.

As the nomadic Baqqara are becoming more and more settled, many villages and rural centres have emerged in the lowland composed of Nuba and sedentary or semi-sedentary Arabs. These recent changing patterns in land use and tenure have produced far-reaching social, economic and political repercussions in the region. For instance, arable land has become increasingly scarce, leading to the emergence of a land market in the form of borrowing, sales, rent, and lease. However, the 'whole question of legal title to agricultural holdings remains ambiguous because officially all land is state owned, and farmers in theory retain only rights of usage' (Roden,1975: 302).

A further response has been that individual and communal disputes over land have begun to increase, leading to more disputes, especially when they involve members of different ethnic groups. At this stage in the process of socio-economic transformation, traditional institutions become increasingly incapable of handling the scale and complexity of these inter-ethnic land-based issues. The result is a drastic shift from small to large-scale land-based conflicts as detailed in the following chapters.

The nomadic[3] Baqqara

The term 'Baqqara' ([pl.]; 'Baggari' [sg.]) means 'cattlemen' and applies to 'an Arab who has been forced by circumstances to live in a country which will support the cow but not the camel' (Henderson 1939: 5). The Baqqara in the region are typical of the pastoral and nomadic groups that roam across Africa's arid and semi-arid lands. In their well-defined and rhythmic spatial mobility, an integral part of their life-style, they constantly adopt different strategies and coping mechanisms to survive changing ecological and human situations (Henderson 1939; Cunnison 1966; Haraldsson 1982; Abdel-Hamid 1986; Michael 1987a, 1998; Azarya 1996; Mohamed Salih et al., 2001; Gertel 2007).

The Baqqara, who arrived in the area of the Nuba Mountains over 200 years ago as pastoral nomadic peoples, represent the major sub-ethnic group of Arab origin in the region.[4] They are part of larger nomadic Arab tribes in Africa who collectively occupy a zone extending from the left bank of the White Nile to Lake Chad, covering in the Sudan the plains of Kordofan and Darfur as far south as the Bahr al-'Arab.[5]

According to Cunnison (1966: 1) and Henderson (1939: 52), after the Arabs' invasion of Egypt, groups which later became the Baqqara drifted westwards along the North African coast to present-day Tunisia, then headed south-east to the Chad region, Bornu and Wadai, and later spread eastwards in the direction of the Nile, via Kordofan. Others, such as MacMichael (1912/67: 276), favour the view that the Baqqara formed part

---

[3] Despite their distinct differences, for the purpose of this book, the terms 'pastoral' and 'nomadic' are used here interchangeably to mean one broad category of mobility as opposed to the sedentary category. For some discussion on the distinction between 'pastoralism' and 'nomadism', see Azarya (1996: 3, footnote 1). See also Gertel (2007: 28, note 2) for some distinctions on 'nomadism' itself.
[4] For earlier studies or notes on the Baqqara Arabs, see Lloyd (1908, 1910), MacMichael (1912/67, 1922/67), Yunis (1922), Henderson (1935, 1939), and Trimingham (1949/83). For more recent studies, see Cunnison (1966), Ahmed (1976), Abdel-Hamid (1980), Adams (1982), Michael (1987a, 1987b, 1991, 1997, 1998), and Ibrahim (1988, 1998).
[5] For a discussion of various nomadic groups in Africa, including some comments on the Baqqara see, for example, Hussein (1998), Azarya (2006), Mohamed Salih et al., (2001), and Gertel (2007).

of the Guhayna Arab group who spread in large numbers over the Nile Valley in the first half of the fourteenth century and in the following centuries appear to have pushed westwards as far as Bornu. By 1803, they were already well established in Darfur (Henderson 1939:58).

The Baqqara of South Kordofan consist primarily of three main groups: Messiriyya, Aulad Himaid, and the Hawazma. According to Gillan (1931: 8), the Arab population in the region in 1927 was estimated at between 65,000 and 70,000, representing 28% of the region's total population. In the first census (1955/56), the figure totalled 351,393, including the Arabicized Nuba of Tegali (Republic of Sudan 1958: 48).

Of these three main groups, the focus here is on the Hawazma sub-groups because of their relevance to the study. The word Hawazma originates from an Arabic term, meaning 'tie together'. During the sixteenth century, there were numerous tribal clashes and many small tribes in Kordofan needed to cooperate. They formed the Hawazma by swearing on the Qur'an that they would always give up their own claim to independence if needed for the sake of the whole tribe; since then, many groups and individuals have sworn the Hawazma oath (Haraldsson 1982: 26).

Over time, the Hawazma has become more than a tribe or even an ethnic group. Today, it is a conglomerate of ethnic groups as it has flexibly extended its alliances to integrate other non-Arab ethnic groups. For example, the six tribes of Zunara, Takarir, Jillaba, Hawara, Jawama'a, Bidayrriyya, and slaves are part of Halafa. None of these six tribes forming Halafa is genealogically Arab, as are most Hawazma groups. These non-Arab groups were integrated into Hawazma in the mid-eighteenth century upon swearing an oath that bound them to the Hawazma alliance (MacMichael 1922/67: 151–52).

The Baqqara move seasonally southwards during the dry season between the hilly Nuba areas and the traditional homelands of the peoples of South Sudan and then return northwards during the rainy season. Although they are historically known to be nomadic, a great number have acquired a more sedentary mode of life today, as they move gradually from nomadism to an agro-pastoralist mode of life that depends on both animals and cultivation on the plains of the Nuba Mountains. Moreover, some of these agro-pastoralists have been completely transformed into sedentary groups with progressive engagement in trade and mechanized rain-fed farming in the Nuba Mountains.[6]

Since Turco-Egyptian rule, the Baqqara have been part of the native administration system introduced at that time in the Sudan and governed by the Nazir, 'Umda, and Shaykh (Warburg 1971: 144). The Hawazma are composed of three main confederated sections: the Halafa, the Aulad 'Abdul 'Ali, and the Rawawqa. Each section is further divided into sub-sections. For instance, the Rawawqa section is composed of Dar Jami',

---

[6] For some discussion of the ecological adaptation and progressive transformation of the Baqqara of South Kordofan, see, for example, Henderson (1939), Adams (1980), Abdel-Hamid (1986), Michael (1987a, 1987b, 1991, 1997, 1998), and Battahani (1980, 1986).

Dilimiyya, and Aulad Nuba (MacMichael 1922/67: 140–53). Recently, non-Arab groups of the Shawabna, the Fellata of al-Bardab and the Takarir, have been co-opted into the Hawazma confederation. At present, the Rawawqa native administration is composed of six 'Umudiyas' of Dilimiyya, Aulad Nuba, Dar Jami', Shawabna 'Agab, Shawabna al-Samma, and Fellata of al-Bardab (Ibrahim 1988, 1998).

As agro-pastoralists, the Hawazma adopt a rhythmic pattern of migration compatible with variations in the natural environment and seasons. They spend the wet (rainy) season in al-makharif in the sa'id (north) as their original dar, i.e. home territory, around the northern limits of the Nuba Mountains and the southern limits of Northern Kordofan. Towards the end of the rainy season, they start their systematic movement along a north-south axis to their respective early dry or winter season grazing zones (al-mashati) in the plains areas within the Nuba Mountains hills.

In the dry season, they move further southwards to the riverain lands of Balu al-Arab in Dalu al-Ghazal and the White Nile in the traditional homelands of the peoples of the South Sudan (al-masaif). They spend approximately eight months in dry season camps in al-mashati and al-masaif, one or two months in rainy season camps in al-makharef, with the rest of the year spent trekking either north or south. At the beginning of the rainy season, they resume their movement northwards to spend the early showers period (rushash) in the plains areas within the Nuba Mountains hills before continuing their journey back to their al-makharif. In this way, the Nuba Mountains region acts as a traditional buffer zone between their wet and dry seasons, with most of the yearly cycle being spent in the region (Salih 1982; Abdel-Hamid 1986; Ibrahim 1988; Michael 1991).

In general, the younger members of the family move with their cattle north or southwards, while the remaining family members stay behind in order to engage in traditional cultivation and horticultural management until they are rejoined with their cattle at the end of the rainy season. Today, the territorial distribution of the Hawazma-Rawawqa section in the Nuba Mountains takes the following rough pattern: the Dar Jami' coexists with the Nuba Keiga, with their centre in al-Kweik, the Aulad Nuba with the Nuba Laguri and Saburi and with Tukswana and Umm Safifa as their centres, and the Dilimiyya with the Nuba of Moro, Masakin Tuwal, and Qusar, whose major settlement points are at Hamra and Reikha.

In their rhythmic movement coupled with partial settlement, the Baqqara are intensively engaged with the local sedentary Nuba through a set of ecological and social intermediaries. These include pastures, water points, market places, farming land, socio-cultural and political functions. Accordingly, they have been progressively integrated into the wider socio-economic system in the Nuba Mountains. They are significantly engaged in local trading and in mechanized rain-fed farming, with their children attending schools, and some of their elites occupying leading positions in the political and public arena at regional and national levels (Henderson 1939; Battahani 1980, 1983, 1986; Ibrahim 1988, 1998).

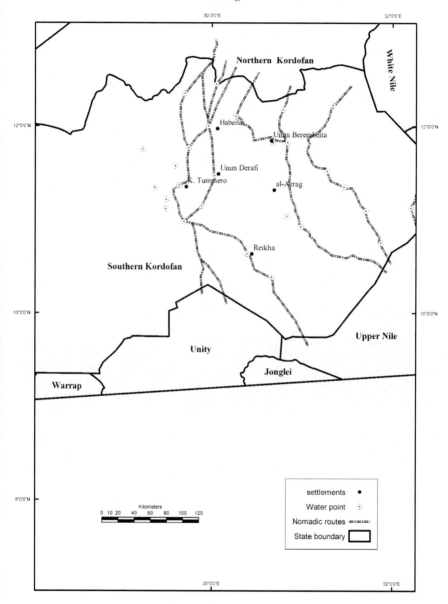

Map 1.2 Baqqara nomads' seasonal migration routes and water points
Source: Field work, 2006–8

Under normal circumstances, the nomads' seasonal migrations follow distinctive and strict routes which regulate the movement and timing of their grazing rights. The British administration implemented a system of stock routes for seasonal migration and had set dates for the beginning of it to coincide with the end of the harvest. There were water points along the way and stock holding areas (Map 1.2). It was a vital arrangement aimed at avoiding damage to Nuba crops.

At the same time, Nuba farmers were not allowed to farm on the stock routes or to delay harvesting unnecessarily. The native administration, which was abolished in the 1970s, was a major catalyst in maintaining this arrangement although this strict colonial arrangement had become greatly weakened. Consequently, livestock started to encroach into farming areas more and more. Two key factors contributed to the deterioration of the stock route system and, therefore, to the acceleration of frequent farmer–nomad conflicts: ecological changes and state institutional failure, coupled with the state's underhand and distorted forms of development intervention in the region.

In the last three decades, the African Sahelian zone, including North Kordofan, has been severely affected by droughts, particularly during the 1970s and 1980s (Adams 1982: 268; Harragin 2003: 12; Abdul-Jalil 2005: 63). Due to these negative ecological changes, the South Kordofan/Nuba Mountains region has been subjected to the influx of successive waves of Arab nomad refugees from North Kordofan.

Due to ecological and socio-economic changes, some of the Baqqara nomads decided gradually to settle, and established permanent hamlets along the traditional migratory routes, thus blocking them. Moreover, it forced the nomads to move southwards with their cattle earlier and therefore they frequently arrive before the Nuba harvest is over. More important, from the end of the 1960s onwards, the region has experienced a sweeping expansion of mechanized rain-fed farming schemes which intersect with certain major stock routes.

As a result of these multifaceted factors, the nomads have started to encroach more and more on the farming zones, causing destruction and damage to agricultural production. As revealed in subsequent chapters, several recent cases of nomad–sedentary conflicts in the region are ascribed to the expansion of mechanized rain-fed farming investments in the region.

The Nuba marginality, enslavement and dislocation: an historical review

As a social world, the present Nuba Mountains region is a product of a long history coupled with different forces in the process of Sudanese state formation (Baumann 1982, 1984, 1987). The historical forces, detailed below, are spread over the precolonial, colonial, and post-colonial eras.

THE FUNG AND TEGALI KINGDOMS AND THE SUZERAINTY OVER THE NUBA HILLS

The Fung kingdom was founded in the sixteenth century by some black groups who joined forces with the Hamaj, the indigenous inhabitants of the Gezira, against the invading Arab tribes. In the middle of the seventeenth century, the allied forces of the Fung and Arabs invaded Kordofan. Those who escaped from the Fung took refuge either in the Northern Kordofan Hills such as Kaja, Katul, Haraza, and Abu Dereg, or in the Southern Kordofan Jebels (Salih 1982: 28). In the latter case, some of them occupied uninhabited Jebels, while others drove weaker communities out of their homes and occupied them themselves. From that time onwards, there were periodic raids, especially to the Tegali hills, but no attempt at permanent occupation seems to have been made by either of these ruling races (Sagar 1922: 138).

The subjugation of some of the hills to Sennar rule was largely symbolic, since communities were allowed to retain their rulers and their indigenous institutions. However, there was a systematic subordination or overlordship by the Sennar kingdom over the Nuba through two channels, first, through the Sultan of the Ghudiyat of Kordofan, and second, through the vassal fiefdom of Tegali (MacMichael 1922/67: 8; Elles 1935:10–17; Salih 1982: 29; Spaulding 1987: 372). Elles recorded that by the middle of the seventeenth century, the kings of Tegali were supreme over the North-Eastern Jebels. To the south-west, many hill communities of pagan Nuba were indirectly subject to Tegali, including the Koalib, Alleira, Heiban, Shwai Nuba, and possibly also those of Otoro.

This early subjugation of the Nuba hill communities by the Fung Sultanate through the Tegali or the Ghudiyat Sultanates marked the beginning of their displacement and enslavement. The pattern was followed by the Baqqara, Jillaba, the Mahdiyya, foreign slave traders, and the Turco-Egyptian rulers.

THE ARRIVAL OF THE BAQQARA AND THE MASS DISPLACEMENT AND ENSLAVEMENT OF THE NUBA

The penetration of the Baqqara Arabs to Kordofan from the west marked the beginning of mass displacement of the Nuba from their ancestral land. Upon their arrival and penetration in waves into the Dar Nuba in the early years of the 1800s, the Baqqara Arabs violently de-territorialized the local Nuba before they participated in precolonial slave-raids, with great success (Pallme 1844; Lloyd 1908; MacMichael 1922/67; Henderson 1939). They divided the country between them with the Hawazma taking the eastern and central Jebels, the Hamr the western, and the Messiriyya a few small Jebels in the north-west of Dar Nuba. At once, they began to raid the Nubas, enslaving everyone they could lay their hands on, and stealing all the grain and cattle they could find. In defence, the Nubas retreated into their Jebels in remote areas, where the raider-horsemen could not reach them, and terraced the land for cultivation (Lloyd 1908: 55).

However, crops grown in the barren soil of the terraced hills were poor and often failed, so that in such failed harvest times, the Nuba were compelled to sell their own people, often their own children, as slaves to the Arabs for grain (Sagar 1922: 140). Thereafter, traders and the local Baqqara Arabs carried out regular slaving raids:

> The raiders were organized in bands of footmen, armed with rifles, and a detachment of Baqqara horsemen, whose function it was to cut off the Nubas from their hills. Each horseman was accompanied by a camp follower, who rode behind him during the preliminary operations, and then dismounted to bind and take charge of the captives. The riflemen then appeared on the scene, ready to repel any effort at a rescue made by the hill men. (Sudan Government 1912: 79)

The severity of these raids resulted in wide-scale deterritorialization of the Nuba from their plains. In some instances, a total depopulation of some lower and more accessible hills took place, and a further exodus of many Nuba groups from the lower slopes and foothills to high valleys and plateaus (Sagar 1922; Colvin 1939; Stevenson 1965; Roden 1975). Such, roughly, was the state of the Jebels when the Egyptian Government arrived in 1821; and from that time, the whole of Sudan entered a new phase.

THE TURCO-EGYPTIAN ERA AND THE UPSURGE OF NUBA ENSLAVEMENT AND DISPLACEMENT

The process of Nuba marginalization, humiliation, oppression, and dispossession of their plains land was reinforced and institutionalized during Turco-Egyptian rule in the Sudan (1821–1885). One of Khedive Mohamed Ali's main objectives in conquering Sudan was to recruit black slaves from the Nuba Mountains, Blue Nile, and Southern Sudan to reinforce his imperial army. Towards that end, in 1823, the Khedive wrote to the Commander-in-Chief of the Sudan and of Kordofan, 'You are aware that the end of our efforts and these expenses is to procure Negroes. Please show zeal in carrying out our wishes in this capital matter' (Salih 1982: 32; Ibrahim 1988: 24).

Given that the Nuba were technologically powerless, their inaccessibility in the hills offered the best form of resistance against the Turkish troops. The Turco-Egyptian rulers did not attempt to conquer the region territorially, 'but took tribute, at first in the form of slaves, for recruits from a number of more accessible Jebels such as Dilling, Ghulfan, Kadaro, and Kadugli. A few of the other smaller Jebels were also attacked, and either reduced or wiped out' (Lloyd 1908: 55; Trimingham 1949: 244).

For several decades thereafter, the Turks, Egyptians, Arab traders, and middlemen from northern and central Sudan raided these areas. As a result, slavery became a major trade activity among many local Arabs and Jillaba. For example, in 1824, four years after the conquest, the number of Nuba who had been taken into captivity was estimated at 40,000, but by 1839 the figure had reached 200,000, excluding the thousands kidnapped by the Baqqara and bought by the Jillaba. The Nuba captives were distributed as follows: the best men were recruited into the army; others were handed over to Turkish soldiers in lieu of pay at an approximate price of three hundred piaster, while the remainder of the captives was sold at public auction (Pallme 1844: 307, 324, 309; Salih 1982: 33–5; Ibrahim 1988: 25).

Turco-Egyptian rule, unable to subjugate the Nuba, used the Hawazma Arabs by giving them a relatively free hand in the Nuba Mountains region in return for taxes payable in Nuba slaves. In outlining the situation in the Nuba Mountains and the Nuba-Arab relations previous to the Mahdiyya, Vicars-Miles (Sudan Archive 1934b: Ref.: SAD 631/10/3) wrote:

> The hills were for the most part under the dominion of the Arabs, who had either reached an agreement with the inhabitants or else regarded them as a reserve for slave-hunting. Hill groups, such as Kadugli and Miri, had real working agreements with the Arabs. Other smaller units, such as Tagoi and Tacho, were more or less used as a source of slaves [...] and sometimes the overlord on his return to a hill would have to conquer it afresh if a new leader had arisen meanwhile who was not prepared to take this state of affairs lying down.

One major conclusion here is that the process of slave raids carried out by the joint efforts of both external (Turkish) and internal forces (Arab traders and the local Baqqara) forced the powerless Nuba to abandon their plains territory and to seek refuge and protection in their inaccessible hilltops, leaving the arable plains land to be occupied by the local slave raiders, the Baqqara. This was soon followed by the official conferring of the Nuba plains land to the Baqqara as their permanent dar (homeland) by the Turco-Egyptian Government, without Nuba consent (Ibrahim 1988: 23; Komey 2008b: 1000). In a nutshell, Nuba land was sold out by the Turkish to the Arabs, in return for getting Nuba slaves through Baqqara involvement.

THE MAHDIYYA AND THE FURTHER ALIENATION OF NUBA LAND

The rise of the Mahdist movement in the 1880s had territorial, social, and political repercussions on the Nuba peoples on their various hills in a number of ways. First, the Mahdiyya movement launched a direct, forced mobilization of the Nuba and the Baqqara into the Jihadiyya to aid the government's Mahdiyya troops in Omdurman (Lloyd 1908; Sagar 1922: 140; Ibrahim 1988: 26).

Second, the Mahdiyya launched offensives on some Baqqara in their homelands in North Kordofan for refusing to submit and support its movement, resulting in an influx of the Baqqara into the Nuba hills (Ibrahim 1988: 27; Sagar 1922: 140–41). By the time they arrived in the area, they 'were reduced to poverty by the raids on their herds, and from being Baqqara became cultivators' in the Nuba lands (Sudan Archive 1934b: SAD 631/10/6; see also Sagar 1922: 141; Trimingham 1949: 29; Roden 1975: 298).

Third, sometimes the Mahdists would arm an allied group of the Baqqara and instruct them to encamp at the foot of the Nuba Jebels (Salih 1982: 38). Fourth, the Mahdiyya brought small goods into the Nuba hill communities such as guns and ammunition and sold them on to the Nuba.

At the outset, the ruling Mahdi and the Dervishes gathered a very large number of recruits, mostly by force, often associated with mass atrocities. Even little children did not escape the massacres 'where they were seized by the feet and their brains dashed to pieces on the rock' (Wingate 1892: 98–9, quoted in Salih 1982: 37). The lucky ones were taken as captives, and there was a slave market in al-Obeid where the women and children, mostly Nuba, were sold, while the full-grown men were recruited into the Jihadiyya. In some cases, almost the entire population was removed to Omdurman. The Nuba's description of these raids is dramatic, with children terrorized by the mere sound of galloping horses (Lloyd 1908: 55; Sagar 1922: 140–41; Gillan 1931: 9; Trimingham 1949; Salih 1982: 38; Ibrahim 1988: 26).

Towards the end of Mahdiyya and the beginning of Anglo-Egyptian (colonial) rule, the state of affairs in the Nuba Mountains was characterized by (i) mass devastation among the Nuba communities, (ii) wide-scale deterritorialization of the Nuba, associated with violent occupation and the full control of the Baqqara over their plains lands, (iii) subjugation of the Nuba by the local Baqqara through suzerainty or what was widely known as the Arab Overlordship of the Nuba, and (iv) the fairly effective armament of the Nuba following the defeat of the Khalifa in Omdurman and later in Kordofan.

COLONIAL RULE AND THE DESIGNATION
OF THE ARAB DAR IN NUBA LAND

Following the overthrow of the Khalifa in 1898, Vicars-Miles[7] noted that the Anglo-Egyptian administration found 'the Arabs in possession of the plains, glad of some sort of peace but resenting their loss of power and freedom, and the Nubas on their hills, well-armed and distrustful of all' (Sudan Archive 1934b: SAD 631/10/9). So the immediate challenge was to put an end to Arab slave raiding, which was still active, to eliminate Arab suzerainty of the Nuba, and to set up some sort of separate administration for each group in the region. As early as 1902, it was reported that there is 'a good lot of both slave dealing and slave raiding going on, and just as much amongst the Nubas themselves as by the Arabs. The establishment of a few Government posts would practically end all slave raiding and dealing which, at present, it is impossible to deal with' (Sudan Intelligence Report 1902: 20).

---

[7] A. L. W. Vicars-Miles (1897–1965) had a long service as an Administrator in the Nuba Mountains and West Kordofan. He was an Assistant District Commissioner for Heiban and Rashad during 1922–28, and then of Heiban only from 1929 to 1930 before he was promoted to full District Commissioner of en Nahud and Dilling (1931–37). (See his memoirs in Sudan Archive 1934b: *Ref: Sud. 631/10/1–62*. Durham: Durham University Library).

The Nuba Mountains Region as Social World

In November 1902, Major O'Connell reported a series of slave raiding cases carried out by the Hawazma and the Arabs of Talodi in Jebel Umm Heitan of Mek Abdul Rahim, Jebel Shwai of Mek Nasir Tagallawi, Jebel Kowarma or Otoro of Mek Kepi Talandi, and Tira Mandi (Governor-General's Report 1902 in Ibrahim 1988: 42). However, the military and political authority of the Baqqara Arabs was progressively destroyed with slave raids being put down (see, Sagar 1922; Sudan Archive 1934b: SAD 631/10/1–60; Gillan 1930, 1931).

One important point to note here is that the colonial government seems to have interpreted the spatial distribution of the Nuba and Baqqara groups in the Nuba Mountains as being the norm, rather than as an anomaly brought about by violence. It went further to assign some kind of land ownership rights to the Baqqara and later to the government, even though the Baqqara only wanted passage rights for their animals rather than full land rights (Sudan Archive 1934b: SAD 631/10/1–60; Harragin 2003).

Given their living memories of slavery, the Nuba avoided any contact with foreign elements, including the British administrators. 'This is hardly strange, as the official language is Arabic and, with exception of the District Commissioner, most of the officials were of Arab stock. The Government, therefore, to the Nuba mind at the time appeared to be almost one with the Arabs and so something to be mistrusted and avoided' (Sudan Archive 1934b: SAD 631/10/12). Also, the Nuba believed that their hills were impregnable to attack, especially after significant improvement of their defence system following the acquisition of more than 20,000 rifles from the Dervishes during their unsuccessful attacks, and with more arms coming in via deserters from the Khalifa's army after the battle of Omdurman (Lloyd 1908: 58; Sagar 1922: 141).

As Arabs sold many of their rifles to the Nubas, the relative balance of power changed slightly in favour of the Nuba hills. They were, for the first time, in a position to defend themselves (Sudan Archive 1934b: SAD 631/10/6). As a consequence, the colonial government soon instituted a series of policies in the region including (i) pacification campaigns among some defiant Nuba hill communities; (ii) the establishment of the Nuba Mountains as a separate province with Toladi as its capital (1914–1928); (iii) the Closed District Ordinance of 1922; and (iv) the introduction of cotton production in 1925 (Gillan 1930, 1931; Trimingham 1949; Stevenson 1965; Sudan Archive 1934b: SAD 631/10; Battahani 1986; Ibrahim 1988).

The pacification process resulted partially in further Nuba movements up into the hills for protection, before they were forced down the hills again (Sagar 1922: 141; Trimingham 1949: 29; Roden 1975: 298). This enforced retreat of the Nuba to the hills gave more opportunities for the Baqqara to encroach further into their previously inhabited plains land. Indeed, the local Arabs were commonly used by the British government on punitive expeditions against the rebels in the early period of pacification (Ibrahim 1988: 35). The pacification process was usually coupled with the Nuba being driven downwards. This factor, and the partial settlement of the Baqqara Arabs on the same plains land, marked a new stage, characterized by emerging reciprocal relations between these two groups. In this regard, Sagar (1922: 142) noted that:

> Meanwhile the Arabs, led by the hand of the Government, are learning to trade and to carry the Nuba produce on their bulls to market. The two races are necessary to one another, the producer and the carrier [...]. I can best conclude this sketch of the history of the country in the words of a prominent Nuba Mek, Government has taught the leopard and the lamb (i.e., the Arab and the Nuba) to sleep side by side.

This arrangement strengthened the Baqqara's intermediary role between the Government and the Nuba hill communities. Through this position they gained the advantage, becoming the principal beneficiary of economic opportunities brought to the area. Moreover, their status strengthened the various forms of control over the Nuba they already had, particularly through 'sid al-darb al-darb', the Arabs' over-lordship of the Nuba:

> The Arabs were not slow to see that it was to their advantage to keep the Nuba in the belief that they were intermediaries between the hills and the Government. It was also to their advantage to retard the progress of the Nuba, so that power should remain in their hands and grain continue to be obtainable for next to nothing. (Sudan Archive 1934b: SAD 631/10/11; Gillan 1930: 24–6)[8]

At the same time, the British were not in favour of allowing Arab culture and Islamic influences to continue penetrating into the authentic Nuba cultural identity. Towards that end, the Closed District Ordinance of 1922 was enacted, followed by Gillan's Nuba Policy in 1931. According to the ordinance, no Muslim Arab was allowed to enter a closed district and no native could leave a designated area without acquiring an exit/entry permit. The ordinance was finally abolished in 1947 having achieved very little (Gillan 1931; Salih 1982, 1990; Battahani 1986; Ibrahim 1988).

The failure of the Closed District Policy in maintaining the Nuba as an authentic culture was partly due to the fact that:

> [...] the government's decision to maintain some of the Arab overlordship had caused a major set-back to the Nuba policy, for the Nuba groups found it extremely difficult to retain cultural identities in these Arab surroundings, and that in turn militated against the building of an authentic Nuba civilization and culture. (Salih 1990: 427)

Thus, Arab suzerainty was kept intact with regard to the following hill communities even when they were demanding liberty:

(i) the Liguri and Saburi Nuba hill communities under the control of the Nazir Hamid al-Likha of Aulad Nuba of Rawawqa;

---

[8] See also Gillan (1930, 1931: 24–26), Salih (1982: 156), Abdel-Hamid (1986: 178), Ibrahim (1988), and Mohamed Salih (1988: 82).

(ii) the Fungor, Nyaro, Kau groups under the control of Aulad Himaid; and

(iii) the Jebel Warni group under the nominal power of the Nazir of Hawazma (Gillan 1930; Salih 1982, 1990).

In 1925, cotton production was introduced with the intention of stimulating exports and promoting socio-economic development in the region (Colvin 1939; Rose 1950, 1951). However, cotton production accelerated the transfer of the Nuba land to more powerful newcomers. Initially, the intention was to provide a livelihood for the Nuba and, hence, restrain their migration to the towns, which exposed them to Arab and Islamic influences (Gillan 1931).

In reality, the policy worked in favour of Baqqara, Fellata and, later, Jillaba merchants. Moreover, it accelerated the process of inequality in Nuba-Arab interactions and relationships (Roden 1975: 298–99). The Nuba were not able to invest in their land reserved by the British government for cotton production. At the same time, the Baqqara were successful in cotton production, which led them to extend once again into Nuba land to increase their production (Salih 1990: 431). By 1939, 40,000 hectares were under cotton annually and eight ginning factories had been built in the region (Roden 1975: 298):

> Arabs in many cases are responsible for retarding the Nuba's progress in cotton growing, for so long as they can induce the Nubas to part with their grain cheap, it is to their advantage to keep the cotton crop entirely in their own hands and let the Nubas concentrate on supplying grain. (Sudan Archive 1934b: SAD 631/10/22)

Over time, it became evident that the process of cotton introduction had subjected the Nuba to systematic land grabbing by local Baqqara, Fellata and Jillaba. The colonial response was the introduction of Gillan's Nuba Policy under the title: *Sudan Government Memoranda No. 1: Some Aspects of Nuba Administration 1931*.[9] The Nuba 'Native Lands' constitute Chapter 5 in Gillan's Memorandum. The main underlying principles of the 'Nuba Policy' as envisaged by Gillan (1931: 20) were:

> [to] preserve or evolve an authentic Nuba civilization and culture, as against a bastard type of Arabization or at least to support this evolution up to the point where the people themselves will be fit to choose with their eyes open, the type of culture which most appeals to them.

A critical look at this policy document reveals that the British administration was in a real dilemma as to how to pursue its desired interests in the region while securing the land rights of the Nuba,

[9] J. A. Gillan (1885–1981) had a long service in the Sudan. He started in 1910 as Inspector in en Nahud, Kordofan; afterwards, between 1928 and 1932, he continued to hold various offices, including the Governorship of Kordofan (including the Nuba Mountains Province). In 1932–34 he was an Assistant Civil Secretary before his appointment as the Sudan's Civil Secretary in 1934, an office which he continued to hold until his retirement in 1939 (see Daly 1984: 3 and 7).

particularly over the agricultural land which was already diminishing. That policy document pointed to the emergence of land scarcity in the region:

> Until a few years ago there was ample land for everyone concerned. [...]. But with the development of cotton growing the situation is rapidly changing. Good cotton land is limited and apart from local claims it has attracted many outsiders, some of them, as Gellaba, quite clever enough to cheat and exploit the more unsophisticated of the local inhabitants. (Gillan 1931: 37)

In short, contrary to British policy aimed at improving the Nuba economy while preserving their identity and land, cotton production resulted in far-reaching economic and social changes with profound impact on traditional tenure customs among the Nuba hill communities. It stimulated the involvement of more powerful actors who presented a further threat to the powerless Nubas' livelihood and survival.

Roden (1975: 299) outlines four prominent transformations among the Nuba communities, namely (i) the choice of new settlement sites and the associated expansion of plain farming; (ii) the change from a frequent condition of land hunger to a general condition of land surplus; (iii) the reappearance of land shortage in certain communities; and (iv) increasing exposure to alien influences. To curtail Baqqara, Fallata, and Jillaba encroachment into what was perceived to be Nuba agricultural zoning land, the British administration strictly divided the region's agricultural lands into three zones:

(i)   Zone A was to extend as a circular expansion from the foot hill … as a centre of a circle with a 3-miles radius. It was an exclusively Nuba zone. Because of its location in the foothill region, it was confined to Nuba dwellings and cultivation of sorghum and sesame.
(ii) Zone B was to extend by another six miles from the radius of Zone A, to form a bigger circle with a 9-miles radius. The Nuba were categorized as having a complete right over two-thirds of this zone with non-Nuba permitted dwellings and nomadic passage over this zone only with written permission from the Provincial Governor.
(iii) Zone C was to extend in circular form, from the margins of Zone B to cover the boundaries of the Nuba Mountains Province. One third of Zone B and half of Zone C were allotted for non-Nuba usage (Ibrahim 1988: 61–2).

Gradually, however, there was a steady expansion in cotton production in the region by the Arabs coupled with their progressive encroachment into Nuba-zoned agricultural land, through 'rent, purchase, and more rarely through invasion' (Ibrahim 1988: 66). As early as the 1930s, the colonial administration had foreseen the emergence of land-based conflicts in the region:

> At present the Nuba may not protest very much against the stranger within his gates; but when we have satisfied (as we must) his desire for education

we shall be faced with a Nuba intelligentsia demanding why, under our stewardship, their birthright was given away. First, then, let us give the local inhabitants full room for expansion and then turn our attention to the problems of using the remaining land for the benefit of the Sudan as a whole. (Sudan Archive 1934b: SAD: 631/10/32, 36)

Despite this advice, no practical action was taken because both the Closed District Policy and the Nuba Policy were falling apart. As an alternative, the British administration introduced two distinct native administration systems: (i) the Mekship for the Nuba, governed by their customary laws and traditions, and (ii) the Nazirate-'Umdaship for the Baqqara Arabs, based on Islamic laws (Salih 1982: 67–74; Ibrahim 1988: 38–48). One direct territorial consequence of this arrangement was the specification of tribal land (dar) for the Baqqara Arabs with juridical and administrative authorities that form the basis for claiming land ownership rights in the region to the present day.

By the 1940s, it was evident that both the Closed District Policy of 1922 and Gillan's Nuba Administration Policy of 1931, aimed at restraining Arab influences on the authentic Nuba, had come to an end with insignificant success. On the other hand, the Nuba-Baqqara social and economic interactions and complementarities were accelerated and consolidated over time, resulting in the transformation of the region into its present social reality.

More importantly, by the time of independence of the Sudan in 1956, the region and its communities were at the margins of the Sudanese state politics and economy. That political and socio-economic position 'crystallized the present socioeconomic structure and stratification in the region where the Jellaba, the Baqqara, and the Nuba occupy the top, the middle, and the bottom of the socioeconomic system respectively' (Ibrahim 1998:6). Within this stratification, the Nuba were ill-equipped, politically and economically, in comparison to other social groups in the region. At the same time, the region as a whole lagged behind on the periphery, functionally tied to the centre through various forms of unequal and exploitative socio-economic and political relations (Battahani 1986; Ibrahim 1988; Saavedra 1998; Mohamed Salih 1995, 1999; Komey 2005a, 2005b; Manger 2007).

Postcolonial state and land grabbing in the region

Following independence, the national state has subscribed to the illusion that mechanized farming is somehow 'modern' and efficient, though in reality it is neither of these things. Rather, it has proved to be a highly destructive use of the land (Abdel Salam et al. 2002: 128). As demonstrated here, the progressive introduction of mechanized rain-fed farming into the region since the 1960s has led to a disturbance of both its ecological and social systems.

Under the 1968 Mechanized Farming Corporation Act and upon the request of the World Bank to facilitate the agricultural development of the Sudan, mechanized rain-fed farming was vigorously pursued, particularly in the Gedarif area in the eastern part of central Sudan, and also in the Blue Nile, Darfur, and the Nuba Mountains, through public and private sectors.[10] Duffield (1990: 5) reported that

> The process began in eastern Sudan and spread south into the Blue Nile Province and then west through southern Kordofan and Darfur. By the end of the 1970s, about four million feddans[11] stretching across the central clay plains was registered under mechanized cultivation, compared with about nine million feddans registered as 'traditional' rain land. By 1982, the area under mechanized cultivation had jumped to about six million feddans. In 1986 it jumped again to over nine million feddans, exceeding the traditional sector.

Under the 1968 Act, 60% of land was to be allocated to local people and no one was to have more than one farm. Despite the priority given to local and agricultural cooperative societies in the distribution of these schemes, the first beneficiaries were Jillaba merchants and allied local politicians and traditional leaders. Following the introduction of the mechanized rain-fed farming schemes in the region, land grabbing has become a consistent government policy, resulting in the strengthening of the privileged ruling elites and their allied merchants, who have acquired land at the expense of rural communities. Set up in 1957 as a national bank, the Agricultural Bank of Sudan (ABS) aggravated the underdevelopment of local communities and further promoted the position of wealthy farmers in the region through its loans policies and specific conditions. It continued to concentrate its agricultural loans on wealthy investors who were more likely to repay their loans. The smaller farmers who were unable to repay loans were forced to rent their plots to merchants at a low rate, in order to keep up their loan repayments (Harragin 2003: 13).

In the process of schemes allocation, local communities and their native institutions were hardly engaged. As a result, many entrepreneurs ended up acquiring land which they had never even seen. This land could be farmed or inhabited by local people, or used as grazing pasture by agro-pastoral groups (Abdel Salam et al., 2002: 129). Over time, the issue of schemes distribution proved to be crucial for the local people when land expropriation became the main state policy in the region. According to Harragin (2003), the mechanized farming area in the region covered 2.5 million feddans in 1993, and by 2003 it had jumped to 3–4 million feddans representing a range of 9%–12 % of the surface of South Kordofan, and around 50% of its plains and fertile areas. As a result, some local wealthy

---

[10] For a detailed account of the mechanized rain-fed farming schemes in the Nuba Mountains, see Saeed (1980), Manger (1981), Battahani (1980, 1983, 1986), Ibrahim (1988), African Rights (1995), Suliman (1998, 2001), Mohamed Salih (1995, 1999), Abdel Salam et al., (2002), Rahhal (2001), and Harragin (2003).

[11] One feddan equals 1.038 acres, or 4200 square metres.

Baqqara, Fellata, and Jillaba, with strong links to the central state, got involved in the expropriation of small holdings of sedentary Nuba communities. Johnson (2006: 132) reports that in the process of the mechanized schemes expansion:

> Nuba villages began to be surrounded by the mechanized schemes, and farmers were frequently fined (or even imprisoned) for trespass. The mechanized schemes also lay across the grazing routes of Baqqara cattle herders, and to avoid prosecution for trespass they frequently re-routed their herds through Nuba farmland. In the absence of the old Native Administration to arbitrate the dispute which arose, the government courts generally took the side of the Baqqara against the Nuba. The dispossessed farmers joined the ranks of marginal wage-labourers seeking work on the schemes or in the main cities.

For example, it was reported that the entire mechanized scheme of the village of Fayo near Habila was encircled by the establishment of a large-scale scheme, and all the villagers, about 500 families, were reported to have lost their traditional farming plots (African Rights 1995: 45). Local farmers and leaders provided extensive testimony about how the encroachment of the mechanized rain-fed farming had devastated the economic and social life of the Nuba and ultimately destroyed their friendly relations with the Baqqara. Suliman (1998: 13) reported the following testimony of one of the Nuba civil leaders whose name was withheld:

> The mechanized farming problem has two ways of taking our land. The government planned mechanized farming schemes which are given from Khartoum …they do not care if there are villages in this land or not; land is just allotted to certain people who are mainly retired army generals or civil servants, or wealthy merchants from northern Sudan or to local Jellaba who have been living in the area for long time and have accumulated wealth … Because the Nuba are not wealthy a small number of them are involved in this distribution of land. What happens is that the Nuba are squeezed and have to choose between two options: either to leave the area to work for the government as soldiers, or become workers in the mechanized farming schemes.

Numerous cases of Nuba farmers driven off their ancestral lands have been widely documented.[12] The exclusion of the local farmers from the majority of these schemes demonstrates beyond any doubt that agricultural development in the region has nothing to do with its rural community development. It also reflects how the region's resources are siphoned off to the core regions through wealthy investors who dominate the region's major schemes.

Thus, the manner in which the government allocates the mechanized farming schemes to outside investors, with no consideration of the rights or

---

[12] For some details, see for example Africa Watch (1992a), African Rights (1995, Suliman (1998), and Rahhal (2001).

interests of the local peoples, is one of the main sources of contention in the region. By 1974, the distribution of the schemes in Habila Agricultural Project was as follows: 11% for local farmers, 6% for cooperatives, 49.8% for merchants, 21.6% for retired officials, 5.8% for government officials, and 5.8% for other government-related entities (Ibrahim 1988: 128). By the 1990s, both African Rights (1995: 41) and Suliman (1998: 8) reported that two hundred mechanized farms in Habila were allocated as follows: 'Four were leased to local co-operatives; one was leased to a consortium of local merchants, and four individually to local merchants. The remaining 191 were leased to absentee landlords, mainly merchants, government officials and retired army officers from the north.'

The heart of the matter is that land expropriation for mechanized schemes, that are monopolized by wealthy outsiders, with no consideration for the rights and interests of local peoples, has brought about new socio-political and economic dynamics, not only along the centre–periphery line, but also along ethnic lines within the region. Local communities resist the encroachment of mechanized farming, and violent conflicts often erupt between them and the absentee landlords who are supported by the government. The conflict becomes multidimensional between (i) the local population and the scheme owners, (ii) the sedentary and nomadic local communities, and (iii) between the local sedentary and nomadic communities, on the one hand, and central and regional government institutions, on the other.

In this way, the mechanized schemes have stirred a series of conflicts involving the state machinery, mechanized farming schemes' owners, the sedentary Nuba and nomadic Baqqara. In other words, the introduction of mechanized rain-fed farming in the region has been achieved not only at the expense of traditional local farmers, but is also quite harmful to Baqqara nomadic groups. With the sweeping expansion of mechanized rain-fed farming schemes, some major stock routes have been intersected by these schemes. They progressively occupy the buffer grazing zone between Bahr al-Arab in the southern region and the sandy quz in North Kordofan.

The location of mechanized farming schemes in the middle of this grazing zone has completely disturbed the fragile balance of the Baqqara transhumance system, jeopardizing the lives of thousands of nomads (Ibrahim 1988: 109). As a consequence, competition over resources between sedentary Nuba groups and Baqqara nomads has intensified and has taken on a political dimension along ethnic lines. Despite this pressing situation for local communities, successive governments have continued their policies of favouring large-scale mechanized farming, while both the sedentary and nomadic communities are being progressively and forcibly pushed to the margins of their livelihood base. Map 1.3 demonstrates the same schemes and the way that they intersect traditional livestock routes, particularly in the Habila scheme in Dilling Province, which is by far the largest mechanized scheme in the region.

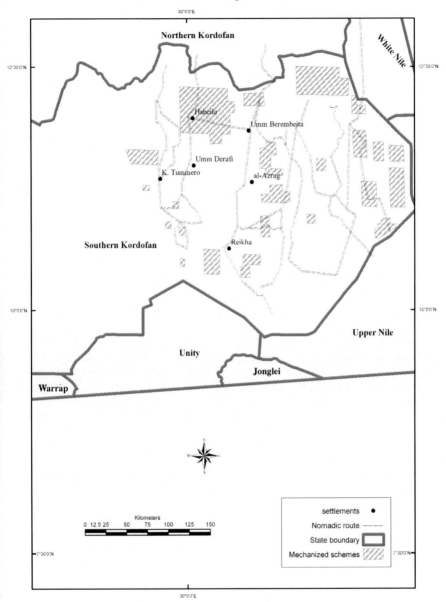

Map 1.3 Mechanized schemes, nomadic routes and sedentary settlements
Source: Modified from Harrigin, 2003, map 1, p. 21

What becomes clear here is that, under the banner of 'public interest', mechanized schemes have been involved in privatizing local resources for the benefit of a few wealthy or politically connected individuals. Based on the slogan that 'land should be given to those who are able to use it for the national interest', most of the best arable land in the region has fallen into the hands of a few. By the mid-1980s, it was widely recognized by both observers and practitioners alike that the mechanized rain-fed farming schemes in the region and elsewhere were economic, environmental, social, and political disasters (Saeed 1980; Kursany 1983; Ibrahim 1988; Duffield 1990; Abdelgabar 1997). In July 1981, the South Kordofan Commissioner lamented, in a letter to the central authority, the adverse consequences of the mechanized schemes for the people of the region:

> We used to be optimistic about the establishment of the mechanized agricultural schemes in our Province, hoping that they would produce real development for our people, raising their standard of living, encouraging resettlement of the nomads and providing cheap food supply for the people, the excess of which could be exported and bring hard currency to the nation [...] unfortunately, what is happening in the Province now due to the mechanized agricultural schemes is completely the reverse. (Ibrahim 1988: 112)

Current literature reveals that this disturbing situation continues to the present day (Abdel Salam et al., 2002; Harragin 2003; Komey 2009a, 2010b). As noted previously, the victims are the local communities, both the sedentary Nuba and the nomadic Baqqara. Map 1.3, which combines the nomad's seasonal main routes and the mechanized rain-fed farming schemes, clearly illustrates how the nomads' grazing rights and interests have been undermined by the state. In this map, the major schemes, such as Habila, block off major traditional stock routes. The land of the sedentary Nuba has been seized, the people evicted and driven from their ancestral land without compensation. In this way, the mechanized rain-fed farming schemes have brought suffering to the entire region as a spatial and social world by causing widespread ecological deterioration resulting in further social dislocation and conflict over diminishing resources, with far-reaching political implications.

It is obvious that the initial factors that led to the deterioration of sedentary Nuba–nomadic Baqqara relations were externally generated. In the subsequent discussion, it will be demonstrated that the causes of the escalation of local and normal low-scale conflicts into large-scale conflicts, with uninhibited violence and gross human rights violations, are related to external rather than internal factors.

The conclusion to be drawn is that, with the expansion of mechanized rain-fed farming schemes in the region, both sedentary and nomadic local communities were and still are being systematically squeezed out, not only to the margins of their livelihood base but also to a peripheral socio-economic and political status. It is precisely the introduction of mechanized capitalist agricultural schemes in the region, coupled with political and economic favoritism that has marked the economic ascendancy of the Jillaba traders, who have assumed full control of all economic spheres in the Nuba Mountains.

Although several intermingling factors lie behind the emergence of the conflict in the region, several published works have pointed to the land question, in its wider context, as a key factor that triggered Nuba moves to join the war in the middle of the 1980s. For example, Ayoub (2006: 1–2) argues that in 'the Nuba Mountains, the continuous alienation of Nuba lands and their appropriation by outside investors has been one of the key motivating factors for the Nuba to join the Sudan People's Liberation Movement/Army (SPLM/A).' In emphasizing land as a major root cause of the civil war in the Nuba Mountains, Johnson (2006: 131) asserts that:

> The war currently being fought in the Nuba Mountains combines the new conflict over land with older forms of oppression. It is the starkest example of the new land war which has become so much a feature of the civil wars in the North. Whereas in the South, land ownership and the threat of appropriation of land was not a major factor in the outbreak of the war, in the Nuba Mountains, it has become one of the main issues.

In the same way, Suliman (1998: 9) states that the 'single most important issue behind the outbreak of the conflict in the Nuba Mountains is the encroachment of the mechanized agriculture on the Nuba smallholders farming. It devastated the economic and social life of the Nuba and ultimately destroyed the friendly relations with the Baqqara.' Following this line of argumentation and focusing on the primacy of the land question in the eruption of the civil war in the Nuba Mountains, Pantuliano (2007: 3) states that 'these land grabs led to massive displacement and was a main reason why in the late 1980s, people in Southern Kordofan joined the Sudan People's Liberation Army (SPLM) insurgency.'

It is worth noting, however, that the agricultural land issue was not the only reason for land expropriation. Africa Watch (1992a), Suliman (1998, 2001), Mohamed and Fisher (2002), Johnson (2006), Pantuliano (2007), and Patey (2007), have demonstrated that the government has also employed a violent scorched earth policy in the Nuba Mountains since the early 1990s in the process of oil exploration and subsequent exploitation (Chapter 3). Toward that end, it has deliberately and systematically depopulated, and is still depopulating, huge corridors through the Nuba Mountains in order to safeguard the oil pipeline from the oil fields in the South to Port Sudan, the main port, in eastern Sudan.

Conclusion

Based on this review of the historical and contemporary dynamics that have dominated the socio-political scene in the region, one may draw some important conclusions. First, the progressive penetration of Arabs, particularly traders and religious leaders, from the north into Kordofan and eventually into the Nuba Hills has drawn the Nuba, in spatial, political, economic, and social terms, ever more tightly into relationships of subordination to them and, therefore, to their geographical, political, and socio-economic centres, which have been situated elsewhere in central and northern Sudan ever since. Thus, for a very long time, the Nuba Mountains as both a spatial/territorial and social/peopled world have been subjected to various forms of 'institutionalized insecurity', control, and subjugation.

Second, the progressive and violent occupation of the Nuba plains land by the Baqqara as late-comers and their persistence in alliances with external forces (from the early slave raiders, through the Turco-Egyptian rule, then the Mahdiyya, to the colonial and postcolonial rulers) in subjugating the Nuba have resulted in far-reaching socio-economic and political effects.

Third, the postcolonial regimes did not deviate much from the precolonial and colonial patterns of socio-economic and political marginalization of the Nuba people but consolidated that position with stricter, more suppressive and exclusionary political, economic, and socio-cultural policies.

Fourth, in aggregate terms, the state's underhand and misguided agricultural development interventions within the region, coupled with policies of political marginalization and socio-economic deprivations, stimulated tensions and conflicts, not only along the centre-periphery line, but also along ethnic lines.

Fifth, the postcolonial state land-grabbing policy and related practices of violence and land alienation, created misery and grievances among the local communities who were pushed systematically to the margins and eventually became landless, with their very survival greatly endangered in their ancestral homeland.

Finally, viewing land in a wider social and political context, it is evident that it was a key factor that contributed, in a number of ways, to trigger, sustain or even escalate various types and levels of conflicts at different stages of the country's violent transformation into what it is at present. However, it is necessary to consider the land factor within local conflicts in the region in a wider national social and political context. That context is in itself a result of cumulative historical and contemporary socio-political and spatial dynamics in the process of the Sudanese state formation. This is the subject of the following chapter.

2

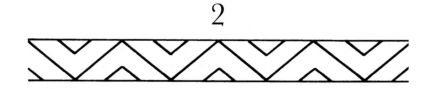

State Land Policies, Politics & Rights in Sudan

'Land rights are always political'
(Shipton 1994: 351)

Introduction

In Chapter 1 it was argued that the Nuba Mountains region of South Kordofan is a typical case of a marginalized region in contemporary Sudan. It demonstrated the unequal and exploitative forms of relations between the periphery and the centre within an overall socio-spatial system and the consequences of the multi-dimensional marginalization process through disguised and distorted forms of development that are linked, but not restricted, to mechanized rain-fed farming and oil exploitation with excessive land grabbing and alienation by the state.

Although it is evident that land is a contributing factor to the marginalization and, consequently, to the conflict in the Sudan in general and in the Nuba Mountains in particular, this chapter takes a broader perspective to demonstrate that the role of the land question in marginalization and conflict is in itself a result of cumulative processes of precolonial, colonial, and postcolonial social, economic and political dynamics underlying the overall Sudanese nation-building project.

This chapter is not intended to provide a systematic and comprehensive study of historical and current land legislation developments. Instead, it will consider some milestones in Sudanese land legislation, tenure policies, and politics, with a focus on their possible contribution to the current conflicts and civil wars in the Sudan.

The intrinsic and multifaceted link between communal land rights and ethnic identity, and conflicts in Sudan, is evident, because land, in the broad sense, plays important political, legal, and social roles. These are governed by a set of modern laws, as well as by a cluster of Islamic customary and traditional laws, particularly in the rural communities (el-Mahdi 1977; Simpson 1976; Gordon 1986; Goldflam 1988). Within all its roles, land contributes to the triggering, maintenance, or escalation of different types of conflicts, and has done so through all the various stages of Sudan's transformation. The cumulative result of these forces is manifested in current land rights, tenure system, policy, and politics in the Sudan.

As argued elsewhere (Komey 2010b: 350–52), and evidenced in many developing societies, the land tenure system in the Sudan is characterized by a sharp dualism: first, the communal traditional land tenure pattern is regulated by customary laws and institutions, with no legal recognition in government courts when it comes to rights of ownership. El-Mahdi (1979: 221) observed that the main problem with customary law is that it is 'uncollected, unrecorded and uncertain'. Second, the modern state land tenure pattern is based on civil laws and institutions. Since its gradual introduction to the present day, the modern state land tenure pattern continues to be concentrated in central and northern Sudan, and in limited urban areas in the remaining parts of the Sudan. Consequently, the bulk of the Sudanese rural communities remain beyond the modern land policies and the related private land ownerships. A burgeoning colonial and postcolonial literature substantiates this view: (Bolton 1954; MacMichael 1954; Simpson 1976; el-Mahdi 1979; Adams 1982; Spaulding 1982; Gordon 1986; Goldflam 1988; Duffield 1990; Simpson 1991; Babiker 1998; Adams and Turner 2005; Abdul Jalil 2005; Abdel Salam et al. 2002; Manger 2003; Kapteijns and Spaulding 2005; Komey 2008a, 2008b, 2009b, 2010b).

The precolonial stage and communal land rights

In traditional communities, land is communally owned with individual rights to use in accordance with tribal custom or as tribal authority directs: hence the importance of the concept of tribal land as the main constituent of traditional land tenure in Sudan, with a strong link to the practice of native administration. According to Simpson (1965: 90), 'tribal land is meant land which has for long been at the disposition of the tribal land authorities.' Tribal land is a major tenure system taken on customary lines where there is no pressure on land in terms of ownership or rights of access to use. The system is derived from tribal territorial rights initially constituted during successive indigenous kingdoms of precolonial Sudan. Within the tribal homeland, collective security of the community is constituted with individual use and inheritance rights without alienating the land from the collective ownership of the community. However, as a society undergoes transformation, the land tenure system shifts towards private ownership. Observing the socio-economic transformation in rural Africa in the nineteenth century, Lord Lugard summarized the process of shift in land tenure as follows:

> In the earliest stage the land and its produce is shared by the community as a whole; later the produce is the property of the family of individuals by whose toil it is won, and the control of the land becomes vested in the head

of the family. When the tribal stage is reached, the control passes to the chief, who allots unoccupied lands at will, but is not justified in dispossessing any person or family who is using the land. Later still when the pressure of population has given to the land an exchange value sale, mortgage and lease of the land, apart from its user, is recognized. (in Simpson 1965: 82–3)

As early as the sixteenth century, land was privatized and traded for on an individual basis in the central and northern parts of the Sudan while it remained a common property with no market value in the rest of the country (Adams and Turner 2005; Kapteijn and Spaulding 2005; Komey 2008a, 2010b). During the Islamic Kingdoms of Funj (1504–1821) in northern, eastern, and central Sudan, and the Keira Sultanate in Darfur, land rights were granted to local administrators and to religious and communal leaders in order to win their favours.

In this way, some land properties were transferred from communal to individual ownership and authenticated by documents known as 'wathiqah' or charter in Funj, and 'wathiqah al-Tamlik' or 'hakura', (concession, monopoly) in Darfur (Mamdani 2009: 114–19). These land granting documents bore the ruler's seal. The policy created a class of landlords owning vast tracts and extracting dues and/or agricultural surpluses from their tenants and/or slaves (Goldflam 1988: 34–6). The policy was further consolidated and expanded during the Turco-Egyptian (1821–85) and the Mahdiyya (1885–1898) periods (Spaulding 1982; Goldflam 1988; Kapteijn and Spaulding 2005; Miller 2005; Abdul Jalil 2005; Adams and Turner 2005; Mamdani 2009, Komey 2010b).

The Turkish Government introduced a series of political–administrative arrangements with far-reaching implications for the Sudan's contemporary political, administrative, and socio-economic structure. According to Spaulding (1982: 2) and Goldflam (1988: 36), it first made the private ownership of land possible in northern Sudan by granting land to certain people of political or religious influence, largely as special favours or from the desire to develop the territory. Second, as reported by Warburg (1971: 144), in 1863, during the rule of Musa Pasha Hamdi, the government introduced what came to be known as the native administration system in the Sudan, tied strongly to land and, therefore, to tribal territories. The system is administered by traditional leaders of Nazir, Omda, or 'Umda and Shaykh from top to bottom respectively. Their administrative units were called Nazirate, 'Umodiya or 'Omodia and Shiakha. In the non-Arab communities including the Nuba, the titles Mek and Mokukiya (Mekship) were used instead of Nazir and Nazirate respectively. Since that time, land tenure policies and related political-administrative arrangements have to a large degree been governed through the native administration system. According to the Report of the First Population Census published in 1958:

OMODIA is essentially a concept derived from the Arab tribal organization, whereby each tribe is ruled by a NAZIR, beneath whom there is a number of OMDAS, each responsible for an OMODIA and beneath the Omda is the SHAYKH, who is the headman of a small group of families [...]. In settled areas Omodia boundaries consist merely of imaginary lines that may be said to run between the fields of a village belonging to one OMDA and those of a village belonging to next. In nomadic areas, of course, the OMODIA boundaries scarcely have any meaning at all, though it is recorded of certain nomadic tribes that the various sections tend to keep to one or any part of the whole tribal territory. (Republic of Sudan 1958: 7, capitals original)

Goldflam (1988: 35) reported that under Mahdiyya rule (1885–98), there was extensive state political interference with the system of land tenure. Ownership of land was taken out of the hands of disloyal factions and transferred to loyal ones. Large-scale massacres and forced migration during the Mahdiyya era left large areas of arable land turned to wasteland with significant changes of the positions of certain individuals and communities in terms of land control, access, or ownership.

The colonial stage and regional differential in land policies

Although politicization and privatization of land rights can be traced back to the times of the Funj Sultanates, through Turco-Egyptian rule and the Mahdiyya, the colonial period (1898–1956) marked an important stage in the process of land tenure politics in the Sudan (Simpson 1955, 1965, 1976, 1984; Simpson 1991; Bolton 1954; Lebon 1965; Warburg 1970; el-Mahdi 1979; Gordon 1986; Goldflam 1988; Komey 2010b). Although the colonial administration accepted existing customary and Islamic rules governing land use, the title to bare land ownership was vested in the government. A policy of limiting land acquisition by merchants and non-Sudanese individuals was adopted, followed by confiscation of large areas of irrigable land in Gezira and Blue Nile, the Tokar Delta, and elsewhere, in order to establish cotton cultivation (Sudan Archive 1946/47: SAD 627/16/11–15; Simpson 1955, 1965; Henderson 1946; MacMichael 1954).

During this period, the politicization of land ownership was vigorously pursued with the Sudanese territory progressively divided into tribal diar ([pl.] dar [sg.]), or homelands. These diar are clearly visible in contemporary maps and demonstrate the link between tribal identity and geography that continues today. They reveal the close relationship between a tribe and its homeland (Ayoub 2006; Komey 2010b). The colonial administration reinforced this by considering the paramount tribal chief (nazir) as their appointee, entrusting him with legal administrative and financial authority, and expecting him to allocate hawakir ([pl.] hakura [sg.]) as he saw fit (Goldflam 1988; Kapteijn and Spaulding 2005; Abdul Jalil 2005, 2008; Komey 2010b).

Following the subjugation of the Sudan, the colonial administration issued its first Land Ordinance in 1899 by which it recognized and registered the continuously cultivated lands in northern and central Sudan as private property. Since that time, the management and practices of land tenure were pursued through a series of land legislations amounting to more than fifteen ordinances enacted during a period of 1899–1930 as detailed below.[1] Through the creation of series of authoritative land ordinances, the administration converted customary occupancy of land into legally sanctioned ownership of property, while at the same time recognizing the concept of government ownership of unregistered land (Goldflam 1988: 153). According to Warburg (1970: 156), one major policy of these ordinances was to expand cultivation while safeguarding the inhabitants' rights and encouraging the formulation of a Sudanese proprietary class. All lands which were regularly cultivated were regarded as 'mulk', or in private full ownership, and the full rights of their owners were recognized and guaranteed, except when it was required for public purposes. In MacMichael's words:

> The principles adopted for general application were to recognize de facto rights and settle as many natives as possible upon the land with secure titles, except when it was required for public purposes, and to discourage land speculation by foreigners. It was also made clear that land in which private ownership was not proved was the property of the Government, though it might, of course, be subject to village or individual rights of cultivation or grazing. (1954: 81)

According to the Title to Lands Ordinance, 1899 (Sudan Archive 1899: SAD 627/12/7), for individual land to be recognized by the government as an absolute entitlement in the northern region, a mild condition was put forward that 'continuous possession, or receipt of rents or profits, during the five years immediately preceding the date of claim, created an absolute title as against all persons'.

It is worth noting that the application of these ordinances was confined to the northern and central regions of the Sudan excluding the rural regions of the southern provinces, and in the Nuba Mountains, land settlement was not undertaken during this period. Disputes concerning land were adjusted on a tribal basis either by agreement or administrative decision. Hence, no individual private landownership was recognized in

---

[1] For original full texts of these Ordinances, see Sudan Archive 1899 (SAD 627/12/3–44), and Simpson (1965). For some communications and reports of the Land Office or committees commissioned to implement these Ordinances, refer to Sudan Archive 1915a (SAD 542/15/1–24) on the Sennar Land Settlement 1913–15; Sudan Archive 1915b (SAD 678/2/2, 27–40) on the Final Report on Sennar Land Settlement 1915; Sudan Archive 1914 (SAD 542/3/35–49) for Reports on Bara Lands in 1914 and 1935; and Sudan Archive 1954 (SAD 720/3/1–2) for the Land Office's Annual Report 1953–54. In addition, for detailed studies, accounts, reviews, interpretations, and explanatory notes on these Ordinances, refer to Sudan Archive 1903a (SAD 542/1/5–7), Sudan Archive 1930b (SAD 542/23/2–5), Sudan Archive 1934a (SAD 542/24/4–5), Sudan Archive 1930b (SAD 542/23/2–5), Henderson (1946), Hawley 1950 (Sudan Archive 1950: SAD 719/10/2–4), Miskin (1950), MacMichael (1954: 80–85), Sudan Archive 1947/47 (SAD 627/16/6–15), Simpson (1955, 1965, 1976), el-Mahdi (1979); Daly (1986:210–14), Gordon (1986); Warburg (1986: 155–170); Goldflam (1988), and Simpson (1991).

these regions throughout the colonial era (Bolton 1954: 187; Warburg 1970: 159). In the words of the then Legal Secretary of the Sudan, B. H. Bell in 1930:

> The question of individual ownership of particular parts of the tribal lands cannot arise. The only individual right is to use the land in accordance with tribal custom or as the tribal authority directs. The internal economy and administration of the land rests with the tribal authority and subject to the ultimate direction of the Governor with tribal authority alone. The occupation by any member of the tribe of a particular piece of land is in virtue of the direction, expressed or implied, of the tribal authority. (Sudan Archive 1930b: SAD 542/23/2–3)

Later, MacMichael (1954: 80), a prominent British colonial administrator, justified the regional variation in land policy by stating that in the spacious rain lands of the interior and in the south, no particular action under this head was required for years to come: land there was more than ample for the needs of the population and most of it was in tribal or village communal ownership.

An Ordinance for the Settlement of Rights over Waste Forest and Unoccupied Lands and to Provide for the Expropriation of such Rights of 1905, commonly known as the Land Settlement Ordinance of 1905, made general provisions for the settlement and registration of claims to lands which were alleged to be waste, forest, or unoccupied. It contained an important provision that all such land should be deemed the property of the government unless claims to the contrary were proved. In this Ordinance, the 'unoccupied lands' 'include uncultivated land and all land which shall not have been in the uninterrupted occupation of some person or persons for a period exceeding five years next before a notice given by the Governor General with reference to such land [...]' (Sudan Archive 1905: SAD 627/12/13).[2] Although the Ordinance gave the relevant government authority the right to expropriate land, it stipulated that the 'Settlement Officer may award compensation in land or partly in land and partly in money' (Sudan Archive 1905: SAD 627/12/17).

In other words, the local people of central and northern Sudan who owned land which the Government needed for public use were compensated in kind, cash, or both, during the early period of land expropriation confined to these parts of the Sudan. At the same time, the uncultivated and unsettled land of northern and central Sudan and the entire lands of the Nuba Mountains, East, West, and South were classified by the colonial government as government-owned land subject to customary usufruct rights vested in the community. Indeed, as customary usufruct rights are not legally registered, they are also implicitly subject to withdrawal by government (el-Mahdi 1977, 1979; Gordon 1986; Goldflam 1988).

---

[2] The *Sudan Gazette*, No. 80 of 24 August 1905, was a special issue in which the original text of the Land Settlement Ordinance 1905 was published (Sudan Archive 1905: SAD 627/12/13–18).

In 1907, the government issued the Deeds Registration Ordinance in the *Sudan Gazette* No. 9, 1907. It was meant to improve the regulation of the registry of deeds relating to land in the city of Khartoum and the town of Khartoum North and to provide for the establishment of registries of deeds elsewhere (Sudan Archive 1907: SAD 627/12/22–8). In 1908, an order was issued to apply the ordinance to the town of Omdurman and the Provinces of Khartoum, Berber, and Wad Medani town, and amendments were made to the 1899 and 1907 Ordinances in the form of a new ordinance known as 'the Deeds Registration Ordinance 1908' (Sudan Archive 1908: SAD 627/12/29–30). Later, the 1907 and 1908 Ordinances were combined in 'the Deeds Registration Ordinance' of 1920 with the extension of several provisions (Sudan Archive 1920: SAD 627/12/34–5).

In the central and northern regions, the colonial administration conferred land rights upon the religious leaders of the Khatmiyya and the Ansar as well as tribal leaders in order to consolidate and legalize these rights and to encourage these emerging landlords to grow cotton using irrigation pumps along the banks of the Nile, the White, and the Blue Nile. For instance, reporting on the Sennar Land Settlement 1913–1915, Sarsfield-Hall revealed that in 1915, of the total area of the District, '17%, 81%, and 2% were registered as privately owned land, Government land, and Government land subject to tenant rights respectively' (Sudan Archive 1915a: SAD 542/5/10). As a result, most of the privately owned lands were controlled by the religious leaders, who soon came to dominate the political and economic scene of postcolonial Sudan and still do so at present. Indeed, due to these processes of land settlement and registration in northern and central Sudan, some individuals, mostly religious and communal leaders and dignitaries, have ended up owning huge tracts of land as their private property.

For instance, both Bolton (1954: 192) and Goldflam (1988: 112) reported that as early as 1903, the tribal heads of the Shukriyya in the Rufa'a district won their claimed rights of ownership over tribal rain land in the Civil Court. Accordingly, some local landless communities were allowed to buy land from the ruling Abu Sin family. In 1935, however, this situation was redressed when it was decided that such lands would be handed over to cultivators on the family's commuting of a fixed sum of dues which they had been paying to their 'landlords'. Moreover, in 1915, during the process of land settlement and registration in Sennar District, Sarsfield-Hall reported (Sudan Archive 1915b: SAD 678/2/29) that 'it is the case that certain people in the district possess or lay claim to large tracts of land, in some cases land of entire village'. At a later stage, MacMichael (1954: 151) reported that most of these claims were recognized and eventually registered since 'one of the first steps taken was that of land settlement and registration to prove and secure such private rights as existed'. This is an extremely important historical reality, with far-reaching economic and political implications today.

Such early regional and social differentiation in land tenure policies and ownership rights acted and is still acting as the main source of wealth and power for the present influential religious-based political parties in the Sudan, namely: the Umma Party and the Democratic United Party (DUP) linked to the Khatmiyya and the Ansar Islamic sects respectively. Their economic and political domination over the entire contemporary public space of the Sudan, is to a large degree, drawn from these early land tenure policies and politics, which enabled them to accumulate huge tracts of registered lands and related endowments in major urban centres in the central and northern parts of the Sudan.

The early arrangements of empowering the religious and native leaders in northern and central Sudan were reinforced through the Native Disposition of Lands Restrictions Ordinance, 1918, by which the colonial government sought to protect native private landowners against dispossession by expatriates. Again, this same pattern was not applied in the peripheral regions of the South, Nuba Mountains, southern Blue Nile, Beja, and Darfur, where the land was still communally owned with no recognition of private or individual rights.

The colonial government continued to introduce a series of ordinances aimed at consolidating the law of land settlement and strengthening the system of registration of land titles, while maintaining its power to withdraw customary usufruct rights. Hence, the 1925 Land Settlement and Registration Ordinance was introduced, with all previous ordinances being consolidated into one. It was intended to enable anybody who claimed a title or rights to land to be recognized and registered. Title to land governed by common law principles was classified as either freehold or leasehold ownership, which is an individual rather than a traditional tribal ownership system. Apart from making some minor alterations to the existing system, the 1925 Ordinance repeals or consolidates 13 Ordinances or Amending Ordinances. It has become evident since this ordinance was introduced that no person can acquire land in the whole of Sudan with any degree of safety without registration (Sudan Archive 1925: SAD 627/12/36–7).

The Act mainly deals with urban land and infrastructural land, exclusively confined to North and central riverain Sudan. The major impact of this Act on the local population in these regions is that within the framework of government ownership, customary land rights are recognized to some degree. Several studies, for example, de Wit (2001: 9) and el-Mahdi (1979: 9) reveal that tribes, clans, families, and rural dwellers could consider land as *de facto* their 'own' in a communal or cooperative context.

In the Prescription and Limitation Ordinance of 1928, land definition was extended more explicitly with reference to buildings, a development that had gained momentum in several emerging urban areas, particularly in the central and northern parts of the Sudan. It, therefore, redefined the word 'land' to include benefits arising out of land, such as buildings, structures permanently fixed to land, and any interest in land or the general right to use land. It also defined 'usufruct' as the right to use and enjoy land, the bare ownership of which belongs to someone else, and 'usufructuary' as the person having such a right. Having instituted these definitions as legal terms, the ordinance reaffirms that 'Unless and until the contrary is established upon settlement under the provisions of the Land Settlement and Registration Ordinance, 1925, a person in possession, use or enjoyment of waste, forest or unregistered land with or without the express permission of the Government shall be an usufructuary' (Sudan Archive 1928: SAD 627/12/39–43).

The implication of this statement is that, except for privately or communally owned and registered lands in the central and northern parts of the Sudan, all Sudanese inhabitants residing on communally owned land are by law usufructuaries on land whose bare owner is the Government.

It is worth noting that the riverain migrants, mostly the Jillaba, Muslim and Arab-speaking merchants who migrated from northern Sudan and spread all over the country, managed to utilize this policy of recognizing and registering land as private rights to secure and register some rural lands beyond their riverain homelands. This happened at the time the majority of individuals in the rural communities beyond the central and northern areas did not enjoy the same rights. For example, as early as 1916, the very few cases in which individual claims over rural lands were recognized and registered as private property outside the central and northern areas were all linked with the riverain merchants involved in gum plantations and trade in Kordofan Province. Warburg reported that:

> In Kordofan the only land settlement undertaken until 1916, was that of El Obeid and Dueim. Nearly all other lands were either owned by tribes or by the government and the few disputes that arose were settled according to local custom. In the district of Bara, where many claims to private land were put forward by members of the riverain tribes, they were recognized whenever supported by valid evidence. (1970: 159)

In his note to the Legal Secretary on land tenure in the Kheiran of Northern Kordofan in 1936, the Registrar of Lands in Kordofan Province referred to the economic importance of the artificially irrigated fertile lands of the Kheiran ([pl.],khor [sg.]: small watercourse) for Nekhal, Dom palms products, and the onion crop. Apart from the local cultivators of the Dar Hamid tribe, who admit that the land is tribal but subject to strict individual rights of cultivation, it was reported in 1935 that there were the 'descendents of the Danagla whose forbears settled in the Kheiran before the Mahdia [Mahdiyya] and who claim ownership of the land' (Sudan Archive 1935a: SAD 542/3/47). In this way, these riverains, mainly Jillaba merchants, came to have the upper hand in acquiring land as private property in most of the emerging urban centres in the South, East, Darfur, and the Nuba Mountains. Later, they reinforced their positions when they managed progressively to control the best lands for mechanized rain-fed farming, particularly in the Nuba Mountains from the 1960s to the present day. This is evidenced in various studies, including, among others, Battahani (1980, 1986); Manger (1984); Mohamed Salih (1984); Spaulding (1984); Abdelgabar (1997); Saavedra (1998).

The 1930 Land Acquisition Ordinance further paved the way for the government to acquire any land subject to village or tribal rights when it appeared likely to be required permanently or temporarily for any public purpose. However, before the introduction of the 1930 Ordinance, individual ownership of land had already been established in the course of the settlement of the riverain land between Halfa and Kosti and the rain land of the Gezira. In its endeavour to establish the Gezira scheme in central Sudan, the colonial government recognized the rights of affected communities in the area since the Wathiqah documents of title, dating from the Funj kings, still existed, and private ownership had been accepted by the early Land Commissions and Civil Courts. By 1927, land rights in all of Gezira had been settled with different types of community or individuals claims registered, before being compulsorily rented by the government for the establishment of the project. Most importantly, the same land owners were incorporated as tenant-holders (Bolton 1954: 191; Goldflam 1988: 60–4).

The Land Office started a cadastre in northern and central Sudan in 1906 and completed it in 1912. The task was complicated by the uncertainty of boundaries, the need to sift thousands of claims, some valid, some baseless, yet all conflicting, the continuing migratory habits of the population, and above all, by the Mohammedan laws of inheritance, which enabled men, women and children living perhaps hundreds miles away, to claim the rights of inheritance to minute fractions of land. Despite this, one of the first steps taken by the colonial administration in the northern and central regions in the process of land settlement and registration was to prove and secure such private rights as existed. In the event, when the settlement and survey had been completed:

> the Government compulsorily rented the whole area from its registered owners at the rate current for underdeveloped land before the inception of the scheme, and then, having divided it into manageable units of uniform size to conform with the needs of systematic irrigation, re-allotted it to its owners in the form of tenant-holdings of uniform size as near as possible to the site of their original holdings. (MacMichael 1954: 151–52)

The process of the Gezira scheme illustrates this land policy. Informing the British Parliament, on behalf of the Sudan Government, about the progress of their policy in the Gezira scheme in 1924, the British Foreign Secretary stated that:

> The result of this policy has been that practically the whole of the land in the Gezira remains in native ownership divided into comparatively small holdings so that it might be said that, not only has the foreign land speculation been kept out, but also the wealthy native absentee landlord and the whole of the land remains in the ownership of the actual cultivators that work upon it. (Goldflam 1988: 64)

The establishment of the Gezira scheme in central Sudan in the 1920s demonstrates how the interests and the rights of the local communities in central and northern Sudan were harmonized with public interests pursued by the colonial administration. In his written note on the issue of 'individual rights in tribal lands', addressed to the Director of Lands, Mr. B. H. Bell, then Acting Legal Secretary of the Sudan, affirmed the recognition of the tribal lands by modern law; and that rights had been practically guaranteed in central parts of the Sudan on the basis of the claimed tribal lands: '[in] the Gezira, certain harik and 'ugud lands have been settled and registered to Government subject to the rights of certain tribes or section of tribes to cultivate etc. [...] It is thus apparent that tribal lands are well recognized by law' (Sudan Archive 1930b: SAD 542/23/1).

In the same way, Simpson, who served as Commissioner of Lands and Registrar-General (1945–53) in the colonial Sudan, noted how the interests and rights of the locals were maintained while pursuing public interest in establishing the Gezira scheme:

> The land was first settled and registered to prove and secure such private titles as existed. It was then compulsorily hired at a generous rental under a special ordinance which gave the Government power to make use of the land for the purposes of the scheme but at the same time retained to the owners their interest in the land [...] The scheme is in fact an outstanding example of how the best possible development has been secured whilst private interests have been fully safeguarded. (Sudan Archive 1946/47: SAD 627/16/11)

The same policy was pursued in the pump schemes along the White Nile in central Sudan and the Nile River in the northern part of the country. In establishing these schemes, it was emphasised that the 'interests of the local population who have to earn their living on the land must override the interests of those who merely wish to draw income out of rents' (Sudan Archive 1946/47: SAD 627/16/12). Fair compensation was paid to individual land owners and no land was confiscated by the Government without proper settlement or direct sales. For example, Bolton (1954: 191, 194) reported that the salika land holders along the White Nile were compensated in kind and in cash in 1936 when their agricultural lands were designated to be flooded by the Jebel Aulia Dam. A similar state of affairs existed in Halfa district, where registered owners lost use of their lands on account of the raising of the height of the Aswan Dam in Egypt.

Also, in its Annual Report of 1953–54, the Registrar General of the Lands' Office (Sudan Archive 1954: SAD 720/3/1) reported that all land cases which were sold or expropriated and registered to the Sudan Government were preceded by compensation paid to the local individual owners in Gezira, the Blue Nile, and the Northern Provinces during the period 1950–54. So by the1950s, according to Miskin (1950: 81), it was evident that registration of agricultural land was practically confined to the Northern, Khartoum, and Blue Nile Provinces, where most of the narrow land of alluvial soil and all the rain lands of the Gezira were registered as individual property. Bolton (1954: 188–97), MacMichael (1954), and

Goldflam (1988) noted that the Sudanese societies were experiencing a transition stage in land tenure patterns with the following three major categories of land rights in practice:

(1) Government land subject to no rights: in the delta of Tokar and the Gash the Government has refused to recognize rights in these two delta lands, treated as Government lands, not subject to tribal or private rights. However, the Government admitted that the original cultivators should be treated in a preferential manner as a privileged class. Preference was given to indigenous tribesmen in a unit called a 'dimin', in Tokar or 'shaibut' in Gash. Both these terms refer to a large tribal holding scattered over the delta, and also to small individual holdings. In the process, both types of holdings were recognized and registered despite the fact that the delta land was considered to be government land, subject to no rights. When an irrigation scheme was introduced in 1923, preference was given to the registered holders of shaibut or dimin. At a later stage, Government land was allotted rent-free on a system of annual tenancies to cultivators, with 70% of the total allotment being on a tribal basis with reference to registered holders and members of tribes which had exercised cultivation rights.

(2) Government land subject to rights vested in a community, such as a tribe, section, or village, or sometimes in individuals. Generally, tribal land ownership was the main pattern for the nomadic and sedentary groups all over the Sudan except the riverain land between Halfa and Kosti and the rain land of the Gezira. This includes the large areas occupied by nomadic and semi-nomadic tribes in the Provinces of Kassala, Kordofan, and Darfur, which were tribal lands. The Beja tribes in the Red Sea Hills, the Kababish and Kawahla of northern Kordofan and the Baqqara tribes of southern Darfur and Kordofan have almost unrestricted enjoyment of a large area of territory known as the tribal dar (homeland). In Kordofan, Darfur, Southern Blue Nile, the Nuba Mountains, and in Southern Sudan, land is held communally and, since the inhabitants are mainly sedentary, the unit is the village or hill community.

(3) Land individually owned: individual ownership of land was established in the course of settlement of the riverain land between Halfa and Kosti and of the rain land of the Gezira. Saqiyya as well as saluka lands were for the most part held in private registered ownership in small holdings. There are instances of unregistered land held in individual ownership in Berber and Shendi Provinces and in the Kheiran in Kordofan.

In summary, when Sudan gained independence in 1956, all agricultural land held individually or communally in the central and northern Sudan was recognized and registered, while in the remaining regions, land remained unregistered and communally held but subject to government appropriation for public purpose without undermining the interests of the traditional rights of the affected communities and individuals. As this discussion moves to the postcolonial stage, the following significantly important principles governing the colonial land tenure policies and politics must be kept in mind:

First, 'unless and until the contrary is established upon settlement under the provisions of the Land Settlement and Registration Ordinance, 1925, a person in possession, use or enjoyment of waste, forest or unregistered land with or without the express permission of the Government shall be an usufructuary' (Sudan Archive 1928: SAD 627/12/39). In 1950, D. F. Hawley insisted 'until legal ownership has been established by a settlement, the bare ownership of all land is vested in the Government in trust for the native and subject to all rights of user belonging to natives in community or individually' (Sudan Archive 1950: SAD 719/10/2).

Second, tribal lands were well recognized by law. Thus, the colonial Government empowered the native authority with legal, administrative, and financial arrangements to exercise powers not only to address land disputes but also to 'if [it] thinks fit and subject to tribal custom, let out portions of its land to strangers charging them a rent in cash or kind' (Sudan Archive 1930b: SAD 542/23/1–2).

Third, in the areas where the processes of land settlement, registration, and expropriation were taking place, namely in the central and northern parts of the Sudan, 'the interests of the local population who have to earn their living on the land must override the interests of those who merely wish to draw income out of rents.' That is why 'the land was first settled and registered to prove and secure such private titles as existed' (Sudan Archive 1946–47: SAD 627/16/11–12).

Fourth, the colonial Government retained power

> to make use of the land for the purposes of the scheme but at the same time retained to the owners their interest in the land. Power to deal with these interests has been progressively restricted, in order to prevent merchants and persons with no local connection from acquiring land solely for the purpose of investment or speculation. (Sudan Archive 1946–47: SAD 627/16/11)

Fifth, the colonial Government maintained a consistent and strict policy of paying compensation in land or partly in land and partly in money:

> If the compensation consist[s] of land and the Government delayed in settling that compensated land at the time it effectively took over the concerned land, then the Settlement Officer shall award compensation by way of rent from the date when the Government enters into the possession of such rights to the date of the actual compensation. (Sudan Archive 1903a: SAD 627/12/17)

Sixth, several writers including MacMichael (1954: 80) and Bolton (1954: 195), have suggested that the settlement of land rights, followed by registration, has not been extended to the Southern Sudan, Southern Blue Nile, and the Nuba Mountains for three major reasons. First, because there is plenty of land; secondly, because the inhabitants are for the most part in a stage of development in which land is held in common by a tribe or group, and an individual has no rights except as a member of such a tribe or group. Thirdly, the inhabitants are pagans and unaffected by the recognition given to individual ownership of land by Mohammedan law prevailing in the rest of the Sudan. As a result, the policy of 'all unregistered land is government land in trust for the people who habitually exercise rights over it' has never been put to any practical test.

Finally, registration of land as private property means the acquisition of an asset of significant and durable economic value. Despite this, the process of recognition and eventual registration of individual land rights was not applied to the indigenous peoples of the Nuba Mountains, Blue Nile, the South, and Darfur throughout the colonial period. In these regions, lands remain communal with no recognition of individual rights of ownership apart from rights of use. Based on this reasoning, it is argued here that these early regional variations in land rights policy and practices formed, to a large extent, the basis for the economic differentiation between the communities in the central and northern parts of the Sudan, on the one hand, and those in the rest of the country, on the other, with far-reaching socio-economic and political implications up to the present day.

The postcolonial state policy and institutionalization of land grabbing

The following discussion shows that the postcolonial state not only undermined the land rights principles prevailing during the colonial period but also subjected unregistered and communally owned lands in the peripheral regions to excessive appropriation and grabbing, with no consideration for the interests of the local communities.

With population pressure on land, particularly for agricultural development, the prevailing view during the colonial era that land was abundant (MacMichael 1954: 80) in areas other than central and northern Sudan is historical rather than current. Land was commoditized and became an important source of wealth and power for individuals, communities and the state. Thus, after independence, it was assumed that the postcolonial national state would continue the same process of recognition, settlement, and eventual registration of the customarily and communally owned lands in the remaining regions of the Sudan.

Most importantly, it was assumed that the postcolonial state would preserve the interests and rights of the local communities whose land was required for public purposes, by maintaining the favourable principles applied under the colonial administration:

(i) Recognizing and, therefore, registering the communal or individual claims of lands as they existed;

(ii) Paying compensation in kind, cash or both in case of land confiscation for public interests; and

(iii) Adhering to policy of restraining merchants and persons with no local connection from acquiring land solely for the purpose of investment or speculation (also see Komey 2010b: 356–57).

Instead of adhering to these fundamental principles, successive national governments introduced more repressive land policies and practices so that the situation deteriorated. Unregistered communal lands in the peripheral regions were subjected to a systematic and violent practice of land grabbing and expropriation for public and private investment, which again benefited mostly the Jillaba and a few ruling elites while impoverishing local communities of indigenous dwellers. To consolidate its land policies and practices with the clear intent of undermining the interests of the local people, the Sudanese national state introduced a series of repressive land legislations. Among these is the 1970 Unregistered Land Act. A burgeoning literature reveals that the Act represents a major negative shift in land rights in postcolonial Sudan with far-reaching implications as far as the rights of communal land ownership are concerned (Simpson 1976; el-Mahdi 1977, 1979; Gordon 1986; Goldflam 1988; Mohamed Salih 1999; de Wit 2001; Manger 2003a, 2008b; Komey 2008a, 2008b, 2009a, 2009b, 2010b).

Combining the state practice of land grabbing with the problem of excessive regional disparities in national development demonstrates that postcolonial Sudan is a typical example of an exclusionary state in contemporary Africa (Komey 2009a). Thus, as argued in more detail in the next section, the state's exclusionary practice in land rights is responsible for current conflicts, both large and small. It evokes all kinds of appeals and emotions about belongings and identities, in the excluded indigenous communities who find themselves landless in their own homeland and with their very survival greatly endangered (Komey 2009a, 2009b).

It is worth noting that although the postcolonial state brought in a series of land legislations, it has continued to use some colonial land ordinances in land settlement, registration, and expropriation to the present day. However, despite this fact, there has been a significant shift in the actual practices by the national state. Following recent developments in postcolonial land policies and practices, Gordon (1986: 146) concludes that 'there is often no relationship between formal legislation and what actually takes place on the ground.'

In the contemporary state of Sudan, contrary to colonial administration policy, the interests of private investors—basically the Jillaba of the riverain areas who merely wish to draw income out of rent—override the interests of the local population who rely on the land for their livelihood. This is a striking setback in land tenure policy, particularly for the rural communities where all land remains communal and unregistered. Moreover, the strict colonial policies of compensation in kind, through the offer of alternative land, cash compensation, or both, have ceased to exist as strict practice. Compensation is valid only in the case of registered lands in the northern and central regions as well as for urban registered lands in the remaining parts of the Sudan. In this respect, el-Mahdi (1979: 9) claims that:

> Registered private ownership of land along the Nile Valley and generally in
> the Northern Sudan Provinces and in the urban areas in the southern

Region, and Western Sudan is recognized and respected. No person shall be deprived of such property except in the manner provided for by law and upon payment of fair compensation. If the Government is in need of land for a public purpose, it acquires it under the Land Acquisition Ordinance, 1930 and fair compensation is paid to the person whose land is expropriated.

An important distinction here is that the bulk of registered land in the urban areas in western, eastern, and southern Sudan is again controlled by the riverain Jillaba and state officials the majority of whom are socially linked to the central and northern regions of the Sudan. They are the primary beneficiaries, as they usually receive fair compensation when such lands are expropriated by the government for public purposes. At the same time, and to the contrary, the bulk of unregistered land owned customarily by rural communities in these peripheral regions remains subject to grabbing and expropriation with no compensation or commitment to local communities' interests. In this way, land as a source of wealth and power becomes one of the main differentiating factors between individuals and communities of the central and northern core regions, and also for those of peripheral regions in postcolonial Sudan.

Within this process, the postcolonial state has promulgated a series of legislations designed to encourage private investment[3] with an enormous expansion in both irrigated and rain-fed mechanized farming. With the sharp demand for arable land for public and private projects, the land tenure system becomes a bone of contention between the state and rural communities.

The 1970 Unregistered Land Act introduced an important modification to earlier legislation, particularly in section 4(1) which stipulates that:

All land of any kind whether waste, forest, occupied or unoccupied, which is not registered before the commencement of this Act shall, on such commencement, be the property of the government and shall be deemed to have registered as such, as if the provisions of the Land Settlements and Registration Act of 1925 have been duly complied with. (Unregistered Land Act, 1970, in el-Mahdi 1979: 221, Egemi 2004: 4)

Effectively, this section repealed Section 7(ii) of the Land Settlement Ordinance of 1905, which stated that 'all waste forest and unoccupied land shall be deemed to be the property of the Government until the contrary be proved' (Sudan Archive 1903a: SAD 627/12/15). It also repealed Section 14 (iv and v) which allowed for compensation in kind (i.e., alternative land), in money, or both for the affected community or individual (Sudan Archive 1903a: SAD 627/12/17). One major change to be noted here is that, for the first time, 'occupied' land which is not registered is deemed automatically to be government land, with no chance of any recognition, settlement, or eventual private or communal

---

[3] This legislation includes the Approved Enterprises (Concessions) Act, 1956; the Organization and Promotion of Industrial Investment Act, 1967; and Mechanized Farming Act, 1968. For a discussion on these and other economic legislation, see Gordon (1986).

registration of such land, or of an alternative fair payment of compensation as previously.

Evidently, the Act repealed the rights and, consequently, the interests of the majority of rural communities. It deprives them of their customarily owned and effectively occupied lands and sometimes even evicts them. No doubt, this repressive practice has enormous socio-economic consequences for the livelihoods of rural communities nation-wide. Thus, de Wit condemns the Act (2003:11):

> ...[it] deprives prior users from the right to be compensated for loss of land use rights, or for opportunities to be incorporated in the planned agricultural programme. An immediate consequence of this Act is that 'traditional' land uses, including agriculture are being pushed to more marginal areas, the better land being reserved for state interventions.

In practical terms, under the 1970 Act, a communal customary land right that was legally recognized by the colonial administration is no longer secure because '[it] is reduced to a mere license or "tenancy" at will which may be revoked at any time when the Government invokes Section 8 of the Act and evicts the occupant' (el-Mahdi 1979: 9).

The Act was enforced nation-wide despite the fact that all rural communities in western, eastern, and southern Sudan have or had no previous system of land registration in force. Moreover, the Act 'does not provide a transitional period for land users to register eventually their rights under the 1925 Act. On the contrary, according to article 7.1, any registration process in [the] pipeline shall abate on the commencement of the Act' (de Wit 2003: 10). The main intention is to make it 'easier for the Government to expropriate land for large agricultural schemes regardless of claims to ownership' (Simpson 1991: 102). In sum, the Act becomes 'a government tool to facilitate the acquisition of large tracts of land for agricultural schemes, at the expense of rural dwellers' (de Wit 2003: 10).

Thus, the Act has even more repressive and detrimental arrangements than the colonial version. All rural lands became government lands, while large portions of the land in central and northern Sudan are already privately owned land because they were recognized, settled and registered during the colonial period. To ensure the suppression of a community or individual wanting to resist the process of land grabbing and to disable any protests, three interrelated measures were put into place. First, the Act gave the government the right to use force in safeguarding land designated as its own. According to Article 8 of the Unregistered Land Act, 1970: 'If any person is in occupation of any land which is registered or deemed to be registered in the name of the Government, the Government may order his eviction from such land and may use reasonable force if necessary' (de Wit 2003: 10).

Second, the government weakened communal social organizations and structures by abolishing the native administration, an important institution for regulating land and managing inevitable land-related conflicts, among others (Babiker 1998; Mohamed 1998; Abdul Jalil 1985, 2008).

Third, the government was also enabled to implement a development policy based on the expansion of mechanized farming, and the exploration, production and transportation of oil by allocating vast tracts of land to private investors (both local and foreign) at the expense of rural communities' traditional land rights.[4]

Concurrently, a specific form of tenancy, instituted in the development of the mechanized rain-fed large-scale projects in the central rain land and in the Nuba Mountains during the 1960s, was reinforced (Battahani 1980; Saeed 1980; Manger 1981; Ibrahim 1988; Harragin 2003). 'Being unregistered the government claimed ownership and distributed in holdings large enough to make the use of a tractor economic, initially of 400 hectares (952 feddans)' (Simpson 1991: 102). Since this is the same land which largely constitutes the livelihoods of sedentary and nomadic communities, the new-rich non-local merchants came into ownership of huge tracts of land while local communities were confined to small, fixed, and increasingly infertile plots.

The radical reversals in rights and the repressive aspects of the 1970 Unregistered Land Act were further strengthened by the 1984 Civil Transaction Act and its amendments of 1991 and 1993. As a result, any case against the Government pertaining to unregistered land has no legal basis; therefore, no court of law is competent to receive a complaint that goes against the interests of the state. These amendments also incorporated the Islamic concept of land as a public utility 'owned by God' and regulated by the Islamic Sharia principles in an Islamic state. It stipulates that 'Land belongs to God' (Civil Transaction Act 1984: Section 559(1) in Gordon 1986: 149). It also legalizes some elements of Sharia law, such as the official recognition of unregistered land rights connected with Islamic 'urf (de Wit 2003: 11).

A further consequence of these new legislative developments, which were driven by political Islam from the 1980s onwards, is to have institutionalized another form of social difference in land rights along religious lines. It has reinforced the rights of Muslim communities by accepting Islamic 'urf in legalizing unregistered land. It thus provides an opportunity for a Muslim claimant to transfer Islamic-based customary rights into full legal rights of ownership. No equivalent opportunity is granted for the bulk of African pagans and Christians, not only in southern Sudan, the Nuba Mountains, and the southern Blue Nile, but also in the northern and central parts of the country, where a sizeable number of non-Muslim minorities exist.

Despite the fact that both the 1970 and 1984 Acts have never been

---

[4] For a detailed account of the mechanized rain-fed farming schemes in the Nuba Mountains, see Saeed (1980), Manger (1981), Battahani (1980, 1986), Ibrahim (1988), African Rights (1995), Suliman (1999, 2002), Mohamed Salih (1995, 1999), Abdel Salam et al. (2002), Rahhal (2001a), Harragin (2003). For some accounts on the role of oil investment in Sudan in alienating rural communities from their livelihoods, see, for example, Suliman (2001); International Crisis Group (2002), Mohammed and Fisher (2002); Rone (2003), Johnson (2006); and Patey (2007).

widely applied on a routine basis, the Government continues to use them whenever and wherever it deems appropriate, instigating a high degree of communal insecurity among the affected communities particularly in rural Sudan (Mohammed Salih 1999; Mohamed and Fisher 2002; de Wit 2003; Harragin 2003; Egemi 2004; Johnson 2006).

Conclusion

In summary, contrary to the fundamental and strict land policy of protecting the interests of the local population while pursuing public development as practised, to some degree, during the colonial administration, successive postcolonial national governments have undermined the interests, rights, and livelihoods of the local people. The above discussion has demonstrated that the postcolonial governments in the centre reinforced the negative aspects of the colonial legacy, while undermining the major and positive aspects pertaining to the interests, rights, and livelihoods of the local people. This process has worked to the advantage of the small ruling elites and the state-linked Jillaba merchants. This state land policy manifests itself in the following three distinct, discriminatory and exclusionary aspects:

First, the expropriation of land for public and private development associated with a strict policy of compensation in kind, cash, or both was replaced by a policy of land grabbing associated with alienation or displacement of local communities. This is more evident in the peripheral regions of the Sudan where the bulk of the land is unregistered and where most of the recent major mechanized farming projects and oil explorations are being conducted.

Second, the colonial land registration practices, which were used to first settle, register and secure such private titles as existed, and to prevent merchants and persons with no local connection from acquiring lands solely for the purpose of investment or speculation, were not only undermined but replaced with more oppressive regulation. Consequently, the state-linked Jillaba merchants and state officials became progressively the real beneficiaries of any new land settlement and registration, particularly the agricultural lands in the peripheral regions.

Third, the persistent undermining of the rights of local people resulted in an incredible devastation of their livelihoods and mode of life with far-reaching political and socio-economic repercussions, particularly in the South, Darfur, Southern Blue Nile, and the Nuba Mountains.

The cumulative result is a wide-scale crisis in the Sudan's subsistence economies with serious socio-economic and political repercussions, particularly in the peripheral regions of the country. This, in turn, has led to extensive differentiations and disparities in development between the centre and the periphery.

The emergence and extension of the civil war to include most of the marginalized regions in the Sudan can only be fully understood through its historical and contemporary dynamics pertaining to land politics, policies and practices in the context of the overall process of Sudanese state formation. The root causes, dynamics and manifestations of the extension of the war into the Nuba Mountains region is the main subject of Chapter 3.

Part II

The War: Causes & Impact

3

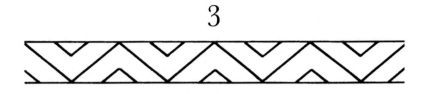

The War

Root Causes & Ramifications in the Region

The previous discussion revealed that the root causes of the civil war in Sudan are multi-dimensional in nature and scale. They range from factors related to the historical legacy of Sudanese state formation to the present governance, national politics and policies, and their regional and ethnic manifestations. The task of this chapter is to trace the root causes, dynamics, and ramifications of the civil war, and the trajectories of its extension from southern to northern Sudan via the Nuba Mountains. It reviews in brief the pre-war political situation in the region while focusing, in details, on the war's dynamics and effects. These local events are analyzed from a broad state- and governance-based perspective. It is within this broader context that land, as a source of wealth, power and identity, acquires significance in local and national conflicts.

Nuba marginalization and their peaceful political striving

After Independence in 1956, the Nuba people, among other marginalized communities, realized that, despite their contribution to the struggle for the new state, they were being purposely denied access to, and participation in, power and wealth sharing, coupled with socio-cultural exclusion and suppression of their identities (Abbas 1973; Ibrahim 1988; Battahani 1998; Rahhal 2001a; Komey 2005a, 2005b; Ylonen 2009).

Due to this multi-dimensional marginalization and exclusion, the Nuba started to voice their grievances in different peaceful forms of resistance against the national state's exclusionary policies. This peaceful political striving proved fruitless (Abbas 1973; Battahani 1980, 1986; Munir 2006; Komey 2005a, 2009b). The Nuba Mountains General Union (NMGU) was established in 1957 with a strong political commitment to redress

Nuba marginalization and promote Nuba African identity. The late Philip Abbas Ghabush (1922–2008), a prominent Nuba politician, was one of the NMGU's founding leaders.

The NMGU strove to foster development opportunities, the region's political participation, and the promotion of African identity as an essential ingredient in the formation of the national character (Abbas 1973: 37, see also Ibrahim 1988: 213–61). This was to be achieved by promoting Nuba unity, re-establishing the Nuba Mountains Province, and representing the Nuba in central government institutions (Abbas 1973: 37, Rahhal 2001a: 38). In outlining the main principles of the first NMGU constitution, Fr. Philip Abbas Ghabush states that:

> A constitution was drawn up calling for the unity of all the Nuba, revival of the Nuba Mountains Province, abolition of the poll tax, a program of school building for western Sudan, parliamentary representation of the Nubas by Nubas, implementation of an acceptable solution to the southern question, a policy of 'Africanizing' Sudan rather 'Arubizhig it, and eventual black rule over the whole country. (Abbas 1973: 37)

The manifestation of this political agenda was evident in the 1965 election when the NMGU managed to contest and defeat the dominant ruling elites of the Khatmiyya-based National Unionist Party and the Ansar-based Umma Party by winning eight of the thirteen seats in the region. In the same year, it submitted a petition to the central government demanding the abolition of the Poll Tax still imposed on the Nuba, despite its abolition nationwide.

The marginalization of the Nuba people in national political, socio-cultural and economic spaces was evident during both the military and democratic regimes (Battahani 1986; Kadouf 2001; Rahhal 2001a; Komey 2005a, 2005b; Ylonen 2009). For example, during the first democratic national government of Ismil al-Azhari (1956–58), the ruling elite pursued strict policies of Islamization and Arabization in the education system of the whole country, with no consideration for any cultural, religious, or linguistic distinctions. To achieve complete cultural assimilation, indigenous languages were forbidden, including their banning in schools in the Nuba Mountains; Nuba children were not allowed to attend school unless they adopted Arabic names and spoke no language other than Arabic in the school (Johnson 2006: 131; Saeed 2001: 19).

The military regimes of Ibrahim Abud (1958–64) and Nimairi (1969–85) pursued the same policies but with greater determination towards excessive Islamization and Arabicization among Nuba children. In an interview conducted by Ende (2006a: 2) with Neroun Philip, a member of the Nuba elite and a prominent SPLM/A commander, Philip was highly critical of the education policies:

> The curriculum wasn't good. It was a pro-Arab curriculum anyway, but at that time we wouldn't know that it was bad. We were just learning whatever [they told us]. The first year in the primary I started learning the Qur'an

and I was very brilliant. The headmaster, who was giving us the lessons, was very happy and encouraging. He was telling me: 'You're a brilliant pupil; why don't you become a Muslim?' Usually they persuaded pupils who had names in their mother tongue, like Kuku; they would write it and then they would try to convince them: 'No, this is not a good name; you should better be given an Arabic name.' That's why you will find that most of the Nuba in the Nuba Mountains have Arabic names, even though they also have their local names.

During the Nimairi military regime (1969–85), some young Nuba leaders decided to establish several interlinked underground movements, namely al-Sakhr al-Aswad (the Back Rock), Nahnu Kadugli (We are Kadugli), and Kumalo (Kadouf 2001; Munir 2006). The emergence of these underground movements marked a turning point in the Nuba political struggle. Through their secret activities among the Nuba, these movements, particularly Kumalo, succeeded in the 1980–82 one-party-system elections to push through their own active members into the government legislative system at local, regional, and national levels, (Salih 1989; Battahani 1998; Kadouf 2001).

In the midst of this socio-economic and political environment the late Yusuf Kuwa Mekki (1945–2001) emerged as an important figure. After his graduation from the University of Khartoum in 1980, Mekki returned to the Nuba Mountains and led the Kumalo movement in Kadugli. Neroun Philip, a Kumalo activist at that time, describes his experience:

> When I entered the secondary school, we were in the underground cells of the Komolo [Kumalo], which were being organized, by that time, by Yousif Kuwa [...] We held our meetings in secret places where we knew that no security person, or anybody else who wasn't one of us, could be listening [...] We had our meetings there, and [the leaders of Komolo] would brief us: this is what we want; our objectives are so and so. One day we have to liberate our people; it's already happening all over the South. (Ende 2006b: 4–5)

In 1981, Kuwa was elected as representative of the Kadugli constituency and as Deputy Speaker in the People's Regional Assembly of the Kordofan Region. With this political participation, Kumalo leadership hoped to redress Nuba's political, social, and economic grievances and injustices in a peaceful way. At that time, land grabbing for mechanized farming schemes in the region was already a highly contested issue in Kordofan regional politics. For example, in 1981, Ali Abu 'Anga, a Nuba member in the People's Regional Assembly in the Kordofan Region, accused

> [some] senior government officials in the Ministry of Agriculture of making certain Khartoum residents the beneficiaries of the agricultural schemes which were distributed in Southern Kordofan (Habila and Dilling), and charged that these actions had severely undermined the livelihoods of those who depend on the land for survival and demanded quick redress. (Salih 1989: 14)

However, the government continued the policy of land grabbing with more intensity and brutality. The Nuba became strangers in their own land, with many forced to migrate to urban centres in central and northern Sudan in search of new means of livelihood. In these places, however, the Nuba and other persecuted groups faced other forms of marginalization, a growing threat of destitution, with tangible evidence of being treated as 'second-class citizens' by the state in their own country.

Moreover, a brutal and forced deportation campaign, known locally as Kasha, was launched in Khartoum against all those without identification cards or employment on the pretext that they were a threat to public security and order. They were taken against their will to the area of their respective ethnic origins or otherwise to agricultural schemes in central Sudan as forced labour. According to Kadouf (2001: 51) 'The Nuba, and all those with obvious African features, were the main target. The army was deployed in the streets of Khartoum to implement the decree [...] the kasha was performed in a brutally humiliating and inhumane way.'

In the midst of these political grievances and socio economic marginalizations, active members of Kumalo, including Kuwa, realized their peaceful political movement was ineffective in redressing the issues of the region. However, the 1985 event of 'al-intifadh', i.e., a popular uprising, overturned the Nimairi Government and created an opportunity for political freedom that encouraged the Nuba underground movements to surface. Several Nuba parties were formed: (i) the Sudan Labour Party, whose main agenda was to 'propagate and portray Nuba African identity in contradiction to the claims of Arabism that was used indiscriminately in the Sudanese politics' (Kadouf 2001: 55); (ii) the NMGU, led by Professor al-Amin Hamuda, dominated by the Nuba elite with less popular support at the grassroots level in the region; and (iii) the Sudanese National Party (SNP), led by Fr. Philip Abbas Ghabush.

In October 1985, the transitional military government claimed to have uncovered a 'racial coup' led by Philip Abbas Ghabush that was planning to overthrow the government. He was arrested along with many Nuba soldiers and civilians. The latter were released three months later without charge, while 'the soldiers remained in prison for up to four years after conviction in a court that was a mockery for justice – no witnesses or documentary evidence were produced' (African Rights 1995: 58). Despite this, the SNP, under the leadership of Fr. Philip Abbas Ghabush, came to dominate regional politics in the Nuba Mountains through the election of 1986, winning eight seats in the region in the National Assembly. Despite this political representation, the Nuba and the entire region of the Nuba Mountains remain at the margins of Sudan's economy, politics and culture.

When the civil war broke out in the South in 1983, the Nuba, particularly the active Kumalo members, were ripe for rebellion (African Watch 1995: 32; Suliman 1999: 212; Johnson 2006: 131). The following year signified a shift to armed struggle in the Nuba Mountains when the prominent Kumalo leader Yusuf Kuwa Mekki, among others, joined the

Sudan Liberation Movement/Army (SPLM/A). In an interview conducted by Ende (2001), Kuwa argued that:

> We wanted some equality, some services; so that people could feel that they were belonging to the same country. [But] it wasn't possible, because whenever you talked, you would be [...] described as a racialist, a separatist, this and that and always they would try to find something to condemn you for. That is why we were enthusiastic to read the SPLA manifesto of 1983, which talked about fighting for the united Sudan, for equality and share of power, share of economy, freedom of religion, freedom of speech, freedom of practicing culture. That is what made us join the SPLA in 1984. We were disappointed with the situation.

The Nuba involvement in the civil war arises from a long history of political, economic and social marginalization and discrimination. Thus, as detailed in the following section, the spill over of the war from southern Sudan to the Nuba Mountains region in the north was politically driven though multiple factors.

The Nuba Mountains Region as a conflict zone

The actual extension of the civil war from south to north Sudan started when the encounters between the SPLM/A and the Government army blocked the grazing lands of the Baqqara around north-south frontiers. Two nearly simultaneous events occurred, neither of them directly connected with the Nuba. One was the raid in July 1985 on the Baqqara village of Gardud, just beyond the internal North-South border, by an SPLA unit based in the South; the second was the government's response, arming Baqqara militias to confront the SPLA as they approached northern Sudan. From that time the central government took a chance by arming the Baqqara in a systematic manner and encouraging them to form a pro-government militia force against the SPLM/A. This was a significant step towards transforming the Baqqara Murahaliin into a well armed force. The new militia immediately began small-scale raiding of Nuba communities (Africa Watch 1991: 5; African Rights 1995: 60).

THE BAQQARA: FROM MURAHALIIN TO ARMED MILITIAS

The formation and arming of the Baqqara militias was initiated by Fadlalla Burma Nasir, then Minister of Defence of the transitional military government of Swar al-Dahab (1985–86). Himself a Messiriyya Zuruq, he created the first Messiriyya militia, widely known as the Murahaliin, which became a powerful force. Initially, it was directed against the SPLA forces and Dinka of Bahr al Ghazal, who frequently threatened Baqqara access to land and water during their movements north. It soon became evident that the Baqqara had another agenda of their own besides protecting themselves along their north-south seasonal routes.

Thereafter, with or without the assistance of the Sudan military forces, they began raiding Nuba communities who were not yet part of the SPLM/A. These Arab militias used the weapons provided by the government indiscriminately, raiding, killing, and looting Nuba villages, and committing numerous massacres. These events polarized Nuba public opinion further, not only against the central government, but also against the local Baqqara (Africa Watch 1992; African Rights 1995; Suliman 1998; Johnson 2006; de Waal 2006).

Fadlalla Burma's militia policy was reinforced under the 1986–89 parliamentary government of al-Sadiq al-Mahdi. The Kordofan Region including Southern Kordofan Province was ruled by Umma Party leaders with close links to the Messiriyya militia. The transformation of the Messiriyya Murahaliin into armed militias subsequently led to the militarization of the other Baqqara groups in the region. This situation immediately created fear and havoc in many parts of the Nuba Mountains. Several Nuba informants who were interviewed by African Rights (1995: 62–5) reported several cases of terror and atrocities committed by the Arab militias in Kawalib, Miri, Fama, Lagawa, Saburi and Laguri areas, among others.

The fact that a group of Nuba had joined the SPLM was reason enough, from the Baqqara point of view, to attack the Nuba. What was distinctive about the militia activity was the scale of its military support, not only from the government, but also from some international economic allies of the government. In this respect, Johnson (2006: 83, fn. 3) asserted that: 'Even the Chevron Oil Company financed a Messiriyya militia, ostensibly to protect its camp at al-Muglad in Southern Kordofan.'

POLITICS OF LIBERATION AND NUBA RECRUITMENT IN THE SPLA

Before the SPLM/A penetrated into the Nuba Mountains, its radio broadcasts were very effective in disseminating the SPLM/A's doctrine of liberation movement among the Nuba elite. Inspired by a 'New Sudan Vision', the SPLM/A's political doctrine was enshrined in its manifesto. The New Sudan Vision, crafted by the SPLM/A leader, the late Dr John Garang (1945–2005), was and still is an inspiring force in the politics of liberation and resistance within marginalized groups and regions fighting against the institutional structures and functions of the 'Old Sudan' (Khalid 1987; Kameir 2006).

By the time of actual recruitment into the Liberation Movement in the Nuba Mountains, there was a sizeable number of the Nuba elite and a younger generation who had already been indoctrinated by the SPLM/A's politics of liberation and armed struggle through the radio broadcasts. Mobilization and eventual recruitment started among the Kumalo activists in Kadugli and other large urban centres, particularly Khartoum. All Nuba recruits were taken clandestinely to the SPLA's military camps in Ethiopia over Sudan's eastern border.

Although the Gardud incident of July 1985 marked the beginning of the extension of the war to the Nuba Mountains, it was not until 1986 that small task force groups of the Abushok Battalion, under the leadership of 'Awad al-Karim Kuku, Telefon Kuku, Yusuf Karra, and Yunis Abu Sadur, secretly entered the Nuba Mountains to recruit Nuba. They were soon followed by the first fighting force, the Volcano Battalion, under Commander 'Abdul Aziz al-Hilu. With its arrival, the recruitment took on a larger scale. The intensification of the recruitment campaigns among the Nuba created terror and havoc among the local Baqqara, who started to encounter a different attitude amongst the Nuba in their neighbourhoods.

For example, my informants, from the 'Yatqa Arabs who had lived for quite a long time with the Nuba Leira in al-Azraq, remarked that the emergence of the war in the area caught them by surprise. In their own words:[1]

> When some of our close friends from the Nuba Leira youth joined the SPLM/A, they did not inform us about their intention. Instead, we were told by some government circles that the Nuba had/have decided to wage war against the Arabs in the region. Thereafter, several signs started to surface and gave us frightening feelings that there was/is something unusual happening around us. More Leira youth started to systematically disappear from us. Moreover, some Leira started to separate their livestock from that of the 'Yatqa and took them to the Jebels.
>
> Additionally, some of the Leira would advise their 'Yatqa friends not to visit them anymore in their hilltop settlements, and not to show up in the weekly local markets or in the Leira villages. At a later stage, some Leira told their 'Yatqa close friends to leave the area altogether. Soon, we started to see the return of some Nuba youth who had been absent from the area for some time. This time, however, they avoided meeting or mixing with us. In the night, we could hear gunfire. Under such circumstances, we were forced to evacuate and got out of al-Azraq, a very risky situation.

The fact that the Nuba had sided with the rebels gave the Baqqara militias the pretext for stepping up their raids even in areas not yet experiencing the presence of the SPLA forces. In May 1987, Yusuf Kuwa returned to the Nuba Mountains to find almost one thousand young men had already been recruited. He took them for training in the SPLA military camp in Ethiopia. It was not until January 1989, that Yusuf Kuwa Mekki commanded the New Kush Division Six as a fighting unit and re-entered the Nuba Mountains (African Rights 1995: 66).

Despite the Nuba's declaration that their original intention was to fight the government and not their local partners, Nuba-led SPLA forces were persistently accused of targeting the Baqqara during their military operations (Fadl[2] 2002, and Muhammad Al-Haj 2006). SPLA leaders insisted that their main targets were the government army and institutions,

---

[1] Author's interview with 'Umar Ahmed Khair and others, Umm Beremeita, 2 February 2007.
[2] Mohamed al-Tayeb Fadl was an army officer who served as Commissioner of Kadugli Province 1991-93. His book: *Kadugli wa-Massirat al-Salam 1991-1993* (Kadugli and Peace March, 1991-93) represents, to a large degree, government perspectives on a number of issues related to war dynamics in the Nuba Mountains including the Jihad declaration, 'peace villages', and 'peace from within'.

and that some of their engagements with the Baqqara militias were forced on them by the Baqqara themselves (Ende 2001: 10).

Thereafter, the Nuba-led SPLA engaged in successive battles against the government army and the Baqqara militias alike. Thus, the tensions and eventually the war took on a new dimension, intensifying the antagonism between the two communities along ethno-political divides. From a Nuba perspective, the Baqqara were supposed to join hands with the Nuba and their armed forces in the SPLM/A to fight against the central government, which continued to marginalize whole communities in the region, including the Baqqara.

But the Baqqara decided to side with the government, which promised them Nuba land in return for their military support. From a Baqqara perspective, as shown in the above testimony of the Baqqara of 'Yatqa, the Nuba did not seek their opinion when they decided to join the SPLM/A. From the Baqqara point of view, the Nuba had decided in secrecy to go it alone, with subsequent evidence revealing that their intention was to target the Arab groups in the region

In this situation of accusation and counter-accusation, the government took a risk and redirected the war—originally between the central government and the armed Nuba—into a conflict between two marginalized local groups. In this way, two local and disadvantaged communities, the sedentary Nuba and the nomadic Baqqara, were made to fight each other for reasons externally generated from the centre of power (African Rights (1995: 23–4).

ESCALATION OF THE WAR
AND THE FORMATION OF THE PDFS

As the war intensified, the al-Sadiq al-Mahdi government started to form the Quat al-Difa' al-Sha'bi, or Popular Defence Forces (PDFs), with the aim of legitimizing the Murahaliin militias by turning them into a paramilitary force in close coordination with the army (African Rights 1995: 71). With this move, financial support, weaponry and training were provided to the militias by the provincial administration and security agencies.

On 30 June 1989, the National Salvation Revolutionary Council, led by Lt.-General Omer al-Bashir, seized power. It was ideologically backed by the National Islamic Front (NIF). The NIF had itself been active in trying to win the Murahaliin away from Umm Party loyalty. In October 1989, the new government passed the PDFs Act, prompting a number of Baqqara members in the Umma Party to join the NIF and consequently the ruling military regime (African Rights 1995; Rahhal 2001a).

On the expansion of the SPLA forces into the Nuba Mountains, the Rawawqa section of Hawazma Baqqara held a meeting in Tilo, Kadugli in 1987 and decided formally to organize armed militias, on the grounds that they were Arab groups targeted by the khawarij, (outsiders), i.e. the SPLA. The militias were to defend the religion of Islam and the Muslims in the region, and to protect their dignity, property, and the country. For that purpose, a 45-man-committee was formed from the native leaders representing the six 'Umudiyyat. It was divided into two wings, the military and political. The latter was chaired by Abu al-Bashar and the former by Ahmed Mahmud al-Kalas, a member of the NIF. Al-Kalas, who was later killed in combat near Kadugli, was responsible for military operations in terms of preparation, coordination with the military and security organs, military training, and the issuing of directives related to operations. This military wing became a basis for the formation of the PDFs which took place in Kadugli on 8 May 1989 with al-Kalas as the first commander (Muhammad al-Hadj[3] 2006: 120–40).

Subsequently, the PDFs participated separately or jointly with the army forces in operations that devastated Nuba villages. The main target appears to have been the young educated Nuba, and there was a widely held belief among the people that the army had drawn up a list of all educated Nuba, with the intention of killing them all, systematically. Mohamed Salih and Harir (1994: 197) revealed that suspicions of a tabur khamis (fifth column) were in wide circulation. Demands were made to kill, imprison or remove anyone openly supporting the SPLM/A to another region; hence, public condemnation of tribal militias became synonymous with a tabur khamis, especially in areas with mounting inter-ethnic tension or previous incidents of tribal warfare.

In this situation, some Nuba in government-controlled areas were forced to join the PDFs, mainly to protect themselves from Arab militia raids or security interrogations. Although, unlike the Baqqara-armed Murahaliin and militias, the PDFs were multi-ethnic, the Baqqara were gaining the upper hand in their orientation and operations. By the end of 1991, the pattern of violence had become well established in the region, with gross human rights violations being committed by both sides. Several human rights organizations and activists reported in detail that both sides raided villages, killed civilians, and/or kidnapped leaders. They also engaged in indiscriminate violence against civilians during military engagements.[4]

However, the atrocities committed by the government among Nuba civilians in their villages and the educated generation all over the country remain the most tragic aspect of this war. Rahhal (2001a: 127–33, Appendix 3) provided a detailed list of 308 well educated Nuba citizens who were arrested in the early 1990s and summarily executed by the

---

[3] 'Isa Abkar Muhammad al-Hadj, a member of the Baqqara elite from al Hamra village in east Kadugli, was himself one of the founding members of the Rawawga-Hawazma Arab militia and a subsequent active member of the PDFs in Kadugli. His book: *Jibal al-Nuba bein Tomuh al-sassah wa-dai'a al-foqra'*, 2006 (*Nuba Mountains between the ambitions of the politicians and the poor people's loss*) documents in detail, from the view of a pro-government member of the Baqqara elite, how the Nuba-led SPLA armed struggle was initially perceived as a Nuba war against Islam, Arab groups, and their dignity and property. It was this initial Baqqara position that led the government to seize the advantage and shift the war to ethnic and religious lines.
[4] See Africa Watch (1991, 1992a, b), African Rights (1995, 1997), Suliman (1998), Mohamed Salih (1995, 1999) and Rahhal (2003).

government's military intelligence service. These atrocities were committed after the government was successful in sealing off and isolating the Nuba communities from all national or international connection and support.

NUBA FACING JIHAD AND GENOCIDE BY ATTRITION

At the start of the 1990s, reports from Africa Watch (1991, 1992a, b) revealed, for the first time, that the Nuba Mountains had been sealed off by the government. No foreigners were permitted access, and Sudanese citizens had to obtain passes from the military authorities to travel in the area. The government embarked on a large military operation followed by an intensive campaign to eradicate the Nuba identity through ethnic cleansing. In great secrecy, physical genocide and cultural genocide (ethnocide) were to be perpetrated. As a result, by the early 1990s, some 60–70,000 Nuba had been killed in government military operations – brutal campaigns virtually invisible to the outside world (Meyer 2005: 26).

My key informant, Commander Simon Kalo,[5] who commanded SPLA troops in the Buram area during 1991–99, summarized the situation in the SPLA-held area during those days as follows:

> In October 1991, the government sealed off the Nuba Mountains, prohibiting any travel or contact by foreigners. That was the first step towards an unprecedented military assault, accompanied by a radical plan for the relocation and displacement of the Nuba community. The intent was to clear the whole region of its indigenous people. By 1992, the SPLM/A controlled areas in the Nuba Mountains were subjected to complete isolation with no access to national, regional, or international communities. Moreover, the Sudan government prevented the extension of the UN-led Operations Lifeline Sudan (OLS) to the Nuba Mountains. The aggregate result was the death of thousands because of hunger and disease associated with an enormous suffering of the rest of the Nuba communities who were subjected to the government's systematic campaigns of genocide and ethnocide.[6]

Bradbury (1998: 28) insists that '[the] responsibility for the tragedy in the Nuba Mountains lies squarely in the hands of the successive Sudanese governments who are accused of human rights atrocities, creating famine conditions, war crimes and even genocides'. This situation was maintained throughout the 1990s and only brought to an end in late January 2001, when the government allowed the delivery of international aid to the Nuba Mountains for the first time since 1986. This came as a result of the Senator John Danforth's peace initiative, which culminated in the signing the Cease Fire Agreement in January 2002. Three months later, Danforth (2002: 3) reported that:

> This area of African and Christian influence had been under siege for

---

[5] Simon Kalo is a senior Commander in the SPLM/A; after peace he served as political advisor for the Governor of the Southern Kordofan State, and the SPLM's Secretary–General in the region.
[6] Author's interview with Simon Kalo, Kadugli 9 January 2007.

almost two decades by the Government, which used military force and starvation as weapons, and which applied cultural and religious pressures against the people who live there. The government had allowed no relief into certain targeted areas of the Nuba Mountains for thirteen years to reinforce food pressures upon the population.

The government not only pursued military campaigns against the Nuba but also an ideological and religious strategy aimed at destroying Nuba culture, identity, and even their very survival as an ethnic group. At the centre of this strategy was a politically driven Jihad (Mohamed Salih 1989, 1995, 1999; African Watch 1992; African Rights 1995; Moszynski 1998; Rahhal 2001a).

POLITICIZATION OF THE RELIGIOUS FACTOR: THE JIHAD

Socio-economic marginalization, political oppression, and military campaigns against the Nuba people reached a climax with the emergence of the politicization and mobilization of the religious factor in the civil war that took place under the al-Bashir military regime (Mohamed Salih 1989, 2002; Africa Watch 1995; Rahhal 2001a; Kadouf 2001, 2002; Manger 2001–2002; Komey and Wassara 2008).

As the military confrontation between the government and the PDFs on the one hand, and the SPLA forces on the other, intensified in the region, the government started to change its war tactics by evoking the religious factor. It declared a Holy War, the Jihad, against the Nuba. The Jihad was carried out as part of a wider and comprehensive political and social scheme aimed at eradicating the Nuba identity through a series of coercive religious, social-cultural, political, and military measures. It was part of the government's campaign, code-named al-Da'wa al-Shamila (the Comprehensive Call). Compulsory Islamization of the Nuba was to be achieved through at least six separate yet interconnected schemes:

> (a) religious indoctrination, and the imposition of Islam and Islamic teachings among non-Muslim Nuba; (b) political, social and economic favouritism for Nuba Muslims and their instigation to spearhead the religious campaign; (c) Jihad or military campaign against non-Muslims as well as Muslim Nuba who defy the Call; (d) isolation of Nuba Christians and intimidation of clergy and church congregations [...]; (e) resettlement in 'peace villages' to facilitate (a) and (b); and (f) sustained harassment, detention and torture of any Nuba or other Sudanese who oppose the campaign inside or outside the Nuba Mountains. (Mohamed Salih 1995: 75)

Despite the fact that the declaration of Jihad in the region was religiously irrelevant because a number of the Nuba recruits in the SPLA, and many civilians in the SPLA-held areas, were Muslims anyway, a politically driven justification for fighting and killing these people was established. On 27 April 1992, a fatwa (an Islamic decree) was issued, in a conference in El Obeid, the capital of North Kordofan, on the pretext of fighting the SPLM/A forces (which included a substantial number of Nuba Muslims).

For that purpose, the fatwa extended the definition of apostasy by declaring that:

> The rebels in Southern Kordofan and southern Sudan started their rebellion against the state and declared war against Moslems. Their main aims are killing women, desecrating mosques, burning and defiling the Quran, and raping the Moslem women. These foes are the Zionists, the Christians and the arrogant people who provide them with provisions and arms. Therefore, an insurgent who was previously a Moslem is now an apostate; and a non-Moslem is now a non-believer standing as a bulwark against the spread of Islam, and Islam has granted the freedom of killing both of them. (Rahhal 2001a: 48–9; Manger 2001: 49–50, 2001–2002: 132–33; African Rights 1995: 289; and Johnson 2006: 133)

This widely quoted fatwa and the subsequent supporting Jihad arrangements came to have far-reaching and multifaceted implications for the war waged against all Nuba, Muslim and non-Muslim alike, and their respective religious institutions including mosques in the SPLA-held area Johnson (2006: 133) pointed out that.

> In providing a religious justification for its policies, [the government] defines its opponents as anti-Islam; by this definition its Muslim opponents become non-Muslims. A clear territorial distinction has been imposed distinguishing the *Dar al–Islam* (Abode of peace) from the *Dar al–Harb* (Abode of war). Mosques found outside government control have been destroyed and defaced, and Muslims enjoined to relocate themselves to the *Dar al–Islam* of government garrison.

This call for Jihad was reinforced by overwhelming political and military support from Southern Kordofan's Commissioner, Abdul Wahab Abdul Rahman. Under his leadership the following three decrees were issued, in 1991, in support of Jihad in the region for: (i) the formation of a higher committee for Jihad support in Kadugli Province, (ii) the establishment of an executive committee for Jihad support, and (iii) the formation of a Jihad committee for publicity and propaganda throughout the region (Fadl 2002: 41).

During the Jihad-driven military operations, the Commissioner of Southern Kordofan Province authorized the allocation of whatever booty was gained in any battle to the Mujahidin forces, in accordance with Islamic Shari'a (Muhammad al-Hadj 2006: 141). However, from the viewpoint of the majority of the Nuba, the war being waged was not a religious one. It was, rather, a war against their African identity and for possession of their ancestral land. For them, the declared Jihad was merely an act of politicizing religions along ethnic lines by the Arab-Islamic ruling elite in order to continue consolidating their economic, political, and socio-cultural domination over the Nuba (Kadouf 2001: 57–61, see also Kadouf 2002).

Support for the Jihad reached its peak at a conference of tribal leaders in al Obeid, where President Omer al-Bashir gave an address on the closing day. An eye witness, Khalid 'Abdul Karim al-Husseini,[7] then Head of Security in the Kordofan Governor's office, has testified that Omer al-Bashir was proclaimed the Imam of al Jihad. State governors and tribal leaders were in return named the Amir of al-Jihad in their respective spheres of influence and control. Also, they were promised arms for their Muslim fighters (African Rights 1995: 110–12).

A major success of the government in evoking the religious factor in this war was that it managed not only to gain substantial support from Arab and Muslim groups within Sudan and indeed beyond, but also to divide the Nuba along religious lines. Muhammad al-Haj (2006: 133–46) and Fadl (2002: 19) reported that some Nuba, particularly the native leaders, sided with the government as Mujahidin and PDF members against their own people who were in the SPLA. The involvement of some Islamic countries in support of the Jihad was evident in the Tullishi offensive, in which government forces were aided by Iranian military 'advisors'. It was the largest assault in the history of the civil war in the Nuba Mountains (African Rights 1995: 116; Ende 2001: 12; de Waal 2006: 6).

THE NUBA FACING GENOCIDE AND ETHNOCIDE

Several works including Africa Watch (1992); African Rights (1995); Mohamed Salih (1995, 1999); Fein (1997); Bradbury (1998) and de Waal (2006, 2007) agree that the government's isolation of the Nuba people in the mountains amounted to a 'genocide by attrition'. As one prominent scholar and human rights activist has said:

> Not only did the government aim to defeat the SPLA forces but it also intended a wholesale transformation of the Nuba society in such a way that its prior identity was destroyed. The campaign was genocidal in intent and at one point, appeared to be on the brink of success. (de Waal 2006: 1)

Severe hunger, diseases, collective displacement, forced relocation and mass fatality resulted. Due to the various military assaults in areas held by the government's forces as well as in those held by the SPLM/A, the Nuba were subjected to large-scale depopulation, displacement and forced relocation processes (Africa Watch 1991, 1992a, 1992b). At this desperate period, in early 1992, Muhammad al-Tayyib Fadl, the Commissioner of Kadugli, approached the SPLA commanders in the area to propose negotiations with the Nuba-led SPLA for a ceasefire agreement under the banner of *es-Salam min al-dakhil*, or 'peace from within' (Fadl 2002: 45–132; African Rights 1995: 128–32).

The negotiations collapsed (African Rights 1995: 129–30). As a result, the army and PDFs resumed large-scale military operations with major

---

[7] Khalid al-Husseini is a brother of 'Abdul Karim al Husseini, then Governor of Kordofan in 1992. He defected to Switzerland and applied for political asylum in October 1993 (Nuba Survival, November 2001: 1; African Rights 1995: 110). He was one of the first and rare authentic sources to give detailed information about the government's genocidal intent against the Nuba people when the Nuba Mountains were completely isolated from the outside world.

offensives opening up in November 1992. The consequences were dire, with (i) a series of systematic incidents of mass killing and massive destruction of the people's livelihoods, with many villages reduced to ashes; and (ii) a mass displacement with massive loss of human life. As people fled from the army and the PDFs, many died of hunger and/or thirst (Meyer 2005; Africa Rights 1995; Africa Watch 1991, 1992a, 1992b; Mohamed Salih 1995, 1999; Ende 2001).

By the middle of 1992, the two sides had fought each other to a standstill. On the SPLA side, the sheer scale of human suffering caused commanders and administrators to ask whether they should continue the war or whether it was better to negotiate for a ceasefire agreement in the Nuba Mountains. In the midst of these catastrophic military operations and the outcries of the suffering people, Commander Yusuf Kuwa initiated the formation of a civilian institution, an Advisory Council, in the Nuba SPLA-controlled areas. This significantly boosted popular support for continuing the armed struggle. On 30 September 1992, a five-day conference of the Advisory Council convened in Debi with one topic on the agenda: 'whether or not to continue the armed struggle'. After two days of orientation with speakers reviewing the situation, Commander Kuwa concluded that 'Up to today, 1 October 1992, I am responsible, I take responsibility for everything that has happened in the Nuba Mountains up to now. But, from today, I will not be responsible. If we are to continue the war, then, this must be our collective decision' (African Rights 1995: 131).

On the final day, the Advisory Council voted overwhelmingly to continue the armed struggle despite their total isolation from the outside world and the grave increase in the incidence of genocidal and ethnocidal atrocities in the government's military offensives. The event was described in dramatic terms by many writers, such as Meyer (2005) and de Waal (2006), as a rare situation in which a political leadership has to rely entirely on the wishes and support of its constituency for its own survival. As a civil administration parallel to the military administration in the region, the Advisory Council put 'the Nuba on a unique experiment in popular wartime democracy' (Meyer 2005: 91). This was unprecedented throughout the SPLM/A controlled areas.

In the words of de Waal (2006: 6), 'their resilience bought time: by slowing down the advance of the government troops, they ultimately defeated the genocide'. With this collective will to continue resistance, the Nuba found new reserves of determination and fought on in the following years with resourcefulness and self-belief, while the civil administration opened schools and clinics.

All this was accomplished with no budget and no external assistance. That is why, 'when international agencies began to operate in the Nuba Mountains in 1995, they were first impressed with the self-reliance and pride of the people' (de Waal 2006: 7, see also Meyer 2005). Another important achievement of this civil administration was that it established several secretariats specialized in the fields of health, education, agriculture and animal resources, among others. In close collaboration with some international agencies, the secretariats have played a vital role in delivering basic needs and services to the Nuba people, not only during the war period but also during the current transitional period where the government services in the former SPLM/A controlled areas are negligible.

At a later stage, Jan Pronk, the UN Special Envoy to the Sudan, summed up the suffering of the Nuba in the course of their armed struggle by saying, 'They were evicted from their land, forced to take sides, denied adequate services. They have shown resilience. It is them who have to make the real choice, because it is their life, their land, their destiny' (2007: 2). At a time of total isolation, with no news available from the Nuba Mountains, the Nuba diaspora exerted a tremendous effort to reveal to the international community the atrocities continuing to be perpetrated jointly by the army and security and PDF forces.

NUBA RESILIENCE AND THE ENDING OF GENOCIDES

The above discussion reveals that the Sudan Government succeeded in keeping secret its campaign of genocide in the Nuba Mountains for several years; external condemnation did not arise until 1995. The isolated areas were opened up to international scrutiny when the first plane carrying observers landed in secret in the SPLA-controlled part of the Nuba Mountains. Shortly after, journalists and human rights activists revealed the atrocities committed against the Nuba population during their period of complete isolation. Meyer (2005: 26) reported that:

> A few journalists, notably the British freelance writer Julie Flint and photographer David Stewart Smith braved war conditions in 1995 to document atrocities in the Nuba Mountains. Later that year, Flint made the first major documentary on the Nuba's plight, entitled 'Sudan's Secret War: the Nuba', and returned to the region regularly after that. That same year, the London-based African Rights also managed to do the first full-scale investigation for human rights abuses in the Nuba Mountains: *Facing Genocide: the Nuba of Sudan* which reported its findings, and was published in 1995.

In addition, there were reports from Justice Africa and the BBC, both of which played a significant role in unveiling the government's gross human rights abuses in the region. Subsequently, a number of international organizations became involved and that moved the Nuba cause steadily from the local to the global arena. The Nuba in diaspora played a key role in reinforcing international support to redress this human tragedy through a series of solidarity campaigns, in collaboration with international organizations and human rights activists. As a result, the aims of the atrocities of the secret war, to eradicate Nuba identity or even their very existence, were widely disseminated (Rahhal 2001a; 2001b; Meyer 2005; Komey 2008a, 2008b). Reports revealed that the Nuba resisted this programme of genocide while in complete isolation due to their fearless resistance, self-reliance and unprecedented resilience.

Describing the exceptional performance of the Nuba resistance, de

Waal (2006: 7) asserts that there was 'no humanitarian presence in the region at all. There was no news coverage, and in any case the people in the mountains had no batteries for their radios. The Nuba felt forgotten by everyone. With nothing but themselves to rely on, they found [the] necessary determination and reserves of energy.' Winter (2000: 60) referred to the Nuba experience of resistance, resilience, and self-reliance during the long period of isolation as something unique and unprecedented. He stated that:

> [in] today's pattern of conflict, in which communal and ethnic struggles predominate and civilians rather than opposition militaries are the primary target, much of what is seen in the Nuba Mountains is not unique. What is rare, however, is that such a war by a government against a civilian population is being waged so invisibly. The years-long isolation of the victims is unique in the case of the Nuba. As a result, the Nuba have been forced into a pattern of self-reliance that is also not common.

Through this persistent resistance, self-reliance, and resilience, the Nuba eventually overcame the genocide threat, although mass killing, burning of villages, rape, and displacement continued for some time. In 1997, reports continued to reveal gross human atrocities in the Nuba Mountains. In documenting the ongoing war of attrition directed at the civilian population by the government, an African Rights report (1997) insisted that the 'Nuba are still facing genocide. The threat of massacre has perhaps receded; the Nuba resistance has shown itself remarkably resistant and tough, fighting on with virtually no outside assistance against huge odds. But the future of the people of the Nuba Mountains still hangs in the balance.'

At this stage, the government realized that its genocidal campaign was not only extremely difficult to achieve but also too expensive. As an alternative to comprehensive ethnic cleansing, some Islamic extremists in government circles opted for a new strategy that would achieve the same result, albeit more slowly and messily. During this phase, the government shifted its focus from Jihad to al-Daw'a al-Shamila, i.e., the Comprehensive Call. This strategy was implemented through a combination of transformative programmes such as 'peace from within', 'peace villages', and a forced re-education of Nuba communal leaders among the returnees and in the displaced population still held in the government controlled areas (de Waal 2006: 8; Mohamed Salih: 1995: 75).

Several 'peace villages' were established in Southern Kordofan, six of them around Kadugli including Reikha village, a case in focus below. They were run by paramilitary leaders, security forces, and Islamic organizations such as al-Da'wa al-Islamiya (Islamic Call) Organization and al-Bir International. It is evident from my ethnographic research, discussed below, that, similarly to their counterparts in the SPLA-controlled areas, the Nuba returnees in the displaced camps or in the 'peace villages' demonstrated strong cultural resistance and resilience despite the comprehensive process of forced social transformation pursued by the government with the support of well-funded international Islamic organizations.

Peace villages and forced social transformation: the Reikha case

While the government concentrated its genocidal campaign in the SPLM/A-controlled areas through military offensives, ethnocide through forced social transformation among returnees and the displaced population was the main project in its controlled areas. To create a conducive environment, some Nuba villages were destroyed, people were driven from their lands and relocated in displaced-people camps or in peace villages. Educated Nuba and community leaders were intimidated, stripped of power, transferred outside the region, or systematically assassinated. These practices were widely documented by Africa Watch (1991, 1992a, b), Amnesty International (1993a, b), and African Rights (1995, 1997), while critically analyzed by Mohamed Salih (1995, 1999), Rahhal (2001a), Meyer (2005), and Suliman (1998, 1999, 2001, 2002).

The following results from my ethnographic study support those early analyses. They are based on participatory observations and unstructured yet guided interviews carried out during my fieldwork in the Reikha peace village in three stages over twelve weeks between May 2005 and January 2007.

REIKHA VILLAGE AND THE WAR IMPACT

Rolabe is the original name of Reikha, an Arabised version that appears on some colonial maps and official documents. Changing the names of physical and cultural landscapes from the indigenous language into Arabic has long been part of forced social transformation. Reikha, a homeland of Nuba Daqiq widely known as Massakin Qusar, is located in the northern part of Buram, the capital of the 'Buram Administrative Unit' (Map 6.1 in Chapter 6). Reikha was originally located in a narrow passage that separates the Todoro and Bolo hills in an area known locally as Ndillo. During the war in the late 1990s, the army forced the population to relocate to its present site on the plains at the foot of Todoro hill. Their new location was transformed by the government into a peace village, with a population of 22,000 people. In the process, all the Daqiq people in the nearby hilltops were forced down, settled and mixed with the Arabs and soldiers in the plains area of present Reikha. New leaders were appointed with a specific task to perform: the mobilization and recruitment of their peoples in the PDFs in order to fight the SPLM/A.

The forced relocation process was perceived by the Nuba Daqiq as part of the government's wider agenda of imposing certain socio-cultural and politico-ideological patterns on Nuba communities. This localized process is part of the government's wider Islamic-based ideological strategy forcefully to transform multi-ethnic, multi-religious, and multi-linguistic Sudan into a nation with one ideology, one language, and one religion.

At first glance, upon my arrival in Reikha in 2005, it was not difficult to observe that most of the local personnel who control the institutions of the market, army, and social services are either from the Nuba Daqiq who were in line with government ideology or they are mostly of Arab origin, mainly from Aulad Tayna of the Hawazma-Dilimiyya, in addition to a few non-Daqiq Nuba, Shawabna, and Fellata. My daily participatory observations revealed that, as a peace village, Reikha was more or less acting as a centre for Islamic and Arab cultural diffusions among the indigenous Nuba Daqiq community. Its marketplace and adjacent settlements were dominated by the army and the PDFs. The market was controlled by some local Arab and Muslim merchants. Both the merchants and the army personnel were not, respectively, mere economic agents and military professionals. Rather, both were effective agents of forced socio-cultural, religious, ideological and political transformations.

NUBA DAQIQ AND THEIR RESISTANCE TO THE FORCED TRANSFORMATION

As in many other Nuba communities, a sizable number of the Nuba Daqiq are neither Muslim nor Christian but followers of African beliefs and traditions. Despite this, the management of institutions governing their public affairs in Reikha was and still is controlled by Arab or Islamized Nuba Daqiq leaders. As early as the 1940s, while passing through Reikha, Rodger (1984: 43) reported that although 'the position of under-chief was often held by a Nuba, the chief was usually an Arab'. During the war and thereafter, my observation during the field work indicates that this situation was reinforced by a chain of authorities ranging from pro-government and Islamized leaders, the Arabs, to the military and security personnel.

To ensure its effective control over the local communities, the government usually appoints native administration leaders ideologically transformed in a way that allows them to adhere to, and to accelerate, the process of Islamization and Arabicization in the community. In this respect, Manger (2003a: 15) reported that during 'the period of the current government (National Salvation Government) many Nuba tribal Meks and Arab chiefs have been sacked and replaced by others who revealed a considerable Islamic commitment together with loyalty to the regime which is now the precondition for holding a tribal office among the Nuba and Arabs.'

In Reikha, the Daqiq's appointed native leaders are systematically Arabized and/or Islamized, economically empowered, and politically co-opted to the extent that they become an integral part of the government ideological machinery. The current Daqiq leadership is led by Amir Khamis Abu Kindi,[8] assisted by several 'Umdas including

[8] Khamis Abu Kindi was appointed by the government as leader of his people in the middle of the civil war, following the death of Mek Abu Kindi, his father. Several key informants in the area reported that his brother Kosti was prepared by his father to assume the Mekship. However, after the death of Mek Abu Kindi in the early 1990s, Khamis, who was then a prominent PDF member, was appointed by the government as Amir of all Massakin in 1994. His brother Kosti challenged his appointment and, thus, the legitimacy of his leadership. In the midst of this conflict, Kosti was assassinated reputedly by the government on the pretext that he was a fifth column supporting the SPLM/A. Since his death, many people in the area have allegedly held Amir Khamis responsible for the elimination of his brother Kosti.

Osman Tia al-Ma'mun[9] and al-Tum Harun Kuwa.[10] One of the main roles of these appointed tribal leaders during the war was to mobilize their tribes to fight against the SPLA under the PDFs, which were driven by Jihad ideology. For Khamis Abu Kindi to perform the new Islam-based mission of converting, recruiting, and leading the Mujahidin during the Jihad campaign, the position of the Mek, which his father Abu Kindi continued to hold, was replaced during the Ingaz regime by an Islamic title of 'Amir' as part of a wider process of an entire leadership transformation across the whole of Sudan.

Apart from their new task of mobilizing and recruiting their people into the PDFs, the Daqiq leaders in Reikha advance the Islamic way of life, suppressing any indigenous culture incompatible with Islamic teachings and faith. Two examples demonstrate the process. First, the raising of pigs was systematically discouraged and eventually eradicated in the area by Daqiq-imposed Muslim leaders, backed by a small but powerful Muslim and Arab community centred in Reikha. From an Islamic perspective, the keeping or eating pigs is synonymous with apostasy or the Christian religion. Before the war, in the Massakin area the house farm fields were regularly manured with cattle and pig manure and kept permanently under cultivation. Today, not a single pig can be found, not only in Reikha village but almost throughout the Massakin area.

Second, guided by Islamic teachings, the new leaders became an effective institution used by the government to destroy the Nuba Daqiq's authentic, indigenous cultural identity including a number of social and customary practices usually performed under the auspices of the kujur.[11] They are closely linked to the yearly cycle centred on the rainy season and associated farming activities. The festival of nagad (agricultural maturity) in October, the harvest festival in January, and the diboia[12] festival in May are some of the major socio-cultural events celebrated every year in the Daqiq hill communities. Each of these festivals is freighted with sets of rituals, customs and beliefs inherited from the ancestors (Corkill 1939; Nadel 1947; Rodger 1984).

For instance, the diboia festival, which I attended during my field work in May 2005, is strongly linked with specific sites, symbolic of an ancestral land. Like other such celebrations, it is more than just an event. It is a socio-cultural practice that regulates and reinforces necessary ties, bondage, and solidarity among the successive generations of each lineage and clan and,

[9] 'Usman Tia al-Ma'mun is the Imam of a mosque with its attached Islamic centre on the outskirts of al-Reikha.
[10] Al-Tum Haran Kuwa was an SPLM/A member. In 1993 he defected with a group of his people and joined the government. He was then integrated by the government as a PDF member in order to resist the SPLM/A in the area. Later, he was appointed as Deputy 'Umda of Reikha.
[11] Kujur is a term of the lingua franca of the semi-Arabicized but basically pagan areas in the Sudan for witch-doctors, rain-makers, mediators with occult powers, and magicians generally (Corkill 1939: 206).
[12] Diboia is a local name for antelope. The Diboia festival is held to supplicate rain for a good harvest; and it is important that the antelope is brought to the Kujur alive and sacrificed, not slaughtered; through a specific ritual led by the Kujur (Corkill 1939: 206–7).

thus, the whole tribe. It is performed as a communal event under the auspices of the Kujur with various rituals and roles performed by carefully selected actors who represent the various lineages of different Daqiq clans.

Sadly enough, while participation in the festival is a matter of joy and pride, it was evident that the Daqiq new leaders who were expected to lead the events were not only refraining from attending such communal festivals but were also discouraging the people from attending the festival on the grounds that it is irreconcilable with Islamic teachings and faith. However, the overwhelming participation of the Daqiq people in the diboia festival, despite repression, points to great resistance to relinquishing their authentic culture and identity which they continue to celebrate with pride and enthusiasm.

After the peace, the role of these Nuba leaders was, to a large degree, contained by a counter political move from the SPLM in the area. Most of them were either replaced by individuals who were pro-SPLM or continued in their leadership role but shifted their political and ideological loyalty to the SPLM. To the present day, the rest remain committed to the government, that is, the National Congress Party (NCP). They exercise less influence on their people because, after the peace, they confined their activities to the urban areas, particularly Kadugli, the capital of the Southern Kordofan State.

SOCIAL TRANSFORMATION THROUGH EDUCATION

As in other places in the Nuba Mountains, various social institutions in Reikha village, particularly the schools, were used to reinforce the process of Arabization and Islamization among the indigenous communities. In war-torn areas controlled by the government such as Reikha, some schools were run by Islamic institutions and/or army personnel, with a sharp focus on Arab-Islamic-based political and socio-cultural doctrine and blatant discrimination against indigenous culture, heritage, and languages. Setting up schools in the peace villages was intended in part to produce an educated Nuba cadre with an inferiority complex towards their own ethnic identity, history, and cultural values.

This is not a new educational policy. It has been energetically pursued throughout postcolonial Sudanese history. The late Yusuf Kuwa Mekki, a prominent Nuba political leader and SPLA Commander, described how the philosophy and the content of education in the Sudan contributed towards his becoming convinced of the need for change, a situation that led him to lead the Nuba to armed struggle:

> There was nothing in the history books about the Nuba that was good. [...] We did not read anything that makes us proud of being a Nuba. This is why you find a lot of us Nuba, especially the educated ones, hate themselves for being Nuba. As Muslims, they will hate their Nuba culture, and they would like to distance themselves from being Nuba [...]. They will change their names from Kuwa and Tiya into Arabic names. [...] Up to now this inferiority complex makes a lot of Nuba feel that they don't belong to the

Nuba ethnic group. They feel ashamed of what is called Nuba. The conclusion of course was that there is something wrong in Sudan that must be corrected. And this question of Sudan being an Arab country really is the wrong basis on which Sudanism is built. With this in mind, I started to think we have to do something. (Rahhal 2001a: 31)

Contrary to the intended objective of 'the Comprehensive Call', a survey of the salient features of socio-cultural practices among the Daqiq of Massakin demonstrates that they have not undergone serious and radical alteration or decline, despite their disadvantageous positions in every aspect of their affairs in public space. They adopted a sort of passive resistance by avoiding any government project, including the Islam- and the Arab-biased school system.

As a consequence, the Reikha School, which was established in 1954 as an agent of change, failed to produce its intended effect on Daqiq communities. Indeed, it is still failing to attract a sufficient number of pupils from nearby Daqiq hill communities. Given the nature, content, and objectives of the Sudanese educational curriculum, the Massakin people tend to equate education with Arabization, Islamization, alienation, and, eventually, loss of indigenous identity. Shaykh Abdul Nur Musa Mohammad, a Baqqara from Aulad Tayna and a prominent member of the Reikha school council, describes how difficult it is to get Daqiq children to attend the school:[13]

> Daqiq people have negative attitudes towards education provided by the school. They believe that schooling weakens the boys to the extent that they cannot perform their traditional role as strong wrestlers, fighters, and farmers. We usually exert tremendous effort to recruit Daqiq's children into the school. However, parents, especially mothers, will come and take their children away from the school, especially during the seasonal festivals and the related rituals to ensure their participation as part of their training for their designated traditional roles in the society.

As a consequence, the few educated Daqiq are not socially rewarded or esteemed. Instead, they are perceived by their own society as a source of Arab penetration into their indigenous socio-cultural system, and as such, they are not social assets but threats to the communal identity and survival. With this image in the Daqiqs' minds, schooling with its current contents has been persistently resisted in different ways. The case of the Nuba Daqiq of Reikha reveals that the Nuba identity in government-controlled areas during the civil war was basically subjected to a systematic process of social engineering and alienation partly implemented by their own disempowered, brainwashed and manipulated leaders.

Despite the brutality and intensity of the government's programme of social, ideological and political transformation among the Nuba in the peace villages like Reikha, some realities on the ground suggest that, similar to their counterparts in the areas controlled by the SPLM/A, some Nuba

---

[13] Author's interview with 'Abdal Nur Musa Muhammad, Reikha, 28 May 2005.

communities in the government-controlled areas have equally continued to show a magnificent degree of cultural resilience and resistance. This has happened despite the systematic government process of reproducing and manipulating the communal leadership at different levels of the communal social organizations as shown below.

MANIPULATING TRIBAL LEADERS
THROUGH ECONOMIC MEANS

To induce the new tribal leaders to perform their new role as set by the government, they are often empowered economically through different incentives, including subsidies for agricultural investments and opportunities to exploit the best farming lands at the expense of the traditional farmers and other public interests at large. This is manifested, for example, in the following case, found by the author, involving cooperation between the government (represented by the Kadugli Province authorities), al-Bir International Organization (one of the Islamic organizations working in the Nuba Mountains during the war), and some tribal leaders including Khamis Abu Kindi, the Amir of Daqiq.

The case is documented in the form of a memorandum[14] written by the Deputy Commissioner of Kadugli Province to the Attorney General of the Province. The former instructed the latter to prepare a tripartite contract between (i) the government, represented by the Province authority, (ii) al-Bir International Organization, and (iii) three tribal leaders who were labelled 'citizens' in the memo. The memo specified a project area of 1,000 feddans in the fertile land of Umm Shu'ran between Massakin Tuwal and Hamra.

The memo stipulated that the government and al-Bir International Organization were to provide tractors, all related agricultural goods and food supply for the labourers, while the three 'citizens', or more precisely community leaders, were to supervise the agricultural operations. They were also to mobilize an estimated forty armed men (PDFs) for the work, and to act as guards at the same time. The memo specified that the expected crop production was to be divided equally among the three stakeholders after deduction of the total cost involved. At a later stage, a letter with an official letterhead and the signature of the Deputy Commissioner of Kadugli Province[15] altered the sharing ratio; 25% of the net profit was to go to the three citizens, while the remaining net proceeds were to be divided equally between the other two stakeholders, i.e. the Province and the al Bir International Organization. Although the author failed to trace how the story ended, the case implies the following:

First, it clearly substantiates other reports' claims, such as that of *Nuba Survival* (November 2001: 1) that the government was using a carrot-and-

---

[14] Found by the author in Kadugli Province HQ, file No. 01/A/01: Agriculture, letter dated 9 July 2000.
[15] Kadugli Province HQ, file No. 01/A/01: Agriculture, letter dated 16 July 2000.

stick policy with local leaders, bribing them and giving them privileges for carrying out government policy in the region.

Second, the case of the al-Bir International Organization reinforces a finding arrived at by an earlier study that some Islamic organizations have been and still are being used as a vehicle for spreading political Islam at an accelerated rate, combining spiritual and material rewards among the disenfranchised poor communities, not only in the war-torn Nuba Mountains, but also in many African communities at large.[16]

Third, the project and the stakeholders involved are an exemplary case of bad governance and misuse of public property by an allied group of agencies, namely government officials (state), global Islamic agencies (the al-Bir International Organization), and some reproduced local leaders, in the promotion of interests other than those of the public.

Fourth, it reveals that instead of the new tribal leaders performing their traditional roles as custodians of the communal lands, they have become effective agents of mismanagement and exploitation of the communal land, a source of community livelihood. They are no longer a source of community welfare, but a driving force in bringing misery to their communities and alienation of their ancestral lands, as detailed below.

Land alienation and livelihood destruction during the war

During the war, the government of Sudan pursued a number of policies aimed at alienating Nuba land and destroying indigenous identity. Violent means were used: these include (i) military campaigns to effect the mass displacement of people, by destroying their villages, (ii) forced relocation and resettlement of the displaced far from their homelands, (iii) reallocation of land owned by custom in rural areas and (iv) land grabbing for rain-fed mechanizing schemes as well as for oil exploration.

MASS DISPLACEMENT AND FORCED RELOCATION

The destruction of the villages, as above, was supported by cutting off food supplies and creating the total isolation of SPLM/A-controlled areas bringing hunger and disease. People were forced to flee from the SPLA-controlled areas to the government-controlled areas.

Numerous studies (Africa Watch 1991, 1992a, 1992b; African Rights 1995; Mohamed Salih 1995, 1999) reported numerous cases of the success of this multiple strategy. To exemplify:

> In the central Nuba Mountains, the army destroyed dozens of villages in a campaign that began in November1990 and continues unchecked to the present day. Among the villages burned were: Demba, Koholyat, Miri

---

[16] For some detailed accounts, see, for example, Mohamed Salih (2002); de Waal (2000), Trimingham (1949/1983), and Warburg (1978).

Bara, Miri Gowa, Um Duja, Kufulu, al-Khawal, Loya, Kofa, Kanagha, Lima, and Abu Sunon. The residents of these villages were forced to flee to camps on the outskirts of Kadugli, including Tafri, Hajr el-Nar, Kulba and Murta. (Africa Watch 1992b)

The second phase of the land alienation process was a forced relocation in two sequential steps. First there is a relocation in transit camps within the Nuba Mountains mostly around the major towns of Kadugli, Dilling and Lagawa. These 'camps are run by the government in close coordination with Islamic aid agencies such as al-Da'wa al-Islamiya and Islamic Relief Agency' (Africa Watch 1992b: 4). The second involves the removal of the displaced Nuba from their homeland, the Nuba Mountains, altogether. This is perhaps the most dramatic human rights abuse perpetrated by the Sudan Government during the civil war; their homeland was the base of their economic livelihood and a symbol of their socio-cultural identity. It was a comprehensive plan of social engineering and political repression of the Nuba people on a scale never before seen in Sudan. In April 1991, the Peace and Resettlement Administration for Southern Kordofan was established under the leadership of 'Umar Suliman Adam who, after the peace agreement, became the Governor (Wali) of Southern Kordofan State (2006–2007).

In February 1992, twenty-two peace villages had been prepared for 70,000 thousand forced returnees from SPLM/A-controlled areas. An estimated 20–30,000 Nuba were deported from their homeland to semi-desert areas in North Kordofan. Others were forced to work in the mechanized schemes in lands that belonged to them before they were handed over illegally to wealthy Jillaba, among others. By the end of 1992, a total of over 40,000 people had been relocated in Northern Kordofan in Khor Taggat in el-Obeid, Umm Ruwaba, Sodiri, Bara en-Nuhud (Africa Watch 1992b: 50). 'These and other inhumane practices committed by the Sudan Government,' argues Mohamed Salih (1995: 76), 'amount to an act of genocide.'

STATE INTERVENTION
IN COMMUNAL LAND REDISTRIBUTION

Following this policy of mass displacement and relocation of the Nuba, the government initiated a plan for land redistribution in the region. Small Farmers' Collective Schemes were introduced as part of a wider agricultural investment plan in the 1990s. In theory, the initiative was meant to transform the customarily owned communal lands into individual registered rights. Towards that end, a process of surveying, allocation, and registration based on modern state land laws was pursued in the government-controlled areas. The state authorities publicized that priority would be given to members of households constituting a community, i.e. a tribe, clan, or lineage, in their specific claimed territories. The plan envisaged that each neighboured cluster of 20–40 village-based households would to be treated as a 'collective farming unit' (Imam and Egemi 2004).

The Nuba were suspicious and unenthusiastic about the initiative for three main reasons: first, their traumatic experience of systematic state practices of land grabbing. Second, they feared abuse of state power by some bureaucrats in allocating some of their communal lands to new-comers: wealthy people, and government officials with no local connections. Further, the plan would have the effect of giving some of their claimed communal land to others, including the Baqqara, who had had the upper hand in all public space in the region throughout the war period in government-controlled areas. Third, the Nuba leaders were convinced that the timing of the initiative was inappropriate since most of the Nuba, at that time, had been forcefully displaced from their homelands while others had come in and occupied their lands. They preferred to delay any issue related to land until the internally displaced Nuba returned to their respective homelands when peace was finally brokered.

Soon after the implementation of the initiative, all the above-mentioned concerns and suspicions proved to be correct. In an interview with Muhammad Ibrahim al-Digayl,[17] he confirmed the resistance of some Nuba leaders to a plan that summarily handed over some of their customary owned land to people they do not recognize as having rights of ownership. For example, the 'Umda of Keiga Tummero, al-Yias Ibrahim Koko, opposed the government initiative on the grounds that the Keiga Tummero community does not recognize land ownership rights claimed by other non-Keiga groups in the area though it recognizes their secondary rights of access to use the land and peaceful cohabitation (also, see Komey 2008a, 2008b, 2009a). He went on to state that:[18]

> I initially opposed the proposed small farmers' collective scheme which intended to include the communal land of the Keiga Tummero community. It was another way of the state policy of land grabbing. As a result of my opposing position, some government officials started to by-pass me intentionally while incorporating some of my disloyal Shaykhs in the process of land surveying, plot allocation, and distribution.

Some Baqqara expressed similar opposition as they felt that the government was and is undermining their traditional communal land rights while trying to regulate the land on a private basis. My key informant, al-Bushra Somi Tawir of Dar Jami', complained bitterly about the government's practice of grabbing land from local communities:

> The government involved us, the local leaders, in the initial process of 'the village-based livelihood farming project' in the 1990s. But at the stage of plot distribution, we and our people were excluded except some of those politically linked to the government. They are the ones who got schemes in the name of Dar Jami'. As a result, most of the local

---

[17] He is a Survey Technician in the Land Use and Water Department, Ministry of Agriculture, Kadugli, Southern Kordofan State. He was in charge of surveying the small farmers' collective schemes in 1994: interviewed by author in Kadugli, 21 and 22 February 2007.
[18] Author's interview with al-Yias Ibrahim Koko, 'Umda of Keiga Tummero, Keiga Tummero, 14 February 2007.

communities, both Nuba of Keiga and Arabs of Dar Jami' who customarily own the surveyed lands, were excluded or, at best, given a small portion out of their vast and fertile land.[19]

In spite of opposition from the majority of local communities, the government persisted with the survey and allocation of the Small Farmers' Collective Schemes. Within Keiga communal land, sixty-five schemes were accomplished on a total area of about 50–60,000 feddans,[20] collectively known as al-Zalataya schemes. The average size of each household's scheme varies from 500 to1000 feddans. My field-centred data regarding the pattern of distribution reveals that the majority (about 70%) were allocated mostly to the local Baqqara of Dar Jami' (39.6%), the Baqqara of Aulad Nuba (6.8%), the Fellata of al-Bardab (22.7%), and the Fellata Takarir (2.3%). The Nuba Keiga of Tummero and Luban, who claim communal ownership of the distributed land, got 20.4% of the total 44 schemes.

Some of my key informants[21] confirmed a total of 65 schemes in the area described. This implies that apart from the above 44 schemes, there were another 21 that the author could not trace. However, one of my informants indicated that some of the schemes were allocated to wealthy people outside the area. It suggests that some wealthy outsiders were able to pay the required fees and subsequently completed the registration process.[22]

The whole exercise resulted in major problems between the state and local communities as well as between the local Arabs and the Nuba. In view of this field-centred analysis, two key points deserve attention: first, the contradictions between the communal customary rights and practices of the two traditional communities (sedentary Nuba and nomadic Baqqara), and the application of modern state laws with no recognition of customary land rights are palpable. Second, the state's legality is highly contested by the local community on the basis of their customary legitimacy. This is their inevitable and justified response to the state policy of land grabbing that persistently undermines communal customary rights and legitimacy, with no consideration of all the interests and priorities connected with their members' livelihoods (Komey 2009b, 2010a, 2010b).

SCORCHED EARTH POLICY FOR OIL INVESTMENT

Apart from their land grabbing policy for mechanized farming detailed in Chapters 1 and 2, the government have also pursued a systematic, violent, scorched earth policy in the Nuba Mountains since the early 1990s in the processes of oil exploration and exploitation. This is widely recognised (Africa Watch 1992a, 1992b; Suliman 1998, 2001; Mohamed and Fisher

---

[19] Author's interview with al-Bushra Somi Tawir, al-Kweik, 13 February 2007.
[20] One feddan equals 1.038 acres or 4200 square meters.
[21] (i) Muhammad Ibrahim al-Digayl, Kadugli, 21 February 2007; (ii) Nazir al-Bushra Somi Tawir, al-Kweik, 13 February 2007; and (iii) Nazir 'Usman Bilal, Kadugli, 22 February 2007.
[22] Author's interview with Muhammad Ibrahim al-Digayl, Kadugli, 21 February 2007. In the same interview, my informant revealed that one wealthy Takarir man came from the Gulf States and paid all fees required for the registration of their allocated 4000 feddans on behalf of the Takarir community.

2002; International Crisis Group 2002; Rone 2003; Johnson 2006; de Waal 2007; Pantuliano 2007; Patey 2007).

The practice of enforced depopulation of local communities in the oil fields and along the pipeline line started with the direct involvement of international companies: Chevron, (before its withdrawal in 1992), China National Petroleum Company (CNPC); Petronas of Malaysia; and Talisman and Sudapet Limited—a Sudanese national oil company collectively known as the Greater Nile Petroleum Operating Corporation (GNPOC). In 2002, a Canadian human rights group concluded that, in order to execute offensive attacks on villages in the rebel-controlled areas, the government forces used both the company's airstrips and roads to move heavy military armaments. In 2002, the UN's special rapporteur on the Sudan reported that oil has seriously exacerbated the conflict while causing the overall deterioration in human rights and continuing widespread displacement of local communities. Their 'ancestral land has instead become a theater of war, fueled with inputs from oil interests from Canada, China, Malaysia, and other European Countries' (Rone 2003: 506).

Further, Johnson (2006: 163) described how oil turned into a curse rather a blessing for the local communities in the Nuba Mountains and southern Sudan:

> Oil exploitation has been made possible by clearing the oilfields of their civilian population through the activities of the Sudanese armed forces and the Baqqara militias from Southern Kordofan, and then securing the areas through alliance with the Nuer break-away factions of the SPLA [...] Once installed, the Sudanese military has used the oil company roads and airfields to attack civilian settlements within a widening security radius.

Moreover, Suliman (2001), Rone (2003), and Patey (2007) revealed that the abuse most connected to oil development in Sudan since the early 1980s has been forcible displacement—by military means—of tens or possibly hundreds of thousands of local communities in order to obtain land for international oil companies. One direct recent result has been a series of violent reactions or alternatively legal responses from local communities against the government and the oil companies.

The response of local communities is manifested in a number of court cases filed against the Sudan Government and that currently involve oil companies. One case still in process has been filed by two elite groups from the area, in Dilling Court, on behalf of 98 local farmer households, against the Consortium (composed of oil companies). The plaintiffs are demanding fair compensation for the losses they have incurred since 1995 as a result of an oil pipeline that destroyed their livelihoods including farming and grazing lands, and settlements. It is likely that the local communities will not win their case, given the present land laws that do not recognize customary land rights. Despite this, the case demonstrates beyond doubt that oil investment in the region is one of the key driving forces behind the government's policy of land alienation, forced displacement and relocation of rural communities in the region.

Conclusion

The transformation of the Nuba's peaceful political movement into an armed struggle with actual engagement in war, coupled with militarization of the Baqqara Murahaliin, has marked a turning point in both regional and national politics. At the national level, it has signified a shift in the conflict from a regional to a large-scale national civil war with significant repercussions on the entire Sudanese political landscape. At the regional level, the dynamics of the war have had far-reaching and multifaceted implications for state-society relations as well as on inter-ethnic relations along Nuba-Baqqara divides.

As the war intensified, the previously shared Nuba Mountains territory was progressively divided along ethno-political lines into two heavily militarized administrative zones: (i) areas controlled and administered by the Nuba-led SLPM/A with the Baqqara nomads having no access to their traditional seasonal grazing lands and water and (ii) areas controlled and administered by the Islamic-based Government of the Sudan with the Baqqara having the upper hand in public affairs.

This analysis has revealed that the central government utilized ethnic and religious factors to gain Baqqara support in fighting against the Nuba, even though the Baqqara share with the Nuba the same grievances resulting from collective socio-economic underdevelopment and marginalization, and political misrepresentation from the centre. In pursuing its objectives, the government deployed a series of brutal strategies against the Nuba including, among others: military offensives, the denial of food and other basic needs, a politically driven Jihad, mass displacement through the destruction of villages and forced relocation coupled with land alienation and a radical socio-cultural transformation. The whole exercise, genocidal and ethnocidal in intent, was finally overcome through the Nuba's unprecedented heroic resistance, self-reliance, and resilience.

These spatial and social patterns imposed by war along Nuba-Baqqara ethnic divides were coupled with an almost total collapse of their normal relations and co-existence. Despite this, sufficient ethnographic material demonstrates the continuing existence of some sort of economic-driven cooperation between the Nuba communities in the SPLA-controlled areas, and some Baqqara groups in the government-controlled areas. This is the subject of the following chapter.

4

Baqqara–Nuba Relations
in a War Situation

Introduction

As revealed in the previous chapter, the severe fighting between the Government of Sudan and the Nuba-led SPLM/A dictated its own logic and dynamics in the region. Shortly after its extension from the Southern Sudan into the Nuba Mountains region in 1985, the war took on an ethnic dimension. The majority of the Nuba sided with and therefore were supported by the Sudan Peoples' Liberation Movement/Army (SPLM/A) against the central government. Simultaneously, the Baqqara supported and were reciprocally supported by the government forces. As a result, the two previously co-existing groups were gradually divided into two heavily militarized political-administrative zones along ethno-political lines (see Manger 2003b, 2007; Komey 2008a, 2008b, 2009a, 2009b, 2010a).

Despite the antagonism that war brought between the Nuba and Baqqara a new and sporadic form of cooperation emerged (Suliman 1999). Some key actors from both sides were able to 'strategically essentialize' themselves and to develop a new pattern of shifting market places across the war frontiers: indeed, 'trade has not been dormant throughout the years of wars in Sudan. Trade has bridged the political barriers, infiltrated garrisons and rural areas, crossed both national and international borders, as well as ethnic and religious divides' (Fraser et al. 2004: xi).

The key questions are, therefore, how and why the two groups who were forced to fight each other were simultaneously able to collaborate in economically-driven activities, centred on new forms of market places, spaces, and exchanges in a situation of high insecurity and mounting risk? This chapter gives an analysis of the initiating driving forces, the function, and the spatial pattern of the war-born markets in the context of pastoral–sedentary relations during the war in the region. It describes some of the survival strategies deployed by the parties involved while interacting in a situation fraught with insecurity and risk.

The second part of the chapter focuses on the local market institution as place, space, and exchange in the context of relations between the pastoral Baqqara and the sedentary Nuba in normal situations. It concludes with some notes on pastoral production and its local-national-global link. Part three focuses on the emergence of new forms of local markets as a part of the limited survival strategies in response to the war situation. The Baqqara–Nuba market-centred and locally brokered series of peace agreements is discussed in part four. In conclusion, some key findings are provided in the light of the overall analysis.

The pre-war symbiotic socio-economic relations

The preceding chapter showed that the armed conflict between the Nuba-led SPLM/A and government forces supported by the Baqqara militias and the PDFs brought great suffering to the Nuba and Baqqara alike. Moreover, it impacted severely on the symbiotic relations between the sedentary Nuba and the nomadic Baqqara, who have continued to share the region, albeit with constant competition, for about 200 years. Despite the Baqqara's history of involvement in slave raiding against the Nuba and, subsequently, their forced deterritorialization, the two groups have intermingled, amalgamated, traded with, and enriched each other (Ibrahim 1988, 1998; Komey 2008a).

The two groups continue to engage in a complex process of economic cooperation, through the complementarities and social ties associated with low-scale and self-managed conflicts. Since colonial rule, land and water disputes were resolved at the annual conferences of the Nuba Meks and the Arab 'Umdas and Shaykhs. The cumulative result was that their cultures and modes of life permeated each other, with sizable members of each group embodying dynamic cultural elements of the other. Ibrahim (1988, 1998) demonstrated that their relations were in constant flux with the notions of 'Nubaness' and 'Baqqaraness' being fluid identities, to the extent that the author claims a 'Baqqara-ization' of the Nuba and a 'Nuba-ization' of the Baqqara. However, as shown in Chapter 1, the contemporary Baqqara–Nuba symbiotic relationship has been shaped and reshaped by cumulative and interwoven ecological, socio-economic, and political dynamics. These had been traced throughout the precolonial, colonial, and postcolonial stages of Sudanese state formation. The substantial and various historical and contemporary dynamics that continue to shape the nomadic-sedentary symbiotic relationship have been covered in a burgeoning literature referenced in this work, including Lloyd (1908), MacMichael (1912/67, 1922/67), Henderson (1939), Trimingham (1949) Ahmed (1976), Håland (1980), Abdalla (1981), Battahani (1980, 1986, 1998), Adams (1982), Ibrahim (1988), among others.

What is new, however, is the far-reaching impact of the Sudan's recent civil war (1985–2005) on the symbiotic relationship between the nomadic Baqqara and the sedentary Nuba. A literature survey reveals that little attention has been paid to the impact of war, i.e., forced transformation, on the relationship and the survival strategies of the pastoralist and sedentary communities in the region. Nevertheless, some clues are observable in a few works that appeared during and after the civil war (see Africa Watch 1991, 1992a, b; African Rights 1992; Mohamed Salih 1995, 1999; Babiker 1998; Ibrahim 1998; Suliman 1999; Vang and Granville 2003; Manger 2004, 2007, 2008a, b; Elsayed 2005; Johnson 2006; Pantuliano et al., 2007; Komey 2008a, 2008b).

It is worth revisiting the transformation of nomadic-sedentary relations imposed by war, with a focus on the people's constant striving for their very survival and ways of life. The institution of the local market is revealed as a multifaceted intermediary space where the socio-economic symbiosis that exists between the sedentary Nuba and the pastoral Baqqara persisted throughout the conflict.

Vang and Granville (2003: 6) reported that, before the civil war, there were three types of markets in the region: permanent small shops owned by the local Nuba and Baqqara alike, permanent but usually larger shops owned by the Jillaba traders from northern Sudan, and weekly markets usually located in certain villages as a focus for a wide area. Unlike the two types of permanent shops, the weekly markets, connecting sedentary and nomadic groups, tend to flourish only during the dry season. Thus, the existence of the weekly local markets is an inevitable response to sedentary–nomadic complementarities and symbiotic relationships. In terms of timing and routes, the Baqqara's spatial mobility patterns are compatible with the times and the relative locations of weekly markets.

Accordingly, the seasonal migratory routes of the Baqqara's livestock tend to follow three separate but closely interlinked landscape features: (i) man-made or natural water sources, (ii) sedentary Nuba settlements, and (iii) major weekly local market places along some Nuba settlement points. In addition, the trade routes of the Jillaba merchants between the urban centres in central parts of the Sudan follow similar spatial pattern (see Map 4.1).

Thus, the water sources and the weekly local market places are usually found within the vicinity of sedentary Nuba settlements. Acting as intermediary spaces, these weekly markets bring together farmers with agricultural produce, pastoralists with animal resources and related products, and Jillaba traders supplying goods from the major towns of the northern and central parts of the Sudan.

LOCAL MARKET INSTITUTION AS PLACE, SPACE, AND EXCHANGE

For quite a long time, scholars such as Bohannan and Dalton (1965), Dupire (1965), Synamski et al. (1975) have described nomadic pastoralist, subsistence cultivation, and periodic market systems in Africa as on a

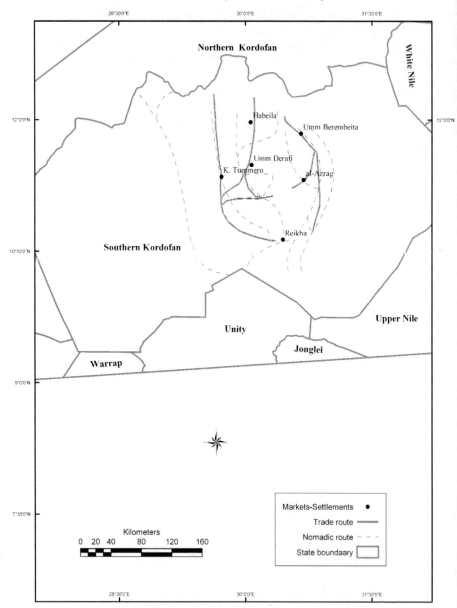

Map 4.1 Intrinsic relationship between settlements, nomadic mobility
and trade routes
Source: Field work 2006–8

mobile–sedentary continuum based on changes in mobility. A recent report on rural market systems in Southern Kordofan showed that:

> Market outlets for different products are built around cluster[s] of small, village-level markets. Each cluster has a central market in which all villages participate. These centres attract traders from other markets in the locality, as well as others from within and outside the State. Village markets gain importance as centres or primary markets. Itinerant, village-level markets (umdawawar) serve as collection points and constitute the building blocks of an overall market structure. Markets usually consist of two distinct levels forming the market chain: a) Primary markets at village level; b) Secondary or intermediate markets (big towns and cities). (Abukasawi 2009: 20)

My observations from visiting a number of local markets in selected field sites reveal that they are not merely places for commodities exchange (also see Komey 2008a: 116–18). Rather, they are multifaceted intermediary spaces, full of interwoven social fields with significant implications for the involved actors.

The weekly market-place of the Keiga Tummero village, about 42kms north of Kadugli, is a good example. It acts as a set of socio-cultural, political, and economic fields in the course of sedentary–nomadic people's interactions. On Fridays, the periodic market brings together different societal actors with their respective functions and interests. The various forms of transactions and interactions observed on that market day demonstrate that the Keiga Tummero local market functions as:

(i) a centre for economic and commercial transactions and exchange among the local communities involved with their different ethnic, political, and economic affiliations. The economic complementarities between pastoral and sedentary products, on the one hand, and the Jillaba merchants' dominant role, on the other, is evident during market transactions: economic interests tend to supersede all other political or ethnic-based divides.

(ii) a meeting point for networking and information exchange between different actors. For example, information related to lost animals is usually found at the market where nomads from different fariq (livestock camps) meet not only for doing their deals but also to exchange information about the possible schedule of their migratory movements, potential grazing zones, available water sources, and other issues of common interest.

(iii) a forum for political campaigning by different political interests. For government and non-governmental institutions, the market-place is still the most effective institution in a rural setting for disseminating information. Most importantly, it also provides an informal and less costly space for state institutional functions, such as immunization, agricultural extension, veterinary services, and tax estimates and/or collection, to mention a few.

(iv) a meeting point for negotiation, mediation, reconciliation, and conflict settlement, including the payment of fines incurred as a result of court verdicts or gentlemen's agreements. Most conflicts are mediated by the elders or native leaders in these spaces because everybody is either voluntarily present or can easily be found. Likewise, as the weekly market brings together people from different ethnic groups it can frequently be the place that triggers collective or individual conflicts and a subsequent tendency to retaliate.

(v) an appropriate medium for developing social ties and acculturation among different socio-economic and ethnic actors. The selection of Friday as market day in Keiga Tummero has a religious dimension, for example. Its main mosque, located at the centre of the market, represents one of the distinctive cultural features of the physical landscape. All Muslims from different ethnic backgrounds come together to perform Friday communal prayers in that mosque. Furthermore, some friendships and personal relationships between people of different affiliations are stimulated and strengthened through market interactions. This can be observed, for instance, in a gathering around a woman who serves tea to customers from different ethnic backgrounds. By its very nature, the market imposes certain conditions of physical proximity to the extent that some warring parties may find themselves forced to engage with each other peacefully, simply because a third party has brought them face to face without prior arrangement.

Apparently; the flow of the Baqqara from their nearby fariq and their effective participation in the market exchanges is a decisive factor in the functioning or non-functioning of the weekly markets established in the Nuba settlement points. Indeed, the weekly markets in the Nuba Mountains that flourish during the dry season are usually characterized by the presence of numerous pastoral Baqqara. As the rainy season approaches, the Baqqara start their rhythmic movement northwards, while the Nuba engage in cultivation. The once-flourishing markets gradually shrink to complete but temporary disappearance, until the Baqqara return.

LOCAL MARKET INSTITUTION AND ITS NATIONAL AND GLOBAL LINKS

While the local market places act as an intermediary space in which pastoral Baqqara and sedentary Nuba interact, Jillaba traders act as the controlling agents of market exchanges. Studies, for example, Manger (1984, 1988), Mohamed Salih (1984), Battahani (1986), and Ibrahim (1998), among others, have documented the Jillaba's long history of exercising effective control over most of the commodities traded at different levels of the market chain. In so doing, the Jillaba traders have been able to supply expensive urban manufactured goods to the local people while siphoning off cheap local agricultural products and animal resources.

In this way, the local market operates as a starting point in a wider set of trade chains that systematically tie in local economies to national and global markets. The multifaceted transactions at the markets, across different social fields, are not merely local dynamics. In most cases, they are instead local manifestations of national and globalization processes, with all their social, political, and economic dimensions (see Manger 1984, 1988, 2001, 2008a, 2008b; Battahani 1986; Johnson 2006, Abukasawi 2009).

Taking pastoral production as an example, it is not difficult to trace its local–national–global link. Local markets are collecting points for pastoral production from different households which is then transported to national and/or global markets. Two examples, one of a local, traditionally processed white cheese, primarily for national consumption and second, the export livestock trade, demonstrate the complexities of the local market institution. During the dry season, some of the pastoral households, as economic units, make a deal with merchants' agents to locate their livestock fariq near a local market, a rural centre, or along a main road leading to a larger town. The households produce a range of dairy products in high demand among urban consumers, including al-Jinba al-Bayda, i.e., the white cheese. During my fieldwork in Keiga Tummero village, I came across numerous clusters of such cottage industries located nearby. They are not separate, but integral parts of pastoral Baqqara households, as economic units. As described in the preceding discussion, the Keiga Tummero settlement is also a local market place.

The processing of cheese is, therefore, a joint venture between the pastoral households who provide fresh milk as the main raw material and some merchants' agents who provide the other ingredients for production, particularly salt, packing materials, and transport. The merchants involved, residing in some major towns, either show up on a regular basis or send their own vehicles to collect and transport the accumulated cheese production to urban markets. Thus, the small, localized economic units of pastoral households are integrated into wider national market and labour systems, coupled with some form of 'sedentarized' pattern (see Michael 1987, 1991, 1997, 1998). Such patterns of survival economies were reinforced during the war period in response to the risks that restricted the mobility of the village producers.

Livestock trade transactions also start at the local market level, then are incorporated in the national and global dimensions of pastoral production and marketing. Indeed, a close monitoring of the chain of livestock transactions shows that pastoral households, as economic units, are not only linked to national economic and market systems, but also to global market and labour systems at large (see Michael 1987, 1991).

During the weekly local markets, local agents, representing some powerful merchants residing in the main cities, are most conspicuous. Their role is to buy most of the livestock brought to the weekly local markets across the region. Then, at some stage, city merchants arrive to take charge of the livestock acquired by their agents to transport or herd them to the capital, Khartoum. This provides fresh meat for national as well as global consumption mostly via exports to the oil-rich Gulf States.

However, the real beneficiaries of these local–national–global market transactions are the Jillaba merchants who live in the main urban centres of the northern and central parts of the Sudan. As a result, the local producers receive only petty returns. What has been depicted in pastoral production and its national-global link is, to a great degree, applicable to the agricultural products of traditional farming households as economic units.

The cumulative result of these local–national–global market links has been the systematic and multiple exploitation and, therefore, marginalization of local pastoral and peasantry communities. This market-linked economic marginalization, among other factors, has also contributed to the political grievances of local communities, particularly the sedentary Nuba: their engagement in violent conflict in Sudan's civil war was partly due to it. Economic marginalization has been widely reflected in the literature including African Rights (1995), Mohamed Salih (1995, 1999), Battahani (1998), Suliman (1999) Kadouf (2001), Rahhal (2001a), Komey (2005a, 2005b), Johnson (2006), and Manger (2006, 2007, 2008a, 2008b).

The war and new forms of local markets and exchanges

In the previous chapter, we saw that the Nuba were forced to resort to an armed struggle when they joined the Sudan Peoples Liberation Movement/Army (SPLM/A) in 1985, during the course of the Second Civil War in the Sudan (1983–2005). No doubt, the impact of war on the entire region as social world was and still is enormous.

WAR IMPACT ON SOCIO-ECONOMIC SYMBIOSES

The conflict has had significant repercussions on the historical political, economic, and territorial relations between state and local community, and between the various ethnic groups, particularly the Nuba and the Baqqara. As noted in Chapter 3 the previously shared territory of the Nuba Mountains was progressively divided up into two heavily militarized political-administrative zones along ethnic lines: (i) areas controlled and administered by the government, with the Baqqara maintaining the upper hand in the political sphere and in public affairs, and (ii) areas held and administered by the Nuba-led SPLM/A, where Baqqara nomads had no access to their traditional seasonal grazing lands. Manger (2006: 2) wrote:

> During the war years, large tracts of the region, particularly at the foot of hills or in-between mountain ranges became off-limits to pastoralists who feared the SPLA. Pastoralists became less present and the interaction between the Nuba and the Baqqara ceased. Traditional migration and transhumance routes were disturbed. Reciprocal agreements, both those rooted in tradition and those that were court-brokered, that had governed the passage of herds over agricultural land, fell into disuse. In other areas, forcefully displaced Nuba no longer interacted with nomads.

Consequently, the previous co-existence of, and cooperation between, the sedentary Nuba and the nomadic Baqqara in the region ceased to exist. Shortly, there was a complete breakdown of the symbiotic relationships, including their normal and regular interactions at the market places (see Ibrahim 1998, 1998; Manger 2006, 2008a; Komey 2008a, 2008b).

Moreover, with the increasing intensity of the war, and the cut-off of trade routes between the region and the north, the Jillaba traders of northern Sudan who had dominated the trade and market exchanges in the Nuba Mountains discontinued their business, (see African Rights 1995; Suliman 1999, 2002; Vang and Granville 2003; Manger 2006, 2008a). Eventually, the Nuba in the areas under the control of the SPLM/A were completely cut off from supplies of all basic urban commodities and services that used to flow from the major towns in the northern and central parts of the Sudan. As reported by Africa Watch (1992a, 1992b), African Rights (1995), Rahhal (2001a), and Manger (2001, 2003b) the Nuba faced extraordinary hardship and suffering apart from the direct impact of the fighting.

Simultaneously, the Baqqara faced a similar but comparatively milder hardship when their livestock was squeezed into limited, poor grazing zones due to insecurity in the south. Moving along the war frontiers was dangerous, with repeated incidents of livestock looting, resulting in an enormous loss of animal wealth for the Baqqara. Most importantly, their own supply of basic subsistence materials, particularly grains, which used to flow from the nearby Nuba hill communities, was also cut off.

In short, both communities were subjected to a set of externally induced, powerful, and unfavourable forces brought about by the dynamics of war. Hence, their livelihoods and modes of life were not only radically transformed, but their very survival was also endangered. It is within this context that new and sporadic forms of economically driven transactions emerged. They were part of the coping mechanisms and survival strategies pursued by the two groups during the war situation.

These emerging, vital working relations manifested themselves territorially in sporadic market exchange places, known as Aswaq es-Salam ([sg.]: Suq es-Salam), or peace markets. Later, they were modified and came to be known as Aswaq Sumbuk ([sg.]: Suq Sumbuk) or smuggling markets. At the same time, these market-centred transactions were reinforced by a series of locally brokered peace deals between some Baqqara and Nuba groups in their respective localities. This new type of 'strategic', 'essential', and 'situational' cooperation emerged as an alternative to the normal pre-war symbiotic relations in order to counteract the severity of the formal war between the SPLM/A and the government forces.

The emergence of these two market places as new forms of transactions and exchanges indicates the necessity and inevitability of Nuba–Baqqara interdependence, for economic survival. With the intensification of the war, the Baqqara needed grain from their traditional suppliers, the Nuba, and the Nuba, in the SPLM/A-controlled areas needed essential urban goods and services, particularly salt, soap, clothes, shoes, medicine, and agricultural tools from the Baqqara.

The conditions of the Nuba in the SPLM/A-controlled areas deteriorated further due to two main adverse political circumstances that reinforced each other: (i) total isolation from the outside world through central government policy (ii) the cessation of the flow of military supplies to the Nuba SPLA fighters from the main SPLM/A in the South caused by the forces of Riek Machar who defected in 1991. Obviously, the Nuba in the SPLM/A-controlled areas were not only in critical need of basic subsistence supplies, but were also in desperate need of an alternative way to get ammunition supplies in order to continue their heroic resistance against the government forces.[1]

ASWAQ ES-SALAM (PEACE MARKETS)

In a taped interview with my key informant, Simon Kalo, in Kadugli, on 9 January, 2007, he confirmed how the markets played a vital role in sustaining the Nuba in the SPLM/A-held areas. Kalo was the second SPLA Commander in the Buram area in the Nuba Mountains during the early 1990s. He was in charge of looking for an alternative form of market exchanges with some pastoral Baqqara in government-controlled areas at the time the government had effectively sealed off the Nuba Mountains region.

By October 1991, the government had applied a ring of security check points along the frontiers, prohibiting any flow of people or goods from and to SPLM/A-controlled areas. By 1992, the SPLM/A-controlled areas in the Nuba Mountains were in complete isolation. The government not only sealed off the region, but also prevented the extension of the UN-led Operations Lifeline Sudan (OLS) to the region, although the OLS was covering all the rest of war-torn Southern Sudan. At the same time, there was enormous suffering in the rest of the Nuba communities, whose survival was endangered in the absence of basic needs. Their military capabilities were so weakened that they were unable to prevent the central government's systematic campaign of genocide and ethnocide (see Africa Watch 1991, 1992a; African Rights 1995; Meyer 2005; Johnson 2006; de Waal 2006).

Aswaq es-Salam (peace markets) emerged in the rural centre of Buram, an area under SPLM/A control in the early 1990s. However, they did not last long: as they were soon discovered and were targeted by the government army. My informant, Simon Kalo, detailed the initiation, operation, and demise of the Buram peace market and the consequent emergence of the Suq Sumbuk.

The practice of peace markets originated in the northern part of Bahr al-Ghazal in southern Sudan, between the pastoral Baqqara of Messiriyya and the SPLM/A forces. Ibrahim (1998: 47, footnote 25) reports that:

> In 1993, the Messiriyya Arab groups … and the Ngok Dinka of Abyei area [...] sat together and through the revitalization of their historic tribal alliances and arrangements came to a peaceful co-existence pact [...] the

[1] For some detailed studies and reports on the conditions of the Nuba in the SPLM/A-controlled areas during the war, see, for example, Africa Watch (1991, 1992a, 1992b), African Rights (1995), and Meyer (2005).

pact has granted the trading rights of all parties through what are called peace market [...] These markets are established inside the SPLM/A held areas in Bahr al-Ghazal. [...] To both the parties, these peace markets are but a symbolic gesture, for an overall peace in all aspects of the two parties' life.

It is evident that the pastoral Messiriyya were not interested in trade relations as an end in itself, but as a means of securing access to their traditional grazing land and water inside the SPLM/A-controlled areas for the dry season. This suggests that the extension of this pattern of market-centred relations to the Nuba Mountains was initiated by the pastoral Baqqara of the Messiriyya Humr, who kept up secret trade relations with the SPLM/A along the north-south border line during the civil war. The initiative was enthusiastically supported by the SPLM/A leaders in the Nuba Mountains. Subsequently, a certain Messiriyya SPLM/A officer acted as an intermediary between the SPLM/A and his own people in the government-controlled areas.

Some pastoral Baqqara of the Messiriyya sent a delegation of merchant representatives and native leaders to the SPLM/A-controlled areas. The aim was to negotiate the possibility of establishing some form of market exchange relations with the SPLM/A leaders. In February 1993, the delegation managed to arrive safely in Buram in the SPLM/A-controlled area in spite of high levels of insecurity in the area. In a short time, the parties successfully negotiated an economically-driven and market-centred peace agreement known as the Buram agreement. In the words of my key informant, Simon Kalo:[2]

> After we discussed and agreed on the practicality of implementing the initiative, a committee was formed under my chairmanship and entrusted with the task of supervising and ensuring safe implementation of the transaction. Security arrangements were the main concern. The challenges were twofold: first, how to provide effective security measures for these commercial convoys during their journeys from and to the SPLM/A-controlled areas; second, how to make sure that the SPLM/A's security and military systems and affairs were not penetrated by some possible pro-government elements within the convoys.

On their return home, the Messiriyya sent a convoy of over twenty merchants, with camels loaded up with the basic commodities desperately needed by the Nuba people. The day the convoy arrived in Buram inaugurated the implementation of the agreement. My informant Simon Kalo continued his testimony and described how relieved the Nuba were when the convoy arrived:

> The first Messiriyya convoy, composed of more than twenty camels, arrived and supplied the Buram market with commodities from the government-controlled areas. It was a historic day for the local people! Not only for the people in and around the Buram area, but all over the SPLM/A-controlled areas in the Nuba Mountains. After several years of deprivation, they

---

[2] Author's interview with Simon Kalo, Kadugli, 9 January 2007.

rushed into Buram market from all directions to find basic commodities, salt, soap, sugar, clothes, medicine and shoes. Most importantly, the Messiriyya also supplied us with some ammunition just when our military supplies from the South were cut off. In return, the Messiriyya went back with a sizeable number of livestock. Initially, the exchange system was almost in the form of barter trade because there was no money in the SPLM/A-controlled areas. After that, commodity supplies continued to flow regularly through the Messiriyya convoys.

In the process, new local markets were opened up in Ekurchi in Moro and other places in Kawalib and Shwai. At a certain stage, government security agents discovered the transactions and started tracing, arresting, and eventually killing some of the parties involved inside the government-controlled areas. Despite the increasing danger, the market continued to flourish, because the Messiriyya involved in the government-controlled areas and the SPLM/A were both determined to sustain it. It was a profitable business for the pastoral Messiriyya, while it was a survival strategy for the Nuba in the SPLM/A-controlled areas.

Due to frequent ambushes by government forces and militias, a new pattern of trade convoy mobility had been invented. The Messiriyya convoys started to move in the form of small but well-armed groups to protect themselves and their property. These pastoral trade convoys continued to encounter government forces and/or militias and often engaged in fighting. In spite of the danger, they continued to pursue economic gain in collaboration with the Nuba in SPLM/A-controlled areas. Simon Kalo described the situation:

> The Messiriyya joined hands with us in resisting the government forces on many occasions. For example, during the big battle of Buram in December 1993 when the government forces launched an attack on a busy market day, the Messiriyya merchants present stood by the SPLM/A against the government forces. In this way, these Baqqara Arabs who were perceived as the enemy of the SPLM/A, proved to be not only very supportive but strategic and trustworthy partners during a very critical period in the history of the Nuba struggle.

Obviously, this economically-driven and market-centred cooperation contributed, to a large degree, to the survival of the sedentary Nuba. It also reinforced the military ability of the SPLA forces through ammunition supplies, at the time when their military supplies from the main SPLM/A in southern Sudan had long been cut off. Apparently, the demise of the peace market due to some drastic war developments on the ground led to its rebirth in another form, which came to be known far and wide as Suq Sumbuk.

ASWAQ SUMBUK (SMUGGLING MARKETS)

Historically, the word 'Sumbuk' refers to the risky but lucrative business of slave smuggling along the Red Sea during the early days of Anglo-Egyptian rule. In his 'Report on Slavery and Pilgrimage, 1926', C. A. Willis, Assistant Director of Sudan Intelligence (1915–26), defined 'sumbuk' or 'sombuk' as an act of 'smuggling or illegal transporting [slaves] across the Red Sea to Saudi Arabia by cheap but poor quality of, and therefore, risky boats, or Dhows' (Sudan Archive 1926: Ref.: SAD 212/2/26). The risk involved was partly due to the harsh punishments that the British Government in the Sudan imposed on slave dealers caught red handed — for the slave trade had already been banned internationally. It seems that the term 'Sumbuk' was somehow revisited, transported, and re-utilized in a similar profitable business, stimulated this time by the dangers and insecurities of large-scale civil war.

The campaign to recapture the Buram area continued until the signing of a Cease-Fire Agreement in 2002. This led to the immediate termination of Messiriyya-SPLM/A market exchanges and connected relations, putting an end to all peace markets in the SPLM/A-controlled area. However, the closure of the peace markets led to the evolution of another pattern of highly localized, clandestine trade and market exchanges, the Suq Sumbuk (smuggling markets). The main distinction between these two market exchange patterns is that the peace markets operated inside the SPLM/A-controlled areas with the formal backing of SPLM/A officials, whereas the smuggling markets were pure community-to-community transactions with no involvement of the SPLM/A or government authorities. In other words, smuggling was practised by community members from both sides behind the backs of the government and the SPLM/A military and security authorities, and their respective political-administrative institutions. It was a sporadic and highly mobile market exchange, operating at a number of strictly confidential, strategic sites in transitional war zones.

After the collapse of the peace market and the withdrawal of the Messiriyya dealers, smuggling markets soon became the prevailing trading pattern along the war frontiers, particularly around al-Hamra, Umm Serdeba, and Umm Derafi, among others. It was practised by local Baqqara of Hawazma Rawawqa in the government-controlled areas and Nuba in the SPLM/A-controlled areas. The pre-war social ties along the Baqqara-Nuba line were quite instrumental in this new form of market exchange. Suq Sumbuk was very lucrative but an extremely risky business undertaken by some Baqqara dealers. For the Nuba in the SPLM/A-controlled areas, the activity was an alternative survival strategy in war.

In Suq Sumbuk, a group of people from the opposing sides meet at a specifically chosen, strategically hidden site, where they exchange commodities as quickly as they can. The site and time for the next market is determined depending on the war dynamics on the ground. Thus, the pattern of mobility for each group of traders, Baqqara and Nuba, is constantly adjusted in a situation of high insecurity and risk. It is secret in timing and location, exclusive in membership, and mobile in nature.

There is a deal of testimony from actors involved on both sides of the conflict on the operations of the markets. The practice reflects the necessity and the inevitability of cooperation between the sedentary Nuba and nomadic Baqqara to maintain their livelihoods. Responding to my question as to whether the Baqqara Hawazma participated in Suq Sumbuk, one of my key Baqqara informants confirmed that:[3]

> Yes, we participated effectively in suq sumbuk dealings. Some of our people used to smuggle some essential commodities such as clothes, sugar, salt and oil, from Kadugli to the SPLM/A-controlled areas especially to Buram, Shat, Kololo, and Saraf al-Jamus markets. They use bicycles, donkeys, and camels to carry the smuggled commodities in small groups. Suq sumbuk was a dangerous and a risky trading and exchange business; but it was worth it for it was such a lucrative business. An estimated eight to twelve of our young people were shot dead by the government army and security agents during their sumbuk transactions along the frontiers.

Apart from market-driven relations, there were other forms of economically or socially driven interests and cooperative activities between some individuals or groups along the divides during the war.

OTHER FORMS OF NUBA-BAQQARA TIES DURING THE WAR

Some ties were motivated by the fixed economic assets left behind in the SPLA-controlled areas by some Baqqara and Jillaba traders. At the same time, many Nuba communities who joined the SPLA left behind their fixed assets, farm land, and well-established villages in government-controlled areas. In many cases, these economic assets seem to have facilitated the continuation of some family-to-family ties along the Nuba–Baqqara divide during the war and after it.

The anonymous informant cited above revealed that the Aulad Tayna of Dilimiyya of Rawawqa-Hawazma in Reikha were forced to relocate to Kadugli in the war. Many left behind most of their fixed assets, such as shops, mills, stores, and houses. After the signing of a peace accord, they were eager to return to the area and resume local trading. Unlike other Baqqara who were unable to return to their pre-war areas, the Aulad Tayna of Dilimiyya's return to Reikha was quite smooth. They ascribe this to their ability to reposition themselves so that they could maintain their economic interests and personal ties in the area during the war. While forcibly detained in government-controlled areas, they managed to maintain their old ties with Nuba community leaders, including some of the SPLA commanders, so that they were able to cut across the war zones and practise Suq Sumbuk at the frontiers.

Hamid Sattar, the Shaykh of the Baqqara of 'Ayatqa, also testified that when the war caught them by surprise in al-Azraq village in the eastern part of Heiban, they were forced to retreat with their livestock northwards into the government-controlled areas in Umm Berembeita and Kortala in South Kordofan and 'Aluba in North Kordofan. Several of the families settled in al-Azraq left behind most of their fixed assets. 'My own family,'

---

[3] Author's interview with a key Baqqara Informant (name withheld by the author), Reikha, 17 February 2007.

he lamented, 'left behind several orchard farms in al-Azraq, with a total of two hundred and twenty-four mango trees, in addition to two shops and houses. At the same time, some of the Nuba cattle which used to be under our care, together with some of their boys, were taken along with us, when the insecurity forced us to move out of the al-Azraq area'.[4] These cross-cutting social ties maintained some sort of group or individual links across the dividing lines of wartime and the following peace.

These narratives, among so many others, indicate that pre-war Nuba–Baqqara ties, in terms of neighbourhoods and social and economic ties, were crucial in the creation and maintenance of the smuggling markets. Suq Sumbuk was an opportunity for some individuals with strong social ties or economic assets across the dividing line to maintain positive connections throughout the civil war. The ultimate objective was to secure a smooth return to their pre-war situation when the war was over.

In sum, the nature of both Aswaq el-Salam and Suq Sumbuk, and the way they were initiated and managed, demonstrates the dominance of economic-based interests. These interests arose from the inevitable complementarities inherent in the ways of life of the sedentary Nuba and the nomadic Baqqara that continued to connect them across the divides during wartime. These various forms of cooperation, particularly peace markets and/or smuggling markets, became an entry point for subsequent locally brokered peace initiatives in the region between the two communities. Peace agreements further strengthened Baqqara–Nuba market relations despite the intensity of the war and the grave risks both sides ran along the frontiers of their zones.

Market-motivated communal peace agreements

In the context of their market relations during the war, different groups of the Nuba and the Baqqara concluded several community-based deals, significantly, the Buram, the Regifi, and the Kain agreements. They were brokered by some pastoral Baqqara communities in government-controlled areas and sedentary Nuba in SPLM/A-controlled areas in 1993, 1995, and 1996 respectively.

There were several driving forces behind the establishment of these agreements. For example, the Baqqara regretted that they were misled by the government and made to fight against the Nuba despite the marginalization of both sides by the same government. They lost many people and sizeable livestock wealth, as well as the displacement of most households. They expressed their strong desire to trade with the Nuba. Simultaneously, the Nuba emphasized their intention to fight the

---

[4] Author's interview with Hamid Sattar, Shaykh of Baqqara 'Yatqa of al Azraq, Khartoum, 10 June 2006.

government and not the Baqqara and expressed their utmost interest in trading with the Baqqara, exchanging crops and animals for manufactured goods, such as clothes, shoes, salt, soap, and medicine from government areas.

In February 1993, the first community-based peace agreement was reached in Buram. Most of the principles enshrined in this agreement were echoed in similar agreements thereafter. Suliman (1999, 215–16) reported that both sides agreed, among other points, to abide by the following terms:

1. To stop immediately all military actions against each other and to exchange relevant military and security information.
2. To safeguard free movement of people and goods from and to both sides and to assist them, if necessary, in safely reaching their final destinations.
3. To settle disputes or cases of peace violation through a joint committee.
4. To collaborate in putting an end to the recurring incidents of animal-looting across the frontier zones.
5. To safeguard trade exchanges between the people of the two territories.

The opening up of the trade route into the Buram peace market resulted from the agreement. As mentioned earlier, the Buram peace market flourished until the end of 1993 when the government troops recaptured the area and closed it down.

On 15 November 1995, the Regifi agreement was reached. It reiterated the principles enshrined in the previous agreement. Both sides acknowledged that the community-based peace agreement was crucial for their co-existence in the prevailing crisis in the region. Suliman (1999: 217) insists that the government did all it could to sabotage the agreement:

> It targeted the leaders of the Baqqara who signed it: 'Abdalla, the Messiriyya leader at the negotiations, was shot dead; others were assassinated or imprisoned; a few were bribed and skilfully used by the government to undermine the spirit of trust and cooperation between the Baqqara and the Nuba which had begun to spread in the region.

The forces that continued to hold off the Baqqara from the Nuba through policies of 'divide and rule' were always generated at the centre, beyond the reach of both peoples. In June 1996, the Nuba took another initiative towards establishing peaceful cooperation with the Baqqara of Rawawqa-Hawazma. A five-man delegation sought out the Rawawqa on neutral ground in Zangura, west of Tima, in the Lagawa area. The Baqqara were invited to move their market close to the 'liberated areas', i. e., those areas under SPLM/A control for better mutual cooperation in trade and market exchanges. The Baqqara accepted the initiative and concluded what came to be known as the Kain peace agreement in 1996. It was almost identical to the previous two agreements. However, this time a special trade committee was established to supervise the implementation of trade and market exchanges. What was remarkable in the agreement, as reported by Suliman (1999: 217–18) was that:

1. The Rawawqa were so confident in the stability of the agreement that they began to bring in ammunition and army uniforms to sell to the Nuba;
2. The Baqqara traders began to come to the markets unarmed and were gradually accompanied by women and children; and
3. The first test of the agreement came shortly after signing it, when an Arab attacked a Nuba, took his weapon, and left him nearly dead: the Baqqara brought the weapon back, paid for the treatment of the victim, and promised to deliver the attacker to the Nuba authority.

Shortly after the implementation of the agreement and the opening of the market, government security forces began to visit the marketplaces out of uniform, to pass as civilians. The attempt was to sabotage the agreement through bribery, imprisonment, or ultimately murder. The Nuba leadership became alarmed and ordered the closure of the market. Yet the government continued to target leaders on both sides of the divide. Suliman (1999: 218) reports that in 'one known case, government officials offered a would-be assassin four million Sudanese pounds and a license for a mill in return for killing a leading Nuba signatory to the agreement.'[5]

To summarize: these community-based peace agreements were driven by the mutual interests of the two groups along the divide. This suggests that the macro-agenda of the central government proved to be neither appealing nor viable for a substantial portion of the common people (Ibrahim 1998: 48). But it is equally true that not all the Baqqara and the Nuba recognized or adhered to these peace agreements, because many individuals from both peoples had sided with the government army and/or the People's Defence Forces (PDFs) in the civil war.

Moreover, there were frequent clashes between some Baqqara armed groups and the SPLA along the frontiers because both were unaware of the peace agreements for some time. Another challenge was that some Baqqara traders were playing a double role for their own economic interests. According to Suliman (1999: 218), 'On the one hand, they traded with Nuba and even sold them ammunition; on the other, they supplied the government with information about rebel troops.' Despite such enormous challenges and insecurity, the two groups managed to engage in a constantly changing form of market relations during the entire war period.

---

[5] In 1999, 2,576 Sudanese Pounds (SDP) was equal to one US Dollar (see Suliman 1999: 218).

Nuba–Baqqara relations assumed a new shape after the signing of the Nuba Mountains Ceasefire Agreement in 2002 and the conclusion of the Comprehensive Peace Agreement in 2005, which allowed for free movement of people and commodities in the Nuba Mountains. The impact of the peace agreement as process and outcome and the post-war dynamics on Baqqara–Nuba relations is one of the main themes in the following chapters.

Conclusion

The symbiotic relationship between the pastoral Baqqara and the sedentary Nuba of the Nuba Mountains region in Sudan has been shaped and continues to be reshaped by cumulative historical and various contemporary forces. However, the main argument of this chapter has been that the Sudan's recent civil war was more repressive, with far-reaching and multiple ramifications not only on Baqqara–Nuba symbiotic relations, but also on their respective ways of life and, indeed, on their very survival.

Focusing on the role of the market institutions in pastoral–sedentary relations in the war situation, this chapter has provided an analysis of the initial driving forces, the function, and the spatial pattern of the economically-driven cooperation between the two groups, born out of war. Through the narratives of some key informants, the chapter has revealed some of the survival strategies and coping mechanisms deployed by the parties involved, while interacting in a period of escalating danger.

The overall analysis has generated some insights that may deepen our understanding of the complex nature of interconnected issues, in the institution of the local market as a multifaceted intermediary space and its primary role in pastoral-sedentary symbiotic relations and the Nuba and Baqqara ways of life in a protracted civil war. First, the empirical dimension of this study not only confirms the inevitability of the pastoral-sedentary symbiotic relationship, but also reinforces it. Sudan's prolonged and severe civil war imposed its own logic and dynamics on the symbiotic life of the pastoral Baqqara and the sedentary Nuba in the Nuba Mountains region. As a result, the livelihood of these two co-existing groups was progressively divided into two heavily militarized political-administrative zones along ethno-political lines. Moreover, the groups were made to fight a proxy war that came to have a far-reaching impact on their way of life, symbiotic relations, and even their survival.

Second, while the two groups were forced to fight each other, some were simultaneously able to essentialize themselves strategically and develop a new pattern of cooperation. This cooperation was chiefly driven by what Gertel (2007: 18) calls 'economies of survival', resulting in the emergence of a new pattern of local market exchanges along the war frontier zones. It was pursued jointly within extremely limited survival choices. Aswaq es-Salam (peace markets), Aswaq Sumbuk (smuggling markets), and a number of related community-based and market-motivated peace deals were manifestations of the survival strategies pursued by the two endangered communities in a vicious war.

Third, the continuation of Baqqara–Nuba relations during the war, though less intense and more sporadic in pattern, indicates that pressures driving them into fighting against each other, in the context of the larger civil war, were not internally generated. Equally, they were not related to the distinction between nomadic and sedentary ways of life, and their respective concerns. Rather, they are externally generated by state-induced factors connected with the failure of modern state administrative institutions and bad governance, with misguided national policies, and distorted national development strategies that disregarded the interests and priorities of both the farmer and herder communities.

Finally; like other pastoral groups in Africa (see Bovin and Manger 1990; Azarya 1996; Mohamed Salih et al., 2001; Gertel 2007), the Baqqara are neither traders by custom, nor have they themselves founded markets. Despite this, they continue to play a key role in the evolution and the continuation of the local market as place, space, and exchange. The weekly local market of Keiga Tummero reveals that the flow of pastoral Baqqara from adjacent livestock camps and their effective participation in market exchanges are decisive factors in determining the success or failure of such a market institution.

The weekly local markets in the Nuba Mountains tend to flourish at times of intensive pastoral Baqqara presence during the dry season. As the rainy season approaches, the Baqqara start their rhythmic movement northwards, while the Nuba engage in cultivation. Consequently, the flourishing markets shrink or even disappear temporarily before they flourish again when the Baqqara return in the following dry season. In this way, Baqqara–Nuba market relations and their persistent, joint efforts to maintain them, in one way or another, during the severity of war reveal the intrinsic and inevitable socio-economic symbioses between the pastoral nomadic and the sedentary peasant ways of life.

Part III

Peace & Post-conflict Dynamics

5

The CPA & the Nuba Questions of Land, Identity & Political Destiny

> They [the Nuba] were evicted from their land, forced to take sides, denied adequate
> services. They have shown resilience. It is them who have to make the real choice,
> because it is their life, their land, their destiny.
> Jan Pronk (2006: 2), the UN Special Envoy to the Sudan.

This chapter aims at examining the Comprehensive Peace Agreement (CPA) as initiative, process, and outcome. The focus is on the question of the Nuba Mountains region, one of the three areas widely referred to as 'contested', 'marginalized', and 'conflict' areas, 'transitional zones', or 'border territories' in the context of the south-north socio-political dichotomy.[1] Apart from the Nuba Mountains, the three areas include the Southern Blue Nile and Abyei.

This discussion is geared towards three major questions. To what extent has the CPA been able to address effectively the root causes of the war in the Nuba Mountains, particularly the questions of land, identity, and political destiny? What roles did the Nuba's various political and civic forces play in the peace process in the context of their peaceful and armed struggle? And how did they respond to the CPA's final outcome?

The three areas: a bone of contention

The Nigerian peace initiative under the Abuja Peace Negotiation One and Two in May–July 1992 and April–May 1993 respectively, and the regional efforts of the Inter-Governmental Authority on Development, IGAD, which started in March 1994 and continued until the signing of the CPA on 9 January 2005, represent the main efforts that put an end to the war. From the outset, the three areas were a contentious issue between the two negotiating parties and the mediators because of their transitional positions along the north-south social and spatial borders that are rich in the land-based resources of fertile soil, water and oil. It is worth noting that the Nuba Mountains and

---

[1] For some detailed discussions on the three 'contested areas', see, for example, Abdel Salam and de Waal (2001), Danforth (2002), Johnson (2006), de Waal (2007), and Manger (2008a, 2008b); and for the Blue Nile in particular, see James (2009).

the Southern Blue Nile are part of the socio-political geography of northern Sudan, while from 1905, Abyei was detached from southern Sudan and annexed to northern Sudan for administrative purposes.

At an early stage of peace negotiations, the GOS rejected the inclusion of the three areas in any agenda for negotiation on the grounds that the IGAD mandate was confined to the problem of southern Sudan. However, the SPLM challenged the GOS's position and insisted that the areas under its control (the liberated areas), including substantial parts of the three contested areas, must be treated as one geo-political-administrative and military block in the negotiations. In this respect, the Nuba fighters who represented 'more than a quarter of the SPLM/A troops' (de Waal 2008: 1), and who fought side by side with their southern counterparts on all fronts, were led to believe, beyond doubt, that their political destiny would be collectively determined along with the people of Southern Sudan in the final peace settlement.

While the SPLM/A fought under the banner of 'one political destiny' as envisaged in the united 'New Sudan' vision, several unfavourable dynamics in the Sudanese political sphere were concurrently at work. Of significant relevance to the discussion is the recognition of the 'right of self-determination'[2] for the people of southern Sudan. The exclusive endorsement of this right was a landmark with far-reaching consequences regarding the contested areas in the outcome of the peace process.

The right to self-determination for southern Sudan was first incorporated in the 1992 Frankfurt Agreement between the Nasir faction led by Riek Machar and the GOS. Thereafter, it also was endorsed in the following agreements and declarations:[3]

(i) the Washington Declaration, October 1993, between the SPLM/A main faction led by John Garang and the defected faction of Riek Machar;

(ii) the IGAD Declaration of Principles (DoP) in 1994 which the SPLM/A endorsed at once, while the GOS did not sign up to it before July 1997;

(iii) the Chukudum Agreement, December 1994, between the SPLM/A and the Umma Party;

(iv) the Asmara Agreements of December 1994 and June 1995, signed by SPLM, the National Democratic Alliance and some trade unions in opposition;

(v) the Khartoum Peace Agreement, April 1997, on the basis of which self-determination was enshrined, for the first time, in the Sudan Constitution of 1998; and

(vi) the Djibouti National Call of 1999 between the Umma Party and the GOS led by the National Congress Party.

---

[2] For discussion of the concept of the Right to Self-Determination and its applicability to Southern Sudan and the marginalized areas of Northern Sudan, see chapters 10 and 12 in Abdel Salam and de Waal, eds. (2001: 199–269). Also, see de Waal and Ajawin, eds. (2002: 221–40).

[3] For the chronology of Sudan's key peace events and agreements, see Johnson (2006: Appendix: 195–221).

During the Nairobi negotiations in March 1994 between the GOS and the SPLM, under the auspices of the Inter-Governmental Authority on Development (IGAD), the GOS continued to reject the 'right for self-determination'. It finally acquiesced to a debate on self-determination for the people of southern Sudan in May 1998. But the SPLM continued advocating the inclusion of the three areas in the rights of self-determination. Deng Alor Kuol, a prominent SPLM/A leader from Abyei, summarized the SPLM argument on the three areas as follows (Kuol 1999: 3):

> Abyei is culturally and ethnically part of the South and was promised a referendum twice in 1952, during the British rule and in 1972 during the Addis Ababa Agreement but no implementation was carried out in both cases. The Nuba Mountains and the Southern Blue Nile are currently fighting as members of the SPLM/A so it is only logical that a solution must be found to end war in these areas. Besides being part of a marginalized fighting Sudan, the people of these areas live in one contentious territory with South Sudan and are not scattered and dotted all over the Sudan. This aspect makes them a natural and geographical part and parcel of the Southern Sudan component of the New Sudan. Hence they have the legitimacy to exercise the right of self-determination together or separately with the people of Southern Sudan.

The contested area of the Nuba Mountains

By the mid-1990s, when the war in the Nuba Mountains was intense on all fronts, the fate of the three contested regions in the peace process was ambivalent. At this juncture, Nuba political and civil forces started to call for a Nuba conference in order to achieve a consensus on the political status of their homeland and people. An International Nuba Conference was organized in London in 1996 under the title: 'What peace for the Nuba?' The conference addressed three major concerns: self-determination, land rights, and religion.

The conference demanded the right to self-determination for the Nuba people. With regard to land rights, the conference referred to the advent of mechanized farming in fuelling the conflict in the region. On the issue of religion, the conferees called for the separation of state and religion on the grounds that 'the Nuba have been victimized regardless of their religious adherence, and have discovered at painful cost that conversion to Islam has not protected them from racial discrimination, gross human exploitation, and from being robbed of their land' (see Rahhal 2001a: 125, Appendix 3).

GOS AND SPLM POSITIONS IN THE PEACE PROCESS

For some time, the GOS continued to insist that the Nuba Mountains region and people were part of the North and, therefore, had no right to self-determination. As part of its divide-and-rule politics, the GOS continued to send signals to the Nuba that it was prepared to address the

Nuba question if it were separated from the southern question, and subsequently from the SPLM/A connection. Unfortunately, as revealed below, some Nuba leaders were led to believe in these intentions, not only in government-controlled areas, but also within SPLM/A-held areas.

During the November 1997 IGAD talks, the SPLM/A reiterated its official position with regard to the Nuba Mountains and the Southern Blue Nile. This position was unchanged for the Addis Ababa peace negotiation round in August 1998 when the leaders of the Nuba Mountains and Southern Blue Nile, respectively Commander Yusuf Kuwa and Commander Malik Agar, informed the Government delegation and the IGAD mediators that 'they were indeed part of the South but should the Government of Sudan reject this argument then it could go ahead to finalize the self-determination process with South Sudan including Abyei. However, they would remain outside such a settlement and continue to fight for their rights. (see Kuol 1999: 4).

Addressing the international community and the Nuba in diaspora in London in December 1998, Kuwa insisted that the Nuba people demand the right to self-determination as a universal human right because of:

1. Their long history of being treated as second-class citizens in Sudan;
2. The threat of genocide that hangs over them;
3. Long and bitter struggle for their right of justice and equality; and
4. The right of self-determination has been recognized for Southern Sudan (Rahhal 2001a: 121–2).

Moreover, he revealed that the Nuba would prefer the people of Southern Sudan to remain within the new united Sudan that was envisaged. But if they opted for secession, the Nuba would respect their choice. This implies that the option for the Nuba's right to self-determination differs considerably from that offered to the South. It was a 'separate but parallel' proposal for self-determination for the Nuba Mountains and Southern Blue Nile. In his clarification in London, Kuwa emphasized the following (Rahhal 2001a: 122):

(1) The Nuba are not demanding secession but demanding the right to choose their own right;
(2) Their preferred option is the unity of the Sudan, in which they wish to enjoy full self-government within a decentralized system; and that
(3) During the interim period between the signing of a peace agreement and the final exercise of self-determination, the Nuba demand the following, among others:
    i) To be treated equally with the South Sudan and in parallel in any peace deal.
    ii) Interim self-determination of the Nuba Mountains under the SPLM/A on the same terms as South Sudan.
    iii) A secular, pluralist and democratic regional administration.
    iv) International guarantees for the future of the Nuba as an integral part of any peace deal from the outset.
    v) The [international] presence to ensure respect of human rights and

the free and fair conduct of the exercise of the right of self-determination.

vi) All Nuba people will exercise their right of self-determination separately after people of Southern Sudan have made their decision in an internationally-monitored referendum.

Moreover, he insisted that in the event that the people of Southern Sudan opted for separation in the exercise of their right to self-determination, the Nuba should have the following options (Rahhal 2001a: 123):

(i)   To choose to be part of Southern Sudan state; or
(ii)   To choose to be part of the Northern Sudan state; or
(iii) To choose to have an independent statehood.

These options reflected the significance of the choice to be made by the South. The separation of the two areas would inevitably dilute the original demand for the right to self-determination, leading to an inferior and an ambiguous type of political exercise called 'popular consultation' in place of the original right to and demand for self-determination.[4] At this stage, the IGAD had not yet taken a clear position on the three contested areas, and this persuaded the GOS to insist that the Nuba Mountains and the Blue Nile were part of the North and not entitled to any rights on self-determination. At the same time, the SPLM/A maintained its position that the three areas were included in self-determination in the context of the separate but parallel proposal as described above. Faced with this standoff, the IGAD mediators came up with a proposal on the Nuba Mountains and the Southern Blue Nile issue for the September–October round of talks held at Lake Bogoria in Kenya in 2000:

> Since the territories were not in south Sudan at the time of independence and since the IGAD peace process was restricted to south Sudan, it did not have the authority to consider the issue itself. However, the secretariat insisted that the matter must be addressed and concluded, since the people in these territories have raised arms alongside the SPLM/A, a separate mediation should be established to resolve the conflict. (UNOCHA 2008:1)

This proposal was immediately rejected by the GOS on the grounds that the IGAD had no mandate to intervene in the issue and that the SPLM/A had no legitimacy to represent the peoples of the two areas, since they were part of northern Sudan. Meanwhile, the SPLM/A not only maintained its position, but went further and appointed Malik Agar and 'Abdul Aziz al-Hilu, the two SPLM/A leaders from the Southern Blue Nile and the Nuba Mountains respectively, as permanent members of its negotiating team. The rejection of the IGAD proposal by the GOS led the three areas to remain formally outside the agenda in the peace negotiations although they

---

[4] For 'popular consultation', see the Protocol between GOS and SPLM on the Resolution of Conflict in Southern Kordofan/Nuba Mountains and Blue Nile States, Naivasha, Kenya, May 26, 2004: 3–5: Online: Retrieved 27 May 2008 from http://www.reliefweb.int/rw/RWFiles2005.nsf/FilesByRWDocUNIDFileName/EVIU-6AZBDB-sud-sud-09janPart%20II.pdf/$File/sud-sud-09janPart%20II.pdf

continued to come up during the discussion of remaining issues, particularly in security arrangements and the question of the south-north borders.

While the question of the contested areas was in a stalemate situation, the GOS intensified its tactical policy of 'divide-and-rule' among the leaders through what it called es-Salam min al-dakhil, or 'peace from within' (see Fadl 2002: 45–132, and African Rights 1995: 128–32). The result was the signing of an agreement between the Sudan Government and Mohamed Harun Kafi on 21 April 1997, stipulating that

> the two parties reaffirm the unity of the Sudanese nation and condemn any separatist tendency. The two parties are committed to the right of the Nuba Mountains citizens to their democratic and fair rights within the context of the Sudan. Moreover, the agreement endorsed the notion that 'the Shari'a and customary law are the main sources of legislation in Sudan'.[5]

In the process of implementation, however, it was evident that the government had no commitment whatsoever to the terms of the agreement. As a result, most of the basic points in it were ignored, with excessive marginalization of the signatories to the agreement. The agreement was invalidated in silence after the signing of the CPA, resulting in further marginalization of the main signatory, Mohamed Harun Kafi. In 2007, Kafi, out of frustration, decided to rejoin the SPLM after he had caused terrible damage and weakened the Nuba political position during the peace negotiation process.

Despite the deadlock in the peace negotiations regarding the three areas, there was a growing conviction that there would be no viable peace without their inclusion in the final peace deal. In this respect, a renowned human rights activist (de Waal 2008: 6) who had extensive involvement in Nuba Mountains affairs insisted at the time that IGAD had a mandate for the Nuba Mountains and Southern Blue Nile 'because the SPLA is present in these areas as well as in the South. So far this leverage has not been exercised: it is time for it to be used. If there is a will to work for peace in the South, it is only meaningful if it extends to the adjacent areas'.

It was obvious that the question of the Nuba Mountains as a region for its people was an inescapable issue in the peace negotiations: it was inconceivable that there could be a peace deal without addressing the Nuba question. Twenty years of fighting could not be ended by ignoring the fate of peoples who had allied themselves politically and militarily with the South Sudan, and who felt, and continue to feel, themselves culturally at risk from the tyranny of Khartoum's Islamist project.

Along the same line, Manger (2008: 31) maintains that the question of the three areas must be confronted if a lasting peace is to be achieved through IGAD negotiations and that 'some solution is critical if the unity of the country is to be promoted along the lines of peace agreement.' Two

---

[5] The Peace Agreement between the Central Committee of the SPLM/-Nuba Faction and the Sudan Government (Ibrahim 1998, Appendix 94: 94, 96).

direct results of this persistent international, regional, and local pressure were (i) the signing of the US-brokered Nuba Mountains Ceasefire Agreement on 19 January 2002, at the Swiss resort of Bergenstock and (ii) the inclusion of the three contested areas in the last stage of peace negotiations and as a consequence in the CPA.

THE NUBA MOUNTAINS CEASEFIRE AGREEMENT

Negotiating a ceasefire agreement in the region was initiated in early November 2001 when Senator John Danforth, US Special Envoy for Peace in Sudan, met with officials in the Nuba Mountains. He proposed a ceasefire agreement for the Nuba Mountains not only to bring an end to the isolation and the suffering of the Nuba people, but also to provide a test case for confidence-building measures between the GOS and the SPLM/A (see Meyer 2005: 172). On 19 January 2002, a ceasefire agreement was signed between the Government of Sudan and some Nuba leaders in the SPLM/A, at the Swiss resort of Bergenstock, resulting in (i) the immediate cessation of hostilities between the warring parties in the region and (ii) the guarantee of free movement for civilians and goods, including humanitarian assistance throughout the region (see Government of the Republic of Sudan and SPLM/A 2002). It detailed how the cessation of hostilities was to be regulated and monitored through the Joint Military Commission (JMC) and its conflict resolution body, the Joint Monitoring Mission (JMM), in accordance with the principles and terms specified in the agreement.[6]

Meyer (2005: 173) reported that the agreement 'was greeted with considerable scepticism by many foreign activists on the Sudan as well as by some elements within the SPLM itself'. Remarkable, however, was its surprising success, which came to be widely recognized by different stakeholders, including the local people, the two warring parties and the international community at large. Several studies and reports have documented this achievement, including Danforth (2002), Vogt (2003), Wilhemsen (2004). Four months after the implementation of the CFA, Danforth (2002: 5) reported that:[7]

> The Nuba Mountains agreement, relating to one of the most hotly contested regions of the country, is extraordinary. The ceasefire in the Nuba Mountains is holding; international monitors are arriving; and a long-term relief and rehabilitation effort is beginning. The impact of this successful agreement has given the people of the Nuba Mountains a new life, and in other parts of Sudan it has provided a powerful argument for peace that is not lost upon the Government or the SPLM.

Moreover, after two and a half years of the CFA, Wilhemsen (2004: 2),

---

[6] For the full text of the Nuba Mountains Ceasefire Agreement, see http://www.reliefweb.int/rw/RWB.NSF/db900SID/MHII-6227SX?OpenDocument, retrieved 28 February 2008.
[7] For the full text of the report from Danforth, the US Special Envoy for Peace in Sudan, see http://www.whitehouse.gov/news/releases/2002/05/20020514-11.html, retrieved 2 March 2008.

the Chairman of JMC and Head of the JMM of the CFA, made his personal assessment of the implementation of the agreement and reported that:

> I believe the JMC has achieved considerable success in this mutually accepted extension of the Mission's role and that enduring bridges have been built between the parties. [...] There have been no clashes of the armed forces in the Nuba Mountains since its [implementation] and complaints from both sides have steadily declined, with 130 cases being successfully resolved to date [...] There have, as yet, been no serious ceasefire violations (CFV) and numbers have fallen from 49 in the 2nd Mandate to 9 for each of the last 2 mandates, shared equally between the parties.

Vogt (2003: 37), an expert on peacekeeping at the Norwegian Institute of International Affairs, believed that this remarkable success was ascribed to 'battle fatigue and stalemate, which might have made the conflict somewhat ripe for settlement', while for others such as Meyer (2005: 174), it was due to 'the presence of international monitors'. Several observers, following Vogt (2003), such as Thompson (2004) and Meyer (2005), argued that the notable success of the CFA was important as a test case, but not necessarily a model for the whole of the Sudan.

Despite this impressive success, the following chapters will reveal that the source of strength and the positive aspects of the CFA were not maintained in the post-conflict situation in the Nuba Mountains when the United Nation Mission in Sudan (UNMIS) took over after the conclusion of the CPA. This is evident in the escalation of inter-ethnic conflicts during the post-conflict situation in the region, particularly between the sedentary Nuba and the nomadic Baqqara.

One direct change brought about by the CFA, after more than fifteen years of intense warfare, complete isolation, and gross human rights violations, was the free movement of people and goods in and out of the region. It has provided a new opportunity for Nuba leaders and elites from government-held areas, SPLM/A-controlled areas, and from the diaspora to meet for the first time, after several years of detachment and enforced separation. It has generated new dynamics with various political and social forces engaging in the then ongoing peace process, as discussed below.

NUBA ENGAGEMENT IN PEACE PROCESS

The peace negotiations at Machakos, aiming at ending the north-south conflict took place behind closed doors with restricted information about their agenda and progress. The secrecy surrounding the negotiations fuelled suspicions and fears among the leaders of the two areas about the future political status of their regions and peoples. These were reinforced by the government-controlled media in Khartoum, which continued to publicize that the Nuba Mountains and the Blue Nile were beyond the mandate of the IGAD forum and, therefore, not a subject for discussion.

In the light of this uncertainty, a strong belief emerged in the contested areas that the negotiating parties might reach a peace deal behind closed doors that excluded their political status. Hence, the Nuba feared that the final peace settlement might impose on them the option of remaining within the Northern Sudan if the southern people opted for secession through the already recognized right to self-determination. Abdel Salam and de Waal (2001: 263) pointed out that for the Nuba, the apprehension stems from the fact that:

> Under whatever government, Northern politicians in power will continue to maintain the same policy of 'divide and rule, Islamization and Arabicization' throughout the Sudan. They [the Nuba] fear that indigenous cultures will continue to be undermined and suppressed and that any guarantees for autonomy can be easily overruled and reversed.

Given this state of affairs, the international community and Nuba political and civil forces in government- and SPLM/A-controlled areas, as well as in the diaspora, exercised an enormous pressure on the IGAD negotiators and the two negotiating parties to ensure the inclusion of the three areas in the peace negotiations. Towards that end, numerous memos were directed to the IGAD Secretariat, the two negotiating parties, and some regional and international actors. For instance, on 5 July 2002, civilian groups representing NGOs, CBOs, youth, women, faith-based groups and professional associations, from the South, the Nuba Mountains, and the Southern Blue Nile, presented a position letter on what they called 'the just and lasting peace in Sudan'. The letter was addressed to Lazarus Sambeyweo, the Special Envoy to the IGAD on Peace in the Sudan, with copies to the SPLM/A, the GOS, and the major regional and international actors, including the UN, EU, African Union and the Arab League. The social movement groups insisted in their memo (Sambeyweo 2002: 2–3) that the peoples of the Nuba Mountains and the Southern Blue Nile

> Shall exercise their right to self-determination before the end of the interim period, and after the referendum in the South Sudan; they shall have the following options: 1. Unity with northern Sudan; 2. Unity with southern Sudan; or 3. Independent Statehood.[8]

On 20 July 2002, the GOS and the SPLM/A signed the Machakos Protocol, in which the two parties reached a specific agreement on the right to self-determination for the people of South Sudan, on the state and religion, as well as on the preamble and principles. The two parties agreed to negotiate and elaborate on the specific terms of the framework, including aspects not covered in this phase of the negotiations, as part of the overall peace agreement. This implies that the question of the three areas may still be included at later negotiation phases. Nonetheless, the Machakos Protocol reinforced the fears of the people of the three areas by

---

[8] For the full text of the memo, see http://www.mafhoum.com/press3/105S22.htm, retrieved 28 February 2008.

stating nothing on their future political status while explicitly affirming that 'the people of South Sudan have the right to self-determination, *inter alia*, through a referendum to determine their future statuses'.[9]

In response to the Machakos Protocol, the Special Envoy received an open letter dated 14 August 2002, from Nuba Relief, Rehabilitation and Development Organization (NRRDO), on behalf of several Nuba civil society organizations in the SPLM/A-controlled areas in the Nuba Mountains. It expressed clear concerns about the future political status of the Nuba region:

> We would like the international community and all the stake-holders to be fully aware of the causes and nature of the conflict in the Nuba Mountains and the aspirations of the Nuba people. Without understanding the root causes of the conflict and the aspirations of the Nuba people, and hence addressing them comprehensively and sensitively, there would be a danger that this present window of opportunity for achieving a just, durable and sustainable peace in Sudan will be seriously jeopardized and your efforts and goodwill will be undermined. (NRRDO 2002: 1)

What is most remarkable about the letter is its assertion that the historical north–south border as of 1 January 1956 has become irrelevant. It challenges its legitimacy and relevance as a basis for determining the political future of the three areas in ongoing peace negotiations. Along the same lines, the letter caught the attention of the international community and the mediators when it stated (NRRDO 2002: 1):

> [...] it is essential that all stake-holders realize that any proposals which leave the people of the Nuba Mountains, Southern Blue Nile and Abyei under the administrative jurisdiction of the current NIF Regime (or any future unrepresentative government) in Khartoum can not hope to succeed in generating a durable peace or cessation of conflict.[10]

In their view, the Nuba should be part of the South for a number of reasons, including, among others, the following (NRRDO: 2002: 2):

1. Nuba have been fighting under the SPLM/A since 1984 against the Khartoum regimes but with common experience in armed struggle since 1975 under Anya-nya 2;
2. They are treated together under the Closed District Ordinance of 1922 by the Condominium Rule;
3. They are part of the New Sudan, and are ethnically, culturally and socially much closer to the black African people of Southern Sudan; and that
4. They continued to be subjugated by the north through slavery, religious persecution, land alienation, ethnocide and genocide atrocities.

[9] GOS and SPLM/A, Comprehensive Peace Agreement, Machakos Protocol, 20 July 2002: 3, point 1.3. For a detailed section on self-determination, see points 1.3 to 2.6: 8. Available online: http://www.reliefweb.int/rw/RWFiles2005.nsf/FilesByRWDocUNIDFileName/EVIU-6AZBDB-sud-sud-09janPart%20II.pdf/$File/sud-sud-09janPart%20II.pdf, retrieved 28 May 2008.
[10] For the full text of the letter, see http://home.planet.nl/~ende0098/Articles/20020814a.htm, retrieved 28 February 2008.

Given these realities, they strongly urged the international community and the other stakeholders in the IGAD negotiations to consider very carefully the key issue of borders that was so critical not only to the three areas, but also to peace throughout Sudan.

The position of the Nuba civil societies in the SPLM-held areas in the Nuba Mountains was supported by numerous open letters from Nuba in diaspora. For example, Suleiman Musa Rahhal, the Director of Nuba Survival[11] wrote a letter in *Nuba Vision*, and another letter was sent from the Nuba diaspora in Australia.[12]

Simultaneously, some Nuba political and social forces in the government-controlled areas submitted their own views on the political destiny of the Nuba Mountains to the IGAD and other international stakeholders. The position of the Nuba Mountains Alliance Parties/NMAPs[13] was the most remarkable contribution, being virtually the same as that expressed by the Nuba-led SPLM/A and its civilian organizations. Before the signing of the Machakos Protocol, the Nuba Mountains Alliance Parties submitted a letter on 4 June 2002 to the American Embassy in Khartoum in response to the Danforth Report of 26 April 2002. In his report, Danforth (2002: 7) seems to have doubted whether the right to self-determination for the people of South Sudan could be achieved, while implicitly dismissing it in the case of the two contested areas of the Nuba Mountains and the Southern Blue Nile.

The NMAPs insisted that the problem of Sudan is not between the South and the North. Most importantly, they argued that the problem of the Nuba people was not only about relief, rehabilitation, and anti-slavery, as stated in the Danforth Report, but rather it is a problem of inequality of development, lack of power sharing, endangered cultural identity, and, indeed, their very survival. They maintained that if the southerners were given the right to self-determination and opted to go on their own, then the Nuba would have to have an equal right to self-determination, to decide whether they wanted to be with the North or South or to form their own independent state, separate from both.[14]

Two months later, the Nuba Mountains Alliance Parties (NMAPs) submitted another letter to the IGAD in response to the Machakos Protocol, signed on 20 July 2002, in which they expressed deep concern about the political destiny of the Nuba people which appeared to be undermined by the protocol. Generally, the NMAPs' position is similar to

---

[11] Nuba Survival is a London-based organization dedicated to promoting the cause of the Nuba people of Sudan.
[12] For the letters expressing Nuba views in the diaspora, see http://www.nubasurvival.com/Nuba%20Vision/Vol%202%20Issue%201/11%20Nuba%20views.htm, retrieved 2 March 2008.
[13] The Nuba Mountains Alliance Parties are: the Free Sudan National Party, formerly chaired by the late Fr. Philip Abbas Ghabush (no chairman has been elected since his death); Sudan National Party, chaired by Professor Elmin Hamuda; General Union of the Nuba Mountains (GUNM), chaired by Yusuf Abdel Alla; and the Sudan National Party, chaired by a collective leadership.
[14] See the full text at http://www.nubasurvival.com/Nuba%20Vision/Vol%201%20Issue%204/7.%20Nuba%20Mountains%20Alliance%20Parties%20Comment.htm, retrieved 2 March 2008.

that expressed by the Nuba-led SPLM/A, but with one major exception. Unlike the Nuba in the SPLM/A, who perceive the Nuba Mountains as part and parcel of the South, the NMAPs maintained that joining Southern or Northern Sudan should depend on securing 'certain guarantees'.[15] Although these were not explicitly set out in the letter, it is safe to assume that the NMAPs wanted to ensure that future Nuba political choices would not again subject them to other forms of marginalization and underdevelopment, whether in the North, as the case is now, or in a future Southern state.

Towards the end of 2002, two major events happened with far-reaching consequences for the positions of the various Nuba political and social forces with regard to the peace negotiations: (i) the Nuba Mountains and Southern Blue Nile Civil Society Forum, held in Kampala, 21–24 November 2002, and (ii) First All Nuba Conference, held in Kauda, Nuba Mountains, 2–4 December 2002.

The Kampala Forum was organized by Justice Africa, hosted by the Pan Africa Movement, and attended by some 40 participants representing a wide spectrum of civil society organizations, political parties, and academics from government-controlled areas in the two regions and in the diaspora. A similar number of representatives from the two regions in SPLM/A-controlled areas was invited but did not turn up. The forum was attended by observers from the GOS, the IGAD, the Joint Military Commission (JMC), and international experts. After serious deliberations, the conferees issued the Kampala Declaration of the Nuba and Southern Blue Nile Civil Society Forum (Kampala Declaration 2002: 1–3). The declaration contains over forty resolutions, including:

> 1. The participants expressed their dissatisfaction about the marginalization of the Nuba Mountains and Southern Blue Nile in the on-going peace negotiation process, which exposes the people of these areas to the risk of either jeopardizing their struggle, or turning them into a stumbling block in the search for peace in Sudan;
> 2. they expressed misgivings that neither the GOS nor the SPLM were willing to involve the people of these areas when discussing their issues, and therefore called for fuller representation of political forces and civil society organizations in the two areas in the peace talks;
> 3. they demanded that the two regions should enjoy autonomous rule in the interim period, with constitutional and international guarantees; and
> 4. they recognized the right to self-determination as the right for all people in accordance with international conventions. However, they opted for the choice of safeguarding the unity of Sudan as the priority based on the principles of equality, justice, and respect of basic human rights.[16]

In contrast to that event, the First All Nuba Conference was held at Kauda in the SPLM/A-held areas in the Nuba Mountains. It was described as an

---

[15] For the full text of the letter, see http://www.nubasurvival.com/Nuba%20Vision/Vol%202%20Issue%201/11%20Nuba%20views.htm, retrieved 2 March 2008.
[16] For the full text of the Kampala Declaration, see http://www.nubasurvival.com/news&events/Nov%202002%20Kampala%20declaration.htm, retrieved 2 March 2008.

unprecedented political event in the history of the Nuba, because it brought together, for the first time, Nuba leaders at one forum to discuss the political future of their people. The conference was attended by 390 Nuba participants, representing delegates from Government-controlled areas, including the leaders of the Nuba Mountains Alliance Parties, the SPLM/A-controlled areas, and representatives of the Nuba in diaspora from Europe, USA, and Canada. It was also attended by key SPLM/A leaders from the Southern Blue Nile and Abyei, some international observers, including the IGAD, the Joint Military Commission (JMC), donors, journalists, and some international NGOs representatives.

What was most important was the unexpected arrival of the late Dr. John Garang, the leader of the SPLM/A. In his address, Garang reiterated the unequivocal commitment of the SPLM/A leadership to the primary importance of the Nuba Mountains, the Southern Blue Nile, and Abyei areas in the final resolution of the peace process. Precisely, Kauda Conference Communiqués (2003: 1) quoted Garang as saying, 'I want to reiterate the commitment of the SPLM/A to these areas. We will not let you down. Whatever agreement we reach in the IGAD we will include you.' On the basis of this strong commitment from the SPLM/A leader, the conferees issued the Kauda Conference Communiqué[17] which contains, among others, the following resolutions:

> 1. A mandate was given to the SPLM leadership to negotiate on behalf of the Nuba people in the on-going negotiations under IGAD mediation.
> 2. A strong commitment from the Nuba people for unambiguous alignment with the SPLM during the interim period as the only means to create the opportunity for a democratic and unimpeded process of self-determination.
> 3. The endorsement of the IGAD process as the means to negotiate a just and secure peace in the three contested areas, but only as part of a comprehensive settlement for the whole of Sudan.

Both the Kampala and Kauda conferences had one common objective. They aimed to address the political future of the Nuba people in the light of the then ongoing peace negotiations in Machakos, Kenya. Both agreed that the question of the three contested areas must be resolved in the IGAD forum in the context of an overall peace settlement for the Sudan problem. However, a careful scrutiny of the two forums' declarations reveals sharp differences in their positions, of which at least two can be highlighted.

First, the Kauda declaration gave a full mandate to the SPLM leadership to negotiate on behalf of the Nuba in Machakos, while the Kampala declaration called for the genuine representation of Nuba political forces and civil society organizations in the negotiations process.

---

[17] For the full text of the communiqué, see http://www.nubasurvival.com/Nuba%20Vision/Vol%202%20Issue%202/7%20Kauda%20Conference%20Communiqu%E9.htm, retrieved 4 March 2008.

Second, while the Kampala Declaration called for full regional autonomous rule during the interim period, with an acknowledgement of self-determination as a universal right for all, the Kauda declaration demanded that the Nuba should be part of the South during the interim period and have the right to self-determination.

The diverse positions expressed by Nuba political and social groups showed some significant disparities on the political future of the region. Nonetheless, the international community, the SPLM, and the IGAD mediators were all convinced that the inclusion of the three contested areas in the negotiations was a prerequisite for a comprehensive and lasting peace in Sudan. However, this shared conviction was stubbornly and constantly contested by the GOS before it gave in after enormous and unyielding pressure from the international community and the SPLM/A. It finally accepted the discussion and the settlement of the question of the contested areas as part and parcel of the envisaged comprehensive peace agreement. Accordingly, the final peace deal included two special protocols on (i) the Nuba Mountains and the Southern Blue Nile, and (ii) Abyei.

The Comprehensive Peace Agreement and Nuba disappointment

The signing of the Comprehensive Peace Agreement (CPA) in Nairobi, Kenya, on 9 January 2005, brought an end to one of the longest and bloodiest civil wars in the recent history of Africa. It consists of six protocols/agreements and two appendices of implementation modalities:[18] (i) The Machakos; (ii) Power Sharing; (iii) Wealth Sharing; (iv) The Resolution of the Abyei Conflict; (v) The Resolution of the Conflict in the Two States of Southern Kordofan/Nuba Mountains and the Southern Blue Nile; (vi) Security Arrangements Agreement; (vii) Permanent Ceasefire and Security Arrangements Implementation Modalities and Appendices; and (viii) Implementation Modalities and Global Implementation Matrix and Appendices (see Government of Sudan and SPLM/A 2005).

This section is not intended as an analysis or assessment of the CPA (see International Crisis Group 2007),[19] but rather to highlight some relevant aspects found in two of the protocols, the first on Wealth Sharing and

---

[18] For the full text of the various Protocols that constitute the Comprehensive Peace Agreement, see http://www.reliefweb.int/rw/RWFiles2005.nsf/FilesByRWDocUNIDFileName/EVIU-6AZBDB-sud-sud-09janPart%20II.pdf/$File/sud-sud-09janPart%20II.pdf, retrieved 28 May 2008. For the implementation modalities, see http://www.reliefweb.int/rw/RWFiles2005.nsf/FilesByRWDocUNIDFileName/EVIU-6AZBDB-sud-sud-09janPart%20III.pdf/$File/sud-sud-09janPart%20III.pdf, retrieved 4 March 2008.

[19] For some analyses and assessments of the CPA, see International Crisis Group Report (July 2007), online at http://www.crisisgroup.org/home/index.cfm?id=4961, retrieved 4 June 2008; The Presidency of Republic of Sudan: Implementation of CPA: Progress Report (2007), online at http://home.planet.nl/%7Eende0098/Articles/20070920.html, retrieved 4 June 2008.

second, on the Resolution of the Conflict in the two States of Southern Kordofan/Nuba Mountains and the Southern Blue Nile. These are the sections dealing with the question of land and the political status of the Nuba Mountains region. Nonetheless, a brief review of salient features of the CPA's protocols/agreements is necessary.

The Machakos Protocol, signed on 20 July 2002, was a framework agreement upon which all the subsequent agreements and protocols were negotiated. In its preamble, the two parties recognized the historical injustices and inequalities in development between the different regions of the Sudan that required a genuine effort to redress. Moreover, the two parties agreed on the nature of the relationship between state and religion during the interim period. The most significant breakthrough in the Machakos Protocol, however, was the agreement of the two parties that the people of South have the right to self-determination, *inter alia*, through a referendum to determine their future status at the end of the interim period. This self-determination was agreed on the grounds that the unity of the Sudan, based on the will of its people, democratic governance, accountability, equality, respect, and justice for all citizens of the Sudan is and shall be the priority of the parties, and that it is possible to redress the grievances of the people of South Sudan and to meet their aspirations within such a framework (see Machakos Protocol 2002: 3). Although it is true that the unity of the country was made a priority for both parties, it is equally true that self-determination, through an internationally monitored referendum, could lead to its disintegration.

The Power Sharing Protocol, signed on 26 May 2004, endorses decentralization and empowerment of all levels of governance as key mechanisms of effective and fair administration of the country. Towards that end, it specified in detail the executive and legislative powers pertaining to each level of governance during a six-year interim period (2005–2011). It created four interlinked administrative layers of governance and administration in the country: Federal, Southern Sudan, State, and local levels of government. It outlined the government structures during the interim period led by the Government of National Unity, and based on the Interim National Constitution.

During the interim period, the two signatories to the CPA, the National Congress Party (NCP) and the SPLM, have dominated most of the executive and legislative powers at different levels of governance, though in varying degrees. On the one hand, the NCP has enjoyed a big majority in the Government of National Unity (hereafter GONU) and the governments of the Northern State, including the two contested States of the Nuba Mountains and Southern Blue Nile. On the other hand, the SPLM enjoys an overwhelming majority in the Government of the Southern Sudan (hereafter GOSS) as well as in the governments of the Southern Sudan States. Other political forces have been under-represented or remain without participation in the CPA-driven government.

The Security Arrangements Agreement provided for an internationally monitored ceasefire with the involvement of UN military peacekeeping forces. It detailed the process of redeployment, disarmament, demobilization, and reintegration of the forces of the two warring parties and their respective militia forces. In the case of the contested area of Abyei, a special administrative status was established for the interim period under direct supervision of the Presidency. Significantly, the residents of Abyei will cast a separate ballot to decide whether their area retains its special administrative status in the north or becomes part of Bahr el Ghazal and thus part of southern Sudan. This right is to be exercised under the Abyei Referendum Commission, but simultaneously with that of southern Sudan.

WEALTH SHARING PROTOCOL AND LAND QUESTION

Land, in its wider context, is the primary source of wealth for local communities and the state alike. In view of this, the CPA dealt with the question of land and natural resources through a separate protocol. However, a critical look at the relevant sections reveals that the question of customary communal land rights was not fully addressed, despite the primacy of the land factor in triggering and subsequently perpetuating the civil war. The Wealth Sharing protocol highlighted the traditional nature of land tenure arrangements, but it avoided any explicit resolution of the core issue: customary communal land rights. Article (2), entitled 'Ownership of Land and Natural Resources', stipulates that:

> 2.1. Without prejudice to the positions of the Parties with regard to ownership of land and subterranean natural resources, including Southern Sudan, this agreement is not intended to address the ownership of those resources. The parties agree to establish a process to resolve this issue.
> 2.3. The parties record that the regulation of land tenure, usage and exercise of rights in land is to be a concurrent competency exercised at the appropriate levels of government.
> 2.5. The parties agree that a process be instituted to progressively develop and amend the relevant laws to incorporate customary laws and practices, local heritage and international trends and practices.

The main institutions stipulated in the CPA to deal with land issues during the interim period are Land Commissions at national, Southern Sudan, Southern Kordofan, and Blue Nile States levels. According to the CPA, Article 2 in the Wealth Sharing Protocol of 2004, (Ownership of Land and Natural Resources), the functions of a Land Commission at any level, should be representative and independent, and should, at their discretion, and among others:

> 1. Arbitrate between willing contending parties on claims over land, and sort out the claims, and the decisions it arrived at shall be binding on the two parties; but on a basis of mutual consent and upon registration of the award in a court of law.
> 2. Apply the law applicable in the locality where the land is situated.
> 3. Recommend to the relevant government level concerning land reform policies, and recognition of customary rights and/or law.

4. Assess appropriate land compensation in monetary or in kind, for applicants in the course of arbitration or in the course of a reference from a court.

5. Advise different levels of government on how to co-ordinate policies on national projects.

6. Study and record land use practices in areas where natural resource exploitation occurs.

The Protocols offer no direct solutions or guarantees for securing ownership rights for the communally owned lands or for incorporating customary land rights, practices, and laws in the new legislation envisaged in the CPA. Instead, the final settlement of land issues was left to the judgment of the Land Commissions. It seems the political sensitivity of the land question in Sudan deterred the two parties from addressing it in depth in the CPA: the two parties were fully aware of their divergent and uncompromising positions. It was mentioned earlier that the Sudan Government continued, and is still willing, to adopt a systematic policy of land grabbing, based on statutory laws, with no legal recognition of customary land rights. Contrary to government policy, the SPLM advocates the recognition of customary land rights as legal rights in statutory laws for collective and individual land claims.

A Sudanese expert on land tenure, Egemi (2006: 1), stresses the political dimension of the land question when he states that

> Its political implications are acute enough so that the peace processes in Sudan have not dared to address the question of land in any depth, deferring much of the work to the post-agreement phase. One of the principal root causes of conflict has therefore been sacrificed to political expediency, remaining unresolved in order not to jeopardize the immediate cessation of hostilities.

Moreover, several academics and practitioners have criticised the CPA for leaving several land issues unresolved.[20] These are:

First, the recommendations of the Land Commissions at various levels of the state administration are not binding on the governments' land policy.

Second, the CPA does not provide for a mechanism that would guarantee the representation of the stakeholders, particularly traditional farmers and nomadic groups in the initiation, formulation, implementation, and evaluation of desired land policy reforms.

Third, it is not clear how such claims to land rights are to be submitted, resubmitted, legitimated, or contested, and whether such claims are to be made on an individual or collective basis, and, if collectively, who represents the communities concerned, and whether that representation should be on the basis of legality or legitimacy.

Fourth, the CPA is silent about the importance of the historical roles and positions of the native administration and grassroots community

---

[20] Reference can be made here to the works of Polloni (2005), Imam and Egemi (2004), Pantuliano (2007), Pantuliano et al., (2007) and Komey (2008a, 2008b, 2009b, 2010b).

leaders in communal land management and, subsequently, about their key roles in resolving land-driven conflicts.

Fifth, in the absence of clear-cut solutions or guarantees in the CPA on issues related to customary land rights, there are uncertainties concerning the nature of laws upon which arbitration will be based, the recognition of customary law, the enforceability of verdicts on land and alternatives for redress in case a commission refuses to consider a claim.

Sixth, despite the fact that the Government of National Unity has been in operation since 2005, the National Land Commission, which was formed after long delay, has not been able to function because of disagreement over the Act.

As a result, no progress has been made on enacting new legislation aimed at incorporating customary land rights in conformity with the CPA. In this respect, a recent report tends to suggest that the GONU was, and still is, unwilling to address effectively the question of land ownership, not only before and during the peace negotiations, but also during the implementation phase of the CPA. The report (Pantuliano et al., 2007: 27) asserts that.

> Because of its complexity, the CPA defers the problem of land ownership to the post-agreement phase. It does not address the ownership of land and natural resources, but institutes a process to resolve this question through the establishment of a National Land Commission and a Southern State Land Commission and State Land Commissions in Southern Kordofan and Blue Nile. However, neither the National Land Commission nor the State Land Commissions in transitional areas have been established as part of the implementation of the CPA.

Finally, the aggregate ramifications of shortcomings listed above, built into the Wealth Protocol of the CPA, suggest that the grievances of the majority of sedentary and nomadic communities pertaining to customary land rights are likely not to be redressed in the foreseeable future, for lack of political will.

THE PROTOCOL ON THE RESOLUTION OF CONFLICT IN THE TWO AREAS

In the Protocol on the Resolution of Conflict in Southern Kordofan and Blue Nile States signed on 26 May 2004, and thereafter referred to as the 'Protocol of Southern Kordofan and Blue Nile States', the two parties agreed on certain modalities and principles as the basis for political, administrative, economic, and social solutions to the conflict in the two regions. These principles were enshrined in the State Interim Constitution of 2006, including, among others, that:

> 1. The State shares two percent (2%) of the oil produced in its territory;
> 2. Seventy-five percent (75%) of the total fund designated to the war-affected areas are to be allocated to the two states;
> 3. During the interim period, power sharing in each of the states is to be allocated as follows: fifty-five percent (55%) of the executive and legislative powers to the National Congress Party and forty-five (45%) to the SPLM;

4. The two states shall exercise the right for 'popular consultation' to assess the effectiveness of the protocol in redressing their political and socio-economic grievances;

5. A Land Commission at state level shall be established in each of the two states to redress the land question in close coordination with National Land Commission; and that

6. The definition and the naming of the region as South Kordofan or Nuba Mountains shall be settled.[21]

The last three points are the most relevant to this discussion. Naming the region as Southern Kordofan or Nuba Mountains was hotly debated during the peace negotiation between the GOS and the SPLM. While the former insisted on 'South Kordofan' as a formal name for the region, the latter made constant reference to the 'Nuba Mountains' as a historical name. As detailed in Chapter 1, for at least more than six centuries, the geographical area where the Nuba tribes live in southern Kordofan has been known as Dar Nuba, i.e., Nuba homeland. In addition, the region was formally named Nuba Mountains Province from 1914–1928: only in 1929 was the name Nuba Mountains abolished and the area amalgamated with Kordofan under the new official name of Southern Kordofan District.

During the formal peace negotiations, no agreement was reached on the question of the region's name. However, the Protocol of Southern Kordofan and Blue Nile States (2004: 2, foot note 1) indicated that 'the name of the State shall be settled before the conclusion of the Peace Agreement by a committee representing the State, formed by the two Parties'. Surprisingly, with no indication as to how and when the issue was settled, it was stated in the Implementation Modalities of the same protocol that 'the name of the State shall be Southern Kordofan and its Capital shall be Kadugli'.[22] For the Nuba, that was and still is a disappointing resolution with far-reaching consequences for their indigenous claims in the region.

As far as the region's boundaries are concerned, the Protocol of Southern Kordofan and Blue Nile States (2004: 3) stipulated that the 'boundaries of Southern Kordofan/Nuba Mountains State shall be the same boundaries of former Southern Kordofan Province when Greater Kordofan was sub-divided into provinces' (of Northern and Southern Kordofan). This necessitated the dissolution of the existing Western Kordofan State while transferring the respective parts to either South or North Kordofan States. Initially, the Nuba wanted to add the Nuba in Lagawa area while excluding the Messiriyya in the remaining western Kordofan from their emerging state in order to strengthen their collective

---

[21] For the full text of the Protocol on the Resolution of Conflict in Southern Kordofan/Nuba Mountains and Blue Nile States, see http://www.usip.org/library/pa/sudan/nuba_bnile_05262004.pdf, retrieved 30 May 2008.

[22] See the Modalities of Implementation, Southern Kordofan Annex, Final and approved Text of 21 December 2004: 88, online at http://www.reliefweb.int/rw/RWFiles2005.nsf/FilesByRWDocUNIDFileName/EVIU-6AZBDB-sud-sud-09janPart%20III.pdf/$File/sud-sud-09janPart%20III.pdf, retrieved 29 March 2008.

movement as a united ethno-political entity. The attempt would have given the Nuba an overwhelming majority in the region, an important requirement for controlling the outcome of the anticipated 'popular consultation'.

However, the Nuba attempt was jeopardized by the ruling NCP when it succeeded in adding the entire Western Kordofan, including the Messiriyya, to South Kordofan State. In this way, the NCP was able to suppress the Nuba's wishes while reinforcing the political and demographic influences of the Baqqara Arabs in the region. By doing so, the CPA added a new complexity to Baqqara–Nuba tensions in the post-conflict situation, with far-reaching repercussions.

What is more, the CPA reduced the struggle of the Nuba people for the right to self-determination to an ambiguous phrase: 'popular consultation'. The term has no standard legal or political definition or connotation. Commander Ismail Khamis Jalab (Ende 2006b: 2), the Chairman of the SPLM and the then Governor of Southern Kordofan State (2005–2006), confirmed that 'Our objective was that the Nuba Mountains should have self-determination. Instead, the CPA came with something called Popular Consultation, of which [sic] we are not even sure what it means'.[23]

To be precise, the CPA diminished Nuba political options to be part of South Sudan or North Sudan or to form their own state if the South opted for secession, by using a loosely defined form of political exercise that would give only limited voice to their views on the Comprehensive Peace Agreement (see Protocol of Southern Kordofan and Blue Nile States 2004: 4). The crux of the matter is that the outlined procedures and principles that would determine the views of the people in the region contain a self-defeating mechanism, particularly for the Nuba. Thus, the protocol stipulates that:

> Should any of the legislatures of the two States, after reviewing the Agreement, decide to rectify, within the framework of the Agreement, any shortcomings in the constitutional, political and administrative arrangements of the Agreement, then such legislature shall engage in negotiations with the National Government with the view of rectifying these shortcomings. (Protocol of Southern Kordofan and Blue Nile States 2004: 5)

Three crucial points can be noted here. First it is clear that the right of the people of the region to rectify the agreement is restricted to 'within the framework of the Agreement'. But, in the Nuba view, it is this very framework which needs to be challenged if a rectification is to be made.

Second, in all circumstances, the National Government is likely to be effectively controlled by the dominant ruling elites of northern Sudan, who have a consistent record of intolerance on the recognition of indigenous peoples' rights, including those of the Nuba. An engagement in

---

[23] For the full text of an interview with Ismael Khamis Jalab, conducted by Nanne op't Ende in Kadugli on 13 March and in Khartoum on 15 April, 2006, see http://home.planet.nl/~ende0098/Articles/20060428.htm, retrieved 8 March 2008.

negotiations with such a government will unquestionably lead to further undermining and suppression of such rights and to the further economic underdevelopment and socio-cultural marginalization of the people.

Third, the NCP enjoys a majority of 55%, as opposed to 45% for the SPLM, in the power sharing plan during the interim period in the region. Obviously, this creates overwhelming political control of the Southern Kordofan State for the Baqqara Arabs and some Nuba loyal to the NCP. In this way, they can exercise a powerful influence on the process, to procure an outcome from 'popular consultation' in favour of the wishes of the central government.

With regard to the question of land rights, the agreement stipulated the formation of a State Land Commission that 'shall be competent to review existing leases and contracts, and examine the criteria for the present land allocations, and recommend to the State authority the introduction of such necessary changes, including restitution of land rights or compensation' (Protocol of Southern Kordofan and Blue Nile States 2004: 13).

Towards that end, the SPLM proposed explicit articulation of the following two crucial land rights principles in the State Interim Constitution: (i) recognition of customary primary land ownership as a legal right for the individual, the family, the group, or local communities settled in the region and (ii) recognition of customary secondary rights of the nomadic communities to have access to their seasonal grazing lands without jeopardizing the primary rights of the sedentary groups.[24] However, these principles were seriously challenged by the NCP. Given its majority in power sharing in the legislative and executive structures of the Southern Kordofan State, the NCP was able to obstruct the inclusion of these fundamental land rights in the State Interim Constitution.

In sum, the CPA in general, and the Protocol of Southern Kordofan and Blue Nile States in particular, have inadequately addressed the Nuba's main political and socio-economic grievances, including the land question. Moreover, the establishment of the Southern Kordofan State Land Commission has been delayed. The lack of NCP political will to address the land question effectively indicates its desire to maintain a policy of land-grabbing from rural communities for investments in mechanized farming and oil projects. Apart from bringing an end to the formal war, the CPA seems to have failed to redress its root causes in the region. It has not provided any real opportunities for de-marginalization and development. Most importantly, it has left the Nuba people in political disarray. This gloomy post-conflict situation is expressively summarized by Jan Pronk (2006: 1), the UN Special Envoy for Sudan Peace at that time:

> Since its inception, peace has not brought much development to the people of South Kordofan. Poverty prevails. This could very well result in a feeling

---

[24] For more details on the SPLM position pertaining to the question of land rights in the Nuba Mountains, see the Arabic version of the SPLM's Proposal of Southern Kodofan State Interim Constitution (2005: 38–40).

of dissatisfaction and frustration and is an indication to take up arms again. The future status of South Kordofan has not been unequivocally established in the CPA. Will it belong to the North or to the South, after the people of Southern Sudan will have used their right of self-determination in the referendum foreseen in 2011? [...] the CPA has only stipulated that their future status should be determined by a consultative process. When? Between whom? How? Nobody knows.[25]

The author's study of the post-conflict situation in the region, presented in the following two chapters, reinforces this gloomy picture. It reveals, beyond doubt, that Nuba political dissatisfaction and insecurity about their livelihoods, coupled with land-based conflicts, have increased to an unprecedented scale and frequency after the uneasy implementation of the CPA.

Nuba responses to the CPA: a discourse analysis

This section traces some major political responses taken by the Nuba in reaction to the final outcome of the CPA. At present, a sizeable number of the Nuba holds the view that fundamental questions regarding their identity, territory, and political destiny have not been satisfactorily dealt with in the CPA. The previously quoted UN Special Envoy, Jan Pronk, said, 'the stories of the Nuba people will make us understand that there is still a long way ahead. But there is no way back' (Pronk 2006, 2). Today, one distinctive aspect of Nuba political rhetoric on the negative outcome of the CPA is their slogan: 'the struggle continues'.

During the peace negotiations, the Nuba hoped that the root causes of their armed struggle would be genuinely addressed. Contrary to their expectations, the Nuba were and still are disappointed with the outcome of the CPA. Indeed, 'the protocol of solving the conflict in Blue Nile and Southern Kordofan doesn't address all issues: it has several loopholes and there are so many questions unanswered regarding the Southern Kordofan. We had wanted it to be more like the protocols that address the issue of the South Sudan,' says Khamis Jalab, the chairman of the SPLM and the Governor of Southern Kordofan State 2005–2006 (see Ende 2006b: 2).

In reaction, Nuba leadership in the SPLM has embarked on a set of political and socio-economic initiatives. The aim is to safeguard CPA achievements while transforming its weaknesses into further possible strengths. The Nuba Land Action Strategy, 2004, outlined below, is one such. However, the Second All Nuba Conference, held in Kauda, Nuba Mountains, 6–8 April 2005, just three months after the CPA, was the major event that shaped Nuba political responses. It has acted as a significant 'road map' for Nuba political discourse during the post-conflict situation of the CPA's transitional period, ending in 2011.

---

[25] For the full text, see http://www.janpronk.nl/papers/no-way-back.html, retrieved 9 March 2008.

In these two events, SPLM political and social leaders have called on Nuba identities, strongly linked to their ancestral homeland, in order to unite their people as an ethno-political body, empowered to hold key collective and strategic positions in the post-war era. Specific forms of belonging, rather than 'civic citizenship', are drawn from their ethnic, indigenous or even autochthonous roots (also see Komey 2009a, 2009b).

THE SECOND ALL NUBA CONFERENCE AND ASSESSMENT OF THE CPA

The Second All Nuba Conference of 2005 was devoted to assessing the CPA, its impact on the Nuba struggle, and possible scenarios emerging in the post-war situation. It was attended by about 800 representatives of the Nuba people from all walks of life, including the Nuba diaspora in Europe (Holland, France, and the UK), Australia, Canada, USA, Japan, some Arab and African countries, and from different parts of the Sudan. At the heart of their agenda were (i) the assessment of the CPA, (iii) Nuba unity, (iii) the land question, (iv) Nuba heritage and cultural identity, and (v) development in the Nuba Mountains region (see Final Communiqué of Second All Nuba Conference 2005).[26] The conferees thoroughly assessed the CPA and enumerated its pros and cons from a Nuba perspective.

On the one hand, the CPA was perceived as a positive turning point in the recent political history of the Nuba people. The conferees recognized that the CPA had brought an end to the war and provided a basis for destroying the 'old Sudan' and establishing the 'new Sudan'. For the Nuba, it had put an end to external domination and restored their dignity and internal integrity. Precisely, the conferees acknowledged the following positive points in the CPA: (i) the designated share of wealth for the region, (ii) the decentralization and democratization of powers providing opportunities for the participation of local communities in the administration of their own affairs, (iii) the recognition of national languages, cultural identities, and religious freedom, and (iv) the articulation of the right of 'popular consultation' for the people of the region (Final Communiqué of Second All Nuba Conference 2005).

On the other hand, the conferees identified some shortcomings in the CPA including the denial of the Nuba's demand for rights to self-determination, and their right to rename the region with its historical appellation (the Nuba Mountains). They noted with disappointment that the CPA suppressed the right to compensate local communities who were and still are affected by expanding mechanized farming and oil extraction, with a pipeline that passes through the region's traditional livelihood base; and that the CPA is silent with regard to the atrocities, gross human rights violations and acts of genocide and ethnocide committed by the GOS during the war against the Nuba. Furthermore, the CPA favoured the

---

[26] For the full text of the Final Communiqué of the All Nuba Second Conference, see http://www.sudantribune.com/spip.php?article9487, retrieved 10 March 2008.

Baqqara Messiriyya of the dissolved Western Kordofan State in the distribution of national wealth. It has allocated 2% of net oil revenue produced in their area to the Messiriyya while excluding the Nuba, who coexist with them in the same area. This is a clear case of the state discriminating against its own citizens on the basis of ethnic categorization.

The conferees feared that these negative points might offset and subsequently jeopardize the CPA achievements at large. In the light of these shortcomings, among others, they urged the Nuba to show zeal and political commitment towards 'popular consultation' as a mechanism that may provide an opportunity for the Nuba to rectify the drawbacks of the CPA.

Since existing state land policy offers no legal recognition to customary communal land, the conferees concluded that the CPA did not meet the Nuba's aspiration for legal recognition of their collective or individual customary land claims. They called for a Nuba collective and community-based movement as the only viable option to secure and control their ancestral land. They also reiterated that the Nuba local communities, with their different social organizations, are the real owners of the land, inherited from their forefathers according to custom and tradition since time immemorial. The conferees made a plea that:

> All tribes are requested to maintain and protect their boundaries under the auspices of native authorities. Tribal boundaries must be checked and negotiated before being fixed. This is to ensure that there is no 'no-man's land' and that intertribal boundaries are direct and concrete. At the same time, different neighbouring tribes must encourage intertribal complementarities through land use including settlements. This process is instrumental for the unity and eventual integration of the whole Nuba people. (Final Communiqué Second All Nuba Conference 2005: 9)

TOWARDS NUBA LAND STRATEGY AFTER THE CPA

Shortly after the Second All Nuba Conference, a workshop on land issues was organized in Kauda, 30–31 May 2005. The main objective was to avert any possible intertribal conflicts and tensions while embarking on a boundary-fixing process. At the end of the workshop, the following points, among others, were emphasized as matters of great concern:

> 1. There is a need for mutual recognition of exercising control over the traditional tribal land by the tribal authorities which regulate and guarantee use rights for all citizens in the territory.
> 2. All individuals or groups of people who encroached or who were forced to be relocated into others' land should abide with the customs governing that tribal community, and they shall have no rights to inherit the land they have occupied under such circumstances.
> 3. Tribes with no abundant land may utilize other tribal land in accordance with the custom and tradition regulating the hosting community.
> 4. Tribal boundaries shall be negotiated and fixed through peaceful arrangements governed by tribal customs and traditions. (SPLM 2004: 1–3)

The Rashad County workshop was soon followed by the Traditional

Leaders' First Conference held in Julud, 17–22 June 2005. Three main issues were deliberated: peaceful co-existence between the communities in the Nuba Mountains including the Baqqara Arabs, the role of traditional authorities in the New Sudan, and the question of land:

> It was recognized by all the participants that land laws and land distributions undertaken since the 1970s, and especially in 1983, were intended to disown and displace the people of the Nuba Mountains. It was felt that new laws would be required to redress the injustices of the past and that wronged parties would have to be compensated. (Nabudere 2005: 2)

It is worth noting that the positions taken at the Second All Nuba Conference, the resolutions pertaining to the question of Nuba communal land rights, and subsequent actions have been much influenced by the Nuba Land Action Strategy of 2004. The strategy is critically analysed below as part of the Nuba response to the apparent failure of the CPA to address the land issue.

Nuba Land Strategy
as a base for ethno-political identity and unity

The assessment of the CPA has already revealed that the question of communal land rights was treated ambiguously despite its key role in extending the civil war into the region. In response, the Nuba evoked their autochthonous identity politics, a strong attachment that has persisted through the civil war, and continues to inspire their political struggle thereafter. The 'SPLM Nuba Land Action Strategy' is one of the manifestations of such political struggle.

As argued elsewhere (Komey 2009b: 7) 'Nuba Land Strategy' was perceived as an operational dimension of the Nuba's emerging collective movement in the post-conflict situation. It projects Nuba as a territory-based, unified socio-political entity, capable of taking strategic collective actions including securing their communal lands. The intrinsic link between Nuba *identity* and *territory* is crucial to their collective socio-cultural, political and economic survival.

This land strategy is focused on a process of identification, negotiation, and fixation of tribal boundaries. It envisages the mapping and eventual registration of tribal land as common property, possessed in undivided shares by all members of the community (SPLM 2004: 4). However, in a traditional situation where tribal boundaries always remain loose and flexible, the challenge is how to negotiate fluidity in boundaries while under pressure to fix them. Such flexibility has its own logic in a long history of tribal interactions along the region's frontiers. The difficulty in fixing such fluid boundaries stems from the long history of ethnic intermixing, while competing. This co-existence is manifested in the pattern of neighbourhoods, shifting cultivation, and shared natural resources, particularly water resources. Inevitably these flexibilities have been coupled with various land-based conflicts and an overall political fragility before, during, and after the civil war.

The Nuba Land Strategy was facilitated by land tenure specialists from the 'Land and Natural Resources Project for the Contested Areas of the Nuba Mountains and the Southern Blue Nile', and funded by the USAID/USDA. It was divided into ten sequential stages ranging from 'laying foundation', 'mobilizing community', 'identifying community land area', 'confirming and mapping the boundary', 'establishing local land authority', to 'registering common properties', among others (see SPLM 2004). The strategy was meant to empower Nuba communities in administering their claimed lands. Specifically, it has sought to institutionalize and legalize communal land rights through various means including (i) protecting all existing customary land interests; (ii) legalization of the registration of the communally owned land as such under modern common hold tenure; and (iii) legal recognition of two different types of customary land rights: customary ownership rights for the indigenous Nuba people; and customary use access rights for nomadic groups with longstanding seasonal access to the same lands (see SPLM 2004: 1).

A Customary Land Office was established within the SPLM/A political-administrative structure. The office's main role is to act as a catalyst to empower Nuba communities in negotiating, identifying, fixing, and eventually mapping their respective tribal land boundaries. To make the strategy operational, a set of step-by-step guidelines was made available to each tribal land committee, in the following sequence:

(1) Each tribal community identifies its perceived boundary. Certain indications are considered as supportive evidence to the boundary identification process.
(2) The identified boundaries are then negotiated and perhaps undergo some adjustment, with the Customary Land Office team acting as technical facilitator, mediator, and secretariat during the different stages of the negotiation process.
(3) A map of the agreed boundaries is then drawn using the information which the concerned committees had made a consensus.
(4) The community seeks and receives provisional registration of the community land area.
(5) The committee negotiates occupancy by non-locals who have long-standing rights.
(6) If they accept that they live within the concerned tribal territory, a final map is made.
(7) A Community Land Council is established as trustees and manager of the land.
(8) The Community Land Council seeks final declaration of its area and its authority from the State Land Commission.
(9) If successful, the Land Commission devolves state ownership of the land to the community, naming the Council as trustees and manager of the community land.
(10) Where the submission is contested, the Land Commission considers

the case. It may require that some modifications to the proposed community land area are made. (see SPLM 2004)

Despite these clear steps, the implementation process faced serious challenges. One obvious implication is that, in theory, boundary fixation does not aim at the exclusion of one neighbouring Nuba tribe by another. Rather, it aims at effective control and management of tribal land and its natural resources. It is meant to consolidate the collective identity and political unity sought by the Nuba vis-à-vis the 'other'. In practice, however, tribal boundary fixation seems to have caused serious tensions and disunity among some Nuba themselves.

In order to involve the communities in implementing the strategy, a series of public awareness and mobilization campaigns were launched through communal/tribal conferences,[27] workshops, and community leaders' meetings. Pantuliano et al. (2007) reported that the process first started in former SPLM/A-controlled areas, namely in Rashad County,[28] before its gradual expansion into some hill communities in former GOS-controlled areas.

To a large extent, the implementation of the strategy relies on the communities, particularly in the process of boundary identification, negotiation, and fixation. The experience of the Heiban-Aboll community illustrates how the Nuba land strategy evolved from a top-down approach to the community level. Most importantly, it shows how difficult it is to fix a tribal boundary with a long history of flexibility.

At the Third Heiban-Aboll Tribal Conference, 13–16 April 2005, a substantial period of time was devoted to debating and adopting some of the resolutions of the second conference. The first to be adopted were those on securing tribal land boundaries. The members of the 'land boundary committee' were carefully selected among the most experienced and knowledgeable elders in land affairs before they were given the tasks of tracing the historical geographical boundary of the Heiban 'Umudiya, often by identifying supporting material evidence from human and natural landscape features.

One year later, the committee delivered a progress report to the Fourth Heiban-Aboll Tribal Conference held in Heiban, 10–13 April 2006. It outlined its achievements and difficulties in the process of negotiating boundaries with neighbouring tribes, namely the Shuwai in the west, the Otoro in the south, the Leira in the north, northwest, and northeast, and the Tira in the southeast. Contrary to the land strategy

---

[27] The author was able to trace, through a 'participant observations approach', numerous Nuba tribal conferences, including Heiban-Aboll Third Conference in Kobang, 13–16 April 2005; Leira Third Conference in Hagar Bago, 16–18 April 2005; Irral Payam Conference in Shuwai, 21–22 April 2005; Korongo-Messakin Tribes Conference in Farandella, Buram County, 29 May – 1 June 2005; the All Keiga Second Conference, Keiga Tummero, 12–14 April 2006 and the Temein Third Conference, 13–18 April 2007.

[28] The administrative divisions in the SPLM/A-controlled areas start with the County (Rashad, Kadugli, Lagawa and Dilling). Each county is composed of Payams, e.g. Rashad County includes Ildo of Tira, Kombor of Otoro, Iral for Aboll, Leira and Shuwai, and Kawalib for the Kawalib tribe. It is composed of 76 villages and has an estimated population of 200,000. In each Payam the number of villages ranges from 3 in the case of *Tulushi* Payam to 37 in the case of *Saraf Jamus* Payam in Kadugli County. (NMPACT 2002: 3)

objective, the report emphasised the difficulties in attempting to fix tribal boundaries which had remained fluid for centuries.

Despite the fact that the Land Office and the tribal leaders exerted tremendous precautionary efforts, the boundary fixing process gave rise to several disputes, between different neighbouring tribes on an unprecedented scale in their long history of co-existence. The author's ethnographic observations in the field between 2005 and 2007 indicate that the work of the boundary committees has been significantly hampered by intertribal differences over boundaries. Thus, instead of uniting the Nuba communities, empirical material shows that land strategy actions have triggered intertribal antagonism, disunity, and major disputes over control, access, and ownership of borderlands among the Nuba.

Several disputes have occurred among neighbouring communities in Rashad County, particularly among the five tribes of the greater Heiban area: (i) Otoro and Shwai, (ii) Otoro and Tira, (iii) Otoro and Heiban-Aboll, and (iv) Leira and Heiban-Aboll. Although most of these disputes remained at a low level, some escalated to the point of intertribal fighting. For instance, a dispute erupted a few years ago between the Otoro and Shwai communities over the contested border area of Debe. In 2007, fighting broke out between these two communities, resulting in several deaths and a number of injuries on both sides. The very reports of these intertribal land-based tensions caused problems, as noted by Pantuliano et al. (2007: 28):

> [...] the [land strategy] process was enthusiastically supported, but it has also created a number of problems because it has led communities to believe that their land is now officially registered. This has heightened tension between Nuba communities living in 'border areas', such as Ghulfan and Timaeen in Dilling locality and Atoro-Lira-Abul in the Heiban area.

Instead of securing the collectively claimed land, it is suggested that the very strategy is stirring feelings of disunity among the Nuba themselves.

Tribal boundaries:
a challenge to the Nuba ethno-political unity

One major finding explored in Chapters 1, 2, and 3 is that almost all the plains and fertile Nuba land were either occupied by the Baqqara or systematically grabbed by Jillaba investors linked to the state. It is this type of land, and not the hilly areas, which has been historically and still is a major source of Nuba grievance and a central cause of their armed struggle. Therefore, unless the plains and fertile land are placed at the centre of any land strategy, the question of the communal land rights in the region will not be effectively addressed in the foreseeable future. In direct contradiction of this obvious factor, Nuba land strategy has been focused on the hilly areas, far away from Baqqara habitation and well beyond the interests of state and private investments, whether in mechanized farming or oil extraction. This counter-strategy has shifted the fight over land from one between the Nuba as a collective unit versus the state and non-Nuba groups, to open conflict between the Nuba groups.

The notion of tribal boundary fixing built into the Nuba Land Action Strategy seems to counteract the aim of consolidating Nuba ethno-political unity because of its incompatibility with the history of flexible tribal boundaries. Any attempt leads inevitably to conflicting versions of oral narratives from each claimant. According to Lentz (2007: 43)

> In oral cultures, which lack maps [...] territorial boundaries have to be constantly interpreted and reaffirmed through narratives and rituals. Indeed, narratives are central to the constitution of property because they help to build consensus. Yet narratives are also crucial for articulating challenges to existing property rights.

In supporting their respective claims, different Nuba claimants make excessive references to non-existing (mental) maps of their tribal boundaries dating back over centuries. Such oral narratives are very difficult to trace or prove: available archives and records offer very little when it comes to official maps of tribal land boundaries in colonial and post-colonial Sudan. Despite this, every claimant insists that there has been a map since colonial times for their orally described tribal boundaries and such claims are widely shared among Nuba communities. Several works point to this problem, including Vicars-Miles in 1934 (Sudan Archive 1934: Ref.: SAD 631/10/62), Harragin (2003: 8), and Komey (2008: 108–11). Vicars-Miles, a District Commissioner with long work experience in the Heiban area, testified that 'When the Government first started there [in the Nuba Mountains], few settled boundaries existed and it was not necessary to define them to any great extent; but with the development of the country they have become a more important factor' (see Sudan Archive 1934: Ref.: SAD 631/10/25).

The archival records available make clear that the mufatish (British Inspector) or the mamur (British Administrative Officer) used to set up the Nuba native authorities on the basis of hill communities with no definite but rather fluid tribal boundaries. And because these boundaries shift situationally, the British administrators made no attempt to fix them with formal mapping. Careful scrutiny of the colonial archives and literature suggests that there were no officially drawn tribal land boundaries between neighbouring hill communities. Reviewing the state of affairs in this regard in Africa with special focus on Sudan, Barbour, a well known specialist on the classic geography of Sudan, (1961: 75) concluded that:

> Boundaries between the lands of one family and another or between one village and another or even between one tribe and another generally exist and are recognized by the parties concerned, but they are not usually recorded on maps unless they happen to coincide with the boundaries of the larger administrative framework imposed on the countries by Europeans. Thus, in almost all the colonial and former colonial territories, only a strictly limited number of boundaries are shown on the topographic maps.

In spite of this, it was common for the colonial administrators to draw some explanatory sketch maps of respective hill communities as part of their informal organizational setting for managing the local peoples. For instance, an archive document at Durham University Library, which contains the 1935 Diary of G. W. Bell, the Assistant District Commissioner in Talodi, substantiates this line of argument (see Sudan Archive 1935b: SAD 698/8/31–2). The Diary contains detailed information and sketch maps of all hill communities within the Heiban sub-District. It includes lists of local leaders, the villages they administer, and tax payments demanded. To make things manageable, Bell made several sketch maps in his personal diary. After careful scrutiny of several similar administrators' diaries and personal memoirs, it is safe to suggest that perhaps those sketch and hand-drawn maps are frequently remembered and, therefore, referred to by the elders of Nuba communities today as their evidential base. The crux of the matter is that they were neither official maps nor made to authenticate such claims.

The well remembered annual campaigns of cleaning the roads on the basis of tribal lands during the colonial period and the persistent presence of some major natural barriers such as hills or water courses may sometimes establish a few more concrete boundary points. However, they are hardly sufficient for the identification of entire tribal boundaries.

Hence, any effort aimed at transforming existing flexible inter-ethnic/tribal boundaries into fixed and stable ones, for whatever reason, is likely to provoke serious communal tension between historically coexisting communities. Yet ethnic/tribal distinctions do not go hand in hand with an absence of social interaction and with a lack of mutual acceptance. Quite the contrary, ethnic and tribal distinctions, and partly even low-scale conflicts, are often the very foundation on which embracing social systems are built; and ethnic/tribal differences can persist despite inter-ethnic/tribal contact and interdependence through flexible social and spatial boundaries. The flexibility of Nuba tribal boundaries must be envisaged in itself as a source of Nuba unity. Accordingly, it should be cherished and maintained, rather than dismissed.

In short, the fluidity or flexibility and, therefore, the changeability of both social and spatial boundaries among different Nuba groups are an integral part of their cohabitation pattern. Historical tribal boundaries in the cases studied display all these characteristics, varying in population dynamics and in traditional leadership decisions on the ground at different times. This case supports an old empirically grounded and theoretically informed line of argument that social and spatial boundaries in such societies do not keep people apart: rather they are always a source of dynamic processes of social engagement through a set of economic, socio-cultural, and political fields. This perception is well-established, having been explored by several specialists, including Barth (1978, 1969/1998), and Manger (2007).

However, 'tribal boundary fixing' as a device for securing communal land rights is still problematic in the case of the Nuba Mountains. At the present stage of Nuba development, the flexibility of tribal boundaries seems to have its own logic, dictated by social, economic, political, and ecological realities. Given the prevalence of shifting cultivation as a major mode of economic livelihood among Nuba hill communities, such flexible tribal boundaries are likely to maintain their significance not only at present but also for the foreseeable future. They may continue to act as crucial socio-economic connecters and intermediary spaces, and not as barriers or dividers. This line of argument does not lead to the compromising of genuine efforts to secure the communal land rights of the Nuba people. These rights are worthy, legitimate, and central to the Nuba struggle in particular, and to the marginalized communities of the Sudan in general.

At the same time, the promotion of Nuba unity and the stability of the people's social and spatial organizations are fundamental, not only in securing their communal land rights, but also in safeguarding their identity and political destiny. The continuation of emerging intertribal tensions caused by the tribal boundary scheme is socially, economically, and politically a very disturbing phenomenon. It may jeopardize or even defeat the very purpose of empowering the Nuba to secure their communal land, a central factor in their political struggle in the past, present, and future. In view of this, a socially sound, politically desirable and practically feasible alternative land strategy must be sought if such fundamental rights are to be achieved without causing internal tensions and disunity. The aim must be to contribute to social harmony and political unity among the Nuba communities.

Conclusion

No doubt, the Sudan Comprehensive Peace Agreement as initiative, process, and final outcome was successful in putting an end to the bloodiest and longest war in the recent history of Africa. From the Nuba perspective, however, the outcome of the CPA fell far below their political expectations. It denied them the right to self-determination: it failed to address the root causes of their political and armed struggle, particularly the question of communal land rights.

In response, Nuba political and social leaders embarked on the construction of a set of political discourses and socio-economic actions. The aim was to safeguard the CPA's achievements while transforming its weaknesses into further triumph. Towards that end, they made political use of the notion of an indigenous identity strongly attached to the Nuba Mountains territory as ancestral homeland. The intention was to unite the Nuba people as an ethno-political identity capable of taking collective decisions and strategic positions in the post-war era. This activated specific forms of ethnic belonging to promote their political struggle. Tracing the dynamic trajectories of Nuba emerging identity politics, and the counteractions of other ethnic groups, provides the main themes for the following two chapters.

6

Territory, Ethnic Identity &
Boundary Making

At present the Nuba may not protest very much against the stranger within his gates; but
when we have satisfied […] his desire for education we shall be faced with a Nuba
intelligentsia demanding why, under our stewardship, their birthright [land] was given away.
(A. L. W. Vicars-Miles, in Sudan Archive 1934)

Introduction

This chapter offer an analysis of the identity politics constructed and
pursued by the sedentary Nuba as a group indigenous to the region. At
the same time, attention is paid to the nomadic Baqqara's responses
within the overall national political setting after the CPA. This analysis is
based on the author's fieldwork and theoretically informed by several
overlapping concepts such as region, territory, autochthony, indigeneity.

During the war, the Nuba were fairly successful in summoning their
perceived essential attributes in order to create a strategic unity. Such
attributes were not naturally or intrinsically essential, or, put another way,
not already in place and in use. Rather, they are constructed and invoked
when politically useful. Once these certain essential attributes were called
upon by the endangered Nuba, they were essentialized as an unfailing
link between all the Nuba, as a people belonging to a common origin and
now facing a common threat. In order to maintain unity through the
struggle, the Nuba were able to symbolize these attributes and eventually
absorb all differences between them for collective cultural and physical
survival. The focus here is on how the Nuba constructed their claim to
an autochthonous identity and how they articulated their ethno-political
identities in the struggle.

In many ways the war itself transformed the Nuba community. It
endangered their physical and cultural survival, thus accelerating the
pace of their struggle, and increased awareness amongst diverse
groups facing one common assault, manifested in the government's
Jihad against them with its active policies of genocide, ethnocide, and
land alienation. In the process of their political struggle, the Nuba
were left with no option but to create a sense of common ethnic
belonging.

On this subject, Manger (2007: 72) comments that:

> [...] the Nuba's contemporary struggle can be said to generally represent a violent phase of a situation that has always characterized the region's history and the adaptation of various regional groups. Two basic themes stand out: the one of territory, and the one of identity. Both contribute to a constant struggle of the regional population for their sovereignty and for their right to deal with their own development.

The Nuba's attachment of their identity to their region was a dominant discourse in their doctrine of liberation during the civil war, but has also remained central throughout their contemporary political struggle.

Territory/region as a basis for communal identity politics

The concept of region is fundamental because it is a basis upon which the notion of autochthony rests. I have argued elsewhere (Komey 2008b: 992–94) that region as a concept is usually loaded with social, ethnic, economic, and, thus, political meanings and symbols. Therefore, region is conceived not as a mere geographical space, but as a societal arrangement full of dynamic political, ideological, socio-cultural, and economic realities. To paraphrase Murphy (1991: 27), region is conceptualized as i) a local response to historical dynamic processes of external/internal forces and realities and ii) a focus of identification, i.e., the inter-relationship between land territory and ethnic/community identity, and iii) a medium for social interaction and for the creation of regional patterns and characteristics. Therefore, a national or sub-national territory or region is more than a spatially demarcated political or administrative unit.

> It is a source of identity and self-sustaining resources; it is an 'historic' territory, a 'homeland', a rightful possession of one's forefathers through generations. It is distinctive and a unique territory; and the identity of the nation is bound up with memory, and this memory is rooted in a homeland. (Murphy 1991: 27)

Murphy (1991) has also commented that, with the rise of the idea that societies are defined territorially, socio-cultural and political identities have become fundamentally linked to this affiliation. Given the importance of ideas about territory for the ways in which individuals and groups see themselves and the world around them, some discussion of the role of territorial affiliation is necessary within the context of the nation-building process. What lies behind the framework of political territories or formal ethnic regions are spatial constructs with deep ideological significance that may or may not correspond to political or formal constructs. These ideologies are forged in territorial struggles that produce particular regional arrangements and understandings; and these, in turn, shape ideas, practices, and the overall orientation of the group involved.

In the Sudan, a country of complex diversities in its physical and ethno-cultural landscape, the term 'region' has emerged as a self-identifying concept that serves as a focus of cultural, linguistic, and historical identity. It also functions as the context within which precolonial, colonial, and postcolonial problems of resource allocation and distribution of political power are contested. Ethnic groups occupying a particular region make their demands on central governments on the basis of their region. Thus, the concept of region has obviously been concretized as a political category, a contiguously definable geographical space with specific character, image, and status in the minds of the inhabitants of each region (see Komey 2008b). As shown in Chapter 3, the formation of ethno-regionally-based political organizations, primarily in the 1950s and the 1960s, which later developed into armed struggle movements, has gone some way to support this theory.

Ethnic regions are therefore explicitly understood to be places whose distinctiveness and identity formation rest on socio-political grounds. As social constructs, regions are necessarily ideological and no explanation of their individuality or character is complete without explicit consideration of the ideas, perceptions, attitudes, and aspirations that are developed in the move towards regionalization within the context of the nation-building process (see Beshir et al., 1984; Murphy 1991; Mohamed Salih 1998a, 1998b).

In the context of the Nuba Mountains, identity politics and the game of inclusion and exclusion or 'we' versus 'they' are not only problematic for the relationships between the nomadic Baqqara and sedentary Nuba, but also for inter-relations among the various Nuba hill communities. Nuba communities are unaccustomed to making clear-cut territorial boundaries, as we have seen in the preceding chapter. Their feeling of 'Nuba-ness' as a unifying factor of their ethno-political identity is still in the making. This collective movement is still emerging through their politics of resistance and liberation, and the struggle for territoriality and ethnic identity. Therefore, the collective Nuba position is more about becoming than being. Furthermore, the process of forming a collective identity strongly tied to the Nuba Mountains region is emerging while also being invoked by the government and the other ethnic groups co-existing with them in the region, particularly the Baqqara.

It is within this conceptualization of the region as an ethno-political entity, an ancestral homeland, and a base for livelihood and survival that the Nuba claim to autochthony and its associated territorial attachment and political expression can be understood. Such an analysis is linked to the Baqqara and other ethnic groups in the Nuba Mountains who make up the region's whole social construct, with interrelated local social fields operating within broader socio-economic and political arenas, on the national level and beyond.

The Nuba autochthonous myth
and its political and territorial attachments

Nuba self-identification as an indigenous or even autochthonous group is manifested in their oral history and myths of origin, their cultural and religious practices, and in their contemporary political struggle. It is worth noting here that 'Indigeneity' (see Knight 1982; Kuper 2003, 2006; Thuen 2006) and 'autochthony' are key analytical concepts that inform the discussion in the remaining two chapters (see Geschiere and Nyamnjoh 2000; Mbembe 2000; Geschiere 2005; Geschiere and Jackson 2006; Komey 2008a, 2009a).

Chapter 1 has shown that despite the Nuba's strong feelings as indigenous people for the land they inhabit, little is known about their ancient history. Their own traditions and memories yield sparse information. Despite this, writers such as Sagar (1922), Nadel (1947), and Kramer (1987) have pointed to the prevalence of some sort of vague tribal mythology linking the origin and past of the different Nuba groups with their different localities within the Nuba Mountains region and Sudan as a whole. In fact, Nadel (1947: 5) reported that most Nuba summarize their past in one sentence: 'We have always lived here.'

Moreover, most of the self-attributed indigenous names of individuals, social organizations, and habitats are loaded with meanings strongly attached to their claimed autochthony. For example, Kramer (1987: 1– 2) found that the Krongo people, living southeast of Kadugli and north of Lake Abyat, do not call themselves Krongo but Katu-mo-di, meaning 'people of the home', a term which they not only apply to themselves, but also to other Nuba people nearby. In an interview with my key informant, Sulayman al-Ahaydib of Keiga Luban,[1] a similar narrative was reported. The Keiga people, living north and northwest of Kadugli, believe that all Keiga communities originated from the Kolo sub-hill in Keiga Tummero hill, from where they gradually spread all over the present Keiga territory, i.e., the four hill communities of Tummero, Luban, al-Khayl, and Dameik. Keiga's first legendary ancestor, Kolo, is believed to have been propelled out of the earth onto the top of a hill which came to be named after him. Successive generations of Kolo to the present, throughout the Keiga land, call themselves Kado-de-madi. In their own language, 'kado' means 'nation or people', and 'de-madi' means 'the land' or 'the home': thus kado-de-madi means 'the people/nation of the land', or 'the indigenous people'. This is in contrast to the 'Kamal-ga' people, which means 'the strangers' or 'the camel riders/owners' from North Kordofan who joined them much later.

---

[1] Author's Interview with Sulayman al-Ahaydib in al-Kweik in Keiga Luban, 15 February 2007.

Today, the Kolo sub-hill is an icon of identity and a religious point of reference for Keiga communities. It is a sacred place where ancestor worship and rituals are performed annually with the exclusive participation of kado-de-madi affiliated families from all their local communities. Kolo hill becomes a unifying factor which continues to give the Keiga a sense of territoriality, not only as a religious reference point but also as a source of their autochthonous identity and a basis for their socio-economic livelihood and survival. This highly localized case is typical of the different Nuba hill communities, each with its variations in the details of their narrative.

It is worth noting that concepts of indigeneity or autochthony are increasingly attractive to some human rights activists in global forums, including the UN (see UN 1992, 1994, 1995). Several of the UN's non-binding declarations on the rights of indigenous peoples calls on countries to give more control to tribal peoples over the land and resources they have *traditionally possessed*, to return confiscated territory, or to pay compensation (see UN 1992, 1994, my italics).

With this global environment in mind, a group of elite individuals, particularly those in exile, were able to portray the Nuba internationally, during the severe period of the civil war, as endangered indigenous communities. They opted for the construction of a collective identity, centred on autochthonous claims to an historical land. Towards that end, several Nuba entities were formed in the 1990s in Europe and elsewhere: these included Nuba Solidarity Abroad; Nuba Survival Organization and its newsletters *Nafir* and *The Nuba Vision* in London; and Nuba Relief, Rehabilitation and Development Organization (NRRDO) founded in 1996 in Nairobi, Kenya. These groups launched advocacy campaigns to draw the attention of the international community to the tragedy of an indigenous people facing genocide and ethnocide, having been intentionally and completely isolated from the outside world. Several international actors joined the advocacy campaign including Africa Watch (1991, 1992a, 1992b); African Rights (1995); Mohamed Salih (1995, 1999), Suliman (1999); Rahhal (2001a, 2001b); Mohamed and Fisher (2002); and Ende (2007). Some of these contributions, such as that of Mohamed Salih (1999) and Mohamed and Fisher (2002), were part of global campaigns on the rights of endangered indigenous peoples in Africa and the Middle East.

The world was progressively informed through a series of reports and publications that unveiled the Sudanese government's genocidal intent towards the Nuba. These included *Sudan: Destroying ethnic identity: the secret war against the Nuba* (Africa Watch 1991); *Sudan: Eradicating the Nuba* (Africa Watch 1992); *Facing genocide: the Nuba of Sudan* (African Rights 1995); *Resistance and response: ethnocide and genocide in the Nuba Mountains, Sudan* (Mohamed Salih 1995); *Land alienation and genocide in the Nuba Mountains, Sudan* (Mohamed Salih 1999); *The right to be Nuba: the story of a Sudanese people's struggle for survival* (Rahhal 2001a); *Modernization and resistance: the plight of the Nuba People* (Kadouf 2001); *War and Faith in Sudan* (Meyer 2005); *Averting genocide in the Nuba Mountains, Sudan* (de Waal 2006); *Proud to be Nuba: faces and voices* (Ende 2007); and Ende's internet website titled *Nuba Mountains Homepage*. In supporting the Nuba struggle, a Sudanese scholar, Mohamed Salih (1999: 36, 38) declared

> The Nuba are indeed the indigenous peoples of the Nuba Mountains; they have the strongest ties to their lands and have lived in this region since or before colonization. The Nuba are now dominated by other groups with markedly different cultures. Like other indigenous peoples, the Nuba were not incorporated into Sudanese's mainstream political culture. Further, the Nuba do not accept Islam as their religion, or 'Arabism' as their racial ideology. These two notions of exclusion are often used by the state to justify the oppression and appropriation of Nuba land and natural resources [...]
>
> Hence, the Nuba share at least two predicaments with indigenous peoples the world over: state-sponsored policies assist in the systematic appropriation of their land and natural resources by colonists, capital, and private business interests. Also, their human rights are denied and political persecution, ethnocide, and genocide continue even after European colonialism has ended.

The Nuba autochthonous movement took a new shape following the conclusion of the CPA with outcomes that did not meet Nuba expectations. The post-conflict era allowed for the gradual return of internally displaced persons (IDPs), refugees, members of the diaspora, and SPLM/A-led fighters and leaders to their homeland. The emerging Nuba autochthonous identity was strengthened by this influx of people and their new politics were systematically promoted through a series of tribal conferences. The goal was to foster the sense of being Nuba as a united ethnic group with one political destiny, anchored to an ancestral homeland. The conferences focused on issues related to Nuba identity and cultural revival, forging strong links between ethnicity and territoriality.

One consequence was that the Krongo-Massakin Conference, 2005, resolved that their inhabited places of Buram, Reikha, and Teis (all Arabic words) would henceforth be known by their original Nuba names of Tobo, Tolabi, and Tromo respectively. Further, the Nuba would speak of their overall claimed territory as the 'Nuba Mountains', which was the first name to be officially recognised, during the colonial administration of 1914–28. Simultaneously the Nuba claimed that the regional name, Janub Kordofan, (South Kordofan) was an Arab marker, imposed by successive national governments and their local Arab or 'Arabicized' alliances.

The mythic nature of Nuba autochthonous identity politics will be explored further in the rest of this chapter and the one following. The ethnographic material presented here is based on studies in two relatively small but important villages of al-Azraq and Umm Derafi. During the civil war, the inhabitants of these two settlements abandoned them completely. Toward the end of the war, the settlements re-emerged, but in different locations, provoking intense land-based disputes along ethno-political divides. These two cases demonstrate how the Nuba attempt to represent themselves as unified ethnic groups in their enthusiastic effort not only to secure their claimed communal land, but also to ensure effective control over the entire Nuba Mountains territory after peace. The whole exercise seems to have been driven by the SPLM-led doctrine of liberation within a wider political scheme enshrined in the 'New Sudan' vision.

In practical terms, this Nuba liberation doctrine claims that the only way for all Nuba ethnic groups to cherish their identity and secure communal land for individuals, family, clan, tribes, is by liberating the entire region from the power of central government and its local allies, particularly the Baqqara. This strategy has its own logic, with the inevitable tendency to exclude the 'other' socially and territorially. The two following cases reveal how the practical manifestations of this doctrine can be traced back to certain local dynamics in Nuba–Baqqara relations following the signing of the CPA.

Territory and politics of liberation: the al-Azraq case

LOCALE AND POLITICS OF NAMING

Al-Azraq is a relatively small village approximately located at latitude 30°37'E, longitude 11°18'N. This position lies about 15km from the eastern part of Heiban, or about 106km east of Kadugli, the capital of South Kordofan State (see Map 6.1). The area represents one of the most fertile plains in the region, and was well known for its high yields of cotton from the colonial period to the 1960s.

'Al-Azraq' is Arabic for black, the name given to the area by Arabs in the 18th century when they arrived in the area. As noted previously, the issue of place-names in the region is highly contested, for both physical and cultural landscapes, and they are crucial in claiming land rights or in challenging others' claims in the region. Names are usually loaded with serious political and socio-cultural meanings and metaphors with direct repercussions on claims and counter-claims on land rights. As discussed in the previous chapter, the politics of naming came to the fore during the peace negotiations and continues to be influential in the present post-conflict situation.

It is worth noting that the replacement of the original/indigenous names of Nuba places or tribes with those related to Arab culture has long been common practice for the Arab nomads and the Jillaba. The colonial government institutionalized the practice by integrating Arabic names into official records and maps. At that period, the local Arabs were the sole mediators and interpreters between the British administrators and the Nuba chiefs in their respective hill communities. Thus, the practice of replacing the names of Nuba peoples and/or their places with Arab ones was and still is part of identity politics in the region. For the Nuba, it is part

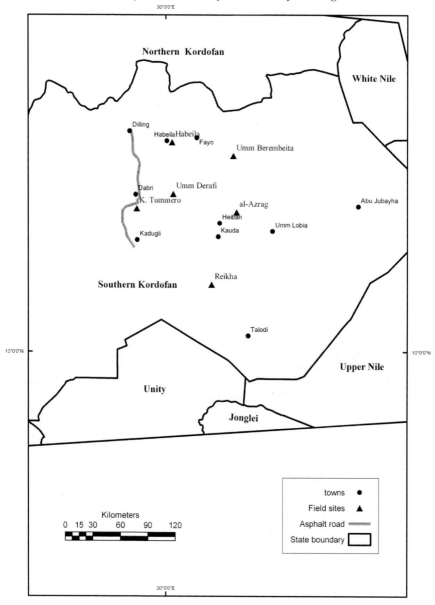

Map 6.1 Main fieldwork sites
Source: GPS Observations 2008

of the long history of the marginalization of their identity and culture by the overriding Arab power and culture. Moreover, it is seen as a concerted attempt by Arabs to strengthen their ownership claim to any contested land.

As with so many other names of locales or Nuba tribes, this name, al-Azraq, is the one that went into official records and maps during the colonial period and that has been maintained by post-colonial regimes to the present day. Originally, the Nuba Leira,[2] the main inhabitants, called it 'Gi-diya', or 'Gi-diwa', the latter meaning 'place of the enemy'. Some Leira elders have no difficulty recalling how their ancestors defended their land in a series of battles in al-Azraq against Arab slave raiders during the Turco-Egyptian era (1821–85). From those battles, the name Gi-diwa was given to the area to mark the presence and actions of the Arabs, the brutal strangers and slave raiders.[3] Memories related to such history in Nuba–Baqqara relations are deeply inscribed in Nuba political narratives. During the war and after, these memories were constantly evoked and used strategically to 'essentialize' their crucial need for unity against that same enemy, although the circumstances were entirely different.

AL-AZRAQ AND WAR DISRUPTION

Due to its strategic location, al-Azraq village was the centre of the highest intensity of warfare in and around the area, and was subsequently left completely deserted. Towards the end of the war, the government authority took possession of al-Azraq itself, excluding its surroundings. As it is located in low land surrounded by hills, the Sudan Army Forces opted for security reasons to position their military garrison on hill Dobo, two to three kilometres south of the original site of the depopulated al-Azraq village. That military base became the site for the re-emergence of the al-Azraq village of today. Meanwhile, the surrounding hilly areas continued to be the stronghold of the Nuba Leira-led SPLA in the area. In the absence of real integration of SPLM/A-liberated areas and government-controlled areas, these patterns of war continued to prevail after the CPA, throughout the transitional period.

Al-Azraq and its surroundings are a crucial part of the Nuba Leira tribal territory, with 'Ayatqa agro-pastoralists representing the nomadic group of Baqqara in the area. Genealogically, the 'Ayatqa trace themselves back to the al-Shuwayhat section of the Bidayriyya tribe in North Kordofan. According to MacMichael (1922/67: 151–2), some of the Bidayriyya who migrated to South Kordofan were long integrated into the Hawazma alliance. They and five other tribes, the Zunara, Takarir, the Jillaba, Hawara, Jawama'a, and slaves, compose the Halafa, one of the three major sections of Hawazma, the other two being Rawawqa and

---

[2] The peoples are called Leira, their territory is known locally as Laro and on some official maps as Alleira. These terms, however, are used interchangeably in different records to mean the people and/or their territory (see Nadel 1947: 85 and Stevenson 1965: 13, 23). For consistency, Leira and Alleira are used here to mean people and territory respectively.

[3] Author's interview with Ali Cornelius, a Leira informant, in Hajar Bako, 3 May 2005.

Abdul 'Ali. MacMichael insisted that none of these six tribes of the Halafa is genealogically Arab, as is the case for most of the Hawazma groups. They were integrated into Hawazma in the mid-18th century after they swore a solemn oath binding them to the Hawazma alliance.

In my interviews with Hamid Sattar,[4] a prominent leader of the 'Ayatqa of al-Azraq, he rejected this assertion and denied any linkage with Hawazma. He claims that the 'Ayatqa nomads in the Nuba Mountains are composed of the three clans of Aulad Abu Zuna in al-Azraq, Aulad Harazalla around Delami and Umm Berembeita, and Aulad Wad 'Abdul Rasul in Umm Derafi, al-Murra, and Shwai. According to the 'Ayatqa's own version of the past, they were forced to move from their homeland in North Kordofan southwards into the Nuba land during the Mahdiyya wars of the 1880s. Although the 'Ayatqa came to the area as nomads, some gradually started to settle and practise farming, including orchard-planting, in the fertile areas in al-Azraq. They pointed to their peaceful relations with the Nuba Leira throughout the pre-war period, when they continued to share many activities of daily life in terms of grazing, water sources, market exchange, and farming, co-existing in the neighbourhoods.

During the dry season, the whole family stays in the fariq (cattle camp) in the areas surrounding al-Azraq, and as the rainy season starts, the younger members of the family move gradually northwards with their livestock. Some family members stay behind and engage in trading, traditional cultivation, and/or horticultural management until they are reunited with their livestock at the end of the rainy season. Due to this cyclical movement, centred in al-Azraq, the 'Ayatqa were systematically integrated into the wider socio-economic system in the area. As a result, some were engaged in local trading, some children attended the schools, and a few prominent elders were co-opted as members of the native administration and local courts.[5]

Towards the end of 1989, the local people suffered some encroachment of militias from the Sudan People's Liberation Movement/Army (SPLM/A), composed mostly of young, local Nuba recruits. The cooperative relations between the Leira and 'Ayatqa turned antagonistic because both sides were soon absorbed by the warring parties, i.e., the Government of Sudan (GOS) and the SPLM/A. As the latter moved deeper into the area, those 'Ayatqa nomads who felt apprehensive started

---

[4] Author's interview with Hamid Sattar, Khartoum, 11 June 2006. He is the prominent Shaykh of 'Ayatqa Aulad Abu Zuna. Following the escalation of the war in the mid-1980s, he and his family were forced to retreat northwards into the Bidayriyya area of 'Aluba in North Kordofan. As prominent elder of the 'Ayatqa, he was co-opted as a member of the local native administration and its court in al-Azraq and Heiban from the 1950s to the time of his departure from the area in the mid-1980s.

[5] Author's interview with 'Ali Cornelius, Hajar Bako, 3 May 2005; and with Mukhtar Hamid Sattar, al-Azraq 6 May 2005. The latter is a teacher and the son of Shaykh Hamid Satar. He decided to come back to the area after the Cease Fire Agreement in 2002 to be a teacher in al-Azraq Primary School.

to retreat with their livestock northwards into government-controlled areas, notably Umm Berembeita and Kortala within South Kordofan, while some others went further, settling permanently in their wet season dwelling area of 'Aluba in North Kordofan.

According to one of my key informants,[6] upon their arrival in Umm Berembeita, some 'Ayatqa swore an oath to attack the Nuba Leira areas. The informant, whose name is withheld upon his request, is one of the few Leira of al-Azraq who happened to be in Umm Berembeita during the war when the 'Ayatqa arrived there. His presence among them gave him the opportunity to witness some of the government and 'Ayatqa militia operations against the Leira areas in and around al-Azraq. He revealed that some young 'Ayatqa were mobilized by the government and eventually recruited as militia forces as well as informants within the government army that launched offensive military campaigns against Nuba villages including al-Azraq and its surrounding hilly settlements. Apparently, some of the al-Azraq operations were later widely reported by human rights organizations including African Rights (1995: 133).

THE DISPLACED 'AYATQA
AND THE POLITICS OF LIBERATION

As presented in the previous chapter, the Nuba Mountains Ceasefire Agreement (CFA) of 2002 granted free movement of civilians and goods and the voluntary return of internally displaced persons to their respective areas in the region. Like many other nomads, the 'Ayatqa, wanted to return to al-Azraq which they perceived as their homeland. They not only own some immovable material assets such as orchards and shops in al-Azraq, but also maintain a wide range of social ties acquired from the long history of amicable co-existence with the Leira community. However, their return to al-Azraq has not proved to be an easy process, because of Nuba resistance, which is driven by the SPLM/A's politics of liberation, focusing on Nuba tribal land as a source of autochthonous identity and livelihood. From the Nuba viewpoint, the recognition of their ownership rights as indigenous people over their customary lands is something that cannot be compromised at this stage of their political struggle.

Accordingly, the Nuba Leira, who control most of their claimed territory since the CPA, argue that, historically, the 'Ayatqa Arabs were generously hosted and given access to the Leira customary land by permission of their ancestors. The 'Ayatqa came to the area after abandoning their own ancestral homeland in northern Kordofan due to the Mahdiyya wars of the 1880s. Moreover, like other Nuba, the Leira claim that when conflict arose in the Nuba Mountains, it was directed against the central government and not against the local Arabs. The 'Ayatqa, like so many other Baqqara in the region, decided not to join

---

[6] Interview with an anonymous informant in al-Azraq, 28 May 2006.

forces with the Nuba in defending land at that critical period in the Nuba's struggle. Instead, they fled and sided with the government against the Nuba, before returning as militias in order to eradicate the Nuba and take over their ancestral land, as was promised to them by the government.

By doing so, the Leira continue to argue, the 'Ayatqa had become local agents of the government during an unjustified war, thus excluding themselves from any land rights in the area, after the successful resistance of the Nuba. The Leira position is that the 'Ayatqa will not be allowed to regain access to the liberated territory including al-Azraq without the consent of the Leira community as collective owners of the land. This view is widely shared among the Nuba in the SPLM/A-held areas. Consent must be based on new terms aligned with the spirit of 'liberation' anchored on the recognition of the Nuba's unquestionable rights over their ancestral land.

The 'Ayatqa felt the need to respond to this line of argument, which could see even their secondary rights to land use being rescinded. They accept that some of their members were recruited into the militia and/or had been members of Quwat al-Difa' al-Sha'bi (Popular Defence Forces or PDFs) and actually fought against the Nuba-led SPLM/A. At the same time, they deny the Nuba claim that the intention of these Arab militias was to wipe out the Nuba Leira and appropriate their land. In an interview with their key leaders, the 'Ayatqa insisted that:[7]

> The 'Ayatqa militias did not go back to attack our people in al-Azraq, never. However, some of our members participated in some of the major joint military operations which include the army, Quat al-Difa' al-Sha'bi, and the tribal militias including those of some Nuba as well. Such operations are usually launched and commanded by the Sudan Army Forces, though in some cases some militias may have launched their own campaigns in search of cattle and loot. Our participation was limited to many formal military operations in different places including some Leira areas such as Ormi and Sarf al-Nila.[8]

The assertion is that PDFs were not an exclusively Arab institution but included Sudanese people of different ethnic backgrounds, including some of the Nuba who were loyal to the government. Thus, these 'Ayatqa leaders maintain that the 'Ayatqa as a community can not be held responsible for PDF atrocities against the Nuba. Those of the 'Ayatqa who participated did so as government recruits and not as representatives of the community. In other words, the 'Ayatqa assert that the joint operations were carried out as part of the war dynamics led by the two main warring parties, i.e. the GOS and the SPLM/A.

---

[7] The author was able to trace, meet, and interview several members of the 'Ayatqa community who consider themselves internally displaced persons in Khartoum, Umm Berembeita, and 'Aluba in North Kordofan and who are waiting to return to al-Azraq in the future. The interviews were conducted as informal but guided discussions with a group of over twenty 'Ayatqa leaders in Umm Berembeita including Hussayn Hassan al-Daba, Muhammad Sanad, Hamuda Digayl Sa'id, Hussayn al-Zayn, Umar Ahmed Khayr, Hamid Sa'id Umar, Shannan Mugadam, and Sa'id al-Tum al-Digayl.

[8] Author's interview with Hamid Sa'id Umar and others, Umm Berembeita, 2 February 2007.

The 'Ayatqa's defensive position may appear reasonable. But the contrary argument is that there were many operations carried out by Arab tribal militias beyond the reach of government authorities. Such widely documented operations (see, for example, African Watch 1992, African Rights 1995, Suliman 1999, de Waal 2006) were, to a large degree, motivated by the potential gains of the individuals or tribes involved. In this regard, de Waal (2006: 2), succinctly noted that:

> The early period of war was marked by militia massacres and extra-judicial executions by military intelligence. In a mixture of reprisals and counter-insurgency, some of it pre-emptive, a coalition of military offices and local militia commanders escalated violence against the Nuba. The first step was arming of local Arab tribes by the government, initially as panicked response to an SPLM/A attack in the region in 1985, and in 1989 they were formalized into 'Popular Defence Forces'. The militia committed the worst massacres of the war, driven not only by orders from their paramilitary command, but also by their own search for cattle, loot and cheap labor.

The Leira claim to their perceived tribal land is firmly grounded on the SPLM Nuba Land Action Strategy and the resolutions of the Second All Nuba Conference reviewed in the preceding chapter. The main principles related to land rights laid down during these two events have found their way into the collective mind of local Nuba communities, including the Leira. The Leira held successive tribal conferences in their liberated areas such as that of Ghidrro, April 2004; Hajar Bako, April 2005; and Sarf al-Nila, April 2006. The 'Ayatqa were eager to participate for the sole purpose of securing their return to al-Azraq. However, they were barred from the 2004 event, except for the opening ceremonial sessions.

The Leira justified their lack of enthusiasm on the grounds that the relationship between the two communities had been severely damaged during the war and was still tense despite the CFA and subsequently the CPA. However, the 'Ayatqa did not give up. They gradually repositioned themselves in the emerging post-war political situation in the region. My informant, Say'id al-Tom al-Digayl, one of the 'Ayatqa's political figures, pointed to some of the political initiatives taken since 2003 toward the SPLM/A as the newly emerging military and political leaders in the region:

> After the Nuba Mountains Ceasefire Agreement in 2002, the 'Ayatqa sent a delegation composed of ten leaders in 2003 to Kauda, the SPLM/A regional headquarters. They met with 'Abdul Aziz al-Hilu, then Governor of the SLPM/A-controlled areas in the Nuba Mountains Region. In the meeting, the 'Ayatqa delegation congratulated the SPLM/A leaders for reaching the CFA agreement, expressed their political support for it, and declared their decision to join the SPLM/A.[9]

---

[9] Author's interview with Sa'id al-Tum al Digayl and others, Umm Berembeita, 2 February 2007.

As a result, when the Leira's second conference took place in 2005, the 'Ayatqa delegation was allowed to attend for the first time. Both sides were able to discuss their damaged relations, recognizing the need for reconciliation. They realized that the whole process required a tremendous effort and considerable time before it could become reality on the ground. As a result, the 'Ayatqa were formally invited to participate with a delegation at the Leira's third tribal conference of 2006. According to my informant, Say'id al-Tom al-Digayl, the delegation was composed of some community leaders accompanied by a team of al-Mardum[10] dancers led by some of their famous hakamat.[11] Though the 'Ayatqa delegation was allowed to remain at the conference, they were in reality excluded when the Nuba Leira decided to convene the conference in their own native language throughout the first day. It was only on the second day of the conference that the 'Ayatqa were able to participate, when the conference switched to a bilingual system of Arabic and Leira. However, many key issues and resolutions, particularly the ones pertaining to Leira communal land rights, had been settled during the closed session the day before.

In an interview with 'Wad Say'id Komi, one of the young Leira leaders in the SPLM/A and the administrative officer of Irral County, which includes the Leira area, he outlined the general SPLM/A policy related to the Nuba's indigenous land. Each Nuba tribe is encouraged to identify and fix the boundary of its own traditional territory without expelling any other ethnic groups living within that defined territory. Nonetheless, he insisted that:

> It is vital for the other ethnic groups to recognize and respect the Nuba rights of communal ownership over their land. We here in the liberated areas of Irral County perceive groups such as the 'Ayatqa, Shawabna, and Aulad Ghabush, among others, as groups which have rights to co-exist if they adhere to this fundamental policy. We considered them part of the marginalized groups which the central government used against our people during the war. Such people deserve to be made aware of their rights and to be encouraged to side with us for better co-existence. For this reason, there is a great need to embark on an inter-ethnic reconciliation process in the area. The Nuba of Leira, for example, should be prepared to forgive the 'Ayatqa for the atrocities they committed against them during the war, provided that the 'Ayatqa is equally prepared to recognize the indisputable rights of ownership of the Leira people over their communal territory in which they co-exist and share in usage.[12]

---

[10] Al-Mardum is a famous Baqqara traditional dance widely shared by some Nuba groups, particularly in the plain areas of the central and northern sections of the Nuba Mountains.

[11] The hakamat ([sg.]: hakama) institutions were instrumental in mobilizing tribal militias and the mujahidiin during the civil war through their songs, centred on praise for the Jihad mission, the heroes and martyrs of what is believed to be a holy war. These same institutions have gradually shifted focus in the post-war era from a 'culture of war' to a 'culture of peace and reconciliation'. This is a response to the political changes and the repositioning exercised by some Arab tribal leaders for the sake of the possible collective survival of their communities in a region currently characterized by political fluidity and a fragile peace.

[12] Author's interview with 'Awad Sa'id Komi, Heiban, 27 February 2007.

This seemingly positive political rhetoric was necessary but not sufficient to restore peace and security among the 'Ayatqa when they were contemplating their return to al-Azraq. Most of the 'Ayatqa families in Umm Berembeita believe that they cannot return to al-Azraq at the present time because of insecurity and the domination of a 'culture of war and exclusion' instead of a 'culture of peace and inclusion'. Despite this, the 'Ayatqa have not lost hope of returning to their perceived homeland in the foreseeable future. In the words of their own leader:

> We have no land other than al-Azraq. We have a valid oath with Leira and other Nuba communities. Therefore, we were not supposed to betray this oath during the crisis, though, unfortunately, some of us did so when they participated with the government against the Nuba. Today, the 'Ayatqa people need to negotiate and reconcile with their brothers the Leira, before they can consider the possibility of returning home. Right now, there is no social peace, no security, and no effective government institutions to put things in order. Unless this situation is reversed, our return will remain a remote but not an impossible event.[13]

Three key points may be noted, based on the above discussion of the al-Azraq situation. First, it is obvious that this is a highly localized ethnography. Nevertheless, an analysis from the evidence is, to a large degree, applicable to several lower or higher levels of scale, including the entire region itself, which is the main focus of this study. This study has shown that the 'Ayatqa nomads were forced into evacuation as a result of the war. But later, some of them were consciously or unconsciously mobilized by the government army to participate in attacks on Leira villages.

Second, despite the accomplishments of the CPA, the political and social situation is still ambiguous as to how to restore the previously mutual co-existence and wide-ranging use of land resources between these two competing ethnic groups. The urgency of the situation stems from the fact that one party (in this case the 'Ayatqa Baqqara) has been completely denied access to this traditionally shared territory. At the same time, the Nuba of Leira have exclusively and effectively controlled their claimed territory with just the possibility of 'others' having conditional access of use to their 'liberated land'. For the 'Ayatqa and possibly many of the nomadic Baqqara in the region, the restoration of pre-war peaceful co-existence is still possible, although the challenges ahead are enormous.

Third, for some Leira and perhaps the majority of the Nuba, however, the damage caused by their previous partners, the Baqqara, is beyond repair and they liberated their autochthonous claimed territory in order for it to remain theirs alone. This position represents the view of the young generation of the Nuba who have been indoctrinated with the 'New Sudan' vision. This vision is associated with the politics of liberation and resistance against the institutional structures and functions of the Old Sudan, which the young believe must be persistently challenged to the

---

[13] Author's interview with Hamid Sattar, Khartoum, 9 June 2006.

point of extinction. That system was and still is, the cause of the Nuba's institutionalized socio-economic marginalization and underdevelopment, political subordination, and land loss. The war brought ethnocidal and genocidal atrocities, leading to the loss of their indigenous identity. The new generation firmly believe that the Nuba's very survival is still at risk.

Imagined boundaries in a contested territory: the Umm Derafi case

LOCATION AND ECONOMIC IMPORTANCE

Umm Derafi is a small but relatively strategic rural centre about 32km to the west of Heiban and about 70km northeast of Kadugli. It lies at approximately latitude 30°12'E and longitude 11°18'N (see Map 6.1). The Umm Derafi area represents the western edge of Alleira tribal land, bordered by Kawalib land near Hadra to the north, Laguri and Saburi land to the west, and Shwai land to the south. The Khur (water stream) Umm Derafi, running northeast to southwest, is one of the distinctive natural features that attracts sedentary and nomadic peoples alike. Fertile plains around water sources are ideal for cultivating orchards, while they offer important grazing and watering areas during the dry season for nomads.

More importantly, Umm Derafi is one of the richest areas of natural resources in the region, particularly for a certain type of tree locally known as deleib (*Bot. Barassus flabellifer Linn.*). Apart from its edible fruits, the wood is widely used for the construction of houses in both rural and urban settlements. As an important economic resource base, deleib attracts many traders and government officials who engage legally or illegally in its lucrative trading.

ETHNIC CO-EXISTENCE AND THE DISRUPTIONS OF WAR

Before the civil war, Umm Derafi was administratively part of Heiban Rural Council. At the same time, it was and still is part of the Leira 'Umudiya. Umm Derafi was composed of numerous clustered hamlets inhabited by various ethnic groups, with the Nuba of Leira and the Shawabna as the dominant communities, in addition to seasonal nomadic groups, namely Aulad Ghabush,[14] Fellata (Waylla and 'Iyal Zahra groups), and Shanabla Humr ('Iyal Abu Hamiya). These various ethnic groups continued to interact and mix in the course of settlement, market exchange, farming, and herd grazing in the area. In this process, some ethnic groups, particularly the Shawabna, Leira, and Aulad Ghabush, initiated some collective actions. For instance, as early as 1954, their leaders jointly demanded that the government deliver some basic services to their

---

[14] Aulad Ghabush, along with Dar al-Gawad, Dar Berti, and Dar Nay'la, are the four sub-sections that form the 'Abdul 'Ali section of Hawazma. For more details, see Sudan Government 1912: 40.

communities. This collective effort resulted in the establishment of a police station in Gardud Tia, one of the Umm Derafi settlement points, followed by a school, and a health centre.

From that period to the outbreak of the war, these groups confirm that they cohabited peacefully, with a real process of inter-ethnic integration on socio-economic and political-administrative levels. For example, it was mentioned that the chairmanship of the Umm Derafi administrative rural unit during the pre-war period was consecutively held by several leaders of different ethnic groups. Precisely, it was chaired by Sharif Ibrahim of Shawabna, Adam 'Abdulrahman Hakim of Aulad Ghabush, and Muhammad Tia of Leira, respectively. This situation demonstrates the high degree of ethnic solidarity and harmony in the area at that time.

With the expansion of the war into the area, all these features of ethnic solidarity and harmony were greatly damaged by the civil war dynamics. Events worked progressively against the continuation of their peaceful co-existence. A series of violent incidents resulted in the complete displacement of the area's inhabitants. The Shawabna were able to relocate in government-controlled areas and afterwards became allies of the government forces against the Nuba-led SPLM/A. Like most of the Nuba, the Leira people of Umm Derafi were politically and, therefore, territorially divided: some joined the SPLM/A while others went over to the government-controlled areas.

A brief background of the Shawabna group follows. They are one of the main inhabitants and key players in disputes over land rights in the Umm Derafi area. A sedentary people, the Shawabna are neither Nuba nor Arabs, but are of mixed origins, creoles, with a long history of interactions with both those local people. Following the migration of their forefathers into the region from their place of origin, the Shawabna interacted with these two groups widely across the region, through intermarriage and cohabitation.

Due to historical and contemporary ethno-political dynamics in the region, the Shawabna were able to establish their own native administration before they allied with the Baqqara of the Rawawqa-Hawazma. At present, they are formally integrated into the Rawawqa native administration system composed of the Aulad Nuba, the Dilimiyya, the Dar Jami' and the Shawabna themselves. Jebel Shaybun near Umm Derafi, which was a famous traditional gold-mining base during the 15th-16th centuries, seems to have been the Shawabna's first settlement point in the region. As early as 1912, the British administration reported that:

> Their ancestors migrated from Messelemias [in the Gezira] some five generations ago, and settled at jebel Sheibun, whence they established their authority over the neighbouring Nuba hills. Three generations ago, the Shawabna were defeated by Shaykh El-Amin of the Ghodiat tribe and forced to take refuge at Jebel Shwai, whence they ousted the Nuba inhabitants. (Sudan Government, 1912: 48)

Due to historical and contemporary ethno-political dynamics in the region, the Shawabna moved gradually towards strengthening their alliance with the Arabs of Rawawqa while establishing their own native administration. Stevenson (1965) reported that they were formally integrated into the broad federated system of the Rawawqa native administration in 1933. At present, the Shawabna are socio-politically part of the Baqqara of Rawawqa, though they are territorially and administratively scattered among several Nuba communities in Tira Mandi, Shwai, 'Aggab, Suma near Kadugli, and in Umm Derafi, the case in point.

NUBA-SHAWABNA CONFLICT OVER UMM DERAFI

As in the al-Azraq case, the name of this area seems to be part of ongoing ethno-politics along Nuba and non-Nuba divides in the region. We have already mentioned that the area was completely deserted during the war in the mid-1980s. Towards the end of hostilities, a series of military campaigns were carried out by the government army and the PDFs against the SPLM/A in the area. At the time, government strategy was that any recaptured village was to be maintained by its own community through their militias and/or PDFs. The militarized groups usually formed the basis for military and security organs providing protection for the re-emerging settlements against SPLA attack. Some community leaders (Shaykhs, 'Umdas, and Amirs), with strong loyalty to the government, were instrumental in the realization of this process within a broader strategy known as 'es-Salam min al dakhil', i.e., peace from within.

The government's main intention was to stimulate demographic restructuring and territorial remapping in favour of the people in the areas it controlled as opposed to those in SPLA-held areas. Moreover, within government-controlled areas, the government granted special support for non-Nuba groups in comparison with Nuba communities in controlling the recaptured areas, as the case below demonstrates. War dynamics coupled with this government policy made it possible for some ethnic groups, such as the Shawabna, to expand their territorial jurisdiction at the expense of the Nuba Leira in Umm Derafi. As a result, the Leira claim to the Umm Derafi area as part of their communal land was and still is being seriously and practically challenged by the Shawabna, who managed to gain some real political and administrative powers on the ground during the war and thereafter.

According to the government strategy described above, the Shawabna were the first to return to the deserted Umm Derafi area on 4 April 2000, after some military campaigns in the area. With the assistance of the government army, the Shawabna decided to resettle at 'Alali hamlet on the western bank of Khur Umm Derafi instead of at the original site of Umm Derafi which is situated on the eastern bank of the Khur. They not only changed Umm Derafi's original site but also replaced the name 'Leira' with 'Shaybun'. Thereafter, instead of 'Umm Derafi Leira' as it was called by the Nuba Leira, 'Umm Derafi Shaybun' was adopted in government and NGO circles. The Shawabna claim that theirs is the original name of the area and not the name claimed by the Leira. Moreover, they justify their decision to relocate Umm Derafi to 'Alali by claiming that the original Umm Derafi site was sited on open lowland and thus was a poor location for self-protection and defence in the case of possible SPLM/A attacks.

In contrast, the Leira people, in both government- and SPLM/A-controlled areas, seem to have a different explanation for the Shawabna move. They claim that the latter's unilateral decision to go back to Umm Derafi ahead of them, without regard to the pre-war ethnic territorial distribution, co-existence, and cooperation, reveals the Shawabna's ulterior motive: to assume control of what the Leira regard as their own autochthonous territory. Moreover, they perceive government support for the Shawabna's unilateral return as a reward for the latter's support of the government during the war. Muhammad Tia, the pro-government Amir of Leira, who was based in Kadugli during the war, was alarmed by the Shawabna's return to Leira traditional land, without his consent as the native leader of the area. Leira worries were substantiated by reports of excessive and illegal exploitation of delieb wood in the area by the Shawabna, the army, and some state-linked merchants. As a consequence, the Leira Amir himself decided to return to Umm Derafi in 2002, following the Nuba Mountains Ceasefire Agreement.

As happened with the Shawabna, the Leira Amir was able to mobilize some of his own people within government-controlled areas, with the assistance of the government army. Upon their arrival in Umm Derafi, the Leira decided to not join the Shawabna in their newly established village at 'Alali. They moved on, past the village, and resettled at a different site within Umm Derafi called Abu Hamama, 4–5km north of the Shawanba settlement – a response to the latter's unilateral and precipitate move and renaming of their site. They also decided to rename 'Abu Hamama' as Umm Derafi 'Leira', claiming it as the principal Umm Derafi settlement, with more legitimacy than the Shawabna one. Mistrust between these two ethnic groups became palpable as they continued to argue for their respective positions. This is confirmed by the Amir of the Nuba Leira:

> We, the Leira people, could not return and resettle together with the Shawabna in 'Alali village this time, because they not only imposed a new name on the area but they also started to claim that this is their territory. For this reason, we decided to go and re-open Abu Hamama village and started to resettle under our original name of Umm Derafi Leira.[15]

The bone of contention is the name. For the Leira, it is Umm Derafi Leira; for the Shawabna, it is Umm Derafi Shaybun; and for the Arab nomads of Aulad Ghabush, it is simply Umm Derafi, with no further labelling of ethnic connotations. Differences over the name of the territory, however, are a cover for deeper conflicts. 'Leira' and 'Shaybun' are loaded with identity connotations that strengthen the rival claims to the land.

---

[15] Author's interview with Muhammad Tia, Amir of Nuba Leira in the government-controlled areas, Umm Derafi, 16 May 2006.

In the Shawabna view, this situation is nothing new. What has changed is the complex dimension it assumed as a result of the civil war. Otherwise, the dispute can be traced back as far as 1956, when the government demanded local representation in the local council. The Umm Derafi multi-ethnic community unanimously selected 'Isa al-Duma of Leira as their representative in Kadugli. In 1957, he fixed a signpost on the Shaybun road with the words, 'to Umm Derafi Leira'. The Shawabna reacted immediately, confronted 'Isa al-Duma and took the signpost down.[16]

In the Shawabna's opinion, this incident signifies the beginning of the conflict over the Umm Derafi territory. According to my informant, Adam Hakim of Aulad Ghabush, in the mid-1970s, the Commissioner of South Kordofan, Mahmud Hassib, visited Umm Derafi, and it was agreed that he would be received in the hamlet of Gardud Tia, the seat of the Leira native administration. The Shawabna were of the opinion that the Commissioner should be received in their hamlet. On the day of the visit, the Shawabna were able to persuade the Commissioner to do so, leaving the Leira waiting in vain in their settlement, a great insult to their honour and dignity. Since then, tension between the two ethnic groups has continued to escalate, with each party attempting to consolidate its position in different ways, including territorial claims and counter-claims drawn from their histories.[17]

Since the war, it is obvious that each party has sought control over the area by way of controlling the new central settlement point at 'Alali or Abu Hamama, each with sharp ethnic distinctions. Each settlement expanded into a village with a separate military base, school, health clinic, markets, stores, and above all, separate native administrations. This territorial separation along ethnic lines clearly indicates that a new type of conflict is emerging in the area, one which has been concretized through the support of the state institutions, UN organizations, and national and international NGOs. It is a point to which we will return.

THE BASIS OF THE LEIRA COMMUNAL LAND CLAIM IN UMM DERAFI

In the Leira view, all historical records and official documents reveal that the area is known as Umm Derafi Leira and not Umm Derafi Shaybun. For instance, they refer to several official fixed signposts with their own designation, claiming that these were set up during the colonial period. Indeed, some still exist along the roads leading to Umm Derafi from Heiban or from Kadugli via Shaybun hill. The Amir of Leira claimed that he presented several complaints in 2002 and 2003 to the government in Kadugli about the Shawabna's attempt to rename the area, but without any response. From the Leira standpoint, the political authorities in Kadugli are apparently backing the Shawabna's ambitions to take over what they perceive to be their own lands.

---

[16] Author's interview with 'Umda Hamid Salatin and Ibrahim Sharif, Umm Derafi, 22 May 2006.
[17] Author's interview with Adam Hakim, Umm Derafi, 19 May 2006.

Amir Muhammad Tia Koko supports the Leira claim, confirming that Umm Derafi has historically been known as Umm Derafi Leira since the colonial period, as well as being part of the Leira's ancestral territory. Before the war, Umm Derafi was under the administration of Mek al-Duma Angelo of Leira, followed by his successor Kajo Bakhit, although it continued to accommodate different ethnic groups. Leira territory itself was and still is part of the Heiban administrative area. The Amir revealed that there are three places called Umm Derafi within the Heiban administrative area. They are: Umm Derafi Tombola, Umm Derafi Tira, and Umm Derafi Leira. Thus, there was a need for official clarification. The additional labels, 'Tombola', 'Tira', and 'Leira', indicate which community the respective territories belong to. The Amir claimed that Umm Derafi is now part of the Leira Imara (native administration), although before the war, it was inhabited by Leira, Kawalib, Hadra, and Aulad Ghabush, intermingled in numerous hamlet clusters including Cardud Tia, Lolla, hilat Shawabna, Koko al-Amin, 'Alali, Abu Hamama, Tabaldiyat al-Nus, al-Nasur, hilat Ramadan, er-Churr, Klayoum, and hilat Shaykh Mugdam Delami.[18]

An interview with another senior Leira informant, Shaykh al-Nur Daldum Angelo, produced another historical account of the emergence of Umm Derafi as a settlement and also confirmed its territorial boundaries as part of the Leira's overall communal land. The Shaykh is one of the few remaining people of the Leira who moved from a hilly area of Hajar Hatab and settled in the plains and fertile land of Umm Derafi in 1942. He believes that the Kochocho and Koko al-Almin were the first settlers and, therefore, the founders of Umm Derafi. Later, the Leira were joined by Kawalib and the Arab nomads of Aulad Ghabush, whose leaders were Korchano and Yusuf respectively. He insisted that the Shawabna were latecomers to the Umm Derafi area. However, he affirmed that all these ethnic groups managed to live together amicably and to establish numerous common institutions, such as the famous Friday local weekly market at Hajar Tia.

Ethnic mixing in neighbourhoods was the norm, but equally significant was the overlap in shifting cultivation patterns and orchard management Shaykh al-Nur was able to mention a number of families who still have orchards in the fertile valley of Khur Umm Derafi. The Leira farmers may be the majority, but the presence of orchard owners from other ethnic groups, including the Shawabna, is evident. In the Shaykh's view, the Shawabna were given secondary rights of use access, not primary rights of land ownership as they now claim. Shaykh al-Nur claimed that Leira tribal boundaries were drawn by a committee formed by Mek al-Duma of Leira at some point in the 1950s. The committee was composed of Mukhtar Almin, Juma' Hamad, Shaykh Kelalo, Kodi Kajima, Nasir Hamid of Kawalib, and Kachocho of Njkur.[19]

---

[18] Author's interview with Muhammad Tia Koko, Amir of Leira, Umm Derafi, 15 May 2006.
[19] Author's interview with Shaykh al-Nur Daldum Angelo of Leira, Umm Derafi, 19 May 2006.

My two key informants of Leira, Muhammad Tia Koko and al-Nur Daldum Angelo, gave an identical description of the imagined boundary of the Umm Derafi as part of the overall Leira territory, as follows. It starts at Hijayr al-Abayd at its northwest frontier to Am Sisi, Tabaldi al-Nus, al-'Adibe al-A'war, and Engini and that forms the Leira border with Kawalib. From Zilaytaya in the southwest it is parallel to the Shaybun hill near Zangor, Shabun well (saniya), rijl al-Nabak and from there it passes through north 'Aggab toward Shwai. It then proceeds from south to east near Kochamba, Ghi-Lo-Ghinda, and from Mirr upwards to Nine in Alleira hill. From this rough boundary demarcation, it is clear that the Leira do not recognize any territorial boundaries with either Shawabna or Baqqara Arabs. They insist that their boundaries have always been with their Nuba neighbours.

This suggests that the Leira, like so many Nuba groups, perceive all non-Nuba ethnic groups living within their claimed tribal territory as communities with rights of access and not rights of communal land ownership. Consequently, the Leira leave no room for the establishment of a Shawabna native administration within their territory. What is feasible is the possibility of co-opting Shawabna communal leaders within the overall Leira native administration. In this respect, reference was made to more recent precedents, when the Shawabna Shaykhs such as 'Ibayd, Kalol, and Dawud were part of the Mek al-Duma native administration during the 1940s and the 1950s.

However, as in many other Nuba communities, the Leira argument does not end here. Rather, the argument is linked to the history of Nuba conglomerated ethnic groups as firstcomers to the region as a whole. This contrasts with the other ethnic groups who were the 'latecomers'. The collective claim of the Nuba's firstcomer status which includes the whole Nuba Mountains region is based on and persists at this macro-level. Moreover, the Nuba-claimed plains and fertile lands, the argument continues, that look like a 'no man's land', have been fully occupied by the Nuba since time immemorial. As discussed in Chapter 1, the Nuba were forced, at a later stage, to abandon their fertile lands following the expansion of external forces including the Baqqara.

THE SHAWABNA COUNTER-CLAIM

Contrary to the Leira line of argument, the Shawabna claim to have definite tribal boundaries that were recognized and drawn up by the colonial administration during the Kanuna Hilal 'Umdaship in the 1950s. These boundaries start in Orertti at Hajr Zera at the Shawabna-Shwai-Aboll meeting-point in the east. The line moves counter-clockwise towards their border with the Leira near Hajr Hatab, Gardud Komi or Komimi, Nugrat al-Shaqa, and continues to Lolla, al-A'rdebi, Tabaldiyat al-Nus to form their border with the Hadra people in the north. It proceeds westwards toward Hijayr al-Abayd and Zilaytaya crossing the Bat-ha toward Witayt, Umm Tibis, and Kashmm to border with Dilimiyya

Rawawqa; then it proceeds toward Hijayr al-Barani of Aggab, Tarong, Karif, Tarror, and then Torbat Komi (currently Eire market), then back to their boundary with the Shwai.[20]

In this context, Sharif Ibrahim remarked that 'because this described territory was recognized by the colonial administration as our own customary communal land, we were annually forced to clear the Kadugli-Heiban road from Shaybun to Shwai and then from there the enforced task used to be taken up by the Shwai and later by the people of Aboll to Heiban.' Practically speaking, this Shawabna-defined territory not only includes the Umm Derafi area and 'Aggab but also cuts across several places which are part of other Nuba tribal land, including some northern parts of Moro, Otoro, and Shwai. For the sake of counteracting the claim of the Nuba Leira as firstcomers to Umm Derafi, several key Shawabna informants gave a detailed historical account of how some Shawabna ended up settling in Umm Derafi, in order to falsify the Leira claim. For instance, their leader 'Umda Hamid Salatin insists that the Shawabna are indigenous to Umm Derafi land:

> This area, with its boundaries that include Umm Derafi, 'Aggab, and the plain land in the western bank of Khur Shwai, represents our forefathers' land. It has been a livelihood base for our last five to six generations. We, the Shawabna, therefore have no land other than this to go to. Though the Shawabna genealogical origin can be traced back to the Arab Peninsula, its present generation is a product of successive intermarriage between their Arab ancestors and the Nuba groups, because our ancestral fathers did not bring their wives along with them upon their arrival here. They came and married Nuba women, and continued this intermarriage process with the surrounding ethnic groups, particularly the Nuba of Shwai, Aboll, Leira, Moro, and Kawalib, as well as the local Arabs of the Hawazma group. The result is our present Shawabna generation, which is original to this soil as their irreplaceable indigenous homeland.[21]

On the basis of his birth in Shwai in 1929, a key Shawabna informant, Shaykh Sharif Ibrahim, insists that the Shawabna initially lived very peacefully with the Nuba Shwai following their relocation from Jebel due to a water shortage in that area, during the colonial period. In 1937, they moved from Shwai back to Jebel Shaybun following a dispute regarding their administrative affiliation. Arno Kepe, a famous and powerful Mek of Otoro, claimed that the Shawabna were part of his Mekship domain, while Shawabna leaders were of the opinion that they were an administrative unit of their own. As a result of this dispute, the colonial administration decided to relocate the Shawabna from Shwai to their previous settlement place at Jebel Shaybun. Although the Shawabna resisted their move out of Shwai, the colonial administration presented them with an ultimatum: to leave by a set time, or have their houses burned to the ground.

---

[20] Author's interview with 'Umda Hamid Salatin, Shaykh Tirab and Sharif Ibrahim, Umm Derafi, 22 May 2006
[21] Author's interview with 'Umda Hamid Salatin, Umm Derafi, 23 May 2006.

In Shaybun, they suffered from a water shortage during the dry season. In 1938 the colonial administration decided to dig a saniya [water well] for them of which remnants exist today. But this well did not satisfy their daily water needs. As a consequence, they started to move into Umm Derafi, which was by then a thick forest and a completely uninhabited jungle. By 1948 almost all the Shawabna families in Shaybun had moved and resettled in Umm Derafi. Later, other groups followed, mainly the Aulad Ghabush migratory nomads, the Hadra people from their nearby hill, and Aulad Mumin from Zilaytaya. At that point, there was no Leira presence at all. It was only in 1949 that the Leira started their flow from their nearby hills in the east into Umm Derafi. They were first led by Majan and his brother Kalas, who stayed in Lolla hamlet in 1950; in 1951, Kuku al-Amin came from Leira hill; and in 1952, Tia Koko, the father of the present Amir Muhammad Tia, arrived. He did not stay with his people in their own hamlets but lived with the Shawabna and established friendly relations with Shaykh Nasir Abdul. They swore an oath of co-existence, and he was given a piece of farming land by Muhammad Kenani. Later, Tia Koko moved and established his own hamlet, which came to be named after him as Gardud Tia.[22]

The Shawabna intended to refute the Leira claim to be the founders of Umm Derafi with these historical narratives, while representing themselves as the firstcomers and the real founders of Umm Derafi as a settlement point. Thus, both sides continue an endless dispute over Umm Derafi territory.

In order to consolidate their position on the ground, the Shawabna managed to establish a new 'Umudiya with its seat in Umm Derafi Shaybun at 'Alali village. Their native leader, Hamid Salatin, who led them back into Umm Derafi, has formally been recognized by the government in Kadugli as 'Umda of Shawabna in Umm Derafi Shaybun. However, the territorial boundaries and the political authorities of this new Shawabna native administration overlap considerably with those of the Leira under Amir Muhammad Tia. Politically and administratively, it is affiliated with the Shawabna's greater native administration under the leadership of Amir Mahmmud al-Murad at Sama, east Kadugli. From the Leira standpoint, this Shawabna 'Umudiya, if it is to exist at all, should be under the larger Leira native administration, which covers all the Leira territories including Umm Derafi.

Hamid Salatin of Shawabna has not yet been given court responsibilities by the judiciary system, but he was recognized by the political-administrative system in Kadugli as an administrative 'Umda. Yet the Shawabna in Umm Derafi seem to be reluctant to take their case to the Leira court: any recognition of the Leira court by the Shawabna might weaken their position in seeking the establishment of their own court in 'Alali. And that may imply their subordination to the Leira native authority, a situation which they have resisted since the colonial period.

[22] Author's interview with Ibrahim Sharif, Umm Derafi, 22 May 2006.

In short, it is evident that the present division of Umm Derafi into Shaybun and Leira is a product of an accumulated historical process of conflict between these two ethnic groups. The Shawabna and Leira versions of their respective histories and geographies of settlement in Umm Derafi are significantly different. It is obvious that each party claims to be the firstcomer and therefore the founder of Umm Derafi as a settlement point. According to the Leira, they established Umm Derafi in the early 1940s at a time when there were no Shawabna there. Moreover, they perceive the area as an integral part of their overall customarily owned territory; even if it is proved that others were the first to settle there. The Shawabna, on the other hand, claim to be the founders of Umm Derafi in the late 1940s when the Leira were still on their jebels. However, a third position comes from the Arab nomads of Aulad Ghabush who have a longstanding presence and co-existence with both Shawabna and Leira in Umm Derafi. One of the prominent leaders of Aulad Ghabush in Umm Derafi testifies that:

> Umm Derafi was founded jointly by the Leira people led by Tia Koko, Morjan Kodi, Koko al-Min, on the one hand, and Aulad Ghabush led by Adam Hakim, on the other, in the 1940s. Later, the Shawabna expanded into the area from 'Aggab and Jebel Shaybun. Historically, Umm Derafi was known as Umm Derafi without 'Leira' or 'Shaybun' attachments. At the same time, it was taken for granted by the Leira that it was part of their overall, customary owned territory before they realized that their claim was being contested by the Shawabna.[23]

In the view of my informant, Adam Hakim, the Leira added the name 'Leira' to Umm Derafi for the sake of consolidating their communal claim to the area because of their fear of the growing Shawabna political hegemony there, since the 1940s. Although the Aulad Ghabush testimony, as presented by Adam Hakim, seems to favour the Leira position, it can also be interpreted as a clever attempt by the Aulad Ghabush to keep Umm Derafi a neutral place for everyone, including themselves. The dilemma of firstcomer and latecomer is palpable in this never ending debate, because firstcomer claims are far from unambiguous.

According to Lentz (2007: 40–1), the key issue in this debate is related to who is recognized as a firstcomer? Was it the discovery of the site of the new village, the actual clearing of the bush, or some form of conquest? The second issue is the delineation of the territorial and social reach of the group that claims firstcomer status. A group may insist on having been founders of a village, including its various subsequently established sections and satellite settlements. However, the founders of the latter may, in turn, claim to be firstcomers in their own right, particularly in relation to others who came yet later. The relative chronology of the foundation of settlements can be manipulated in multiple ways. In addition, firstcomer claims can be extended from a single lineage to entire ethnic groups or

---

[23] Author's interview with Adam Hakim, Umm Derafi, 19 May 2006.

even conglomerates of ethnic groups, as is the case with Nuba firstcomers who claim the entire region of the Nuba Mountains.

At this stage, it is interesting to note that, unlike the case of al-Azraq, the emerging ethnic tension in Umm Derafi described above does not lie along the Government-SPLM/A political-administrative and military divide, but along the ethnic boundaries of two ethnic groups, both of whose leaders embrace the same government political doctrine. This implies that ethnic identity and belonging, and not political or religious affiliations, seem to be the key factor when it comes to the question of communal land rights. However, the situation became even more complex on the arrival of the SPLM, as a new political player, in Umm Derafi after the CPA.

SPLM ARRIVAL AND INVOLVEMENT
IN LOCAL ETHNO-POLITICS

After the peace agreement, the SPLM emerged as a powerful political player in the region. It soon moved into Umm Derafi and established a political office in Abu Hamama village as part of its ambitious plan to expand politically into the government-controlled areas. For the SPLM, Umm Derafi is an area of political significance because it is part of the Leira territory, whose peoples were among the first to join the SPLM/A. This political affiliation to the SPLM after the CPA remains a strategic political issue for the SPLM in general and the Leira in particular.

Upon their arrival, the SPLM started a process of political and administrative involvement in Umm Derafi affairs, especially those related to land management. In an attempt to promote its land strategy, centred on the Nuba autochthonous claim, the SPLM summoned all pastoral nomads present in the area and conveyed the message, as al-Nil 'Usman, a Leira SPLM activist in Umm Derafi, recounts, that 'The pastoral nomads are here in Leira land to enjoy rights of use access and not ownership rights which is an exclusive right for the Leira community.' Moreover, the SPLM office in Umm Derafi took the initiative of forming a joint committee from different ethnic groups in the area to deal with some land-based conflicts in a peaceful manner. However, in al-Nil 'Usman's words: 'The committee did not work.' The first problem that faced the committee was the Shawabna's unilateral attempt to register their claimed orchard plots without others' consent. The committee discussed the issue in the presence of the Shawabna representatives and found that this unilateral move should immediately be stopped. But apparently, as described below, the Shawabna did not comply with the decision and continued the registration of their claimed plots in a highly contested area.[24]

With the arrival and involvement of the SPLM in the area, the political tension between Muhammad Tia, the Amir of Leira, and the SPLM reached its peak. Through my participatory observation, it became evident that the SPLM in Umm Derafi was not only undermining but contesting

---

[24] Author's interview with al-Nil 'Usman, Umm Derafi, 18 May 2006.

the authority of Amir Mohamed Tia because of his strong political link to the ruling National Congress Party (NCP). One major criticism launched against him by the Leira in the SPLM was that he was too weak and was not only controlled by the Shawabna, but also used against his own people. They accused him of collaborating with the Shawabna and the government officials in grabbing Leira land and exploiting their communal natural resources, particularly in timber production.

From the Leira viewpoint, his weakness stems from a conflict of interests in maintaining his business as a merchant and a politician, and assuming responsibilities as a community leader and a custodian for their collective interests. Various informants revealed that some of his current economic assets, such as the flour mill, were granted to him on behalf of the community by the government in Kadugli. However, he has used them to his own benefit. In response to this accusation, the Amir acknowledged that the flour mill was donated by the government, but to him in person and not to the community. Whatever the truth of this case, his answer reveals a government policy of appointing and empowering native leaders who support its political and ideological agenda.

Against this background, the SPLM, led by some Leira activists, started to establish a parallel community leadership for Leira in Umm Derafi, thus undermining the Amir's authority. Some local Leira Shaykhs shifted to a different chain of command that can be traced back to the SPLM political-administrative structure in the area and beyond. Furthermore, new business entrepreneurs with strong links to the SPLM emerged in the area. Since the return of the Leira to Umm Derafi in 2002, there had been only one retail shop and one flour mill, and both belonged to the Amir. By 2007, more than ten new shops and three flour mills had been established, mostly by the SPLM supporters following their return to the area. These new political and economic realities put enormous pressure on the existing institutions controlled by the Amir who is loyal to the ruling NCP. In other words, while his native administration and political powers were being challenged, his monopolistic trade in the area also faced intense economic competition through the expansion of local enterprises led by his political rivals within his own kinfolk.

Leira–Leira political rivalry in Umm Derafi escalated to frequent incidents of violence, exemplified by the following accounts. According to Amir Muhammad Tia, an unidentified person burned down a shelter, part of his native court erected near his house, as well as part of his house in 2006. Despite the lack of evidence, the Amir is convinced that the fire was started by an SPLM supporter to destroy his socio-economic standing and political authority in the area. The second incident took place during my presence in Umm Derafi when, on the night of 2 February 2007 a newly installed flour mill was burned down, with its contents of more than fifty sacks of sorghum grain, the estimated loss of which amounted to an equivalent of US$6000, a substantial sum in a war-torn, subsistence-level rural economy. This time, the property belonged to a prominent SPLM activist—the Amir's main business competitor and political rival in the area.

As in the first-mentioned case, the culprit has never been found. Nevertheless, the owner of the burned mill apparently has a strong but unproven claim that the incident was politically motivated economic sabotage, probably executed by a NCP supporter, perhaps with the direct or indirect encouragement of the Amir himself. In my discussion with the owner, he claimed 'they have destroyed my entire economic livelihood base with the aim of forcing me to leave the area. The ultimate aim is to make the SPLM Office here ineffective or even closed down. I have no enemies except my political rivals among the Leira here in Abu Hamama, and some Shawabna over there, at 'Alali'.[25]

In this tense situation, the members of the Leira community in Abu Hamama village, though ethnically homogenous, found themselves polarized along the SPLM/NCP political divide, creating deep fissures in their social ties. Apart from such violent incidents, this polarization is manifested in a number of daily socio-economic activities and inter-personal relations in the area. For instance, a Leira household's decision to use a certain shop for daily shopping is no longer a purely economic choice. Rather, it is, primarily a political decision that will bring economic benefit to an SPLM or to an NCP shop owner.

The Baqqara and the Fellata nomads as well as the Shawabna households were also politically divided through market interactions. Through my participatory observations at the Abu Hamama local market, it was evident that the majority of Shawabna households were doing most of their shopping in the Amir's retail shop and flour mill, as opposed to the ones owned by persons linked to the SPLM. Interestingly, the Baqqara, Shanabla, and Fellata seasonal nomads seem to have taken a strategic and situational position by dividing themselves among the businesses of these Leira political foes. Their direct interests lie in maintaining positive relations with the Leira as a block, irrespective of Leira internal issues. Each of these two Leira political rivals may exercise some form of authority over some parts of the overall Leira-claimed territory where the nomads roam for grazing. Therefore, these nomads are likely to lose access to some or all of the grazing land within the Leira territory if they side economically or politically with one or other of the Leira competing parties.

Thus, the area was not only divided along the Nuba/non-Nuba ethno-political divide but also along the Nuba/Nuba line, within people of the same tribe in the same locale. In short, the Umm Derafi case demonstrates that the political scene in the post-conflict situation of the Nuba Mountains is extremely complex, fluid, and unpredictable.

SOME ETHNIC TENSIONS OVER LAND RESOURCES IN UMM DERAFI

During the civil war, with the collapse of community-based traditional systems of resource management in the area, the huge deleib timber forest

[25] Author's informal discussion with Ahmed, the owner of the burned flour mill, Umm Derafi, 3 February 2007.

was subject to illegal over-cutting. This activity was further intensified when the area was opened up to traders with the free movement of people and goods, as a result of the Nuba Mountains Cease Fire Agreement in 2002. The Leira peoples, both in the SPLM/A- and in the Government-held areas, who claim communal rights over the Umm Derafi territory, protest against this mismanagement and over-exploitation of their land resources by outsiders. They believe that the Shawabna and the government army stationed in Umm Derafi are the main actors in the timber industry, and are engaged in recurrent conflicts with both on their return to Umm Derafi in 2002. As a consequence, Muhammad Tia, Amir of the Leira, was summoned along with others and questioned by government authorities in connection with their allegedly unnecessary and repeated objections to tree-felling in the area. The Amir of Leira was warned to refrain from such interference. In his own words:

> We had recurring cases of conflicts over timber resources because we wanted to sustain our resources and use them rationally while others wanted to maximize their gains from it at the expense of the present and some generations to come. Despite our efforts to stop this over-cutting, the business is going on, particularly in the areas beyond the control of the Leira Native Administration.[26]

This testimony is in line with a recent report from Pantuliano et al., (2007: 28) which depicts conflicts over natural resources in the Nuba Mountains, post-war, as one of the main land conflicts in the region, including the Umm Derafi area:

> Many key informants reported that insecurity has significantly increased in the areas where farmers are clashing with traders who are exploiting local natural resources. This was said to be a particularly acute problem in the Rashad and Abu Jebeha localities, where traders were reported to have been illegally logging timber, gum Arabic and palm trees (delieb), with the complicity of the military. The areas most affected by logging are khor al-Delieb (palm trees), Umm Durafi (where last year 700 palm trees were said to have been cut), Kao Nwro (gum arabic), Abu Jebeha (gum arabic), and kawalib (gum arabic).

Fruit production is another area that involves serious confrontation between the Leira and the Shawabna communities in the post-war situation. Recently, some Shawabna initiated a process of formal registration of their orchards in Umm Derafi with state support through the al-Zakat Fund. This is known officially in Arabic as Diwan al-Zakahal-Zakat, and is one of several Islamic institutions controlled by Muslim elites in the government. It is part of an endeavour to promote Islamic political ideology and its programmes nationwide. This religious-based economic institution, among others, was widely used and is still being used by the state to empower its political supporters economically (whether individuals

---

[26] Author's interview with Muhammad Tia, Amir of Leira, Umm Derafi, 16 May 2006.

or communities), and sometimes along ethnic lines as this case will demonstrate. Thus, Mohamed Salih (2000: 3) suggests, al-Zakat 'becomes an important political tool'.

The initiative of orchard registration seems to have been confined to Shawabna community members in the area. It was led by the Shawabna native leader 'Umda Hamid Salatin. During my fieldwork in May 2006, the 'Umda arrived from Khartoum with a truck full of improved seedlings of Mango trees supplied by the al-Zakahal-Zakat Fund. Upon his arrival, he held a meeting with those Shawabna households who own orchards. He explained how the first bunch of seedlings was going to be distributed among some families who had already prepared their respective plots. However, he promised that there would be a series of such trucks coming in until all interested families were supplied.

It is worth noting that all the orchards that belong to different ethnic groups overlap with others in the fertile lowlands along the Umm Derafi Khur. Before the war, it was the custom for the boundaries of each neighbouring farm to be maintained by mutual consent, with a process of give and take. During the war, the orchards were abandoned resulting in the disappearance of boundary markers. Up to the end of the time of my field work (2005–2008), a sizeable number of orchard owners had not yet returned, stranded as IDPs somewhere, waiting to return. This implies that any attempt to re-demarcate an orchard in the absence of its neighbouring landowner is likely to create disputes over already loose and fluid boundaries.

For this reason, the Shawabna's unilateral move to identify the boundaries of their orchards coupled with their intention to pursue some form of registration, was categorically opposed by the Leira people and their native authority in the area. According to Amir Muhammad Tia of Leira, they wanted to wait for the other owners to return before a formalization of the boundaries of orchards was pursued. Despite this seemingly sound reasoning, it is evident that some Shawabna households have unilaterally taken practical steps towards some form of registration of their claimed plots, resulting in further inter-communal tensions.

Conclusion

An ethnographic analysis of the al-Azraq and Umm Derafi cases has shown that the territorial co-existence of various ethnic groups was the dominant social form in the region in the pre-war period, although there was constant competition for land resources. During the civil war and thereafter, this pattern suffered drastic erosion. As a result, the return of various stakeholders to their previous territories has been a tense process in the post-conflict era. The new dynamics, still in the making, mean that each ethnic group exerts tremendous effort to consolidate its control over land under its actual use, while contesting others' claims.

The Umm Derafi case in particular reveals the dilemma for peace makers (local, national, and global) in restoring the pre-war situation in the region, where previously co-existing local communities, have become divided territorially along sharp ethnic lines.

Both cases demonstrate that the Nuba claim to land rights is increasingly articulated in terms of autochthonous claims with strong ties to perceived ancestral land. This is part of emerging Nuba movements aimed at reconstructing themselves as one unified ethno-political group in order to be able to take collective political action. However, this position is being systematically contested by the other ethnic groups in the region. They use different forms of alliances, solidarity, power, and control at various levels of governance, including the manipulation of the native administration, to counteract the Nuba's emerging collective movement.

The cases suggest that the settlement of the land question is a vital step toward achieving sustainable social and political peace and security in the region. However, due to a lack of 'comprehensiveness' in the CPA with regard to the land question, associated with the disappointing performance of the Government of National Unity at federal and state levels, it is doubtful whether the CPA and its institutions are capable of redressing the deeply rooted, land-driven grievances of the indigenous Nuba, among others.

The nature, trend, and scale of continuing land-based conflicts in the region create an alarming situation, and the likelihood of a resumption of civil war. In the absence of political will effectively to address the land question, a central factor among the root causes of the recurring Sudanese civil wars, there is no reason to assume a restoration of political and social peace and security, not only in the Nuba Mountains but also in the other regions of Sudan.

7

Contested Communal Lands,
Identity Politics & Conflicts

Claiming communal land ownership on the basis of customary rights is nothing new in the Sudan in general and in the Nuba Mountains in particular. What is new in the region is an upsurge of land claims with a strong tendency to exclude others who share the same claimed territory, particularly in the post-conflict situation (see Elsayed 2005, Komey 2008a, 2008b, 2009a, 2009b, 2010a). This trend, particularly among the Nuba, has been described in previous chapters. This chapter presents a further analysis based on selected field sites offering a view of the long history of Nuba-Baqqara cohabitation and symbiosis.

It focuses primarily on the post-conflict discourse of the increase in Nuba claims to communal land ownership, the Baqqara's disputes over those claims, and the subsequent resource-driven conflicts over the land. Two sides of the situation are presented: first, the Nuba's autochthonous, or lesser 'firstcomer' claim to communal land rights, deeply rooted in their historical and traditional legitimacy; second, the Baqqara Arabs counter-claim to have rights not only in terms of their traditional secondary rights of access and use of land and water, but also in terms of equal rights of ownership of the same land. In the working out of these claims and counter-claims at various levels of scale in the social organizations of the two groups, a range of land-driven conflicts occur of varying magnitudes and with various consequences.

The Nuba claim, however, is not only contested by the local Baqqara but also by the state's modern land policies, laws, and practices. Thus, the issue involves a confrontation between the 'legality' of the modern state's legal framework regarding all matters of land ownership and usage, and also the 'legitimacy' of the traditional ethnic institutions and authorities of indigenous communities, as we have discussed in previous chapters. The state/society land-based confrontation stems from the fact that the state's legal and political-administrative institutions tend to undermine the legitimacy of any communal land claim on the basis of customary rights. At the local community level, confrontation takes place at various levels of scale in traditional social institutions and authorities of the sedentary Nuba groups as indigenous and firstcomers in the region and those of agro-pastoral Baqqara groups as the people who came later. These claims, counter-claims, and consequent actions occur in the course of the constant and unavoidable competition between the two groups over shared land resources.

Nuba and Baqqara contest over a shared territory: the Keiga case

The Nuba of Keiga represent a sub-ethnic group within the Kadugli-Krongo ethno-linguistic group, with an estimated population of 10,000 in north, northwest, and west Kadugli on and around the five hill communities of (i) Keiga Damik, (ii) Keiga al-Khayl, (iii) Keiga Luban, (iv) Keiga Tummero, and (v) Keiga Jerru. However, according to MacDiarmid and MacDiarmid (1927, 1931) and Stevenson (1984), the Keiga Jerru is part of the Temein, a different Nuba ethnic and linguistic group. Like other Sudanese rural communities, the Keiga people traditionally managed their communally claimed land through their socially credited leaders and the associated native institutions.

At the early stage of colonial administration, the various Keiga hill communities were brought under the control of the native administration of Dar Jami' Arabs before they were brought under the Nuba Kadugli federated native administration in the 1930s. Somi Tawir, an Arab leader of Dar Jami', was appointed by the colonial administration as 'Umda of Dar Jami' and all Keiga, a decision that marked a consolidation of the former's suzerainty of the Keiga. This situation continued up to the mid-1930s, when the Nuba and Arab native administrations were separated under the Closed District Policy (1922–47). Thus, in 1933, the colonial government formed an independent Keiga Confederation after the Arabs' suzerainty proved to be exploitative (Gillan 1931: 21; also see Salih 1990: 427). Tio Danda Tio was the first 'Umda of the newly established, separate Keiga native administration (1933–37) with Rahhal Andu, Mek of Kadugli, as paramount Chief. From that time until the mid-'70s, Keiga communities were governed by their own native leaders, namely Hamdun Rahmatalla Wad Kafi (1937–40); Haren Kafi (1942–64); 'Abdalla Hamdun (1968–75).

In 1975, the native administration in the whole of Sudan was abolished by the government, and replaced by *al-Mahakim al-Sh'abiya* (Peoples' Courts) that continued in effect until the early 1990s when the native system was reinstated, albeit in different form and functions. This change was the result of the breaking up of the previous 'Umudiyat which happened for several reason but mainly for political control by the new ruling regime at that time. As a result, the Keiga and Saburi-Laguri 'Umudiyat separated from Kadugli and transformed into Imara under the name of *Imarat al Reif al Shargi* (the Imara of the Eastern Rural Areas). The new designation was under the leadership of the late Amir Ahmed Musa Haren, with Honowa Hakim, 'Umda of Saburi-Laguri, as his Deputy.

Today, each Keiga tribe is headed by 'Umda (leaders) and they are working collectively towards establishing their own separate Keiga Mekship instead of being part of Kadugli . The present native leaders in Keiga are as follows: Keiga Tummero under 'Umda al-Yias Ibrahim Koko, Keiga Jirru under 'Umda Hussayn al-Zubayr Mulla, Keiga Lubun under 'Umda Idriss Abu Jalha, and Keiga Damik under 'Umda Idriss Jibril.[1]

Although each of the Keiga hill communities or tribes has its own loosely defined social structure and territorial boundaries within the overall Keiga communal lands, they believe that they all originated from the Kolo sub-hill in Keiga Tummero. Chapter 6 gave the story of how Kolo, the Keiga's legendary ancestor, was believed to have been somehow propelled out of the earth to the top of a hill, which came to be named after him. The legend implies a strong tie between Keiga ethnic identity and the claim on this site as communal land. Based on this autochthonous myth and its subsequent related narratives, the people of Keiga, like other Nuba groups, believe that they are indigenous or even autochthonous to the region and that they inherited their present land territory from their forefathers a long time ago. Therefore, others who have lately joined them through settlement, or for grazing, farming, or trading purposes are entitled to enjoy only rights of access, not rights of ownership to these lands or resources.

Within this traditionally claimed Keiga land, several other agro-pastoral and sedentary groups of Baqqara Arabs have made their homes, particularly the Dar Jami' Tuwal in al-Kweik and the Fellata in al-Bardab, among others. These non-Nuba groups are allied under one federated native administration inside the Keiga communal land. At present, part of the Baqqara of Dar Jami', a sub-tribe of the Rawawqa of Hawazma, have established their Imara (native administration unit), headed by their Amir (the paramount chieftainship), inside the Keiga Luban territory centred at al-Kweik settlement point. In addition to the Dar Jami' group and their allied sedentary Fellata, locally known as Takarir,[2] there are other smaller but equally influential Arab groups including the Aulad Nuba based mainly at Tukswana in the Laguri area; some Zunara and Bidayriyya Arabs of North Kordofan who migrated to South Kordofan during the drought of the 1970s and 1980s and settled in the fertile land of al-Jughan and other areas within the Keiga land; and several nomadic Arab groups,

---

[1] Interviews with various Keiga key informants: Sambo Sa'id Tia, Keiga Luban, 10 February 2007; 'Umda al-Yias Ibrahim Koko, Keiga Tummero, 5 June 2005; and Suliman al-Ehaydib Kafi Tio Dein, Kadugli, 15 February 2007.

[2] All Fellata and other tribes that come from the west and pass through Kordofan on their way to Mecca for the Hajj [Islamic pilgrimage] are subsumed under the umbrella term Takarir (see MacMichael 1967: 152). They are part of the Dar Jami' native administration and subsequently part of the overall Hawazma Arabs' Alliance, despite being of different ethnic genealogies.

namely Dar Na'yla, Shanabla, Humr, Messiriyya, and Dar Shalango. These groups engage in agro-pastoralism, traditional and mechanized farming, and trading.[3]

Recently, however, these nomadic groups have tended towards claiming land ownership rights inside Keiga territory. In this way, the Nuba Keiga communal territory, claimed on the basis of the autochthonous or firstcomer status, has been seriously and consistently contested by these groups (Komey 2008a). The territorial overlapping of the Nuba and the Baqqara native administration authorities is a source of dispute, leading to many land-driven conflicts along ethnic lines.

The way that the Fellata migrants came to permanent settlement in the fertile land of al-Bardab inside Keiga Luban territory provides a useful example of the issues here. My key informant, Sambo Sayed Tia of Keiga Luban, kept a record in his hand-written memoirs, of how the al-Bardab area was designated by the British administration for the Fellata upon their arrival from their original settlements in West Africa. He claims that he witnessed and sometimes participated in some important events in the area in his capacity as personal guard of Haren Kafi, Mek of Keiga (1942–64), and then as court guard from 1969 until his retirement in 1997. Most of his notes have a high degree of reliability when checked against archival documents obtained from the Sudan Archive at the University of Durham in United Kingdom.

Today, al-Bardab has grown not only into one of the largest settlement areas for the Fellata in the region, who have developed their own horticulture there, but also into an Islamic missionary centre. The Fellata have already gained full status as Sudanese citizens. Over time, the Fellata have increased in number and spread out into Keiga territory beyond al-Bardab. For example, in recent years a group known as Salamat broke away from al-Sharif 'Abdulla's leadership in al-Bardab and allied with Dar Jami' to establish their own 'Umudiyya within the Dar Jami' native administration. Its seat is located at al-Kweik, inside the Luban claimed communal land.

It is clear that the institutionalization of two or more native administrations over the same territory, as revealed here, leads to friction over land jurisdiction among other problems. The Keiga people have a strong notion of communal land ownership through their native administration and perceive territoriality as a base for community identity, livelihood, and survival. At the same time, the establishment of the Dar Jami' native administration on the same territory is evidence of an emerging sense of proper land ownership, at least, for the area they actually control within the shared territory. Several cases of land-related conflicts, outlined below, show that the native authority has been the main institution upon which the Nuba have constructed territorially-based communal claims which the Baqqara, as well as the state at large, progressively challenge.

---

[3] Interview with 'Umda al-Yias Ibrahim Koko, Keiga Tummero, 5 June 2005.

Keiga line of argument in claiming land

While this general discussion covers Keiga as a whole, most of the ethnographic materials employed here are derived from Keiga Tummero as the focal site of the fieldwork. Towards that end, a brief survey of Keiga Tummero as ecological, economic and political-administrative social space is fundamental to the subsequent analysis.

KEIGA TUMMERO AS SOCIAL SPACE

Keiga Tummero is a cluster of interconnected homesteads, about 42km north of Kadugli, and less than 5km east of the Kadugli-Dilling asphalt road at al-Kweik settlement point (see Map 6.1 in Chapter 6). It is a hill community which is part of the Keiga sub-ethnic group.

The structure of the social system of the Keiga Tummero and its territorial boundaries were studied through direct interviews and participatory observations during my fieldwork. The Keiga Tummero area, with its four villages of Kolo, Keidi, Tummero, and al-Joghba, represents a typical example of Nuba hill communities, where each hill or sub-hill community represents a clan or a lineage with loosely defined social and territorial boundaries in settlements and farmlands. Each clan or lineage is, in turn, ruled by one or two Shaykhs, depending on the size of the households. The total population of the Keiga Tummero is about 3000, governed by one 'Umda and several Shaykhs. The author's interview with the 'Umda and a group of Shaykhs of Keiga Tummero, Keidi, on 4 December, 2006, resulted in a description of this area as loosely organized, territorially and socially:

(1) Kolo sub-hill, a territory for the Kolo clan, is composed of the four lineages Ghamile, Gum Swadi, Gado De Madi, and Ghardik with a total of 63 households. The present 'Umda of Keiga Tummero, al-Yias Ibrahim Koko, comes from this Kolo sub-hill community.

(2) Keidi sub-hill, a territory for the Keidi clan, is composed of the six major Shaykh-headed lineages of Kasmago, Danadudri, Kadak, Keidi, Ghadbrug, and Kafuk with a total of 68 households. The Kafuk lineage has disappeared in the area, but some elderly people still remember some of its remnants in urban areas;

(3) Tummero sub-hill is a territory for the Tummero clan and is composed of the five major lineages Ghadidi, Kosobidi, Kadimidogo, Kashadi, and Kadingre with a total of 129 households; and

(4) Al-Joghba sub-hill is the territory of the al-Joghba clan and is composed of the four main lineages of Gasmo, Godmile, Kaduk, and Kasslu with a total of 78 households.

Each of these clans represents a sub-hill community or village with its

189

own perceived settlement and farming land. However, the spatial overlap of settlements and farm zoning patterns, and of social ties from intermarriages between these four sub-hill communities are all evident. The whole system of social organization is fluid and dynamic, with some form of continuous change in the titles, structures, and powers of leadership at each social level, i.e. lineage, clan, tribe, or ethnic group.

Territorial and social boundaries exist but are flexible, a feature of their social and spatial boundaries that allows the people of Keiga Tummero to act to some degree as a collective social entity when it comes to communal land and its imagined boundaries with 'others'. Depending on the source and magnitude of the perceived or actual threat, this collective action can be initiated at a single family level, then pushed up to clan level or even higher up to Keiga (tribal level), and on rare occasions, if necessary, to the Nuba (ethnic level) as a unified ethno-political entity.

The four sub-hill communities of Kolo, Keidi, Tummero, and al-Joghba, which represent the Keiga Tummero sub-tribe, are situated at the foot of Keiga Tummero hill. Before them lies a wide plain of arable land that continues to their perceived borders with the Laguri and Saburi hill communities. This open land constitutes a farming zone during the rainy season and grazing land for nomads' livestock during the dry season.

Two major water courses run through the plain, providing a permanent water source known as bat-ha, but there are also numerous seasonal water points known as mashaqqa. They provide a water supply for humans, livestock and horticulture during the dry season. Within both these natural and man-made settings nomadic and sedentary peoples constantly encounter one another, with frequent disputes over limited land and water resources.

KEIGA LAND CLAIMS: NARRATIVES AND PRACTICES

The people of Keiga Tummero have several legends and stories supporting their claim as autochthonous or firstcomers to the area. For instance, based on their oral history, several elders and key informants from Keiga narrated how the Arabs of Dar Jami', were hosted upon their arrival in Keiga territory. Intertribal conflicts broke out between the two sections of Arab tribes, Dar Betti and Dar Jami', in their original place called Baraka in al-Quz of North Kordofan during the Mahdiyya wars. Having lost the battle, the Dar Jami' were forced to flee southwards to the Nuba lands, seeking refuge and protection. Upon their arrival, they divided into groups, each one choosing a specific Nuba hill community in search of hospitality, refuge, and protection.

This Keiga narrative is not only widely held among the different Nuba communities, but it is also well supported by a wide range of primary and secondary sources, some of which were reviewed in Chapter 1 (for example, see Sagar 1922, Trimingham 1949, Ibrahim 1988). These sources describe in some detail the Mahdiyya's offensive attacks on some Baqqara who refused to submit and support the Mahdiyya movement in

North Kordofan, resulting in their influx to the Nuba hills in Southern Kordofan. In the words of Vicars-Miles (Sudan Archive 1934: SAD 631/10/6), they 'were reduced to poverty by the raids on their herds, and from being Baqqara became cultivators' following their reception and accommodation by the local Nuba in their respective hill communities.

In this respect, the Keiga's narrative continues, a group led by Shaykh Somi Tawir approached the Keiga leaders at the top of Kolo hill. They were well received and accommodated on the Kolo hilltop together with their horses. Some of the remnants of their material culture still exist in the area today. However, through time and in the process of Sudanese state formation, coupled with their assistance by the successive post-colonial state authorities, these later arrivals, the Baqqara, strengthened their presence as sedentary people as well as nomads on Keiga communal land. Today, local dynamics and discourse suggest that these Dar Jami' Arabs, as latecomers, are progressively contesting the Keiga's communal land claims.

It is worth noting here that the colonial legacy pertaining to native administration coupled with the notion of tribal homeland (*dar*) played and continues to play some role in contemporary claims and counter-claims between the Nuba and the Baqqara in the region. Part of that legacy is that, at the early stage of the Condominium rule, Somi Tawir, the founder of the Dar Jami' in the Keiga area, was appointed by the colonial administration as 'Umda of Dar Jami' and Keiga. As mentioned before, he continued to rule Keiga up to the mid-1930s, when the Nuba and Arab native administrations were separated. His appointment as 'Umda over the Nuba Keiga was justified by the British with the assertion that they would prefer a native leader who spoke Arabic, which was not common among most Nuba, including the Keiga, at the time (see Gillan 1930; Sudan Archive 1934: SAD 631/10/6).

In their relentless effort to represent the Dar Jami' as late-comers who are entitled to enjoy secondary rights over their communal land, several key Keiga informants offered numerous narratives to support their representation of the Dar Jami' in the area. The annual Nuba campaign of clearing roads under the supervision of the Nuba native leaders during the British colonial period is one such story. Again, it is a widely shared narrative among the Nuba in general and the Keiga in particular to substantiate their collective ownership rights to their customary land as indigenous territory (see Harragin 2003: 8). My informant, 'Umda al-Yias Ibrahim Koko of Keiga Tummero, explained that during the British colonial period, the people of Keiga Tummero, under the leadership of the local chiefs, used to clear off the bushes and grass along the Dilling-Kadugli road annually at the end of every rainy season. In the campaign process, the people of Keiga Tummero used to receive the work from the Nuba of Debri at al-Ganaya area and hand it over, in turn, to the people of Keiga Luban, who, in turn, passed it on to those of Saburi.

The Nuba wanted to convey the significance of this historical practice:

it showed that there were no kilinki (borders) between the Nuba and any Baqqara group despite their permanent or seasonal presence inside the Nuba land. My informant insists that these Arabs never participated in the annual road clearing campaign. He continues to argue that whenever the Baqqara were asked to participate, they used to respond to the mufatish (the British inspector) or mamur (the British administrative officer) that they had nothing to do with the Nuba land, that they were not inhabitants of this territory but merely seasonal nomads who were simply passing through, and that their permanent homeland was in Kordofan.[4]

From the Nuba point of view, this reveals a recognition by the Baqqara of Nuba rights over their communal land. However, these are the same Baqqara who are contesting these same Nuba rights to this day, because of several ecological, ethno-political, and socio-economic changes. This emerging agro-pastoral Arab strategy, of claiming ownership rights over Nuba historical homeland territory has intensified conflicts at the grassroots level.

The Keiga Tummero people related numerous historical and current cases of land-related conflicts between themselves and agro-pastoral Arabs in the area. For instance, in an interview with Muhammad Hussayn Sabun, Keiga Tummero, June 7, 2005, he portrayed Nuba communal land as a source of unity and collective action. In 1952 a dispute erupted over farmland between Keiga Tummero and Dar Jami' when the 'far farm' of Sharif Koko of Keiga Tummero, located in the al-Tash arable land south Keiga Tummero was deliberately set on fire, with all its harvested crops, by a Fellata-Takarir man. Each party claimed to be the real owner of the land.

The conflict escalated from an individual to a communal level, resulting in loss of lives on both sides. The people involved were put on trial in a court in Kadugli and some were given jail sentences of several years. The prisoners on the Keiga side were portrayed by their communities as heroes, defending their ancestral land. Furthermore, all the Takarir families who had settled inside Keiga claimed territory were transferred, by court decision to territory beyond the Keiga Tummero land, south into Tesse 'Abdul es Salam.

After some time, however, some of these Takarir started to return to traditional farming and grazing within the southern parts of the Keiga territory. Some of their wealthy households were able to shift from the agro-pastoral mode to permanent settlement and got involved in mechanized farming investments. They were able to legalize their mechanized farming activities by getting approval from government authorities for their schemes inside Keiga territory but without Keiga consent. The case has led to recurrent tensions between the Takarir and the Keiga in the area to the present day, as revealed later in this chapter.

Another land-centred narrative was reported by the same key informant, Muhammad Hussayn Sabun, who returned from Khartoum to

---

[4] Author's Interview with 'Umda al-Yias Ibrahim Koko, Keiga Tummero, 5 June 2005.

his homeland Keiga Tummero after his retirement from police service in 1980. Upon his arrival, he found there were serious conflicts over lands between the Keiga and Dar Jami'. 'Umda 'Usman Bilal was then a chief of a native court that brings some Baqqara and Nuba court cases together. My informant claimed that the Baqqara native leaders were the main source of land disputes between Keiga and the Baqqara in the area.[5]

My informant was astonished to see how the government imposed leaders to rule over cases of land disputes in which they are involved. His belief is that these leaders misused their court authority to rule against several genuine Nuba land cases. In order to protest at this injustice, Sabun set up a committee of several Keiga elders to deal with the issue. It filed a complaint against 'Umda 'Usman Bilal in Kadugli, in his capacity as paramount court chief in the area. Instead of considering the complaint, the committee members were first jailed then asked collectively to pay L$360 (approximately US$ 200 at the time) as an alternative penalty. Muhammad Hussayn Sabun commented:

> Despite the fact that we were unjustly punished, 'Umda 'Usman Bilal was not allowed to continue chairing the court sessions in Keiga Tummero. No doubt, that was a victory for the Keiga people because under his chieftainship many Keiga peoples lost their farming land cases in favour of others.

As early as the 1980s, the 1952 dispute mentioned above resurfaced when some wealthy Takarir demanded either a payment of Diya[6] or a piece of farmland as compensation for three of their people who had been killed during the 1952 conflict. The demand for land was rejected in a native court held in al-Bardab. The Takarir's claim was rejected when the 'Umda of Dar Jami' and Ahmed Malik, a Takarir leader, swore before the court an acknowledgement that the Takarir had no land throughout the Keiga territory to which they could claim ownership.

Shortly before the war started in the Nuba Mountains, another conflict occurred between the Nuba of Keiga Tummero and some agro-pastoral Baqqara. It started with a dispute between some Keiga farmers and the Baqqara of Aulad Nuba over some arable land in the al-Jughan area along the southern border of Keiga Tummero territory, bordering Laguri. As a result of government intervention, a fact-finding committee was formed, visited the area, and adjudicated on the claims of the contesting parties.

After thorough investigation, the committee's verdict went in favour of the Keiga farmers. Some official documents were given to both parties to that effect. The verdict was based on the grounds that the disputed area has been part of the Keiga Tummero's cotton production zone since the colonial period. However, at a later stage, the Arabs of Aulad Nuba appealed against the verdict which was revoked and subsequently nullified. My informant claims that some officials cooperated with the Baqqara

---

[5] Author's interview with Muhammad Husayn Sabun, Keiga Tummero, 7 June 2005.
[6] Diya is an Islamic-based compensation paid by a murderer or his/her family to the family of the murdered person.

native leaders involved in manipulating or destroying some documents related to the first verdict, thus making it possible to reverse the previous court's decision.

In an interview with Shaykh Makin al-Wakil al-Zubayr of Keiga Tummero, 8 June 2005, he made it clear that, like so many Nuba, the Keiga seem to have no confidence in all the actors involved in settling their land-related disputes, including some state officials. In their view, the Baqqara and these officials are nothing but two sides of the same coin, both linked to the state which is dominated by the Jillaba institution. Interestingly, this accusation seems to be substantiated by widely reported cases of Nuba land alienation by the courts, among other institutions. Some of these cases can be traced in Mohamed Salih (1995, 1999), African Rights (1995), Suliman (1999), and Harragin (2003). In its summary findings, the NMPACT (2002: 21), i.e. the UN-sponsored Nuba Mountains Programme for Advancing Conflict Transformation, concluded that 'tension and discrimination, including in the court system, between nomads and settled farmers, between Arab and Nuba remained one of the root causes of the conflict which is unaddressed in the region.'

During the height of the war in the region, most of the Takarir households and the nomadic Baqqara retreated to their places of origin in North Kordofan. After the CFA of 2002, and the subsequent CPA of 2005, land conflicts resurfaced when the Takarir came back to the area. This time, they returned with more family members from the drought-hit areas of Jafil, al-Birka, and Umm Sa'da in North Kordofan. They resumed their mechanized farming as well as livestock grazing inside Keiga territory. Tensions revived when the Keiga people discovered that some of the Takarir had managed to get approval from the relevant government authority in Kadugli and were granted seven mechanized projects in a wide area within the shifting cultivation zone of the Tummero community.

The people of Keiga Tummero claim that the territory currently occupied by the Arabs of Aulad Nuba along the Keiga-Laguri border is part of their ancestral land, which has been famous for its cotton production since the 1940s. It includes the areas of Hijayr al-'Ajal, al-Tash, Khashm al-Girba, al-'Iriq, and Shaq al-Gidayl. Over time, however, the Baqqara of Aulad Nuba gradually moved from the Laguri side and settled on Keiga Tummero land. Subsequently, they started to claim ownership over the territory in spite of the fact that the Keiga peoples perceived them as users and not owners of the land. An elder from Keiga Tummero declared:[7]

> When these Arab peoples sought refuge in our homeland, our forefathers protected them and gave them access to our land, after they took an oath to respect our hospitality. But now they have betrayed this oath by their involvement in grabbing our arable land. Also, those who came recently from Kordofan are deliberately encouraged by their leaders to expand territorially at the expense of our customarily owned lands. As these

---

[7] Author's interview with Adam Abu Shuk, Keiga Tummero 9 June 2005.

peoples continue to create many problems including claiming land ownership, we cannot continue to co-exist peacefully with them, unless all of our land-related grievances are fairly redressed and all of our inherited territory is restored.

These successive narratives and arguments of the Nuba Keiga show their unshaken conviction that they perceive the Arabs of Dar Jami', who have co-existed with them for several centuries, as people who only have secondary rights of use access but not full rights of land ownership. One of my key informants confirmed this view:

> Places such as Chalib and Umm Salaf between Laguri and Keiga are traditionally part of the Keiga lands, but they were allocated to the Dar Jami' Arabs by the Keiga for farming. Also, the al-Bardab area, which is part of Keiga Luban, was allocated in 1934 to a group of Fellata on their arrival from West Africa. We, the Keiga, and these Fellata have peacefully co-existed and we had no intention of removing them after they had become Sudanese citizens. Thus, they may enjoy life-time rights of usage over al-Bardab but its ownership remains an exclusive right for the Keiga people.[8]

By implication, the Nuba recognize only the existence of farm boundaries between them and some agro-pastoral Arab groups who continue to co-exist amicably and practise some traditional farming. These types of boundaries, from the Nuba point of view, are meant to allow 'others' to have access to rights of use while ownership remains exclusively theirs, as indigenous groups. In summary, the Nuba recognize no territorial boundaries with any non-Nuba groups, even if they encounter them along farming or grazing boundaries, because they perceive them as mere land users, with no rights of ownership.

Despite unyielding efforts to strengthen their claim through traditional narratives and historical evidence, the claims of the Nuba in general and the Keiga in particular have not only been systematically contested by the agro-pastoral Baqqara, but have also been critically undermined by different levels of state authorities. In this position of disadvantage, a new dynamic situation is emerging within the wider Nuba political context in the region, following the CPA.

LAND-BASED COLLECTIVE POLITICAL EXPRESSION IN KEIGA

In Chapter 5 it was noted that the Nuba Land Action Strategy of 2004 and the Second All Nuba Conference of 2005 played instrumental roles in mobilizing Nuba communities to secure their communal lands, after the peace. The movement was in response to the outcome of the CPA which had failed to redress the Nuba political, socio-cultural and economic issues, including the recognition of their collective or individual customary land rights. After the war, the Nuba opted for a new movement through which

---

[8] Author's interview with Sambo Sayed Tia, Keiga Luban 10 February 2007.

they played down their differences and strategically essentialized what they still have in common, to secure their communally claimed land. The movement is based on 'Nuba territory' perceived as an ancestral homeland and source of livelihood, ethno-cultural identity, and political heritage. Towards that end, the question of land rights has been widely disseminated and popularized among Nuba communities, particularly in their social and political forum. The Nuba Keiga group is very much part of this movement.

In keeping with this overall Nuba strategy, some Keiga elites and community leaders set up a land committee in 2005. Its task was to trace, identify, and fix the boundaries of their communal territory. The terms of reference and the mandate of the committee were endorsed during the First Keiga Conference held in Keiga Tummero, 12–14 April 2006. They managed to mobilize their people through the Keiga Council, a community-based organization (CBO) with its headquarters in Khartoum. According to the Council's chairperson, Shamsun Khamis Kafi, land-related problems were the driving force behind the formation of this Council. Its mandate is to (i) unite all Keiga people, (ii) identify and fix Keiga territorial boundaries, (iii) lay out a strategy for dealing with other ethnic groups who claim rights of ownership over Keiga ancestral land, and (iv) establish a separate native administration for the Keiga people.[9]

In its introduction, the communiqué of the First Keiga Conference demonstrated the solidarity and the will of the Keiga people to take immediate collective action for the protection of their communal land:

> With all our consciousness and free will, we, the people of Keiga Tummero, Luban, al Khayl, Damik and Jerru, have decided as one voice, to adhere to our communal unity, to respect democratic practices and principles, to recognize citizenship as a base for rights and obligations, and to work collectively for the protection and prosperity of Keiga by defending its territory, people and resources. (Kafi 2006: 01)

The final communiqué enumerated several land-related recommendations and resolutions, of which the following are the most relevant to this discussion:

1. Formulation of a High Commission for Keiga communal land;
2. Confirmation of indisputable ownership and control of their communal land and the need for fixed boundaries;
3. Nullification/cancellation of all contracts related to the sale or allocation of land which proves to be part of the Keiga communal land;
4. Compensation for the Keiga people, who have been affected by the construction of the oil pipeline, on a basis equal to the compensation paid to similarly affected groups in northern Sudan;
5. Representation of Keiga people in the Southern Kordofan State's Land Commission;
6. Reconsideration of the overlapping native administrations on the same territory within the Keiga land;

---

[9] Interview with Shamsun Khamis Kafi, Khartoum, 23 June 2006.

7. Revival of the indigenous Nuba names among the Keiga peoples and of the Nuba place-names within the Keiga territory;

8. Prevention of the intrusion of nomads' livestock into the farming areas until the crop harvest is completed. Severe punishments should apply in cases of violations; and

9. Redress on the question of Keiga land alienation, and the people's displacement before, during and after the civil war. All Keiga land occupied by others during the course of the conflict must be restored. (Keiga Council 2006: 1–2)

Contrary to the well-defined Nuba-Keiga line of argumentation as illustrated above, which has been pursued through traditional rights and their present socio-political predicament, the Dar Jami' Baqqara have challenged their position, with strong counter-arguments as discussed below.

The Dar Jami' Baqqara: counter-claims and collective responses

It is worth noting that the Baqqara counter-claim pertaining to land rights is grounded on some historical practices in Arab-Nuba relations, namely 'Arab overlordship over the Nuba'. The overlordship (sid al-Darib) literally means the owner or master of the road/passage. It was an institution that gave the Baqqara native leaders the power to exercise full suzerainty over the Nuba during the precolonial and colonial eras. In practice, it meant that the Nuba were prevented from leaving their hills or establishing any external contact without prior permission from their respective overlords. Lloyd, the British Governor of Kordofan in 1908, describes how the Baqqara brought Nuba under their suzerainty upon their arrival into the region:

> The Baggara at once began to raid the Nubas, enslaving all they could lay their hands on, and taking all the grain and cattle they could find. The Nubas in defence retired to their Jebels and terraced them for cultivation in remote areas, where horsemen could not approach them. Gradually each sub-tribe of Baggara took their own zone of Jebel round which they settled, and which they protected as far as they could from the raids of other sub-tribes, in return for supplies of slaves and grain. (Lloyd 1908: 55)

Vicars-Miles, another British administrator, reported that in 'most cases, this overlord visited the hill every three or four years, demanding slaves and tribute, then left it to its own devices until next time' (Sudan Archive 1934: SAD627/10/3). This early hegemony came to have far-reaching implications on Nuba communal claims over their traditional land in terms of accessibility, usage, and ownership rights. Moreover, this original unequal and exploitative nature of Baqqara-Nuba relations continued to prevail throughout the Turco-Egyptian, the Mahdiyya, and the first half of the Condominium, despite the British Closed Districts Policy in the region. In his note to the District Commissioner of Southern Kordofan, Gillan, then Kordofan Governor, reported that Arab overlordship of Nubas occurred basically in three areas in Southern Kordofan Province as follows:

1. Aulad Hameid overlordship in the Fungor group (and certain shadowy claims by the Nazir of the Hawazma Halfa over the Werna Nubas);
2. Hawazma Rawawqa claims over certain hills in Kadugli District including the Aulad Nuba (Nazir Hamid al-Likha) claim over Laguri and Saburi;
3. Dar Jami' ('Umda Somi Tawir) claim over Keiga; and Dilimiyya (Muhamadan Bahlul) claim over certain Moro hills (Gillan 1930:1).

In the same note, Gillan expressed his intention to put an end to the practice, suggesting to the District Commissioner of Southern Kordofan that 'I think the system of the Arab overlordships of Nuba hills wants putting an immediate stop to even at the cost of some trouble to ourselves' (Gillan, 1930:1). From the Nuba perspective, this historical legacy is the basis for the present Baqqara assertion of some sort of legitimacy in their current land claims to the Nuba lands, not only in terms of access to use, but also in terms of customary rights and/or legal ownership.

In an interview, Muhammad al-Shafay' al-Ma'mun, a Kadugli-based merchant from Dar Jami' Tuwal, claimed that the Dar Jami', like all other Hawazma-Rawawqa, are real partners with the Nuba in communal land rights, not only in terms of land access, but also in terms of full right of ownership. In justifying his argument, al-Ma'mun claims that[10]

> Our ancestors fought for, defended, and died on this land. When we, the Hawazma-Rawawqa, were defending the plains from successive external forces, the Nuba were fortified on their respective hilltops leaving our ancestors to face the common enemies alone. Therefore, our present strong attachment to this land is a result of our historical reality.

This view is strongly supported in another interview with Muhammad 'Alwan Hamid, a nomad from Aulad Nuba of Rawawqa. Contrary to the Nuba claim, he asserts that each Baqqara group has a definite territory controlled by their respective native administration authorities. With the example of Aulad Nuba, he attempts to show the existence of shared boundaries with their Nuba neighbours:

> We, the Aulad Nuba of Hawazma-Rawawqa, physically co-exist with Nuba of Keiga Tummero and those of Laguri and Saburi, with the al-Darut area as the centre of our own territory. We share boundaries with Dar Jami' in the west, Nuba Laguri and Saburi in the south, and Nuba Keiga Tummero in the north. Our territory includes rijil al-'ajal, al-Bukhsa, Umm Garin, Hijayr al-Batil, al-Jughan, and al-Tash.[11]

Other Baqqara nomads interviewed complained bitterly about experiences of mistreatment by some Nuba, especially the young male elite, not only during the war, but after the peace settlement. Hassab al-Nabi 'Abdul Fadil

---

[10] Author's interview with Muhammad al-Shafay' al-Ma'mun, Kadugli, 10 January 2007.
[11] Author's interview with Muhammad 'Alwan Hamid, Keiga Tummero, 9 February 2007.

and al-Nur Fadl 'Abdul Rahim are two nomads from Aulad Rahma of Aulad Nuba of Hawazma-Rawawqa. They were interviewed in their fariq near the Keiga Tummero hill community. They recognize the difficulties facing the agro-pastoral Arabs and the sedentary Nuba in regaining their peaceful pre-war co-existence, despite their long history of socio-cultural interaction, including intermarriage and cooperative customs in habitation and movements. In their own words:[12]

> Despite the achievement of peace and the end of war, Nuba-Baqqara relations in the region have not gone back to normal. Somehow we manage our daily life with our neighbours, the Nuba of Keiga, Liguri, and Debri. But we are unable to practise our pre-war periodic migratory movement southwards into the Jebels of Moro and Krongo. Some of our people went there, but they were forced to retreat with their cattle after being mistreated by some local Nuba. We often encounter some armed Nuba youth or elite groups who tell us, 'This is not your land and we do not want you here with us anymore.' These new, educated generations are the ones who want to upset the long history of peaceful co-existence and mutuality between us, the nomadic Arabs and the sedentary Nuba, in the area.
>
> In the past, all of our problems were sorted out more easily, even though we, both Arabs and Nuba, were almost all illiterate. But with the advance of education among the new generation, conflicts among us are becoming more frequent and complex. Accordingly, their solutions are increasingly becoming beyond our reach today.

Al-Bushra Somi Tawir, a prominent politician and a native leader of the Dar Jami', rejects the notion of tribal boundaries between the already physically and socio-culturally mixed Nuba and Baqqara at the same locale for centuries. Instead, he calls for Nuba-Baqqara unity and solidarity as the only way to reverse the marginalization process continuing to be practised by the successive central governments. He also demonstrates his strong political commitment to opposing the government's practice of land grabbing from local communities. In an interview, he explained that:

> With Nuba, especially the Keiga, we have no territorial or social boundaries. This is so because we continued to co-exist in peace over the same territory for generations. We always shared land resources amicably, and willingly combined our socio-cultural practices including inter-marriage. In short, we were gradually becoming one through this long history of co-existence, cooperation, and mutuality. The time is thus ripe for the Hawazma Arabs and Nuba alike to realize and appreciate this history of their own making. They ought to unite because they are all marginalized by the successive central governments which exploit their land resources including oil for the development of the central and northern regions of the Sudan.[13]

It is evident that 'Usman Bilal Hamid al-Likha, the paramount Nazir of

---

[12] Author's Interview with Hassab al-Nabi 'Abdul Fadil and al-Nur Fadl 'Adul Rahim, nomads' camp in Keiga Tummero, 12 February 2007.
[13] Author's interview with the late al-Bushra Somi Tawer, al-Kweik, 13 February 2007.

the Hawazma-Rawawqa Nazirate since 1989, holds the same view but with a sharper rationale. He rejects the notion of tribal boundaries in the way that the Nuba conceive them. In his view[14]

> The region had never experienced any formal tribal boundaries. The practice has been that the Nuba utilize the hilly land and its immediate surroundings while the Arabs exploit the vast plains beyond these hilly areas. So, for every two adjacent Nuba hill communities, there were always Arab communities on the plains in between. This territorial arrangement was reinforced by Nuba–Arab alliances, such as the ones between the Rawawqa of Dar Jami' Tuwal and the Nuba of Keiga, the Rawawqa of Aulad Nuba and the Nuba of Saburi and Laguri, and the Rawawqa of Dilimiyya and some Nuba in the Moro hills. These Arab–Nuba neighbourhood patterns and alliances resulted in some sort of territorial boundaries, not between the Nuba hill communities, but between a group of allied Nubas and Arabs with another similar alliance in the neighbourhood.
>
> For example, although they were overlapping, there were traditional territorial boundaries between Dar Jami' and Keiga as two groups, the first under the leadership of Somi Tawir, and the second, of the Arabs of Aulad Nuba and the Nuba of Laguri and Saburi under the leadership of Hamid al-Likha. These are not tribal boundaries but territorial arrangements agreed upon by the leaders of these co-existing Arab and Nuba communities.
>
> The notion that Nuba have territorial boundaries with their counter Nuba and not with Baqqara Arabs, and that the Baqqara have no land here, can hardly stand against the obvious historical and contemporary realities. No doubt, this is a recent political position constructed by some Nuba elites, with the intention of deconstructing the long history of Arab-Nuba co-existence.

In sum, these examples of Nuba claims and Baqqara counter-claims reveal the representations and self-perceptions held by each group, and their sharp assessments of each other's case.

Nuba and Baqqara representations and self-perceptions

It is clear that different Nuba ethnic groups have long perceived themselves as indigenous to the region. This is supported by their autochthonous myths that define the Nuba Mountains territory as ancestral homeland and symbol for their socio-political identity. For their part, the Baqqara hold the view that their roughly 300-year presence also qualifies them as indigenous to the same territory. The war increased Nuba self-awareness as a unified ethnic group facing one common enemy, manifested in the government's Jihad against them, coupled with policies of genocide, ethnocide, and land alienation. Since the peace agreement, political discourse in the

---

[14] Author's interview with Nazir 'Usman Bilal Hamid al-Likha, Kadugli, 22 February 2007.

region has perpetuated rigid ethnic distinctions, freighted with negative representations of each other and uncompromising claims on both sides.

The historical legacy of Nuba-Baqqara relations is still a powerful driving force in this battle over land. The Baqqara's argument that the Nuba used the hilly land and its immediate surroundings while the Arabs exploited the vast plains below is highly contested by the Nuba. It was and still is a major point in Baqqara–Nuba conflict, owing to the fact that the main line of Baqqara argumentation seems to be based on an assumption that the current spatial pattern of the Nuba and Baqqara groups in the Nuba Mountains is the norm.

To the contrary, substantial literature and archival records (reviewed in Chapters 1 and 3) reveal that the present Baqqara-Nuba spatial pattern is an anomaly brought about by a systematic and enduring process of intense violence. The bloodshed began with the arrival of the Baqqara in the region. It was then progressively 'institutionalized' and reinforced by the precolonial, colonial, and postcolonial powers. Therefore, the Nuba conceive the contemporary pattern of Nuba–Baqqara spatial distribution in the region as a result of an historical anomaly which has been reinforced by the post-colonial state. Thus, redressing this abnormality is fundamental to any process seeking to establish an everlasting and just peace.The struggle over land ownership can be strongly sensed in the daily discourse among the common people of the Nuba and Arab groups. It is still true that they cohabit, but their different perceptions on land rights run right through their communities. For example, while I was in al-Kweik market in Keiga Labun, I asked several people of the Keiga and Dar Jami', at random, 'Whose land is this?' I meant the al-Kweik neighbourhood. Although the question was simple and direct, it immediately distinguished the respondents by group, and, subsequently, by their associated territorial representations of each other. One Nuba Keiga responded: 'of course, it is al-Kweik of Keiga Luban.' I asked: 'and what about the Dar Jami' who have lived here with you for quite a long time?' One elder Keiga man responded, 'It is true that we hosted the Dar Jami' for quite a long time on our communal land; they became part of our social life and shared our land. But it is equally true that the Dar Jami' have no land here because a guest, no matter how long he stays, will never be an owner.' This Nuba position is deeply rooted in their principle that 'land may be loaned to a friend or a guest for the purposes of cultivation or building, but it remains the property of the family who may exercise their rights at any time' (Hawkesworth 1932: 187).

One Dar Jami' Arab responded to the first question by saying, 'al-Kweik belongs to the Dar Jami''. I asked that Dar Jami': 'where then is the limit of the Keiga Luban's territory?' Following the Baqqara line that the plains are for the Baqqara while the hilly areas are for the Nuba, my Dar Jami' respondent pointed to the Keiga Luban hill areas nearby (excluding the adjacent plains where al-Kweik is situated), as Keiga Labun homeland. The conflict over the plains on which al-Kweik is situated is obvious.

Although these two opposing views are drawn from the Nuba and the Baqqara groups in a very limited locale such as the al-Kweik, they represent, to a large degree, the Nuba-Baqqara claims and counter-claims at different levels of scale in their respective social and political organizations. The view expressed by the Nuba Keiga above is typical of that articulated in the recent mainstream political discourse of the Nuba as a unified ethno-political entity, capable of taking collective action.

In reaction, the Baqqara have decided to oppose this emerging Nuba collective position, as manifested in the Keiga case, among others. They have initiated their own collective political position by holding conferences in parallel to that of the Nuba. The recent Nuba attempt to articulate their ethno-political identity in the struggle over land is perceived by the Baqqara as a deliberate move aimed at ethnic exclusion of all non-Nuba groups from land entitlement in the region. The opinions of the Baqqara above, illustrate how the Baqqara perceive themselves as indispensable participants of the Nuba Mountains' demographic, economic, cultural and ethno-political landscape. To them, exclusion is quite simply impossible and impractical.

These views were embedded in the discourse of the two consecutive Rawawqa conferences held respectively in Ekurchi in Moro, 20–21 May 2005 and in Kadugli, 21–23 June 2006.[15]

1. There is a pressing need for renewing the longstanding pre-war Nuba-Baqqara alliances based on new principles of co-existence, mutual understanding and respect;
2. The other ethnic groups in the region need to understand, and therefore accept the reality that the Baqqara of Rawawqa are part of the indigenous communities of the Nuba Mountains region;
3. The composition and function of the expected State Land Commission in South Kordofan should reflect the ethnic, cultural and religious diversities of the region;
4. There is a need to reopen seasonal migratory routes that were blocked during the civil war and thereafter, coupled with the need to provide essential services (security, water, human health and animal welfare), along these routes by the requisite state agencies;
5. All citizens of the region are equally entitled to the rights of lands for farming, grazing and settlements, among other purposes; and that
6. There is a great need for the representation of the nomads in legislative and executive institutions at state and local levels during the transitional period.

These resolutions reflect a strong desire to rebuild Nuba–Baqqara inter-ethnic ties as the only way to ensure sustainable and peaceful co-existence between the two groups in the region. At the same time, and contrary to the Nuba position, as analyzed above, these resolutions demonstrate that the Baqqara perceive themselves as indigenous inhabitants of the region

---

[15] See *Al-dwaa*, daily newspaper, Issue No. 996, Khartoum, 25 June 2006:8.

with full land entitlement and rights to political representation, based on the principle of citizenship.

These claims and counter-claims over land rights between the Nuba and the Baqqara led to disastrous political and military mobilizations along ethnic lines in the war, and hostility has increased in the post-conflict situation. As a consequence, a culture of war and violence continues to dominate Nuba–Baqqara relations, leading to a serious erosion of peace and tolerance, despite the CPA. However, this tendency towards violence, particularly in land disputes, has also been accelerated over the post-war period by (among other factors) state intervention. Disguised as 'development', this has forced changes in livestock migratory routes, and created other negative interventions, ostensibly 'ecological', in the wider national and continental context.

Some key factors aggravating land conflicts in the area

Based on the Keiga Tummero case, three separate but closely interrelated processes have been identified as major factors systematically triggering and/or accelerating local land-driven conflicts. First, the state's imposition of seasonal livestock routes through Nuba farming and settlement lands; second, the forced displacement, migration, and resettlement of some nomads from North Kordofan due to the severe ecological changes that hit the African Sahelian dry zone, including the northern parts of western Sudan; and third, the state's establishment of privately owned, mechanized farming schemes on communal territories with no consideration of local people's claims, interests, and priorities. It is worth noting that all these factors have been externally imposed on both the sedentary and the nomadic populations.

IMPOSED LIVESTOCK ROUTES

The Keiga Tummero territory is classified by the government as a formal route of passage and a water-point for nomads during their seasonal migration (see Map 1.3). According to the Southern Kordofan State Act No. 3, 2000, entitled *Agricultural and Grazing Regulation Act*, Keiga Tummero's bat-ha (permanent water source) is recognized as a farming and horticultural zone as well as an 'Id point', i.e. a water source for livestock during dry season migratory movements. The same Act prohibits farmers from blocking the water points during the entire dry season. However, the dilemma here is that orchard cultivation, practised at these same water points, is an important income generating activity for many farmers during the dry season. The result is severe competition over water resources coupled with unavoidable and recurrent water-based conflicts.

The Arab nomads cling to their rights of access to the water sources described by the Act. At the same time, the sedentary Nuba people feel that this is their own communal land and, therefore, they have first rights to utilize its resources, including water. Shaykh Makin al-Wakil al-Zubayr of the Kolo sub-hill community in Keiga Tummero spoke in grief when he said[16]

> We want to develop our rich lands around the water sources and transform them into large-scale horticultural schemes. But we are not able to do so partly because of the nomads' intrusions into our land during the dry season. Their intrusions are backed by the Act and various government institutions and policies. The government is favouring nomads while preventing us, the farmers, from using our fertile lands around the water sources. It wants us to remain underdeveloped in our rich territory. This is unfair.

Several sedentary–nomad conflicts are related to the frequent intrusion of livestock onto fields before they are harvested. During my six weeks of participatory observations in Keiga Tummero in 2006, I observed and documented 35 instances of farmer–nomad conflicts during the harvest season in Kolo village due to livestock break-ins that cause partial or at times total crop damage. Another 23 cases occurred and were recorded in Keidi village in the same period. These repeated cases took place not only during the day but also at night. Previously, the intrusion of livestock onto a farm was always reported to the concerned native leader by a livestock owner, a farmer, or even a third party. Today, this is no longer the case, as both parties tend to resort to violence to settle their disputes. With the ascendancy of a culture of war and the dwindling of the culture of peace and tolerance, traditional institutions that used to manage these conflicts effectively, are unable to do so today.

The tendency to violent action and reaction was demonstrated when some young farmers from Keiga Tummero bypassed their native leadership and resorted to force to put an end to recurring livestock intrusions into their fields, before their crops could be harvested. They decided to block access to any Arab nomads' livestock for grazing or watering within Keiga farming and horticultural areas. In retaliation, the nomads also resorted to force. The situation remained highly confrontational until the nomads reluctantly accepted a negotiated written agreement with some harsh conditions. One of these was that as of the following year (2007) the Dar Na'yla livestock would not approach any part of the Keiga area before the crops were completely harvested. In spite of this, during the 2007 dry season, the nomads managed to cooperate peacefully in sharing the water resources.

Although this particular confrontation was resolved peacefully through a direct and locally negotiated agreement, similar cases escalated when pursued along ethno-political lines. At times this resulted in fatal skirmishes involving automatic weapons, as was the case in the Debri area near Keiga

---

[16] Author's interview with Shaykh Makin al-Wakil al Zubayr, Keiga Tummero, 6 June 2005.

Tummero, between the sedentary Ghulfan and the nomadic Aulad 'Ali of Dar Na'yla in 2005, 2006, and 2008. The conflict spilled over into neighbouring Keiga Tummero with the result that there was an excessive presence of weapons in the hands of young people day and night in the area, throughout the conflict period. However, it is interesting to note that some conflicts were settled by direct negotiation, mediation, or court settlements while other similar cases resulted in confrontation on a limited or even a widespread scale. Moreover, some of these local conflicts certainly escalated when they were played on by ethno-political factors and caught up in larger, more complex dimensions. The distribution of weapons among sedentary and nomadic people alike is a stimulating factor, leading to the frequent use of force to resolve some of these recurrent conflicts, which, historically, were resolved quite simply by peaceful means through intermediary, socially accredited, local institutions.

ECOLOGICAL CHANGES

In the 1970s and 1980s, dry regions in northern Sudan, particularly northern Kordofan and Darfur, experienced a series of severe droughts as part of the African Sahelian zone's desertification (see Adams 1982: 268; Azarya 1996: 39; Abdul-Jalil 2005: 63). Several nomadic groups in the drought-affected zones moved south into more fertile areas, increasing the pressure on arable land and causing conflicts with local farmers. In this context, South Kordofan was subjected to two new processes.

First, due to the negative ecological changes caused by drought, the nomads were forced to respond with adaptive coping mechanisms. Accordingly, their rhythmic north-south-north movement was radically altered, in terms of routing and timing. It is vital to understand that the nomads' seasonal migratory movement is not a matter of choice; rather, it is a function of year-by-year ecological variations. For example, as their northern base (makhraf) started to dry up earlier than usual due to less rainfall, the nomads found themselves having to start their southwards migration earlier, in search of water and grazing lands. By doing so, they arrived in the Nuba Mountains while the harvest season was at its peak. Also, it is worth noting that the Nuba traditional farmers' decision to harvest their crops is not a matter of choice but a function of rainfall patterns every year. In short, the lower the amount of rainfall, the earlier the journey of the nomads southwards; likewise, less rainfall delays the Nuba farmers' harvest. This earlier movement of the nomads, coinciding with late harvest of the farmers leads unavoidably to recurring conflicts between sedentary– nomadic groups entirely due to ecological factors.

Second, the 1970s and the 1980s droughts led to an influx of successive waves of displaced Arab nomads from North Kordofan to the Nuba Mountains. On arrival, they became partially sedentary and engaged in farming while maintaining such livestock as remained, after their drastic reversals. Several local farmers in Keiga Tummero complained that, despite the fact that the government had demarcated passage routes for nomads' livestock, some of these displaced nomads had settled down and established permanent hamlets along the official migratory routes. In this way, they blocked traditional migration movements, forcing regular nomads to deviate from the prescribed routes. Thus, they frequently encroach on farming zones, causing destruction and damage to agricultural production.

Empirical evidence has showed that several cases of conflict in the area can be ascribed to this drought-driven situation. For example, the al-Darut plain areas, south of Keiga Tummero hill, and the al-Jughan area along the Keiga Tummero-Umm Heitan border, comprise the main 'far farm' lands for the people of Keiga Tummero. Several migratory nomadic routes pass through these farming zones. However, due to the change in climate patterns, the area was gradually transformed into a settlement by the Zunara nomads, who fled from drought conditions in the al-Guz area of North Kordofan. The Keiga people claim that they have frequently hosted these Arabs as they fled southwards with their livestock from the parched fields of their homeland. Some returned home voluntarily when the situation improved, while others did not.

These newly settled Zunara created problems by claiming ownership of the most fertile areas in Keiga Tummero. This claim became a practical reality during the civil war in the 1990s, when the people of Keiga Tummero felt threatened and retreated from their plain areas towards the foothills of their region. This temporary retreat persuaded several Arab groups, namely Dar Jami', Aulad Nuba, Zunara, and Jummuiyya, to expand their settlements and farming activities into Keiga Tummero lands. Thus, they started developing a sense of ownership of the land, even though only recently under their new usage and control. After the Nuba Mountains Ceasefire Agreement of 2002, the people of Keiga Tummero intended to resume the cultivation of their 'far farm' land in the al-Jughan area. However, they found that the area had been occupied and was being farmed by these newcomers. The result was conflict and confrontation, with far-reaching implications for the local sedentary Nuba.

First, the permanent settlements of the newcomers associated with their farming activities inside the Keiga Tummero land have alienated the local people from their traditional livelihood base. Second, these new settlements blocked the designated migration routes, forcing the actual routes to be modified at the expense of the local farmers' arable lands resulting in recurrent tensions and conflicts between the sedentary Nuba people and the agro-pastoral Arabs. Third, these newly sedentary Arab groups, were supported by some state institutions, in fostering a sense of ownership of the land in the course of their settlement and began mechanized and traditional farming activities.

Some of my informants in Keiga Tummero believe that this demographic and territorial restructuring in favour of Arab groups (nomads, sedentary, and merchants) is happening with the support of the regional and central governments. As the Nuba see it, this is part of a government plan aimed at empowering the Baqqara while weakening and eventually endangering their own livelihood and, indeed, their very survival. As a result, the plan has been met with strong resistance among different Nuba groups. One recent study (Pantuliano et al., 2007: 27) reported that, in 'areas like Keiga al-Khayl, Nuba communities resented what they perceived as government attempts to resettle Baqqara pastoralists on Keiga lands'.

STATE BAD GOVERNANCE AND DISGUISED DEVELOPMENT INTERVENTIONS

The factor of mechanized farming schemes has been discussed at length in preceding chapters. In summary, it has been shown how the government's allocation of mechanized farming schemes, taking no consideration for the interests and priorities of the local communities, has aggravated farmer-nomad tensions. Indeed, members of both groups tend to be squeezed out as the mechanized farms expand systematically at their expense.

From the Nuba farmers' perspective, any land allocated by the government for the mechanized farming scheme belongs customarily to certain sub-hill communities as an essential part of their shifting cultivation zone. From the nomads' standpoint, the mechanized farm projects are a major obstacle to their rhythmic movements. This is so because, unlike traditional farming, the activities on mechanized farms, particularly harvesting, usually continue throughout the dry season. This situation inevitably forces nomads to deviate and pass through some traditional farming zones. From the government standpoint, all unregistered lands are government property, and it maintains its rights, based on civil law and regulations, to determine their utilization as it deems appropriate. Thus, despite their claims and counter-claims, both the Nuba and the Baqqara share one common challenge related to the legal framework of the modern state, as it pertains to land policy. The law has consistently undermined both sides' communal claims based on their respective historical and/or contemporary customary legitimacy.

In the 1990s, the government initiated a plan for land redistribution in the region (Imam and Egemi 2004). Within that plan, Small Farmers' Collective Schemes (SFCSs) were introduced as part of a wider agricultural investment plan. In theory, the initiative was meant to transform the customarily owned communal lands into individual registered land rights. Towards that end, a process of surveying, allocation, and registration based on modern state land laws was pursued in the area. In the process of allocations, state authorities publicized that priority would be given to members of households constituting a community, i.e. a tribe, clan, or lineage, in their specific claimed territories. The state has promised to fund the mechanization of agricultural operations of the proposed SFCSs in order to raise productivity per land unit and household. But the bulk of Nuba and Baqqara leaders alike have been suspicious and unenthusiastic about the initiative.

Nuba suspicions were reinforced by two other factors. First, most of Nuba feared that the process would result in some of their claimed communal land being handed over to local Arabs who perceived the Nuba as land users without ownership entitlement. This concern stems from the fact that the local Baqqara supported the central government against the Nuba-led SPLM/A in the region during the war. Second, some Nuba leaders were convinced that the timing of the initiative was inappropriate since most of the Nuba, at that time, had been forcefully displaced from their homelands while other people had moved in and occupied their lands. The plan should have been pursued when peace was fully restored and internally displaced Nuba had returned to their respective homelands.

Soon after the implementation of the initiative, all the above-mentioned fears proved correct. In an interview, Muhammad Ibrahim al-Digayl confirmed the opposition of some Nuba ethnic groups, including the Keiga, to the process of land allocation proposed by the government, because the process involves distributing some of their customary owned land to other ethnic groups whom they do not recognize as having rights of ownership. As a government official, al-Digayl affirms that the government recognizes that all the co-existing ethnic groups in any given territory have equal rights in terms of land ownership or use. Based on this principle, all the people inhabiting the region, Nuba and non-Nuba, have equal rights to land entitlement subject to a package of administrative, financial, and legal procedures and conditions.[17] In this respect, al-Yias Ibrahim Koko, the 'Umda of Keiga Tummero, affirmed that 'Right from the start I opposed the proposed small farmers' collective scheme being carried out in Keiga Tummero because it is another form of land grabbing by the state'.[18]

In the same way, some of the Dar Jami' community leaders expressed similar grievances, feeling that the government is undermining their traditional communal land rights while trying to regulate the land on a private basis. My key informant, al-Bushra Somi Tawir of Dar Jami', complained bitterly about the government's practice of grabbing land from local communities. He revealed that 'most of the allocated schemes went to government officials and their supporters inside as well as outside the area. Some of these outsiders are from places like al-Rahad and other towns in North Kordofan'.[19] Equally, 'Usman Bilal, the paramount Nazir of Rawawqa, seems disappointed about the initiative as a process and the final outcome of the land distribution.

> From the outset, I was in disagreement with the government in the way it allocated the schemes. I was of the opinion that the distribution should be confined at this stage to the land actually farmed by the respective households. The remaining land should be maintained as communal property for future expansion. The problem is that the government

[17] Author's interview with Muhammad Ibrahim al-Digayl, Kadugli 21 February 2007.
[18] Author's interview with al-Yias Ibrahim Koko, 'Umda of Keiga Tummero, Keiga Tummero, 14 February 2007.
[19] Author's interview with al-Bushra Somi Tawer, al-Kweik, 13 February 2007.

allocated some of these schemes to people who are not part of the local communities.[20]

In spite of opposition from the bulk of the Nuba and the Baqqara communities alike, the government continued with the survey and allocation of the schemes to the designated households. Within Keiga communal land, sixty-five schemes were accomplished on a total land area of about 50,000 to 60,000 feddans in a fertile plain that stretches from northwest to north and northeast Kadugli. These are known collectively as al-Zelataiya schemes. The average size of each household's allocation varies from five hundred to one thousand feddan. The distribution patterns of the schemes depicted in Table 7.1 reveal the following:

(i) The majority of the schemes were allocated mostly to the local Arabs of Dar Jami' (39.6%), Aulad Nuba (6.8%), the Fellata Takarir (2.3%) and the Fellata of al-Bardab (22.7%), amounting to a total of about 62% of the schemes.

(ii) The Nuba Keiga of Tummero and Luban 9 schemes representing 20.4% of the 44 schemes as shown in the table.

(iii) My key informants[21] confirmed that the total schemes in the area described amount to sixty-five. This implies that apart from the 44 shown in the table, there are another 21 that the author was not able to trace.

Table 7.1 Allocation of small farmers' collective schemes in Keiga land, 1994

Community	Allocated schemes by serial numbers	Total (%)
Keiga Tummero	1, 2 (partial), 4, 5, 10,11, and 12,	7 (15.9)
Debri (Nuba Ghulfan)	2 (partial), 6, 7, and 13	4 (9.0)
Fellata Takarir and others	3	1 (2.3)
Baqqara Dar Jami'	8, 9, 14,15, 20, 23, 26, 27, 30, 31, 32, 33, 34, 35, 38, 39, and 40	17 (39.6)
Baqqara Aulad Nuba	24, 28, and 29	3 (6.8)
Keiga Luban	35 and 36	2 (4.5)
Fellata of Al Bardab	37, 42, 43, 44, 45, 46, 51, 52, 53, and 54	10 (22.7)
	Total	44 (100)

Source: compiled from data obtained from Land Use and Water Section, Ministry of Agriculture, Kadugli, South Kordofan State, 21–22 February 2007.

---

[20] Author's interview with Usman Bilal Hamid al-Likha, Kadugli, 22 February 2007.
[21] (i) Muhammad Ibrahim al-Digayl, Kadugli, 21 February 2007; (ii) Nazir al-Bushra Somi Tawer, al-Kweik, 13 February 2007; and (iii) Nazir 'Usman Bilal, Kadugli, 22 February 2007.

In the process of the allocation of these schemes, enormous problems arose between the state and local communities and between the local Arabs and the Nuba. In 2001, a joint letter of complaint was submitted by Ahmed Musa Haren, the Amir of the Eastern Imara (the Nuba of Keiga and Saburi-Laguri) and Musa Somi Rahma, the Amir of Dar Jami', to the Minister of Agriculture and Irrigation, Southern Kordofan State. The two Amirs demanded that the government take the following steps, among others, in order to redress the grievances of the local communities affected by the scheme. They called for:

1. Cancellation of the social survey performed unilaterally by the government officials with no involvement of the community-based committees as agreed beforehand;
2. Replacement of the chief surveyor because he was the main source of discontent among the different communities, farmers and nomads alike; and
3. Conducting a new social survey with effective participation of the local communities' representatives at all stages of the process in order to establish a socially accredited base for the distribution of the schemes among the members of the different communities inhabiting the area.

Due to the growing tension between the two competing local communities and between the state and local communities, the execution of the plan was delayed for three years. In the end, some wealthy new owners, mostly among the Baqqara and the Takarir outside the area were able to secure some schemes inside the communal traditional farming zone in Keiga land.

It was only later that the Keiga people discovered that the government had allocated some schemes inside their claimed communal land to Takarir households, particularly the Shaddad family, with whom they had a long history of land-based disputes. After the CPA, in June 2006, 49 Keiga farmers protested against the state plan and claimed customary rights over the area allocated to the Shaddad family. As a result of this dispute, the latter was unable to invest in practical terms in the assigned land.[22] Thus officially recognized owners such as Shaddad could not exercise their legal rights to the disputed land. From the local community perspective, these new owners are, in fact, state-assisted land grabbers. The state's legality has been challenged by the local community on the basis of their customary legitimacy, and to an extent they have won. However, this happens in response to the state policy of land grabbing that persistently undermines the communal customary rights and legitimacy of the local people, with no consideration for interests and priorities connected with their livelihood.

In concluding this part, it is worth noting that this field-centred analysis reinforces two key points outlined in Chapter 3. First, it reveals the contradiction between the communal customary rights and practices of the two traditional communities (farmers and nomads), and the wayward application of modern state laws with no recognition of customary land

---

[22] Author's interview with Shaykh Sulayman Shirra, Keiga Tummero, 14 February, 2007.

rights. Other studies, such as that of Pantuliano et al. (2007) have come to the same conclusion, reporting that 'in Southern Kordofan access to and ownership of land are central issues, both for the reintegration of returnees and for sustainability of the peace process. Customary land rights are generally not recognized by the government, and statutory legislation has often been used to bypass local customs' (2007: 27). Second, ecological changes and state-driven factors including distorted/underhand development interventions and the failure of the CPA to redress the question of land in the region have resulted in an upsurge of land-related conflicts among different stakeholders in the region in the post-conflict situation.

Nuba–Baqqara land conflict after peace:
concrete cases

Today, inter-ethnic/communal land-related conflicts, particularly between the sedentary Nuba and the pastoral Baqqara, are more frequent and more violent than at any time before the signing of the CPA. In a recent report, (see Pantuliano et al. 2007: 27), the state authority in Southern Kordofan estimated that 'clashes around land, particularly between pastoralists and farmers have resulted in between two and three hundred casualties in Southern Kordofan since the signing of the CPA. Killings and injuries related to land conflict are the single biggest risk to returnees as well as local communities.' This is illustrated in Table 7.2 which gives some of the land conflicts which involve interethnic/tribal warfare with significant human loss and material damage. Most of the cases reported are related to Nuba-Baqqara land conflicts that arose after the CPA, with far-reaching consequences. They were either reported, or experienced directly or indirectly during three stages of sixteen weeks' field work between March 2005 and January 2008.

The cases show clearly that land-related conflicts in the region in the post-conflict situation are not only mounting in frequency but also in scale and complexity. Thus, it is not an exaggeration to describe the present situation in the region not as a 'post-conflict', but rather as a 'conflict of the post-conflict'. The empirical evidence offered throughout this book is in line with several recent reports warning of the likelihood of a drift back to war in the Nuba Mountains. For example, *Sudan Issue Brief*, Human Security Baseline Assessment/HSBA (2008: 4: 10), released by Small Arms Survey in August 2008, asserted that 'Conflict over land is resulting in increased tension' and concluded that 'discontent over the CPA's failure to deliver economic development is turning to anger, and many now view the war in the Nuba Mountains as inevitable. An emerging local narrative sees parallels with the events that led to the Darfur conflict.'

Table 7.2 Selected land-based conflicts, 2005–2008

No.	Case description	Consequences
1	**November–December 2005**[a] The conflict between the Nuba Ghulfan and Dar Nay'la Baqqara nomads revolved around water sources in Debri area due to frequent intrusions of livestock into fields of standing crops. Although it started with low-scale violence in 2005, it escalated into large-scale conflict coupled with the widespread use of arms in following years.	In the dry season of 2005, several farms with standing crops were burned, water boreholes were destroyed, and a number of livestock were slaughtered. In the dry seasons of 2006 and 2007, the conflict resulted in an unknown number of dead or wounded men on both sides. Each side sought some sort of support beyond the locale along ethnic and political lines.
2	**13 January 2006**[b] A group of unidentified gunmen hijacked 3 Shenabla nomads and their 15 camels near Reikha in Buram locality. The incident took place in an area of high insecurity being a transitional zone between SPLA and Government-held areas.	The 3 Shenabla were never seen again. Since the incident I have been told many times that there has been no news about the three missing nomads. The Shenabla believe that their men were kidnapped by Nuba SPLA forces, although there is no evidence to this effect, despite the supporting role of UNMIS in the investigation.
3	**January 2006**[c] The Nuba Daqiq and Messiriyya nomads conflict on water sources in Reikha village.	Several people were seriously wounded on both sides. No use of weapons.
4	**April 2006** Thirty unidentified camel riders armed with Kalashnikovs and GM3s raided the unarmed Nuba of Werni.	During the raid, one person was killed and several were wounded. The Werni people were cut off from access to water for several days as they sought refuge on their hilltops.[d]
5	**April–May 2006** Two months of sporadic fighting between the Warni Nuba and the Baqqara of Dar 'Ali due to severe competition over meagre resources of gum Arabic, grazing land, and water.	Unknown loss of human life, looting of livestock, burning of houses, shops, and schools, all associated with the total collapse of the relationship between the two groups and a growing sense of antagonism.[e]
6	**21–23 July 2006** The Nuba of Mandel and the Ma'alyia Arabs 3-day violent conflict in Dilling district. It erupted as a result of disputes over meagre land and water resources in the area.	Automatic arms such as Kalashnikovs and GM3s were used. More than 10 people were reported killed and a sizeable number of properties were destroyed.[f]
7	**5 October 2006** The Messiriyya ambushed the Kasha Nuba as a result of dispute over Messiriyya cattle grazing on Nuba Kasha farms. They had a long history of land-driven conflicts, usually resolved through their local institutions. This time, however, the culture of violence dominated over the culture of peace due to the increase in arms available to both sides.	Automatic weapons such as Kalashnikovs and GM3s were used. Twelve people from the Kasha and Mandel side were killed, including the Kasha senior community leader (Shaykh), and 15 were seriously injured on both sides.[g]
8	**November–December 2006** Recurrent clashes between Keiga Tummero farmers and various nomadic Baqqara of Dar Na'yla and other groups, owing to frequent intrusions of livestock into standing crops. The nomads had arrived earlier than usual in the Nuba Mountains. This is not a matter of choice, but dictated by annual ecological circumstances, depending on rainfall: to protect their herds, designated movement routes change and damage to crops increases.	During fieldwork in the area for six weeks, I witnessed 58 cases of livestock damage to fields of standing crops. Several farmer/nomad clashes resulted. There were no fatalities but several seriously wounded people, slaughter of livestock, and crop damage.

Notes:
[a] During this period, I was in the field site of Keiga Tummero close to Debri.
[b] The incident happened shortly before my arrival in Reikha, one of my main field sites.
[c] This took place during the three days following my arrival in the Reikha field site.
[d] The case was reported widely. See, for example, *Sudan Tribune*, Sunday 26 April 2006 Online Edition: Retrieved 10 September 2008 from http://www.sudantribune.com/spip.php?article15080.
[e] In June 2006, a successful reconciliation agreement was reached under the auspices of the government of National Unity, Southern Kordofan State, sponsored by the USAID-Pact Sudan, and observed by UNMIS. (Subahi 2006: 01)
[f] Reported in a press release. Sudaneseonline. http://www.sudaneseonline.com/, retrieved August 9, 2006.
[g] Reported by Lazim Suliman, NRRDO Executive Director, on http://www.sudaneseonline.com/, retrieved October 7, 2006.

No.	Case description	Consequences
9	**12–13 December 2006** Two days fighting between a sedentary Nuba group and a nomadic Baqqara group took place in Abu Karshula in the eastern part of South Kordofan due to recurring disputes over land. The nomads claimed certain areas as their grazing land along their migratory route. The local farmers disagreed, asserting that the land was part of their shifting cultivation zone.	Some reports stated that 9 people were killed and an unknown number wounded, with wholesale burning of crops and slaughter of livestock.[h]
10	**29 September 2007** Sunut is an area with a perennial lake and water reservoir where cattle graze during the dry season. The Sunut area, claimed by the Nuba Abujunuk as part of their communal land, has a long history of contestation. Although the incident took place on 29 September 2007, tensions arose earlier when the Ajang, one of the Nuba groups of which the Abujunuk are a part, tried to organize their tribal conference there.. They were blocked by the Messiriyya on the grounds of their ownership of the land. The conference was postponed. In response, when the Messiriyya were moving southwards through Sunut, the Nuba Abujunuk blocked the route and denied access water. The Messiriyya were well armed, ready to open the route by force. Covert NCP military and political involvement in favour of the Messiriyya and by SPLM/A in favour of the Nuba intensified the conflict.	Some sources[i] reported 14 Messiriyya and 6 Nuba fatalities, with unknown numbers of wounded. Subsequent figures reported were far higher: 43 deaths, 28 Messiriyya and 15 Abujunuk; total still rising.[j]
11	**February 2008** Fatal clashes between the Messiriyya Baqqara and the Nuba Daju in Lagawa area following a dispute over water boreholes.	The Messiriyya were attacked while watering their animals at boreholes. Two Messiriyya were killed, 4 wounded; 1 Daju fatality and 1 wounded.[k]
12	**January–April 2008** Recurrent fatal clashes between the Messiriyya militias and the SPLA forces around Abyei in South Kordofan. New development of direct or indirect political and military involvement of the two partners in the Government of National Unity and the signatories to the CPA. This conflict is complex in terms of the stakeholders involved, flashpoint of hostilities weapons used, Tribal land was only one factor. This case also indicates potential escalation of land-based conflicts from local to large-scale.	The bloodiest conflict in the area. It was reported on 2 March 2008, that at least 43 Messiriyya were killed and 70 wounded, with 6 SPLA killed and 26 wounded in a clash on 1 March 2008 in the Dalayba area, 30km from Meiram. Tanks, rockets, and light weapons were used.[l]
13	**2 May 2008** Another clash broke out between the Nuba Abujunuk and a group of Messiriyya nomads in the Lagawa area, to the west in South Kordofan. The conflict started at a market place where the two groups mingle on a weekly basis. Livestock intrusion onto farming land was mentioned as the trigger.	The conflict,[m] initially involved few people, then escalated when the two parties mobilized their members and brought out weapons, resulting in 8 fatalities and more than 25 wounded.[n]

[h] Reported by Gamar al Din, Baha al Din in *Ray al-Sh'ab*, daily newspaper, issue No. 322. Khartoum.

[i] See Nuba Mountains homepage, online: http://home.planet.nl/~ende0098/Articles/20071002b.html, retrieved October 2, 2007. See also *Al Sudan* Daily newspaper: Online No. 878: http://www.alsudani.info./index.php?type=3&id=2147521857&bk=1, retrieved April 24, 2008.

[j] See 'Abdullah al Khayr, Sudan New Vision, in Nuba Mountains homepage, online: http://home.planet.nl/~ende0098/Articles/20071002b.html, retrieved 2 October 2007.

[k] UNMIS, 18 February 2008; in Nuba Mountains homepage, online: http://home.planet.nl/~ende0098/Articles/ 20080218b.html, retrieved 19 February 2008.

[l] Reported in Nuba Mountains Homepage, online: http://home.planet.nl/~ende0098/Articles/20080302b.html, retrieved 3 March 2008.

[m] Reported in Nuba Mountains Homepage, online: http://home.planet.nl/~ende0098/Articles/20080302b.html, retrieved 3 March 2008.

[n] Reported in Akhabar al-Yum, online Khartoum-based daily newspaper, http://www.akhbaralyoum.net/modules.php?names =News&file=art, retrieved, 4 May 2008.

Unfolding political events and the Nuba future choices

The overall current political situation suggests that there is no easy political choice for the Nuba people. The April 2010 national election and its consequences indicate a landslide victory for the dominant ruling party, the NCP, though highly contested. This victory indicates its political domination in the foreseeable future. In the Nuba Mountains region, the party from the start planned to sabotage the procedures leading to the proper exercise of popular consultation, as well as a population census, the demarcation of the electoral constituencies, and the subsequent postponement of elections in the region. It gained total political control over the institutions of the civil service, the police and security, and the judiciary which are technically responsible for conducting proper census and securing fair and free elections in the region.

From the start the SPLM raised concerns about the whole process of the population census and preparations for the elections. Subsequently, the SPLM decided to boycott the population census and to prevent the census staff from entering into the areas under its control in the region. Moreover, it decided to boycott the election at state level (state governorship and parliament) until the census was redone. This SPLM position has resulted in a partial postponement of the region's elections for an unspecified period. The census has been redone, and the preliminary results, which are not yet officially published, suggest sharp differences between the two censuses. The prediction is that if the NCP continues its political control over the institutions of the civil service, police, security, and judiciary in the region, there will be no fair election, and subsequently popular consultation may not happen, or if it does, its results may be subject to serious manipulation. This prospect alone may be sufficient reason for political tension in the region with unforeseeable consequences.

Moreover, the unresolved issues of the north-south borders, the Abyei dispute, and the control of the oil fields are all linked, in one way or another, to this region. Indeed, these highly contested and unresolved national questions will, to a large degree, determine the destiny of the indigenous people of Southern Kordofan. This gloomy political scenario is substantiated by several signs of an imminent return to political violence or civil war in the region. These signs include, among others, (i) the retreat and maintenance of the Nuba SPLA beyond the 1 January 1956 north-south line in southern Sudan territory, under the direct supervision of, and logistical support from, the formal body of SPLM/A; (ii) the possibility of the emerging South Sudan state as a source of political, logistic, military support for the Nuba SPLM/A to continue its political or armed struggle along south-north borders; (iii) Nuba discontent with the outcome of the CPA owing to the continuation of their socio-economic and political marginality; and (iv) the highly likely possibility of the escalation of disputes over the oil-rich area of Abyei along the north-south divide.

The impact of the Abyei dispute on the political stability of the Southern Kordofan is worth noting. After a long controversy over the Abyei Boundary Commission Report of 2005, the National Congress Party and the SPLM/A agreed in June 2008 to refer Abyei to the Permanent Court of Arbitration (PCA) in the Hague. On 22 July 2009, the PCA issued its Final Award and concluded that the Abyei Boundary Commission's (ABC) experts had exceeded their mandate in determining the Abyei eastern and western boundaries as well as in what it called 'the shared secondary rights' area between latitude 10°10'N and 10°35'N. It redefined the Abyei area as a homeland for the 9 Ngok Dinka chiefdoms transferred to Kordofan in 1905, with its northern boundary running along latitude 10°10'00"N, from longitude 27°50'00"E to longitude 29°00'00", while its eastern boundary runs in a straight line along longitude 20°00'00"E, from 10°10'00"N south to the Kordofan-Upper Nile boundary as it was defined on January 1956. The western boundary runs in a straight line along longitude 27°50'00"E, from 10°10'00"N south to the Kordofan-Darfur boundary as also defined on 1 January 1956, and continues on that boundary until it meets the southern boundary. At the same time, the PCA ruled that the exercise of established traditional rights within or in the vicinity of the Abyei area, particularly the right of the Messiriyya and other nomadic peoples to graze cattle and move across the Abyei area, as redefined in the Award, remains unaffected (see PCA: Final Award of Tribunal on Abyei Arbitration 2009: 267–268).

Despite the PCA decision being binding on all parties, its implementation remains unachievable. With this new boundary of the Abyei, the Heglig's oil area, el-Mayram, Nyam and Keilak have been excluded from the Abyei area and included in Southern Kordofan State. The economic, political and social repercussions of this new boundary are significant in both the short and long term. Thus, the future of both South Kordofan and Abyei areas, and subsequently the entire north–south relations after the PCA's Final Award depends fundamentally on the will and commitment of the two parties and the two local communities to abide by the PCA's decision.

There is no easy political choice for the Nuba and their political destiny is uncertain. The Nuba question will remain at the centre of national politics, whether the Sudan remains united or divided into two states after the 2011 referendum of the peoples of southern Sudan. Moreover, it is certain that the unfolding political dynamics analyzed above, and their subsequent socio-economic and political repercussions, will significantly reshape the Nuba Mountains/Southern Kordofan region, and determine the political destiny of its communities, if not the entire Sudan as a social, economic, and political space.

Conclusion

To sum up, the increasing complexity of current land-related conflicts is a powerful indicator of the failure of the CPA to redress the land issue, a chief cause of the civil war in the region. Despite all these mounting land-based conflicts in the region, no tangible progress has been made in resolving communal land issues during the five years since the conclusion of the Comprehensive Peace Agreement in 2005. This raises serious questions about the political will and commitment of the two signatories to a process which should have introduced new legislation to incorporate customary laws and practices, local heritage and international trends, and practices at different levels in accordance with the CPA. Land-related conflicts in the area and elsewhere, created by the government's policy of grabbing land from the rural peoples in Sudan in general and in the Nuba Mountains in particular will continue despite the existence of the CPA.

Conclusion

The overall analysis has generated several reflections for practitioners attempting to establish sound and holistic development policies, and also for theorists seeking a deeper understanding of several old issues but with new dynamics and ramifications. The aim has been to revisit the key reflections generated and to synthesize them into more generalized findings relevant for policy implications and, most importantly, for future research agendas in the areas of governance, land and conflicts, particularly in a post-conflict situation.

The ethnography of this study demonstrates the significance of land for basic survival, as an economic livelihood base, and as a symbol for social and political identification in the majority of rural societies. Livelihoods, identities, wealth, and power are often determined by the ability of stakeholders to access, use and own land resources in their different forms. Thus, issues of land tenure, policies, and politics are becoming critically important in political and public arenas, particularly in rural Africa. Rural Sudan is no exception. The material explored here, from the Nuba Mountains region, shows how the interests and rights of the rural communities are barely harmonized with the state's land policies, practices and development interventions at different stages of the state's formation. The issue here is more than a mere land question. It is about governance, coupled with the state's tendency to exclude its own people from their basic rights and needs.

In many cases, tensions may occur or recur over different types of land rights when modern state laws negate traditional or customary rights, or when multiple and competitive rights exist over the same land. The competition of traditional farmers and nomadic pastoralists over meagre land resources and the systematic expansion of state-driven development projects at the expense of the traditional livelihood base of these subsistence communities typify this process.

This study has described land factors as one of the crucial root causes of the recurrent local conflicts and the subsequent civil war in Sudan. It has also shown that land as a contributing factor to the contemporary local and national conflicts of Sudan is in itself a result of historical, cumulative processes of land tenure policies and politics within an overall nation-building process. The most important stage that shaped land rights and tenure system in Sudan took place under the colonial administration that confined the process of land settlement and registration to the northern and central regions of the Sudan. In the remaining parts of Sudan, the south, southern Blue Nile, the Nuba Mountains and Darfur, land remains unregistered and communally owned through customary laws and traditions.

Registration of land as private property means acquisition of an asset of significant and durable economic value. These early regional differences in land rights policies and practices formed a basis for economic, social and political disparities between the communities in the central and northern parts of the Sudan (the centre) and those in the rest of the country (the periphery). The continuation of these early inter-regional disparities in land ownership rights has provided and still provides the main source of wealth and power for the current dominant political parties and their socio-economic institutions in northern and central Sudan. In this way, land as a source of wealth and power remains one of the key differentiating factors between the core and the peripheral regions in postcolonial Sudan. This is an extremely important historical reality because of its far-reaching implications for the social, economic and political dynamics in Sudan today.

Critical examination of the present land tenure pattern shows that the national state did not deviate from the colonial legacy but consolidated it with more repressive laws, policies and practices. Instead of redressing the regional differences in land rights by pursuing land settlement and registration in the peripheral regions, the state subjected their unregistered communal lands to a systematic practice of land grabbing and expropriation for public and private investments. This further benefited the wealthy from the core region while impoverishing local communities indigenous to the land. The introduction of mechanized rain-fed farming schemes in the peripheral regions since the 1960s and subsequent oil explorations since the 1990s are two major development interventions in the name of 'public interest' but at the expense of the local communities and their subsistence livelihoods.

These misguided development interventions have had far-reaching repercussions, not only on the relations between state and local communities, but also between the local communities. Interventions were conducted with violence and land alienation, producing misery and grievance among local communities. They were systematically pushed to the margins, eventually driven landless, with their very survival endangered in their own ancestral homeland. These state interventions acted and still act as a driving force that has evoked all kinds of appeals and emotions to other forms of identities and belongings among the disadvantaged communities, who fight back for what they perceive as their inherent and legitimate rights. In this context, land issues provoke, sustain or even escalate various types and levels of conflicts in the Sudan's unfolding and violent transformation.

Whereas the land question, in terms of customary communal rights, was not a direct major factor in the outbreak of the civil war in southern Sudan (1983–2005), this study confirms that land was one of the key factors in the extension of the civil war from the southern to northern Sudan via the Nuba Mountains. This is the case in spite of the significant contribution of other historical and contemporary causes of conflict. The continuous alienation of Nuba lands and their appropriation by outside investors has been singled out as the prime motivating factor for the Nuba to join the Sudan People's Liberation Movement/Army (SPLM/A) in the mid-1980s. Its central role in sustaining the war in the region is evident in the after-effects of the hostilities on the relationships between the state and the local communities and between the sedentary Nuba and the nomadic Baqqara themselves.

Before the war, the predominant territorial feature of the Nuba Mountains region was the co-existence of sedentary Nuba and nomadic Baqqara communities, even with constant competition between them over the land and water resources. The groups lived in intensive connection with each other, through various forms of cooperation and with locally manageable conflicts at different levels of their social organizations. The salient features of this co-existence are remarkably evident through several intermediary spaces such as local markets, water points, mixed neighbourhoods, and the complementary socioeconomic activities of farming and grazing. This study has shown how the institution of the periodic local market functions as a multifaceted socio-cultural, political, and economic intermediary space, bringing together different actors along the Nuba–Baqqara continuum with their various interests.

One tragic development of the war (1985–2002) was that it transformed this relatively peaceful and symbiotic Nuba–Baqqara relationship into antagonism. These two local disadvantaged communities were compelled to escalate their previously low and locally managed conflicts into large-scale warfare for reasons externally generated at the national level. With the war extending northwards, the grazing lands of the Baqqara nomads around north-south frontiers, including the southern border of the Nuba Mountains, were turned into a war zone occupied by the government army and the SPLM/A.

The central government armed the Baqqara, enlisting them in pro-government militia forces against the SPLM/A, resulting in a protracted proxy war. The acquisition of more sophisticated arms and the gradual collapse of state institutions in the region motivated the Baqqara to develop their own agenda. They soon began raiding Nuba in their hill communities, before they allied themselves (for protection) with the SPLM/A. The Baqqara engaged indiscriminately in raiding, killing and looting the Nuba villages, committing numerous massacres. These raids polarized Nuba public opinion not only against the central government but also against the local Baqqara.

As the war intensified, the Nuba Mountains territory was progressively divided into two ethno-political and geo-administrative territories: areas controlled and administered by the government of the Sudan, with the Baqqara having the upper hand in public affairs, and areas controlled and administered by the Nuba-led SLPM/A, with the Baqqara nomads denied all access to their traditional seasonal grazing lands and sources of water. The war took on an ethnic dimension and intensified the antagonism between the two already divided communities with distinct territorial divisions along ethno-political lines. It reached its climax in the early 1990s when an emerging Islamic regime added a religious dimension that not only reinforced inequitable policies introduced by the previous governments but also launched a systematic military assault, backed by an ideological campaign to uproot Nuba culture, identity, and even their very survival as an ethnic group. The regime soon declared Jihad against the Nuba people. However, for the majority of the Nuba, the war was not waged on the ground of religion. It was, rather, a war against African identity and ancestral territory, and the declared Jihad was merely an act of religious politicization of ethnic distinctions, by the Arab-Islamic ruling elite. In the midst of a war that amounted to genocide and ethnocide, the Nuba were forced to invoke and essentialize some forms of ethnic identities and attachments to their ancestral homeland as a survival strategy against the brutality of such an exclusionary and repressive state.

Despite the enormity of the fractures along Nuba-Baqqara lines, some evidence shows the emergence of mutual survival strategies and coping mechanisms in terms of sporadic economic-driven cooperation, interests, and ties between the two groups, even during the war. These linkages were made possible by some members of the two communities situating themselves along the divides and engaging in trade and market exchange across borders despite the intensity of war. The existence of these positive relations, although tentative and sporadic in pattern, indicates that the causes of their hostilities during the war were not internally generated. Rather, they were externally driven and essentially induced by the interest of the ruling elites at the centre. Large-scale conflict in the region is generally connected to the failure of the state, its bad governance, the collapse of its modern administrative institutions, and the discredit of its misguided and distorted development interventions that undermine the interests and priorities of both these rural communities.

No doubt, the Sudan Comprehensive Peace Agreement concluded on 9 January 2005 was remarkably successful in putting an end to open warfare of the bloodiest and longest war in the recent history of Africa. It guaranteed cessation of hostilities and the free movement of civilians and goods with the broader objective of the gradual achievement of a just, peaceful, and comprehensive settlement to the conflict. But, paradoxically, in the Nuba Mountains region, some of the central features of the CPA, manifested in increased stability, freedom of movement and the opening-up of the tribal areas, reactivated the sources of conflict that had subsided during the war. These were all linked directly to the issue of land. Pastoralists returned with their livestock to their pre-war traditional grazing zone; internally displaced persons (IDPs) and the Nuba soldiers came back to their pre-war settlements and farming lands; and Jillaba investors resumed their trading, mechanized farming, and the exploitation of natural resources in areas which were not accessible during the war. The reoccupation by the various stakeholders of their previous homelands or activities was a tense process, loaded with new types of conflicts as a result of the war in the region.

Thus, the outcome of the CPA, from the Nuba perspective, fell far short of their expectations because it failed to address the root causes of their political and armed struggle. Questions of communal land, cultural identity and political destiny arose with new emphases. The analysis of the CPA, presented here, particularly the Protocol of Southern Kordofan and Blue Nile States has shown that the agreement has inadequately addressed the land question. Moreover, the establishment of the Southern Kordofan State Land Commission has been delayed for no clear reason, and to detrimental effect. Analyzing the political discourse after peace in the region shows that the delay is linked to the ruling elites' persistent tendency towards not recognizing the communal land rights, in spite of the articulation of those rights in the Comprehensive Peace Agreement. Consequently, no tangible progress has been made in redressing land-related grievances after more than five years since its enactment in 2005. The lack of political will to constitutionally safeguard communal land rights demonstrates the desire of the state to maintain a policy of land-grabbing from local communities for mechanized farming and oil investments.

In response to the CPA's disappointing outcome and the excessive delay in its implementation processes, the Nuba political and social leaders opted for the construction of a new political strategy, linked closely to the 'doctrine of liberation' in the context of the 'New Sudan' vision and its territorial manifestations, discourses and socio-economic actions. The intention was to unite the Nuba as an ethno-political identity capable of taking collective positions and strategic decisions that would safeguard what had been achieved in the CPA while continuing the struggle for its desired destiny. As endangered communities, the Nuba soon activated, politicized and deployed the notion of autochthonous identity, with intense dedication. The notion is tied strongly to their communal land and, in fact, to the entire Nuba Mountains territory as an ancestral homeland, a source of economic survival, and a basis for ethno-political identity. Oral history and myths of origin, cultural and religious practices, and the contemporary political struggle have all been invoked in this self-identification of the Nuba as a unified indigenous group facing the risk of cultural or even physical annihilation. The Nuba tendency to play communal identity politics, and to essentialize some of the common attributes that unite them, is a matter of survival, a strategic use of essentialism against the exclusionary state institutions and their disguised/misguided development policies that have persisted since the colonial times.

However, this very communal identity politics and its territorial manifestation has generated its own dynamics on the ground. It has led the Baqqara to fear that they are likely to be excluded from their claimed primary and secondary land rights in the region. This stems from the fact that the Nuba emerging collective movement on the basis of firstcomer or autochthonous status stimulates inevitable inclusion-and-exclusion strategies, or 'we' versus 'they'.

Therefore, the Nuba's emerging communal identity politics in claiming land has been systematically contested by the state institutions as well as by their local partners, i.e., the Baqqara. The Baqqara in turn developed their counter strategy by strengthening their different forms of alliances, exercising the politics of manipulation over territories, and mobilizing key government institutions at national and regional level. Thus, at the state level this multi-dimensional confrontation appears to be between the legality of the modern state's legal framework regarding land ownership and usage and the legitimacy of the traditional communal institutions and authorities of the local communities. The legal and politico-administrative institutions of the state continue to destabilize the legitimacy of any claims to land rights raised by indigenous groups on the basis of firstcomer or autochthony claims. At the local community level, the confrontation is translated into one between the traditional social institutions and authorities of the indigenous group (the Nuba) and those of the other co-existing ethnic groups labelled as latecomers (the Baqqara) — who are backed by the state.

The overall discourse of the Nuba/Baqqara communal land claims is, to a large degree, linked to the issue of the representations and self-perceptions held by each group. The Nuba have long perceived themselves as indigenous to the region. This idea is supported by their autochthonous myths of origin defining the entire region as an ancestral homeland and a symbol of their socio-political identity. For their part, the Baqqara hold the view that their roughly three hundred years' presence in the region also qualifies them as indigenous. Further, they consider themselves culturally superior to the 'primitive' Nuba whom they regard with scorn since the time when the Baqqara Arabs were practising some sort of overlordship over the Nuba. The war provoked Nuba self-awareness as a unified ethnic group sharing historical oppression and now collectively facing another phase of state-induced oppression. Since the peace agreement, political discourse in the region continues to perpetuate these rigid ethnic distinction loaded with negative representations of the two groups. The problem goes even deeper than of that the land crisis; it is a the relic of the past, disastrously reactivated in contemporary social and political discourse and activity.

The main thrust of the Baqqara position is based on an assumption that the current spatial pattern of the two groups in the Nuba Mountains is *normal*. However, the large corpus of literature and archival records examined in this study reveals that the present Baqqara and Nuba spatial pattern is *abnormal*, brought about by systematic and longstanding violence against the Nuba. This anomaly was 'institutionalized' and reinforced by colonial and postcolonial forces. Redressing it is fundamental to achieving any enduring peace in the region.

One key finding of the study, however, is the impossibility of proving autochthonous or firstcomer claims. This is a never-ending exercise that leads to nowhere in the absence of clear-cut, ethnic, territorial boundaries. All there is is a set of loose territorial boundaries in the minds of the different claimants. These fluid mental maps in different ethnic groups overlap in such a way that a whole territory or part of it can be simultaneously claimed by two or more co-existing ethnic groups, or even by two or more lineages/clans within the same ethnic group in a shared territory. These overlapping, perceived, as opposed to physical, maps trigger the recurrent land conflicts whenever one party attempts to exercise exclusive control over a shared land and its resources. The empirical data of this study demonstrate the futility of any attempt to settle the issue through this type of appeal.

In all local political discourses, the desired power relations are evoked through reconstructions of the past that depict these power relations as both inevitable and the historical norm. In this way, group boundaries do not appear as transient, dynamic, and evolving, but rather as eternally constant distinctions based in nature. In reality, the historical inter-ethnic and inter-tribal territorial and social boundaries have been flexible and dynamic throughout time, changing back and forth depending on complex dynamics, including the history of population movements and settlement patterns, community leaders' decisions on the ground at different times, and the cumulative influence of external forces, including the state. Any attempt, for whatever reasons, to reconstruct well-defined and stable inter-ethnic/tribal boundaries is likely to ignite serious disputes between the historically co-existing communities. On the contrary, ethnic/tribal distinctions do not go hand in hand with an absence of social interaction and a lack of mutual acceptance. The study has demonstrated that ethnic and tribal distinctions and even low-scale conflicts are often the very foundations on which inclusive social systems are built. Such differences persist not in spite of, but rather because of, inter-ethnic/tribal contact and interdependence. They are not the cause of conflicts but solid grounds for inevitable social and spatial complementarities.

The continuation of the war-imposed dichotomy, characterized by a divided political-administrative setting with sharp ethnic and territorial boundaries, is a disturbing reality in the post-conflict Nuba Mountains of today. The persistence of this situation, despite the peace, indicates that the two ethnic groups who were able to co-exist socially and mix spatially during the pre-war period cannot restore harmony after the war. It is significant that the war-imposed settlement pattern of boundary-making along ethnic lines in the same locale is being consolidated by certain key peace and development players, including state institutions, UN agencies, international NGOs, and community-based organizations (CBOs). Instead of unifying this divided livelihood pattern, most of those involved have exacerbated the conflict. This is clearly manifested in the provision of services, particularly schooling, health, food relief, water supply, and security arrangements among the two divided communities after the CPA.

The irony is that some government institutions and global actors who claim they are working towards restoring the normal situation seems to have been trapped in this war-imposed dichotomy. This is evident not only along political, but also along ethnic lines, within the same political-administrative territory and/or within the same ethnic/tribal group. Services are allocated in a manner that fosters the institutionalization of the war-imposed spatial patterns of distinctive ethnic boundaries in all aspects of the public space. State institutions and international bodies were expected to act as agents for positive change, facilitators of ethno-social healing, and promoters of political reconciliation. Surprisingly, this study reveals that some of the actors involved are variously being co-opted or neutralized in the course of their involvement. They become part of processes and agencies which are building up, not tearing down, the walls of ethno-political antagonism during the post-conflict situation in the Nuba Mountains.

In short, the Nuba line of argumentation, related actions and manifestations in claiming land or even the entire region and the Baqqara counter line have stirred up a chain of new types of land-driven conflicts at various levels of scale in the social organizations of the two groups. These conflicts are mounting in trend and scale partly because of the post-war proliferation of uncontrolled small arms movement, in the hands of the local people. As a consequence, the culture of war and violence continues to dominate Nuba–Baqqara relations in the region. The result is the serious erosion of a culture of peace and tolerance despite the Comprehensive Peace Agreement which is proving to be unachievable.

This gloomy picture raises serious questions with regard to the political commitment of the two signatories to the CPA, particularly the NCP, to the implementation of the agreement, including the introduction of new legislation that recognizes and safeguards customary land rights under modern state laws. Thus, in view of the prevailing political unwillingness to address the land question, coupled with the government's continuing policy of land-grabbing, it is likely that land conflicts will continue or even escalate despite the existence of the CPA. There is no reason to expect the restoration of political and social peace and security in the Nuba Mountains and the other similar regions of Sudan until the land question, one of the root causes of Sudan's conflicts, is redressed. Instead, it is conceivable that the trend of articulating communal identity politics in claiming land rights may become more complex and widespread in different rural societies in the peripheral regions of Sudan. This, in turn, may accelerate emerging ethno-regional indigenous movements and the associated ethno-political instability. This not only undermines the nation-building process but endangers the very survival of the Sudanese state as a viable political unit.

Finally, contrary to the established view that conflicts in Africa originate from ethnic, religious or cultural differences, this study substantiates a view that some large-scale conflicts and civil wars in Africa may originate also from other factors including land. In the process of war, factors such as ethnicity, religious or cultural differences may be mobilized, moving gradually towards the centre of the event while the original leading factor recedes. Thus, the conflict becomes more complex, with an internal self-generating capacity to reproduce itself in larger scale and effect. In the context of the Sudan, this process appears to operate not only in the Nuba Mountains but also in similar peripheral regions, ravaged by conflicts and civil wars, particularly in the present conflagration of Darfur.

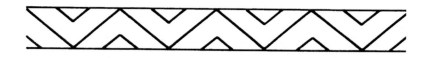

Bibliography

Primary sources

Abdalla, A. J. 1981. 'Sudan pastronomads in transition. Problems of evolution and adjustment', in *Die Nomaden in Geschichte und Gegenwart. Beiträge zu einem internationalen Nomadismus-Symposium*, 11–12 December 1975 in Museum für Völkerkunde Leipzig. Berlin: Akademie-Verlag: 203–211.

Abukasawi, Mustafa J. 2009. 'Assessment of the Rural Market System in South Kordofan State'. Khartoum: Sudan Productive Recovery Programme, North Capacity Building's Report.

Amnesty International. 1993a. *Sudan. The Ravages of War: political killings and humanitarian disaster*. London: Amnesty International Publication.

——. 1993b. *Sudan: Patterns of Repression*. London: Amnesty International Publication.

Danforth, John C. 2002. 'Report to the President of the United States on the Outlook for Peace in the Sudan', from John C. Danforth, Special Envoy for Peace, April 26, 2002. White House release, 14 May 2002. http://www.whitehouse.gov/news/releases/2002/05/20020514-11.html, retrieved 13 September 2008.

Ende, N. Op't. 2001. 'Interview with Yousif Kuwa Mekki'. London 12–13 February. http://home.planet.nl/~ende0098/Articles/20010426.htm, retrieved 5 September 2008.

——. 2006a. 'Interview with Neroun Philip Aju Kuku', by Nanne op 't Ende, Lueri, Sudan 1 April 2006, *Nuba Mountains Homepage* http://home.kpn.nl/ende0098/Articles/20060814.htm, retrieved 4 September 2006.

——. 2006b. 'Interview with Ismael Khamis Jelab, Governor of South Kordofan' by Nanne op 't Ende, Kadugli 13 March and Khartoum 15 April 2006 http://home.planet.nl/~ende0098/Articles/20060428.htm, retrieved 13 September 2008.

——.2005 'Final Communiqué of All Nuba Second Conference', 2005. http://www.sudantribune.com/spip.php?article9487, retrieved 10 March 2008.

Government of Republic of Sudan and the Sudan Peoples' Liberation Movement/Nuba. 2002. 'The Nuba Mountains Cease-Fire Agreement', Bürgenstock, Switzerland, 19 January 2002. http://www.reliefweb.int/rw/RWB.NSF/db900SID/MHII-6227SX?OpenDocument, retrieved 13 September 2008.

Government of Sudan and the SPLM/A. 2005. 'The Comprehensive Peace Agreement 9 January 2005, Naivasha, Kenya', http://www.reliefweb.int/rw/RWFiles2005.nsf/FilesByRWDocUNIDFileName/EVIU-6AZBDB-sud-sud-09janPart%20II.pdf/$File/sud-sud-09janPart%20II.pdf, retrieved 13 September 2008.

International Labor Organization (ILO). 1989. Convention (No. 169) concerning Indigenous and Tribal Peoples in Independent Countries, adopted on 27 June1989 by the General Conference of ILO, at its 67th session but enacted 5 September 1991. Geneva: ILO.

Kafi, Shamsun Khamis. 2006. 'Keiga First Conference's Final Resolutions', Keiga Council, Khartoum.

Kampala Declaration, 2002, 'The Kampala Declaration of the Nuba and Southern Blue Nile Civil Society Forum', 21–24 November 2002. http://www.nubasurvival.com/news&events/Nov%202002%20Kampala%20declaration.htm, retrieved 15 April 2010.

Kauda Conference Communiqués. 2003. All Nuba First Conference, 3–4 December, Kauda, Nuba Mountains, SPLM/A-controlled areas, Sudan. http://www.nubasurvival.com/Nuba%20Vision/Vol%202%20Issue%202/7%20Kauda%20Conference%20Communiqu%E9.htm, retrieved 4 March 2008.

Keiga Council. 2006. The Final Communiqué of All Keiga Council. Keiga Luban, Nuba Mountains.

Nabudere, Dani W. 2005. Comprehensive Report of the First Traditional Leaders Conference in Nuba Mountains, Julud, 17–22 July 2005, http://home.planet.nl/~ende0098/content/documents/Traditional_leaders_conference.htm, retrieved 13 September 2008.

NMPACT Coordination Unit. 2002. NMPACT report of the baseline data collection exercise – Summary findings. Khartoum: UNOCHA.

Nuba Relief, Rehabilitation and Development Organization (NRRDO). 2002. Nuba Reaction to the Machakos Protocol: Open Letter to General Lazarus Sambeyweo from Nuba Civil Society Organizations, regarding the Machakos Protocol, Nairobi, 14 August 2002. http://home.planet.nl/~ende0098/Articles/20020814a.htm, retrieved 13 September 2008.

Permanent Court of Arbitration (PCA). 2009. *Final Award of Tribunal on Abyei Arbitration*, The Hague: The Peace Palace.

Republic of Sudan. 1958. First population census of Sudan 1955/56. Notes on Omodia map. Khartoum: Ministry for Social Affairs, Population Census Office

——. 2006. *South Kordofan State's Transitional Five Year Plan, Part Two: Development Projects (2006–2010)*, Khartoum.

Sambeyweo, Lazarus. 2002. Position of the Sudanese Civil Society on the Just and Lasting Peace in the Sudan, Nairobi, 5 July 2002. http://www.mafhoum.com/press3/105S22.htm, retrieved 13 September 2008.

SPLM. 2004. 'SPLM Nuba Land Action Strategy', Nuba Mountains Region: Governor's Workshop of Land Security Strategy, Kauda-Lwere, 4–5 November 2004, Kauda-Lwere: SPLM Land Office.

——. 2005. Resolutions of Rashad County Land Workshop, 30–31 May, Kauda, Nuba Mountains.

Sudan Archive. 1899. *Sudan Gazette* No. 2. May 27th, 1899. Official Sudan Laws Proclamation. Title to Lands Ordinance, 1899. *Ref: SAD 627/12/3–10*. Durham: Durham University Library.

——. 1903a. Kordofan Land Commission's letter to the Civil Secretary, Government of Sudan, by N.T. Borton, Kaimakam, President of Kordofan Land Commission, Dueim, April 20th 1903. *Ref: SAD 542/1/5–7*. Durham: Durham University Library.

——.1903b. *Sudan Gazette* No. 45, March, 1903. An Ordinance to Amend the Title of Lands Ordinance, 1899. *Ref: SAD 627/12/11–8*. Durham: Durham University Library.

——. 1905. *Sudan Gazette* No. 80 (Special) of 24th August 1905. *Ref: SAD 627/12/13–8*. Durham: Durham University Library.

——. 1907. The Deeds Registration Ordinance 1907. *Ref: SAD 627/12/22–8*. Durham: Durham University Library.

——. 1908. The Deeds Registration Ordinance 1908. *Ref: SAD 627/12/29–30*. Durham: Durham University Library.

——. 1914. Report on Bara Lands by Mr. Corbyn 1914. *Ref: SAD 542/3/35–44*. Durham: Durham University Library.

——. 1915a. Mr. Sarsfield-Hall's Final Report on the Sennar Land Settlement 1913–1915. *Ref: SAD 542/15/1–24*. Durham: Durham University Library.

——. 1915b. Sennar Land Settlement: Settlement Officer's Instructions. *Ref: SAD 678/2, 27–40*. Durham: Durham University Library.

——. 1920. The Deeds Registration Ordinance 1920. *Ref: SAD 627/12/34–5*. Durham: Durham University Library.

——. 1925. The Land Settlement & Registration Ordinance 1925. *Ref: SAD 627/12/36–7*. Durham: Durham University Library.

——. 1926. C. A. Willis (A. Director of Sudan Intelligence 1915–26): Report on Slavery and Pilgrimage 1926. *Ref: SAD 212/2/1–84*. Durham: Durham University Library.

——. 1928. The Prescription and Limitation Ordinance 1928. *Ref: SAD 627/12/39–43*. Durham: Durham University Library.

——. 1930a. Individual Rights in Tribal Lands. *Ref: SAD 442/23/1–5*. Durham: Durham University Library.

——. 1930b. Note on Individual Rights in Tribal Lands by B. H. Bell, Acting Legal Secretary, Legal Department, Sudan Government, August 11th 1930. *Ref*: *SAD 542/23/1–5*. Durham: Durham University Library.

——. 1934a. Note with Reminder to Part of Mr. Evans' note on 'Land Tenure in the Sudan' by M. E. G. Pumphrey, December 14, 1934. *Ref: SAD 542/24/4–5*. Durham: Durham University Library.

——. 1934b. Notes on Nuba Mountains by A. L. W. Vicars-Miles. Written on his return to the Nuba Mountains in 1934. *Ref: SAD 631/10/1–62*. Durham: Durham University Library.

——. 1934c. Eastern Jebel Monthly Diary, October 1934 by Gawain W. Bell. Assistant District Commissioner, Eastern Jebels District, Talodi 2.11.34. *Ref: SAD 695/8/6–8*. Durham: Durham University Library.

——. 1935a. Report on Bara Lands by Mr. Buchanan in 1935. *Ref: SAD 542/3/45–9*. Durham: Durham University Library.

——. 1935b. Gawain W. Bell's Monthly Diary. *Ref: SAD 698/8/31–63*. Durham: Durham University Library.

——. 1946/47. Land Policy. by S. R. Simpson, K. D. D. Henderson and S. K. Smith. 1946/47'. *Ref: SAD 627/16/6–15*. Durham: Durham University Library.

——. 1950. Disputes Concerning Unregistered Lands. by D. F. Hawley, 13 February 1950. *Ref: SAD 719/10/1–5*. Durham: Durham University Library.

——. 1954. Registrar General of Lands Office, Khartoum. Annual Report 1953/54, 1 August 1954. *Ref: SAD 720/3/1–2*. Durham: Durham University Library.

Sudan Intelligence Report. March 1902. Report No. 92. Durham: Durham University Library.

United Nations. 1992. Declaration on the Rights of Persons Belonging to National or Ethnic, Religious and Linguistic Minorities, adopted by the United Nations General Assembly, Resolution 47/135 of 18 December 1992. New York: UN.

——. 1994. Draft United Nations declaration on the rights of indigenous peoples, Resolution 1994/45. New York: UN.

——, 1995. The Rights of Indigenous Peoples, Fact Sheet no. 9 (Rev. 1). Office of the High Commissioner for Human Rights, http://www.unhchr.ch/html/menu6/2/fs9.htm, retrieved 13 September 2008.

UN Office for the Coordination of Humanitarian Affairs (UNOCHA). 2008. 'In-Depth Sudan Peace Process/ Sudan: the road to peace'. *IRIN Humanitarian News and Analysis* (3 March). http://www.irinnews.org/InDepthMain.aspx?InDepthId=32&&ReportId=70688, retrieved 13 September 2008.

Secondary Sources

Abbas, Philip Ghabush. 1973. 'Growth of black political consciousness in Northern Sudan', *Africa Today* 20, 3: 29–43.

Abd al-Rahim, Muddathir. 1970. 'Arabism, Africanism, and self-identification in the Sudan', *Journal of Modern African Studies* 8, 2 : 233–49.

Abdel Ati, Hassan A. ed., 2005. *Sudan: the challenges of peace and redressing marginalization*, Khartoum: EDGE for Consultancy & Research and Heinrich Böll Foundation.

Abdelgabar, Omar. 1997. *Mechanized Farming and Nuba Peasants: An example for non-sustainable development in the Sudan*, Hamburg: Spektrum 48.

Abdel-Hamid, M. O. Abdel-Rahim. 1986. 'The Hawazma Baqqara: Some issues and problems in pastoral adaptations', MA. Diss., University of Bergen.

Abdel Salam, A. H. and Alex de Waal, eds. 2001. *The Phoenix State: civil society and the future of Sudan*, Lawrenceville, NJ, and Asmara, Eritrea: Red Sea Press.

——. Gamal el-Tom and Suleiman Rahhal. 2002. 'Land rights, natural resources tenure and land reform', in Yoanes Ajawin and Alex de Waal, eds., *When Peace Comes: Civil society and development in Sudan*, Lawrenceville, NJ and Asmara, Eritrea, Red Sea Press: 119–44.

Abdul-Jalil, Musa Adam, 2005. 'Land tenure and inter-ethnic conflict in Darfur', in ACTS, ed. *Report of the Conference on Land Tenure and Conflict in Africa: prevention, mitigation and reconstruction, 9th–10th December 2004*, Nairobi: ACTS Press: 53–71.

Bibliography

———. 2008. 'Nomad–sedentary relations and the question of land rights in Darfur: From complementary to conflict', in Richard Rottenburg, ed., *Nomadic–sedentary Relations and Failing Institutions in Darfur and Kordofan (Sudan)*, Halle: University of Halle-Wittenburg, Orientwissenschaftliche Hefte 26: 1–24.

ACTS. 2005. *Summary Report of the Conference on Land Tenure and Conflict in Africa: prevention, migration and reconstruction, 9–10 December 2004*, Nairobi: ACTS Press.

Adams, Martin. 1982. 'The Baggara problem: attempts at modern change in Southern Darfur and Southern Kordofan (Sudan)', *Development and Change* 13, 2: 259–89.

——— and Stephen Turner. 2005. 'Legal dualism and land policy in Eastern and Southern Africa'. *Workshop on Land Rights for African Development: From knowledge to action. Nairobi, 31 October–3 November 2005*. Nairobi: UNDP International Land Coalition.

African Rights. 1995. *Facing Genocide: the Nuba of Sudan*, London: African Rights.

———. 1997. *A Desolate 'Peace': Human Rights in the Nuba Mountains, Sudan 1997*, London: African Rights.

Africa Watch. 1991. *Sudan. Destroying Ethnic Identity: The secret war against the Nuba*, London: Africa Watch.

——— . 1992a. *Sudan: Eradicating the Nuba*, London: Africa Watch.

———. 1992b. *Sudan. Refugees in their own country*, London: Africa Watch.

Ahmed, Abdel Ghaffar M. 1980. 'Planning and the neglect of pastoral nomads in the Sudan', in G. Haaland, ed., *Problems of Savannah Development: the Sudan Case*, Bergen: University of Bergen: 39–54.

———. 2001. 'Livelihood and resource competition, Sudan', in Mohamed Abdel Rahim Mohamed Salih, Ton Dietz, and Abdel Ghaffar Mohamed Ahmed, eds., *African Pastoralism: Conflict, Institutions and Government*, London: Pluto Press: 172–93.

———. ed., 1976. *Some Aspects of Pastoral Nomadism in the Sudan*, Khartoum: Khartoum University Press.

Ajawin, Yoanes and Alex de Waal, eds, 2002. *When Peace Comes: Civil Society and Development in Sudan*. Lawrenceville, NJ and Asmara, Eritrea: Red Sea Press.

Alier, A. 1990. *Southern Sudan: Too many agreements dishonored*, Reading UK: Ithaca Press.

Arkell, A. J. 1961. *A History of the Sudan from the Earliest Times to 1821*, London: The Athlone Press, University of London.

Ayoub, Mona. 2006. *Land and Conflict in Sudan*, Accord Conciliation Resources, http://www.c-r.org/our-work/accord/sudan/Land-conflict.php, retrieved 31 October 2007.

Azarya, Victor. 1996. *Nomads and the State in Africa: The Political Roots of Marginality*, Leiden: African Studies Centre.

Babiker, A. A., H. A. Musnad, and H. Z. Shadad. 1985. 'Wood resources and use in the Nuba Mountains', in H. R. J. Davies, ed., *Natural Resources and Rural Development in Arid Lands: Case Studies from Sudan*, Tokyo: United Nations University Press: 30–59.

Babiker, Mustafa. 1998. 'Land tenure in Kordofan: conflict between the 'communalism' of colonial administrators and the 'individualism' of the

Hamar', in Endre Stiansen and Michael Kevane, eds, *Kordofan Invaded: Peripheral Incorporation and Social Transformation in Islamic Africa*, Leiden: Brill: 197–222.

——. 2001. 'Resource competition and conflict: herder/farmer or pastoralism/agriculture?' in Mohamed Abdel Rahim Mohamed Salih, Ton Dietz, and Abdel Ghaffar Mohamed Ahmed, eds, *African Pastoralism: Conflict, Institutions and Government*, London: Pluto Press: 134–44.

Barbour, K. M. 1961. The *Republic of the Sudan: A Regional Geography*, London: University of London Press.

Barth, Frederik. 1969. *Ethnic Groups and Boundaries. The Social Organization of Culture Difference*, Prospect Heights, IL: Waveland Press.

——. ed., 1978. *Scale and Social Organization*. Oslo: Universitetsforlaget.

Battahani, Atta El Hassan El. 1980. *The State and the Agrarian Question: A case-study of South Kordofan 1971–1977*. Khartoum: University of Khartoum.

——. 1983. 'A strategy for the modernization of traditional agriculture in Southern Kordofan', in Mohamed Hashim Awad, ed., *Socioeconomic Change in the Sudan*, Khartoum: University of Khartoum Graduate College, Monograph no. 6: 67–79.

——. 1986. 'Nationalism and peasant politics in the Nuba Mountains region of Sudan, 1924–1966'. Ph.D. Thesis, University of Sussex.

——. 1998. 'On the transformation of ethnic-national policies in the Sudan: the case of the Nuba people', *Sudan Notes and Records* 2: 99–116.

Baumann, Gerd. 1982. 'Some notes on rural development in the Nuba Mountains (Sudan)', *Journal of Research on North East Africa* 1, 2: 85–94.

——. 1984. 'Development as a historical process: A social and cultural history of development in a Nuba Mountains community', *Anthropos* 79: 459–71.

——. 1987. *National Integration and Local Integrity: The Miri of the Nuba Mountains in the Sudan*, Oxford: Clarendon Press.

von Benda-Beckmann, Franz and Keebet. 2004. 'Struggles over communal property rights and law in Minangkabau, West Sumatra'. *Working Paper No. 64*. Halle: Max Planck Institute for Social Anthropology.

Beshir, Mohamed Omer. 1979a. *The Southern Sudan: Background to Conflict*, London: Hurst.

——. 1979b. *Diversity, Regionalism, and National Unity*. Uppsala: Scandinavian Institute of African Studies.

——. 1984. 'Ethnicity, regionalism and national cohesion in the Sudan', in Mohamed Omer Beshir, Mohamed Abdel Rahim Mohamed Salih, and Musa Adam Abdul-Jalil, eds, *The Sudan. Ethnicity and national cohesion*, Bayreuth: Bayreuth African Studies Series 1: 5–37.

——. M. A. Mohamed Salih, and A. M. Abdul-Jalil, eds, 1984. *The Sudan. Ethnicity and National Cohesion*, Bayreuth: Bayreuth African Studies Series 1.

Bohannan, P. and G. Dalton, eds, 1965. *Markets in Africa; Eight Subsistence Economies in Transition*. Garden City, NY: Anchor Books.

Bolton, A. R. C. 1954. 'Land tenure in agricultural land in the Sudan', in J. D. Tothill, ed., *Agriculture in the Sudan, being a handbook of agriculture as practised in the Anglo-Egyptian Sudan*, London: Oxford University Press: 187–97.

Bourdieu, Pierre. 1985. 'The Social Space and the Genesis of Groups', *Theory and Society* 14, 6: 723–44.

Bibliography

Bovin, M. and L. O. Manger. 1990. *Adaptive Strategies in African Arid Lands*, Uppsala: Scandinavian Institute of African Studies (SIAS).

Bradbury, Mark. 1998. 'Sudan: International responses to war in the Nuba Mountains', *Review of African Political Economy* 25, 77: 463–74.

Ceuppens, Bambi. 2006. 'Allochthons, Colonizers, and Scroungers: Exclusionary Populism in Belgium'. *African Studies Review – Special Issue: Autochthony and the Crisis of Citizenship*, 49, 2: 147–86.

Chabal, P., U. Engel and L. de Haan, eds, 2007. *African Alternatives*, Leiden and Boston, MA: Brill.

Clarke, Adele E. 1991. 'Social worlds/arena theory as organizational theory', in David R. Maines, ed., *Social Organization and Social Process: Essays in Honor of Anselm Strauss*, New York: Aldine de Gruyter: 119–58.

Cloke, P., C. Philo and D. Sadler. 1991. *Approaching Human Geography. An Introduction to Contemporary Theoretical Debates*, London: Paul Chapman Publishing.

Colvin, R. C. 1939. *Agricultural Survey of Nuba Mountains*, Khartoum: McCorquodale and Co. (Sudan) Ltd.

Corkill, N. L. 1939. 'The Kambala and other seasonal festivals of the Kadugli and Miri Nuba', *Sudan Notes and Records* 22: 205–219.

Cunnison, Ian. 1966. *Baggara Arabs: Power and Lineage in a Sudanese Nomad Tribe*, Oxford: Clarendon Press.

Dafinger, A., and M. Pelican. 2002. 'Land rights and the politics of integration: pastoralists' strategies in a comparative view', *Working Paper No. 48*. Halle: Max Planck Institute for Social Anthropology.

Daly, Martin W. 1984. 'Principal office-holders in the Sudan government, 1895–1955', *The International Journal of African Historical Studies* 17, 2: 309–16.

——. 1986. *Empire on the Nile: the Anglo-Egyptian Sudan, 1898–1934*, Cambridge: Cambridge University Press.

Deng, Francis Mading. 1973. *Dynamics of Identification. A basis for national integration in the Sudan*, Khartoum: Khartoum University Press.

——. 1995. *War of Visions. Conflict of Identities in the Sudan*, Washington, DC: The Brookings Institution.

Duffield, Mark. 1990. 'Absolute distress. Structural causes of hunger in Sudan', *Middle East Report* (September–October): 4–11.

Dupire, Marguerite. 1965. 'Trade and markets in the economy of the nomadic Fulani of Niger (Bororo)', in P. Bohannan and G. Dalton, eds, *Markets in Africa*, Evanston/Chicago, IL: Northwestern University Press: 335–62.

Egemi, Omer A. 2004. 'Land Tenure in Sudan: Challenges to livelihood security and social peace', Unpublished paper. Khartoum: UNDP.

——. 2006. 'Land and peace processes in Sudan', *Accord Conciliation Resources*, http://www.c-r.org/our-work/accord/sudan/land-peace.php, retrieved 13 September 2008.

Elles, R. J. 1935. 'The Kingdom of Tegali', *Sudan Notes and Records* 18, 1: 1–35.

Elsayed, Ghefari Fadlallah. 2005. 'The politics of difference and boundary making among the Nuba and the Baggara of Southern Kordofan State, Sudan', M. Phil. Thesis, University of Bergen.

Ende, N. Op't. 2007. *Proud to be Nuba: Faces and Voices*, Amsterdam: CODE X.

Fadalla, Bashir O. M. 1986. 'Unbalanced Development and Regional Disparity', in *Conference of Macro-economic Policies in the Sudan*, 13–16 January, University of Khartoum, DSRC and Friedrich Ebert, Sudan.

Fadl, Muhammad al-Tayyib. 2002. *Kaduqli wa masira al-salam 1991–1992* (Kadugli and peace march), Khartoum: Sudan Currency Press.

Falola, T. and R. C. Njoku, eds. 2010. *War and Peace in Africa*. Durham: Carolina Academic Press.

Fein, Henen. 1997. 'Genocide by Attrition 1939–1993: The Warsaw Ghetto, Cambodia and Sudan: Links between human rights, health and mass death', *Health and Human Rights* 2, 2: 10–45.

Fraser, S., C. Gullick, S. Ling, and K. Vang, eds. 2004. Trading for Peace: An overview of markets and trading practices, with particular reference to Peace Markets in Northern Bahr el Ghazal, South Sudan, Unpublished Reports: SUPRAID, BYDA and Concern Worldwide.

Friedman, John. 1967. 'Regional Planning and Nation-building: An agenda for international research', *Economic Development and Cultural Change* 16, 1: 119–29.

Garang, John and Mansour Khalid. 1987/1992. *The Call for Democracy in Sudan*, London: Kegan Paul International, 2nd edn.

Gertel, Jörg. 2007. 'Mobility and Insecurity: the significance of resources,' in Ingo Brever and Jörg Gertel eds., *Pastoral Morocco: globalizing scopes of mobility and insecurity*, Wiesbaden: Reichert: 11–30.

Geschiere, Peter. 2005. 'Autochthony and citizenship: new modes in the struggle over belonging and exclusion in Africa', *Quest: an African Journal of Philosophy XVIII*: 9–24.

——. and F. Nyamnjoh. 2000. 'Capitalism and autochthony: the seesaw of mobility and belonging', *Public Culture* 12, 2: 423–52.

——. and S. Jackson. 2006. 'Autochthony and the crisis of citizenship: democratization, decentralization, and the politics of belonging', *African Studies Review* 49, 2: 1–7.

Gillan, J. A. 1930. *Arab-Nuba Policy (Arab overlordship)*, Durham: University of Durham, Sudan Archive: 723/8/10–12.

—— 1931. *Some Aspects of Nuba Administration: Sudan Government Memoranda No. 1*. Khartoum, Sudan Government.

Goldflam, Scott H. S. 1988. *The Land Law of the Sudan: Individual ownership of land and the adjudication of rights through land settlement and registration during the Anglo-Egyptian Condominium*, Evanston, IL: Northwestern University Press.

Gordon, Carey N. 1986. 'Recent Developments in the Land Law of the Sudan: a Legislative Analysis', *Journal of African Law* 30, 2: 143–74.

Grönhaug, Reidar. 1978. 'Scale as a variable in analysis: fields in social organization in Herat, Northwest Afghanistan', in Fredrik Barth, ed., *Scale and Social Organization*, Oslo: Universitetsforlaget: 78–121.

Guenther, Mathias. 2006. 'Discussion: The concept of indigeneity,' *Social Anthropology*, 14, 1: 17–9.

Håland, Gunnar. 1980. *Problems of Savannah Development: The Sudan Case*, Bergen: University of Bergen Press.

——. 1991. 'Systems of agricultural production in Western Sudan', in Gillian M.

Craig, ed., *The Agriculture of the Sudan*, Oxford: Oxford University Press: 230–51.

Haraldsson, Ingemar. 1982. *Nomadism and Agriculture in the Southern Kordofan Province of Sudan*, Uppsala: Sveriges Lantbruksuniversitet.

Harir, Sharif and T. Tvedt, eds. 1994. *Short-cut to Decay: the case of the Sudan*, Uppsala: Nordiska Afrikainstitutet.

Harragin, Simon. 2003. *Nuba Mountains Land and Natural Resources Study: Part 1 – Land Study*, Missouri: University of Missouri, International Agriculture Programs and USAID.

Hassan, Sayed Gaafar El. 1963. 'Land use problems in the Nuba Mountains', in *Proceedings of the Ninth Annual Conference on Surveying for Development in Sudan*, Khartoum: Philosophical Society of the Sudan, 47–57.

Hawkesworth, D. 1932. 'The Nuba proper of Southern Kordofan', *Sudan Notes and Records* 15: 159–99.

Henderson, K. D. D. 1931. 'Nubian origins', *Sudan Notes and Records* 14: 90–93.

——. 1935. 'Nubian and Nuba', *Sudan Notes and Records* 18: 325–26.

——. 1939. 'A Note on the migration of the Messiria tribe into South-West Kordofan', *Sudan Notes and Records* 22, 1: 49–74.

Hibou, Béatrice. 2002. 'Fluidity of boundaries and the privatization of the state in Africa', *ULPA University of Leipzig Papers on Africa, Politics and Economics 48*, Leipzig: Max Planck Institute for Social Anthropology.

Hillelson, S. 1930. 'Nubian Origins', *Sudan Notes and Records* 13: 137–48.

Hussein, Karim. 1998. 'Conflict between farmers and herders in the semi-arid Sahel and East Africa: a review', in David Seddon and James Sumberg, eds, *Pastoral Land Tenure Series No. 10*, London: International Institute for Environment and Development: 1–96.

Ibrahim, A. A. 1985. 'Regional inequality and underdevelopment in Western Sudan', Ph.D. Thesis, University of Connecticut.

Ibrahim, A. U. Muhammad. 1977. 'A history of the Nuba Mountains 1898–1947, with special reference to the British policy and administration', Ph.D. Thesis, University of Khartoum.

——. 1985. *The Dilemma of British rule in the Nuba Mountains 1898–1947*, Khartoum: University of Khartoum Graduate College Publications 15.

Ibrahim, Hamid El-Bashir. 1988. 'Agricultural development policy, ethnicity and socio-political change in the Nuba Mountains, Sudan', Ph.D. Thesis, University of Connecticut.

——. 1998. In search of the lost wisdom: the dynamics of war and peace in the Nuba Mountains region of Sudan. Khartoum: Unpublished Manuscript.

Imam, Abdalla El-Tom El and Omer Egemi. 2004. 'Addressing land questions in the Nuba Mountains: capitalizing on previous experiences', Khartoum: UNDP.

International Crisis Group International Crisis Group. 2002. *God, Oil, and Country: Changing the logic of war in Sudan*, Brussels: ICG.

——. 2007. *A Strategy for Comprehensive Peace in Sudan*, Brussels: ICG Africa Report no. 130.

——. 2008. *Sudan's Southern Kordofan Problem: the Next Darfur*, Brussels: ICG Africa Report no. 145.

James, Wendy. 2007. *War and Survival in Sudan's Frontierlands: Voices from the Blue Nile*, Oxford: Oxford University Press.

Jedrej, M. C. 2006. 'Were Nuba and Hadjeray stateless societies? Ethno–historical problems in the Eastern Sudan region of Africa', *PAIDEUMA* 52: 205–26.

Jennings, K. M. 2007. *The War Zone as Social Space: Social research in conflict zones*, Oslo: New Security Program, Fafo Report.

Johnson, D. H. 2006. *The Root Causes of Sudan's Civil Wars*, updated edn. Oxford: James Currey.

Kadouf, Hunud Abia. 2001. 'Marginalization and Resistance: the plight of the Nuba people', *New Political Science* 23, 1: 45–63.

——. 2002. 'Religion and conflict in the Nuba Mountains', in Yusuf Fadl Hasan and Richard Gray, eds, *Religion and Conflict in Sudan*, Nairobi: Paulines Publications Africa: 107–13.

Kaff, Tony. 2002. 'The Nuba dilemma', *New African* (March), http://findarticles.com/p/articles/mi_qa5391/is_200203/ai_n21309159/pg_1?tag=artBody;col1, retrieved 13 September 2008.

Kameir, W. 2006. 'New Sudan: towards building the Sudanese Nation-State,' The General Congress of the Sudanese Writers' Union, Khartoum, 19 September 2006. http://www.sudantribune.com/spip.php?article18400, retrieved 6 September 2008.

Kapteijns, Lidwien and J. Spaulding. 2005. 'The conceptualization of land tenure in the precolonial Sudan: evidence and interpretation' in Donald Crummey, ed., *Land, Literacy and the State in Sudanic Africa*, Trenton, NJ: Red Sea Press: 21–41.

Khalid, Mansour, ed. 1987. *John Garang Speaks*. London: KPI.

——. 2003. *War and Peace in the Sudan: A tale of two countries*, London: Kegan Paul.

Kjosavik, Darley Jose. 2006. 'Articulating identities in the struggle for land: the case of the indigenous people (Adivasis) of Highland Kerala, South India', Colloque international: Les frontières de la question foncière – At the frontier of land issues, Montpellier, 17–19 May 2006, Montpellier: Campus ENSAM–INRA.

Knight, B. David. 1982. 'Identity and Territory: Geographical perspectives on nationalism and regionalism', *Annals of the Association of American Geographers* 74, 4: 514–31.

Komey, Guma Kunda. 2005a. 'Regional disparity in national development of the Sudan and its impact on nation-building: with reference to the peripheral region of the Nuba Mountains', Ph.D. Thesis, University of Khartoum.

——. 2005b. 'Dynamics of the marginalization process in Sudan: the Nuba Mountains case', in Hassan A. Abdel Ati, ed., *The Sudan: The Challenges of Peace and Redressing Marginalization*, Khartoum: EDGE for consultancy and research and Heinrich Böll Foundation: 54–87.

——. 2008a. 'The autochthonous claim of land rights by the sedentary Nuba and its persistent contest by the nomadic Baqqara of South Kordofan/ Nuba Mountains, Sudan', in Richard Rottenburg, ed., *Nomadic–Sedentary Relations and Failing State Institutions in Darfur and Kordofan, Sudan*, Halle: University of Halle-Wittenburg, Orientwissenschaftliche Hefte 26: 101–27.

——. 2008b. 'The denied land rights of the indigenous peoples and their endangered livelihood and survival: the case of the Nuba of the Sudan', *Ethnic and Racial Studies* 31, 5: 991–1008.

——. 2009a. 'Autochthonous Identity: its territorial attachment and political expression in claiming communal land in the Nuba Mountains Region, Sudan', in Roxana Kath and Anna-Katharina Rieger, eds, *Raum – Landscape – Territorium Raum – Landschaft – Territorium. Zur Konstruktion physischer Räume als nomadische und sesshafte Lebensräume, Nomaden und Sesshafte 11*, Wiesbaden: Reichert: 203–27.

——. 2009b. 'Striving in the exclusionary state: Territory, identity and ethno-politics of the Nuba, Sudan', *Journal of International Politics and Development* 7, 2: 1–20.

——. 2010a. 'Ethnic identity politics and boundary making in claiming communal land in the Nuba Mountains after the CPA', in Elke Grawert, ed., *After the Comprehensive Peace Agreement in Sudan: Sign of Change?* Oxford: James Currey: 110–29.

—— 2010b. 'Land factors in war and conflicts in Africa: the case of the Nuba struggle in Sudan'. in Toyin Falola and Raphael C. Njoku, eds, *War and Peace in Africa*, Durham, NC: Carolina Academic Press: 351–81.

—— and S. S. Wassara. 2008. 'Challenges for interfaith relations in the Sudan', in Anne N. Kubai and Tarekegn Adebo, eds, *Strive in Faith: Christians and Muslims in Africa*, Uppsala: Life and Peace Institute: 37–55.

Kramer, F. W. 1987. *The Social Organization of Time among the Krongo of South Kordofan*. Berlin: Institut für Ethnologie, Freie Universität Berlin.

Kuol, Deng Alor. 1999. 'Notes on the Peace Process in the Sudan', http://209.85.135.104/search?q=cache:6OgUFyAC2N4J:www.usip.org, retrieved 13 September 2008.

Kupa, R. and C. Lentz, eds. 2006. *Land and the Politics of Belonging in West Africa*, Leiden: Brill.

Kuper, D. 2003. 'The Return of the Native,' *Current Anthropology* 44, 3: 389–402.

——. 2006. 'Discussion: the concept of indigeneity,' *Social Anthropology* 14, 1: 21–2.

Kursany, Ibrahim. 1983. 'Peasants of the Nuba Mountains region', *Review of African Political Economy* 10, 26: 35–44.

Lebon, J. H. G. 1959. 'Land use mapping in Sudan', *Economic Geography* 35, 1: 60–70.

Lees, Francis A. and H. C. Brooks. 1977. *The Economic and Political Development of the Sudan*, London and Basingstoke: Macmillan Press.

Lentz, Carola. 2002. 'Contested boundaries: decentralization and land conflicts in northwestern Ghana,' in APAD, *Association Euro-Africaine pour l'Anthropologie du Changement Social et du Développement Conference, Leiden 2002*. Leiden: Leiden University Press.

——. 2007. 'Land and the politics of belonging in Africa', in Patrick Chabal, Ulf Engel, and Leo de Haan, eds, *African Alternatives*, Leiden and Boston, MA: Brill: 37–58.

Lesch, A. 1998. *The Sudan: Contested Identities*, Bloomington and Indianapolis: Indiana University Press.

Lloyd, W. 1908. 'Appendix D: Report on Kordofan Province, Sudan'. Sudan Archives: *SAD783/9/40–86*, Durham: University of Durham.

——. 1910a', 'Kordofan. *Bulletin of the American Geographical Society* 42, 7: 521–24.

——. 1910b. 'Notes on Kordofan Province', *Geographical Journal* 35, 3: 249–67.

MacDiarmid, P. A. and D. N. MacDiarmid. 1931. 'The languages of the Nuba Mountains', *Sudan Notes and Records* 14, 1: 149–62.

MacMichael, Harold A. 1912/67. *The Tribes of Northern and Central Kordofan*, London: Frank Cass, 2nd edn.

——. 1922/67. *A History of the Arabs in the Sudan and some account of the people who preceded them and of the tribes inhabiting Dar Fur*. Vol. 1, London: Frank Cass & Co. Ltd, 2nd edn.

——. 1954. *The Sudan*, London: Ernest Benn Ltd.

Mahdi, Saeed M. A. El. 1977. 'Limitations on the ownership of land in the Sudan', *Sudan Notes and Records* 58: 152–58.

——. 1979 *Introduction to the Land Law of the Sudan*, Khartoum: Khartoum University Press.

Makris, G. P. 2001. 'The Construction of Categories: from the era of colonialism to the days of military Islam', in Haydar Ibrahim 'Ali, ed., *al tanu' al thaqfi wa bina al dawulah al wataniyya fi al Sudan* [Cultural diversity and building the national state in the Sudan], Cairo: *Markaz al Drasat al Sudaniyya* [Sudanese Studies Centre]: 36–75, 2nd edn.

Mamdani, Mahmood. 2009. *Saviors and Survivors: Darfur, Politics, and the War on Terror*, New York: Pantheon.

Manger, Leif O. 1980. 'Cultivation systems and the struggle for household viability under conditions of desert encroachment', in Gunnar Haaland, ed., *Problems of Savannah Development: The Sudan Case*, University of Bergen, Department of Social Anthropology: 133–66.

——. 1981. *Public Schemes and Local Participation. Some remarks on the present situation in the Southern Nuba Mountain area*, Bergen: University of Bergen.

——. 1984. 'Traders and Farmers in the Nuba Mountains: Jellaba family firms in the Liri area', in L. O. Manger, ed., *Trade and Traders in the Sudan*, Bergen: University of Bergen: 213–42.

——. 1988. 'Traders, Farmers and Pastoralists: Economic adaptations and environmental problems in the Southern Nuba Mountains of the Sudan', in Douglas H. Johnson and David M. Anderson, eds, *The Ecology of Survival: Case studies from Northeast African history*, Boulder: Westview Press: 155–72.

——. 1994. *From the Mountains to the Plains: the integration of the Lafofa Nuba into Sudanese society*, Uppsala: The Scandinavian Institute of African Studies.

——. 2001. 'The Nuba Mountains: battlegrounds of identities, cultural traditions and territories', in Maj-Britt Johannsen and Niels Kastfelt, eds, *Sudanese Society in the Context of War: Papers from a seminar at the University of Copenhagen*, Copenhagen: University of Copenhagen: 49–90.

——. 2001–2002. 'Religion, Identities, and Politics: Defining Muslim discourses in the Nuba Mountains of the Sudan', *Journal of Arabic and Islamic Studies* 4: 111–31.

—— 2002. 'Reduction of natural resource-based conflicts between herders and farmers', Khartoum: A Report for UNDP: SUD/01/013.

—— 2003a. *Perspectives on Land Tenure and Related Issues in the Nuba Mountains: a desk study for the Nuba Mountains Programme Advancing Conflict Transformation (NMPACT)*. Khartoum: UNDP/NMPACT Report.

——. 2003b. 'Civil war and the politics of subjectivity in the Nuba Mountains, Sudan' in *The XV ICAES Congress, Florence 5–12 July*, Florence: F. de Beer.

Bibliography

——. 2004. 'Reflections on war and state in the Sudan', in Bruce Kapferer, ed., *The State, Sovereignty, War, and Civil Violence in Emerging Global Realities, Critical Interventions 5.* New York: Berghahn Books: 75–88.

——. 2006. 'Understanding the ethnic situation in the Nuba Mountains in the Sudan. How to handle processes of group-making, meaning production and metaphorization in a situation of post-conflict reconstruction'. *The First International Colloquium of a Commission on Ethnic Relations (COER) for IUAES, July 7–9. Florence, Italy.*

——. 2007. 'Ethnicity and post-conflict reconstruction in the Nuba Mountains of the Sudan: Processes of group-making, meaning production and metaphorization', *Ethnoculture* 1: 72–84.

——. 2008a. 'Building Peace in the Sudan: Reflections on local and regional challenges', in N. Shanmugaratnam, ed., *Between War and Peace in Sudan and Sri Lanka: Deprivation and livelihood revival,* Oxford: James Currey: 27–40.

——. 2008b. 'Land, territoriality and ethnic identities in the Nuba Mountains', in Richard Rottenburg, *Nomadic–sedentary Relations and Failing State Institutions in Darfur and Kordofan, Sudan,* Halle: University of Halle-Wittenburg, Orientwissenschaftliche Hefte 26: 71–99.

March, G. F. 1944. *Report of the Soil Conservation Committee: Appendix XX: Note on the Nuba Mountains area of Kordofan.* Khartoum: Sudan Government: 133–37.

——. 1954. 'Kordofan province', in John Douglas Tothill, ed., *Agriculture in the Sudan, being a handbook of agriculture as practised in the Anglo-Egyptian Sudan,* London: Oxford University Press: 827–50.

Mbembe, Achille. 2000. 'At the edge of the world: boundaries, territoriality, and sovereignty in Africa', *Public Culture* 12, 1: 259–84.

Meyer, Gabriel. 2005. *War and Faith in Sudan,* New York: William B. Eerdman Publishing Company.

Michael, Barbara J. 1987a. 'Cows, bulls and gender roles: pastoral strategies for survival and continuity in Western Sudan'. Ph.D. Thesis, University of Kansas.

——.1987b. 'Milk production and sales by the Hawazma (Baggara) of Sudan: implications for gender roles', *Research in Economic Anthropology* 9: 105–41.

——. 1991. 'The impact of international wage labor on Hawazma (Baggara) pastoral nomadism', *Nomadic Peoples* 28: 56–70.

——. 1997. 'Female heads of patriarchal households – The Baggara', *Journal of Comparative Family Studies* 28, 2: 170–82.

——. 1998. 'Baggara women as market strategists', in Richard A. Lobban, ed., *Middle Eastern Women and the Invisible Economy,* Gainesville: University of Florida Press: 60–73.

Miller, Catherine, ed. 2005. *Land, Ethnicity and Political Legitimacy in Eastern Sudan,* Le Caire: Centre d'études et de documentation économique, juridique et sociale.

Miskin, A. B. 1950. 'Land Registration', *Sudan Notes and Records* 31, 11: 274–86.

Mohamed, Adam Azzain. 1998. 'Native Administration and societal change: the case of Darfur Region', in Medani Mohamed M. Ahmed, ed., *Current Studies on the Sudan,* Omdurman: Omdurman Ahlia University, Mohamed Omer Beshir's Centre for Sudanese Studies: 248–73.

——. 2002. 'Intergroup conflicts and customary mediation: Experiences from Sudan', *African Journal on Conflict Resolution* 2, 2: 11–30.

Mohamed, Mona A. and Margret Fisher. 2002. 'The Nuba of Sudan', in Robert K. Hitchcock and Alan J. Osborn, eds, *Endangered Peoples of Africa and the Middle East*, Westport, CT and London: Greenwood Press: 115–28.

Mohamed Salih, M. Abdel Rahim. 1984. 'Local markets in Moroland: the shifting strategies of the Jellaba merchants', in Leif Manger, ed., *Trade and Traders in the Sudan*, Bergen: Bergen Occasional Papers in Social Anthropology 32: 189–212.

——. 1988. 'The socio–economic effects of migrants and returnee migrants in the Nuba Mountains', in F. I. Ibrahim and H. Ruppert, eds, *Rural–urban Migration and Identity Change: Case studies from the Sudan*, Bayreuth: University of Bayreuth, Bayreuther Geowissenschaftliche Arbeiten 11: 79–94.

——.1989. 'The Crescent, the Cross and the Devil's Flute, Islam and the Present Political Turmoil in the Sudan', *Nytt från Nordiska Afrikainstitutet* 23: 31–5.

——. 1995. 'Resistance and response: ethnocide and genocide in the Nuba Mountains, Sudan', *Geo–journal* 36, 1 (May): 71–78.

——. 1998a. 'Other identities: politics of Sudanese discursive narratives', *Identities: Global Studies in Culture and Power* 5, 1: 5–31.

——. 1998b. 'Political narratives and identity formation in post 1989 Sudan', in Mohamed Abdel Rahim Mohamed Salih and John Markakis, eds, *Ethnicity and the State in Eastern Africa*, Uppsala: Nordiska Afrikainstitutet: 72–85.

——. 1999. 'Land alienation and genocide in the Nuba Mountains', *Cultural Survival Quarterly* 22, 4 (Winter): 36–8.

——. 2002. 'Islamic NGOs in Africa: the promise and peril of Islamic voluntarism', Occasional Paper. Copenhagen: University of Copenhagen, Centre of African Studies.

——. and S. Harir. 1994. 'Tribal Militia: the genesis of national disintegration', in Sharif Harir and Terje Tvedt, eds, *Short-cut to Decay: The Case of the Sudan*, Uppsala: Scandinavian Institute of African Studies: 186–203.

——. T. Dietz, and Abdel Ghaffar M. Ahmed, eds, 2001. *African Pastoralism: Conflict, Institutions and Government*, London: Pluto Press.

Moszynski, Peter. 1998. 'Defiant Nuba continue their struggle despite isolation', *The Guardian* 30 June.

Muhammad al-Hadj, 'Isa Abkar. 2006. *Jibal al-Nuba bain Tumuh as-sasah wa diya' al-fuqara'* [The Nuba Mountains: between the politicians' ambition and the vanished poor]. Khartoum: [n.a].

Munir, Shaykh al-Din. 2006. *Komolo: al-halqa al-mafquda fi tarikh al-siyasi al-hadith li Jibal al-Nuba min 1972–2006* [The missing cycle in the modern political history of the Nuba Mountains since 1972–2006], Khartoum: The National Library.

Muñoz, José M. 2007. 'In the name of local development: ethnicity, autochthony and private sector promotion in northern Cameroon', *AEGIS European Conference on African Studies, Leiden, 11–14 July 2007*. Leiden: University of Leiden, African Studies Centre.

Murphy, Alexander B. 1991. 'Regions as social constructs: the gap between theory and practice', *Progress in Human Geography* 15, 1: 22–35.

Nadel, S. Frederick. 1947. *The Nuba: an Anthropological Study of the Hill Tribes of Kordofan*, London: Oxford University Press.

Bibliography

Niblock, Tim. 1987. *Class and Power in Sudan: the Dynamics of Sudanese Politics 1898–1985*. London: Macmillan Press

Nuba Survival. 2005. 'Press Statement: Naivasha accord fails to address Nuba grievances', *Sudan Tribune*, Tuesday 4 January, http://www.sudantribune.com/spip.php?article7354, retrieved 7 September 2008.

Organization for Economic Co-Operation and Development/ OECD. 2005. 'Land and violent conflict'. *OECD Issues Brief*, http://www.oecd.org/dataoecd/26/50/35785480.pdf, retrieved 13 September 2008.

Pallme, Ignatius. 1844. *Travels in Kordofan*. London: J. Madden and Co. Ltd.

Pantuliano, S. 2007. 'The Land Question: Sudan's peace nemesis'. *Humanitarian Policy Group Working Paper*, London: Overseas Development Institute.

——. M. Buchanan-Smith, and P. Murphy. 2007. 'The long road home: opportunities and obstacles to the reintegration of IDPs and refugees returning to Southern Sudan and the three areas: Report of Phase 1', A Report Commissioned by the UK Department for International Development, London: Humanitarian Policy Group, Overseas Development Institute.

Patey, L. A. 2007. 'State rules: Oil companies and armed conflict in Sudan'. *Sudan Tribune*, Wednesday 18 July 2007, http://www.sudantribune.com/spip.php?article22901, retrieved 9 September 2008.

Pelican, Michaela. 2007. 'Mbororo claims to regional citizenship and minority status (northwest Cameroon', *AEGIS European Conference on African Studies, Leiden, 11–14 July 2007*, Leiden: University of Leiden, African Studies Centre.

Polloni, Domenico. 2005. 'Land and the Sudan transition to peace', *Forced Migration Review* 24. Oxford: University of Oxford, The Refugees Study Centre: 21–2.

Pounds, N. J. G. 1972. *Political Geography*, New York: McGraw-Hill Book Company, 2nd edn.

Pronk, Jan. 2007. 'No way back. Preface to book, *Proud to be Nuba* by Nanne op't Ende (2007)'. Jan Pronk Homepage, http://www.janpronk.nl/index331.html, retrieved 7 September 2008

Prunier, Gérard. 2005. *The Ambiguous Genocide*, London: Hurst, 2005.

Rahhal, Suleiman Musa. 2001a. *The Right to be Nuba: The Story of a Sudanese People's Struggle for Survival*, Lawrenceville, NJ: Red Sea Press.

——. 2001b. 'The marginalized peoples of Northern Sudan and the question of self-determination', in A. H. Abdel Salam and A. de Waal, eds, *The Phoenix State: Civil Society and the Future of Sudan*, Lawrenceville, NJ/Asmara, Eritrea: Red Sea Press: 247–67.

Roden, David. 1969. 'Lowland farms for a mountain people', *The Geographical Magazine* 42, 3: 200–06.

——. 1972. 'Down-migration in the Moro Hills of Southern Kordofan', *Sudan Notes and Records* 53: 79–99.

——. 1974. 'Regional inequality and rebellion in the Sudan', *Geographical Review* 64, 4: 498–516.

——. 1975. 'Changing Pattern of Land Tenure amongst the Nuba of Central Sudan', *Journal of Administration Overseas* 10: 294–309.

Rodger, George. 1984. *Village of the Nubas*, London: Phaidon Press.

Rone, Jemera. 2003. 'Oil and War', *Review of African Political Economy* 30, 97: 504–10.

Rose, M. F. 1950. 'Possible Crops for the Cotton Rotation in the Southern Jebels Area of Kordofan, A. E. Sudan', *Empire Cotton Growing Review* 27, 4: 262–74.

——. 1951. *The Nuba Mountains Cotton Crop: Some factors affecting yield: Memoirs of Research Division 20*. Khartoum: Sudan Government, Ministry of Agriculture, Agricultural Publications Committee/Durham: Durham University, Sudan Archive: SUD.A. PK1569.2 ROSE.

Rosivach, Vincent J. 1987. 'Autochthony and the Athenians', *The Classical Quarterly* 37, 2: 294–306.

Rottenburg, Richard. 1983. 'Three spheres in the economic life of the Moro Nuba of South Kordofan', *Zwischenberichte des Sudanprojekts*: 1–9.

——. 2009. *Far-fetched Facts: a Parallel of Development Aid*, Cambridge, MA: MIT Press.

Saavedra, M. 1998. 'Ethnicity, Resources and the Central State: Politics in the Nuba Mountains, 1950 to the 1990s', in Endre Stiansen and Michael Kevane, eds, *Kordofan Invaded: Peripheral Incorporation and Social Transformation in Islamic Africa*, Leiden: Brill: 223–53.

Saeed, Mohamed H. 1980. 'Economic Effects of Agricultural Mechanization in Rural Sudan: the Case of Habila, Southern Kordofan'. in Gunner Haaland, ed., *Problems of Savannah Development: the Sudan Case*, Bergen: University of Bergen, Department of Social Anthropology: 167–84.

Sagar, J. W. 1922. 'Notes on the History, Religion and Customs of the Nuba', *Sudan Notes and Records* 5: 137–56.

Salih, Kamal al Din Osman. 1982. 'The British Administration in the Nuba Mountains Region of Sudan 1900–1956', Ph.D. thesis, University of London.

——. 1990. 'British policy and the accentuation of inter-ethnic divisions: the case of the Nuba mountains region of Sudan, 1920–1940', *African Affairs* 89, 356: 417–36.

Schlee, Günther. 2001. 'Regularity in Chaos: the politics of difference in the recent history of Somalia', *Working Paper No. 18*. Halle: Max Planck Institute for Social Anthropology.

——. 2002a. 'Taking sides and constructing identities: reflection on conflict theory', *Working Paper No. 43*. Halle: Max Planck Institute for Social Anthropology.

——. 2002b. *Imagined Difference: Hatred and the Construction of Identity*, New York: Palgrave Macmillan.

——. 2008. *How Enemies Are Made: towards a theory of ethnic and religious conflicts*, New York: Berghahn Books.

Seligmann, C. G. 1910. 'The Physical Characters of the Nuba of Kordofan', *The Journal of the Royal Anthropological Institute of Great Britain and Ireland* 40: 505–24.

——. 1913. 'Some Aspects of the Hamitic Problem in the Anglo-Egyptian Sudan', *The Journal of the Royal Anthropological Institute of Great Britain and Ireland* 43: 593–705.

——. 1917. 'Nuba'. in J. Hastings and J. A. Selbie, eds, *Encyclopedia of Religion and Ethics* 9, London: Kessinger Publishing: 401–6.

——. and B. Seligmann 1932/65. 'The Nuba', in *Pagan Tribes of the Nilotic Sudan*, ed.[n.a]. London: Routledge & Kegan Paul: 367–412.

Shipton, Parker M. 1994. 'Land and culture in tropical Africa: soils, symbols, and the metaphysics of the mundane', *Annual Review of Anthropology* 23: 347–77.

Bibliography

Simpson, I. G. 1991. 'Land Tenure', in Gillian M. Craig, ed., *The Agriculture of the Sudan*, Oxford: Oxford University Press: 101–16.

Simpson, S. Rowton. 1955. 'Land Law and Registration in the Sudan', *Journal of African Administration* 7: 11–17.

——. 1965. 'Land tenure: some explanation and definitions', in S. R. Simpson, ed., *The Land Law of the Sudan* 1, Khartoum: University of Khartoum, Faculty of Law: 82–103.

——. 1976. *Land Law and Registration*. Cambridge: Cambridge University Press.

——. 1984. *Land Law and Registration, Book 1*, London: Surveyors Publications, 2nd edn.

Small Arms Survey. 2008. 'The Drift Back to War: Insecurity and militarization in the Nuba Mountains', *Sudan Issue Briefs*, 12: 1–12.

Spaulding, Jay. 1982. 'Slavery, Land Tenure and Social Class in the Northern Turkish Sudan', *The International Journal of African Historical Studies* 15, 1: 1–20.

——. 1987. 'A Premise for Precolonial Nuba History', *History in Africa* 14: 369–74.

Spivak, Gayatri C. 1988. 'Subaltern studies: deconstructing historiography', in Ranajit Guha and Gayatri C. Spivak, eds, *In Other Worlds: Essays in cultural politics*, New York: Routledge: 197–221.

Stevenson, R. C. 1965. *The Nuba People of Kordofan Province: an Ethnographic Survey. Graduate College Publications Monograph* 7. Khartoum: University of Khartoum Graduate College Publications.

Strauss, Anselm. 1978. 'A social world perspective', *Studies in Symbolic Interaction* 1: 119–28.

Sudan Government. 1912. *Anglo-Egyptian Sudan Handbook Series 2. Kordofan and the region to the West of the White Nile*, London: His Majesty's Stationary Office.

Suliman, Mohamed. 1998. 'Resource access: a major cause of armed conflict in the Sudan. The case of the Nuba Mountains', in *International Workshop on Community-Based Natural Resource Management, 10–14 May*. Washington, DC: World Bank.

——. 1999. 'The Nuba Mountains of Sudan: Resource Access, Violent Conflict, and Identity', in Daniel Buckles ed., *Cultivating Peace: Conflict and Collaboration in Natural Resource Management*, Ottawa: IDRC and Washington, D.C.: World Bank Institute: 205–20.

——. 2001. 'Oil and the Civil War in the Sudan', Institute for African Alternative, http://www.ifaanet.org/ifaapr/oil_sudan.htm, retrieved 5 October 2007.

——. 2002. 'Resource access, identity, and armed conflict in the Nuba Mountains, Southern Sudan', in Günther Baechler, Kurt R. Spillmann, and Mohamed Suliman, eds., *Transformation of Resource Conflicts: Approach and instruments*, Bern: Peter Lang: 163–83.

Symanski, Richard, Ian R. Manners, and R. J. Bromley. 1975. 'The mobile-sedentary continuum', *Annals of the Association of American Geographers* 65, 3: 461–71.

Thompson, Larry. 2004. 'Sudan Successful Ceasefire Monitoring in Southern Sudan', *Refugees International* (30 December): 1–3, http://www.refugeesinternational.org/content/article/detail/4757/, retrieved 13 September 2008.

Thuen, Trond. 2006. 'Discussion: The concept of indigeneity,' *Social Anthropology* 14, 1: 24–5.

Tonah, Steve. 2002. 'The politics of exclusion: the expulsion of Fulbe pastoralists from Ghana in 1999/2000', *Working Paper No. 44*. Halle: Max Planck Institute for Social Anthropology.

Tothill, John Douglas, ed. 1954. *Agriculture in the Sudan, being a Handbook of Agriculture as Practised in the Anglo-Egyptian Sudan*, London: Oxford University Press.

Toulmin, Camilla and Julian Quan. 2000. 'Registering customary rights', in Camilla Toulmin and Julian Quan, eds, *Evolving Land Rights Policy and Tenure in Africa*, London: International Institute for Environment and Development: 207–28.

Trimingham, J. Spencer. 1949/83. *Islam in the Sudan*, London: Frank Cass & Co. Ltd.

Umbada, S.1988. 'Indicators of developmental grievances in rural Sudan', A discussion paper, No. 80. Khartoum: University of Khartoum, DSRC.

Vang, Ka and John Granville. 2003. 'Aiding Trade: An Assessment of Trade in the Nuba Mountains'. Missouri: University of Missouri and USAID, http://cafnr.missouri.edu/iap/sudan/doc/aiding-trade.pdf, retrieved 22 May 2008.

Vicars-Miles, A. L. W. 1934. *Nuba Mountains – their past and future*, Durham: University of Durham, Sudan Archive: 631/10/1–56.

Vogt, Andreas. 2003. 'The Sudan joint monitoring mission', *Conflict Trends* 4: 37–42. http://www.trainingforpeace.org/pubs/accord/ct403vogt.pdf, retrieved 13 September 2008

Waal, Alex de. 2006. 'Averting Genocide in the Nuba Mountains, Sudan'. *Social Science Research Council* (December), http://howgenocidesend.ssrc.org/de_Waal2/, retrieved 8 September 2008.

——. 2007. 'Scorched earth policy', *Guardian Weekly*, 18 May, http://www.google.de/search?hl=de&q=scorched+earth+policy+de+Waal&btnG=Google-Suche&meta, retrieved 7 September 2008.

——. 2008. 'The Road to Peace in Sudan: Prospects for Pluralism in Northern Sudan', http://www.usip.org/pubs/specialreports/early/ alex-de.waal.pdf, retrieved 11 September 2008.

Warburg, Gabriel. 1970. *The Sudan under Wingate: Administration in the Anglo–Egyptian Sudan 1899–1916*, London: Frank Cass & Co Ltd.

Werbner, Pnina. 1997. 'Essentialising essentialism, essentialising silence: ambivalence and multiplicity in the constructions of racism and ethnicity', in Pnina Werbner and Tariq Modood, eds, *Debating Cultural Hybridity: Multi-cultural identities and the politics of anti-racism*, London: Zed Books: 226–54.

Wilhemsen, J. Eirk. 2004. 'Implementation of a Cease-Fire Agreement', *Sudan Vision* Daily newspaper Official Website, 22 July: 1–3. http://sudanvisiondaily.com/modules.php?name=News&file=print&sid=2272, retrieved 13 September 2008.

Williams, C. H. and A. D. Smith. 1993. 'The National Construction of Social Space', *Progress in Human Geography* 7: 502–18.

Wily, Liz Alden. 2003. 'Governance and land relations: a review of decentralization of land administration and management in Africa', *Land Tenure and*

Bibliography

Resources Series, London: International Institute for Environment and Development.

——. 2004. 'Best practice in emerging land reform in Africa today', *USAID Sudan Task Force, Land & Natural Resources Project, Conflict Area*, London: International Institute for Environment and Development.

Winter, Rodger. 2000. 'The Nuba People: Confronting Cultural Liquidation', An extract from Jay Spaulding and Stephanie Beswick, eds, *White Nile Black Blood: War, Leadership, and Ethnicity from Khartoum to Kampala*, Lawrenceville, NJ: Red Sea Press, http://home.planet.nl/~ende0098/content/documents/Cultural_ liquidation.htm, retrieved 13 September 2008.

de Wit, Paul V. 2001. 'Legality and Legitimacy: a Study on Access to Land, Pasture and Water', *IGAD Partner Forum Working Group*. Rome: Food and Agriculture Organization of the United Nations.

Ylonen, Aleksi. 2007. 'Facilitating development? The Chinese involvement in the Sudan', *AEGIS European Conference on African Studies, Leiden, 11–14 July 2007*. Leiden: University of Leiden, African Studies Centre.

——. 2009. 'Marginalization and violence: considering origins of insurgency and peace implementation in the Nuba Mountains of Sudan', ISS Paper 201 (October). Pretoria, South Africa.

Yunis, N. E.1922. 'Notes on the Baggara and Nuba of Western Kordofan', *Sudan Notes and Records* 5: 200–207.

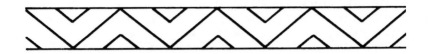

Index

246

Index

Index

Index

253

EASTERN AFRICAN STUDIES

These titles published in the United States and Canada by Ohio University Press